The
CRIME NUMBERS GAME

Management by Manipulation

Advances in Police Theory and Practice Series

Series Editor: Dilip K. Das

The Crime Numbers Game: Management by Manipulation
John A. Eterno and Eli B. Silverman

The International Trafficking of Human Organs: A Multidisciplinary Perspective
Leonard Territo and Rande Matteson

Police Reform in China
Kam C. Wong

Mission-Based Policing
John P. Crank, Dawn M. Irlbeck, Rebecca K. Murray, Mark Sundermeier

The New Khaki: The Evolving Nature of Policing in India
Arvind Verma

Cold Cases: An Evaluation Model with Follow-up Strategies for Investigators
James M. Adcock and Sarah L. Stein

Policing Organized Crime: Intelligence Strategy Implementation
Petter Gottschalk

Security in Post-Conflict Africa: The Role of Nonstate Policing
Bruce Baker

Community Policing and Peacekeeping
Peter Grabosky

Community Policing: International Patterns and Comparative Perspectives
Dominique Wisler and Ihekwoaba D. Onwudiwe

Police Corruption: Preventing Misconduct and Maintaining Integrity
Tim Prenzler

The
CRIME NUMBERS GAME
Management by Manipulation

John A. Eterno • Eli B. Silverman

Forewords by

Sir Hugh Orde, QPM
President of the Association of Chief Police Officers
England, Wales, and Northern Ireland

Andrew Scipione, APM
Commissioner
New South Wales Police Force
Australia

CRC Press
Taylor & Francis Group
Boca Raton   London   New York

CRC Press is an imprint of the
Taylor & Francis Group, an **informa** business

CRC Press
Taylor & Francis Group
6000 Broken Sound Parkway NW, Suite 300
Boca Raton, FL 33487-2742

© 2012 by Taylor & Francis Group, LLC
CRC Press is an imprint of Taylor & Francis Group, an Informa business

Version Date: 20111128

International Standard Book Number: 978-1-4398-1031-6 (Paperback)

Library of Congress Cataloging-in-Publication Data

Eterno, John, 1959-
    The Crime numbers game : management by manipulation / John A. Eterno and Eli B. Silverman.
        p. cm.
    Includes bibliographical references and index.
    ISBN 978-1-4398-1031-6 (soft cover)
    1. Police--New York (State)--New York. 2. Police administration--New York (State)--New York. 3. Criminal statistics--New York (State)--New York. 4. Crime prevention--New York (State)--New York. I. Silverman, Eli B. II. Title.

HV8148.N5E837 2012
363.209747'1--dc23   2011042589

Visit the Taylor & Francis Web site at
http://www.taylorandfrancis.com

and the CRC Press Web site at
http://www.crcpress.com

Dedication

Dedicated to countless victims of crime abandoned
by police organizations

Contents

Series Preface   xi
Foreword   xiii
Foreword   xvii
About the Authors   xxi
Acknowledgments   xxiii
Introduction   xxvii

1 The Unusual Suspects   1

Police under Arrest   1
Numerical Performance: Distortions and Displacement   9
Compstat Conversions   14
Private Sector Performance Shortcomings   16
Unraveling the Puzzle   18
References   19
Suggested Reading   22

2 The NYPD's Untold Story: Crime Report Manipulation   23

Compstat   24
Survey of Retirees   28
Interviews   34
Crime Victims Coming Forward   36
Detective Harold Hernandez   39
Hospital Data   40
New York State Division of Criminal Justice Services Data   42
Recently Released Historical Data   43
The Letter of the Law   45
NYPD Complaint Reports for Illegal Drug Use   47
Admitted Problems with Manipulation by the NYPD
and Other Jurisdictions   48
Audiotapes   49
Our Report Goes Public   52
Conclusion   53
References   54

3   Performance Management: Pitfalls and Prospects   57

Organizational–Managerial Consequences   57
Field Operations Restrictions   60
Societal Consequences   68
Prospects for Reform   71
Performance Management in New York City: The Use
of Symbolic Language   73
Conclusion: The Narrative of Reform   78
References   80
Suggested Reading   82

**4   Police Performance Management: The View from
Abroad   85**

Performance Policing in the United Kingdom   86
Australia   97
France   102
Conclusion   104
References   106
Suggested Reading   108

5   Big Bad Bully Bosses: Leadership 101   109

The Unrelenting Pressures of NYPD Compstat   109
Bullying Behaviors by Management   115
Leadership   130
References   137

6   NYPD and the Media: Curbing Criticism   141

The Condemnations   141
Understanding NYPD–Media Spin   146
The Nature of Police–Media Interactions   148
The NYPD and the Media: Political Ramifications   151
Promoting Favorable Stories   153
Suppressing Dissent   155
Marginalizing Criticism   162
Conclusion—Conflicting Forces   174
References   179
Suggested Reading   186

7   Compstat: Underpinnings and Implications   **191**

Broken Windows Theory and Compstat   192
Limited versus Unlimited Government   198
Transparency   206
Social Science Theory and NYPD Compstat   208
Specific Examples   214
Conclusion   229
References   230

8   Silence Is Not An Option   **237**

Lesson Learned   238
Issues   240
Chapter Ramifications   242
Conclusions   257
References   259

Appendix A   **261**

Appendix B   **263**

Appendix C   **267**

Index   **269**

Series Preface

John A. Eterno, Ph.D. and Eli B. Silverman, Ph.D. have written a penetrating, insightful book that brilliantly captures the essence of the **Advances in Police Theory and Practice** series, of which I am the editor. This volume exposes issues of great concern to worldwide democratic policing. Eterno and Silverman's theoretical and practical findings were presented at the International Police Executive Symposium Annual Meeting in Buenos Aires in 2011. Their research evoked commentaries from numerous participants who recounted similar phenomena in their home countries. Their research has already been heralded as a pathfinding and innovative inquiry into the dysfunctional consequences of police performance management throughout the world. This volume constitutes an extraordinary valuable addition to our series. I am proud to be associated with it.

While the literature on police and allied subjects is growing exponentially, its impact upon day-to-day policing remains small. The two worlds of research and practice of policing remain disconnected even though cooperation between the two is growing. A major reason is that the two groups speak in different languages. The research work is published in hard-to-access journals and presented in a manner that is difficult to comprehend for a layperson. On the other hand, the police practitioners tend not to mix with researchers and remain secretive about their work. Consequently, there is little dialog between the two and almost no attempt to learn from one another. Dialog across the globe, among researchers and practitioners situated in different continents, is of course even more limited.

I attempted to address this problem by starting the IPES (www.ipes.info), where a common platform has brought the two together. IPES is now in its 17th year. The annual meetings, which constitute most major annual events of the organization, have been hosted in all parts of the world. Several publications have come out of these deliberations and a new collaborative community of scholars and police officers has been created whose membership runs into several hundreds.

Another attempt was to begin a journal, aptly called *Police Practice and Research: An International Journal*, PPR, which has opened the gate to practitioners to share their work and experiences. The journal has attempted to focus upon issues that help bring the two onto a single platform. *PPR* completed its 12th year in 2011. It is certainly evidence of a growing collaboration between police research and practice that *PPR*, which began with four issues a year, expanded into five issues in its fourth year, and now is issued six times a year.

Clearly, these attempts, despite their success, remain limited. Conferences and journal publications do help create a body of knowledge and an association of police activists but cannot address substantial issues in depth. The limitations of time and space preclude larger discussions and more authoritative expositions that can provide stronger and broader linkages between the two worlds.

The increasing dialog between police research and practice has resulted in this series, **Advances in Police Theory and Practice**, which seeks to attract writers from all parts of the world. The objective is to make the series a serious contribution to our knowledge of the police as well as to improve police practices. The focus is not only in work that describes the best and successful police practices but also in one that challenges current paradigms and breaks new ground to prepare police for the 21st century. The series seeks comparative analysis that highlights achievements in distant parts of the world as well as one that encourages an in-depth examination of specific problems confronting a particular police force.

It is hoped that through this series it will be possible to accelerate the process of building knowledge about policing and help bridge the gap between the two worlds—the world of police research and police practice. This is an invitation to police scholars and practitioners across the world to come and join in this venture.

Dilip K. Das, Ph.D.
Founding President
International Police Executive Symposium, IPES, www.ipes.info

Founding Editor-in-Chief, Police Practice and Research: An International Journal, PPR, www.tandf.co.uk/journals

Foreword

Police services are, historically, information-based organizations. The information that they acquire comes in many forms—calls for assistance, intelligence, crime reports, evidence, hearsay, and so on. The police are geared up to record information and to prioritize and deploy police officers and staff to deal with a problem. In the past, much of this information was local knowledge carried in officers' heads and, when information was recorded, it was paper-based and used predominantly locally.

Over the last 30 years, two developments have occurred that have transformed this aspect of policing. First, IT systems have been introduced, which not only massively increase the amount of data captured and stored but also exponentially increase the speed and complexity of the associated interpretation, analysis, and reports that are generated.

Second, this technology means that the information is no longer predominantly local. Large amounts of police information are now made routinely available on a much wider scale. We have a multitude of IT-based systems and processes to handle, analyze, and interpret data and to track and account for our activity.

In the United Kingdom, successive governments embraced the opportunities to monitor and drive policing performance. New public managerialism and "policing by objectives" where performance was judged by input and output measures of activity became the norm. As Eterno and Silverman note, Home Office Circular 114/1983 was a seminal text that influenced the thoughts and actions of police leaders for a decade and more. A key paragraph stated, "Chief Officers may wish to consider whether the management information that is necessary for informed decisions to be taken about the deployment of resources in accordance with the force's priorities and objectives has been properly identified."

That more crime has been prevented and solved through the better policing, which resulted in part from these developments, is beyond doubt. Performance frameworks played a role in creating robust comparative data and focusing on many important areas of delivery. In the authors' terms, they served to lower the informational barriers that generally hinder intra- and inter-agency collaboration. In the United Kingdom, crime—measured independently of the police themselves through the British Crime Survey—halved between 1995 and 2010, while public confidence rose. In a very different environment, the remarkable successes of the New York City Police Department (NYPD), which provides a central case study for the authors, are well documented.

Given the widespread enthusiastic adoption of police performance management detailed in Chapter 4, the focus of this book on its manifest disadvantages is a challenge that applies to police forces everywhere. The basic principles of measuring performance and driving local accountability may be sound. However, the integrity of police information relies on it being trusted, acceptable, useable, and available. Transparency, scrutiny, and academic critique make an important contribution to our understanding of how we ensure information systems support frontline police officers without over-burdening them with unintended consequences.

Fundamentally, good policing relies on our police officers having the courage to use their professional discretion, confront risk, and make decisions, in the knowledge that their leaders will support sound decision-making even when things go wrong. This message can be difficult for leaders to communicate to their officers and staff, and it takes time. However, in my policing experience, particularly in Northern Ireland, it was when and where individual police officers were prepared to take risks in order to do the right thing that through their actions they helped to move whole communities forward.

In British policing, it is now well accepted that managerialism went too far, adding cost and bureaucracy and rewarding compliance at the expense of appetite for risk. The debate has shifted in the direction of systems-based approaches, with the current U.K. government pledging to slash bureaucracy and abandon "top-down" targets in favor of locally designed services.

The 180-year history of policing reminds us that most of our decisions are successful in keeping our public safe and upholding public confidence. For all these reasons, a lot of work is underway to put professional discretion based on a clear set of values back into the heart of policing.

Yet, unpacking the measurement machinery remains a work in progress. When things go wrong in policing—as they inevitably will from time to time—inspection bodies are irresistibly drawn toward new compliance frameworks in an effort to safeguard against repeated mistakes. As the authors note, business performance management has a "deep-seated allure" grounded in admiration for its private sector cultural roots. Understanding of the full impact and pitfalls of such approaches is vital to striking the right balance between empowering police officers while gathering information in order to effectively hold them to account for their actions.

Particularly in an environment where public spending on policing is under pressure, police leaders need an accurate picture of crime and disorder problems in communities to deliver value for money. Although the complexity and variety of tasks police officers must confront demands flexibility and discretion, equally important to community confidence is that those officers are visibly and robustly accountable.

Although technology has revolutionized the way the police handle information, it remains as vital a part of tackling crime and protecting the public as ever. This book is an important contribution to a critical debate.

Sir Hugh Orde
President of the Association of Chief Police Officers
for England, Wales, and Northern Ireland

Foreword

Over the past two decades, private sector management techniques with their emphasis on accountability have increasingly been tied to the public sector. And police forces haven't been immune.

The language of managerialism and economic rationalism has accompanied this application: lock ups and convictions supplanted by business plans and performance management, targets, and key performance indicators.

Among the most prominent and celebrated manifestations of this new era for policing was the New York City Police Department's (NYPD) Compstat process, a data-driven accountability regime introduced as a means of promoting police performance.

In a culture of index-driven management that required difficult human and social issues to be expressed in convenient statistical measures, Compstat and the processes it inspired internationally were soon in the ascendant. And to a large extent, two decades on, they still are.

However, in *The Crime Numbers Game: Management by Manipulation*, Eterno and Silverman argue that the improved police accountability and performance that Compstat and like processes promised have not been fully realized. What began as a focus on reducing crime and the fear of crime has shifted to managing—or manipulating—the numbers.

While the authors acknowledge that their research, like all studies, has constraints, their thesis at the very least should have police take pause. Any suggestion that public pronouncements on crime data have strayed into the territory of statistical subterfuge increases the potential for community confidence in police to be eroded. If allowed to go unchecked, crimes will go unreported, victims and witnesses will keep to themselves, and information and intelligence will dry up. Policing loses its very lifeblood.

The corollary is that if we can increase community confidence in the police, we can expect better cooperation from the various communities we serve. In very practical terms, that means victims and witnesses who are more willing to come forward and report matters to us. It means people giving us information and intelligence because they have the confidence that we will respond. It means, ultimately, that we have the community resources on which to draw to solve crimes or, better yet, prevent crimes from occurring in the first place.

Such confidence is only ever in prospect when the police's relationship with a community is built on trust and mutual obligation. Police depend on the community for their livelihood and the information to carry out their roles, and the community's expectation is that its engagement with police will be reciprocated by the police's honesty and a determination to keep it safe.

There is a delicate balance. A preoccupation with numbers is unhealthy if it distracts from the primary need to apprehend the most serious criminals and care for the most traumatized victims; it is unhealthier still if it causes police on the streets to set aside sound judgment and the public good in the pursuit of arrest quotas, lest they attract management criticism or compromise their chances of promotion.

In my jurisdiction, a complementary range of actions redresses that imbalance. Key among them is independent oversight of crime data and police conduct. In the case of the former, the New South Wales Police Force (NSWPF) is not the official source of crime information. At the state level, that responsibility resides within an independent agency, the Bureau of Crime Statistics and Research (BOCSAR). At the national level, crime information surveys undertaken by the Australian Bureau of Statistics verify that NSW-reported crime trends are consistent with the experiences of crime victims.

Vesting the responsibility for reporting of crime data outside the NSWPF significantly frees the Force from that aspect of the crime debate and allows us to focus on our purpose: working with the community to reduce violence, crime, and fear.

However, those factors of themselves do not ensure accuracy and transparency. It remains important that we understand the pressures on policing to achieve crime-related targets and the implications that can have for the veracity and reliability of our data. That understanding has led us to have clear and unambiguous guidance to frontline officers and commanders concerning the appropriate recording of crime and other incidents; auditable and completely integrated systems, from the first phone call or station visit, through dispatch, police attendance, and ongoing recording; and a range of gateways for victims and stakeholders to readily access information.

More recently, we have utilized the services of a commercial and independent provider to conduct hundreds of tests across Local Area Commands to ensure that our interactions with members of the community meet acceptable standards.

This should not create the impression that our frontline police and commanders are not trusted. Sensible data integrity measures reside alongside a high trust management model. To the fullest extent possible within a large public sector bureaucracy, our Local Area Commanders are encouraged to be autonomous; to work with their communities to develop local solutions to local priorities; to communicate with the media without reference to our Public Affairs Branch—or to my office if they so choose.

The search for valid, balanced, and practical indicators of police performance remains a challenge. And no doubt, the numbers do assist our analysis of often complex policing and community issues. Nevertheless, while some numbers are important, they should not become the defining characteristic of policing.

I do not suggest that the current approach in my jurisdiction is perfect. Nor do I believe that we can achieve complete transparency. The security of crucial evidence, the need to protect operational methodology, and other considerations preclude that ideal, however worthy.

Whatever view one holds on the merits of Compstat or on the uses to which it has been put, the expectation that police forces will enumerate and demonstrate results is set to remain. An informed and questioning public and media, a closer working relationship between our elected representatives and public sector leaders, and the global financial crisis increasing pressure to do more with less, are among factors that will see to that.

While the NYPD and Compstat inform the authors' central case study, their research clearly has wider application. How the NYPD debate will play out is yet to be seen and the evidence provided by the authors deserves to be tested. However, key among their conclusions are several worthwhile actions directed at ensuring appropriate oversight and achieving greater transparency, as well as actions that I would characterize as creating partnerships: partnerships with not only the communities police serve, but also trust-based partnerships between headquarters and frontline police officers that eliminate, to the extent that it is possible, micro-management and any obsessive focus on statistics.

Ultimately, police rely upon the community to effectively police our neighborhoods and keep the community safe. Inappropriate crime recording has the potential to significantly impact on community trust and confidence, and this can only make an often-difficult job much harder. As police, we cannot allow mistrust to go unchecked.

Andrew P. Scipione, APM
Commissioner of Police
New South Wales Police Force
Australia

About the Authors

 **John A. Eterno, Ph.D.,** is professor, chairperson, and associate dean and director of graduate studies in criminal justice at Molloy College. He served as a sworn officer with the New York City police department (NYPD) and retired as a Captain. His various assignments included patrol, teaching at the police academy, conducting research, and commanding officer of several units. Notably, his research for the NYPD on physical standards won a prestigious Police Foundation award. He is also responsible for the research leading to increased age and education requirements for police officer candidates. He testified at the New York State Civil Service Commission and before the City's Department of Citywide Administrative Services in this regard. His work on mapping with the NYPD also earned him the *Enterprise Initiative Award* from the New York City Mayor's office.

Dr. Eterno is on the Board of Editors for *Police Practice and Research: An International Journal.* He was also managing editor for that journal from 2006 to 2011. As such, he is an active participant in the International Police Executive Symposium. He is also an active member of the Academy of Criminal Justice Sciences, the American Society of Criminology, Criminal Justice Educators of New York State, and the Captains Endowment Association.

Dr. Eterno has consulted and testified on police management and legal issues. In this regard, he has worked closely with the United States Attorney's office, National Development Research Institutes, and with various law firms. He was recently recognized as an expert witness on police management in federal court.

Publications written by Dr. Eterno include books, book chapters, scientific articles, reports, and many others. His books include *Policing within the Law: A Case Study of the New York City Police Department* (Praeger) and *Police Practices in Global Perspective* (edited with Dilip Das) (Rowman & Littlefield). His peer-reviewed articles are in various publications such as

Professional Issues in Criminal Justice, The International Journal of Police Science and Management, Women and Criminal Justice, and *The Criminal Law Bulletin.*

Most recently, Dr. Eterno received the Faculty Research Award at Molloy College. This was awarded for his outstanding research contributions in the field of criminal justice.

Eli B. Silverman, Ph.D., is Professor Emeritus at John Jay College of Criminal Justice and the Graduate Center of City University of New York. He has previously served with the U.S. Department of Justice and the National Academy of Public Administration in Washington D.C. and was Visiting Exchange Professor at the Police Staff College in Bramshill, England.

He has lectured, consulted with, and trained numerous police agencies in the United States, United Kingdom, Canada, Mexico, Europe, Asia, and Australia. His areas of interest include police performance management, community policing, policy analysis, training, integrity control, Compstat, and crime mapping.

His recent publications include "Understanding Police Management: A Typology of the Underside of Compstat," (with John A. Eterno), *Professional Issues in Criminal Justice,* 5 (2 and 3), 2010; "NYPD's Compstat: Compare Statistics or Compose Statistics?" (with John A. Eterno), *International Journal of Police Science and Management,* 12(3), 2010; *NYPD Battles Crime: Innovative Strategies in Policing,* Northeastern University Press, 2001; "With a Hunch and a Punch," *Journal of Law Economic and Policing,* 4(1), 2007; "Police Practice in Hong Kong and New York: A Comparative Analysis," (with Allan Y. Jiao), *International Journal of Police Science and Management,* 8(2), 2006; "The Compstat Innovation" in David Weisburd and Anthony Braga (Eds.), *Police Innovation: Contrasting Perspectives,* Cambridge University Press, 2006; "An Exploratory Study of the New York City Civilian Complaint Board Mediation Program," (with Elizabeth Bartels), *Policing: An International Journal of Police Strategies and Management,* 28(4), 2005; and "The Anglo-American Measurement of Police Performance: Compstat and Best Value," (with Matthew Long), *British Journal of Community Justice,* 3(3), 2005.

Acknowledgments

Any work of this nature requires the support and assistance of numerous individuals. Many have collectively made this work possible. These special men and women have been critically important to our work. NYPD Deputy Inspector Roy Richter, President of the Captains Endowment Association, provided access to his retired members. We are indebted to his professionalism and transparency. We are especially indebted to Professor Michael Kennedy, Head of Programme, Bachelor of Policing at the University of Western Sydney. This program lies at the cutting edge of policing education. Dr. Kennedy has provided constant support, encouragement, and access to international police experts.

Sir Hugh Orde, Chief Constable and President of the Association of Chief Police Officers in England, Wales, and Northern Ireland, and Andrew Scipione APM, Commissioner of the New South Wales Police Force in Australia provided insightful forewords. Their commentaries offer penetrating and meaningful contributions to our book.

Many current and retired members of the New York City Police Department have assisted us in various ways. Although some prefer not to be named, we are grateful to all. Among those we can name are retired Lieutenant Special Assignment Christopher G. Sullivan, who helped us at various stages with drafts, focus groups, and advice; retired Captain Joseph Pascarella, an inspiration and very helpful at various stages of the project; Retired Deputy Chief John Laffey, who assisted with focus groups and advice; Retired Captain Robert Matarazzo; Lieutenant Special Assignment Ray Manus, who offered helpful ideas; and Retired Inspector James Dean, who assisted with focus groups and ideas. To these colleagues, good friends, and silent partners we appreciate your candid discussions.

We also would like to thank a friend and highly esteemed colleague, Professor Cliff Roberson of Kaplan University. His insightful commentary assisted us at various stages of our work. In addition, we are grateful to another colleague, Professor Harry Levine from Queens College, City University of New York, for sharing his research with us.

We would also like to thank colleagues in the field of education. In particular, we thank Diane Ravitch for her perceptive commentary and encouragement. From the New York City Department of Education, we thank Marc

Epstein for his useful contacts. Sal Rizzo, an expert in Special Education at Molloy College, had helpful comments as well.

There were many others at Molloy College who assisted us. We value the college's focus on VERITAS. We thank the Faculty Scholarship and Research Committee for their critical financial support. The Institutional Review Board, which reviews all college research, made constructive comments. We would also like to thank Scott Salvato for his encouragement. Adjunct Instructor John McLaughlin helped with focus groups and especially insightful comments. We are especially indebted to three Molloy College Department of Criminal Justice graduate assistants—Maddy Yellico, John Osei-Tutu, and Samantha Modik. Their hard work and dedication were indispensable. The department's student worker Armando Rattansingh also assisted. We also acknowledge the Department of Criminal Justice Secretary Maureen Stea for her invaluable service and support.

We also thank the Criminal Justice Educators of New York State (CJEANYS). These dedicated educators represent scholars at their best who encourage research unfettered by prevailing orthodoxy. As invited speakers at their annual meeting in 2010, we were not only warmly welcomed but also supported.

The International Police Executive Symposium was also helpful and supportive. At its annual meeting in Buenos Aires, scholars from around the world offered confirmation, based on their own observations, of our research findings. We would also like to thank Dilip Das for his leadership, especially in the **Advances in Police Theory and Practice** series. Dilip has been a good friend to both of us.

Many victims of crime have contacted us. Two have publicly revealed their stories—Debbie Nathan and Joseph Bolanos. We thank them for their courage and candor.

Very few news journalists have pursued this story with vigor. Reporters Paul Moses, Graham Rayman, Leonard Levitt, and Jim Hoffer have been at the forefront of this issue. We would also like to acknowledge William K. Rashbaum for timely disclosure of our research.

Many at CRC Press/Taylor & Francis have been a pleasure to work with. Carolyn Spence, the acquisitions editor, has been extremely helpful. Jay Margolis, David Fausel, Judy Thomas, Eva Neumann, Gerry Jaffe, Kate Newton, Shayna Murray, and countless others are to be commended for their help as well.

Both of us wish to recognize some people individually. John has a few special people he would like to thank—I especially want to thank my wife, JoAnn (you are the best thing that ever happened to me), and our two children, Julia and Lauren (girls, your hugs and kisses mean everything to me). They are my love, life, and inspiration. Without their support and patience, I could not have written this book with Eli. I also want to thank my brother,

James, and his wife, Camille. Their viewpoints from the educational perspective as well as James' contacts were especially helpful. Of course, I must thank Eli. This book is the treasure it is because of you. Your intellectual power and curiosity have made us an inseparable pair. I consider you the best of friends—even a brother. I also want to thank Susan for putting up with my constant phone calls. She has the patience of a saint. Eli, I hope that God will abundantly bless both you and Susan.

Eli would like to especially thank Susan Tackel—his muse and inspirational wife for her love, support, indulgence, and, yes, patience, for "one more book." Without this bountiful sustenance, this work would have never seen fruition. I am eternally grateful. Family members Karin Otto, Michael Munzer, Mark Silverman, Phil Tackel, and the Black Beauties—Selene and Margot—were wonderful sources of inspiration and encouragement. I wish to thank Michael and Karin for their invaluable cover design contribution.

Friends and former colleagues offered supportive advice and encouragement. They also tolerated my incessant inquiries at offbeat hours. They include Bill Devine, Andrew Karmen, Kimora, Andrea Kroop, Barry Latzer, Tom Litwack, Robert McCrie, Ken Moran, Doug Muzzio, Terry O'Neill, Allan Rabinowitz, Janet Smith, Srijan, Laura Lawson Tucker, Robert Tucker, Anthony and Elaine Viola, and Alex Vitale.

In addition, many friends from abroad made significant contributions. In the United Kingdom, they include retired senior police officers Paul Bompas, Robin Fletcher, Joe Frost, Steve Hallam, Alan Marlow, Ian McKenzie, Malcolm Parry, and Paul Robb. In addition, Francesc Guillen Lasierra from Spain, Thomas Feltes from Germany, Thomas Gilly, Franck Vindevogal, and Emmanuel Didier from France, Peter Versteegh from the Netherlands, Mary and Andrew Hapel from Australia, and Minoru and Yumiko Yokoyama from Japan were extremely helpful.

Finally, John provided the inspiration for our research. Collaboration with John not only yielded this book but also a meaningful relationship filled with my lasting respect, admiration, and affection. John's inquisitiveness, mental agility, persistence, and kindness are unparalleled. I value his friendship and am privileged to know him and his wonderful wife, JoAnn.

Introduction

For the past two decades, New York City's Police Department (NYPD), political establishment, and media have been loudly proclaiming a dramatic decline in serious crime. According to this New York "crime success story"—now proclaiming a "miraculous" 80-percent decrease in official crime statistics—the driving engine has been the NYPD's widely publicized performance management system (Compstat). The NYPD's heralded Compstat system has served as a model that many national and international law enforcement agencies have emulated at their own peril.

As opposed to officialdoms' ever glowing, no warts narrative, it is useful to ask: What about the view from the street—from commanders, frontline supervisors, the rank-and-file? Using a scientific approach, this book uncovers their perceptions of a system gone wild. Regardless of the intentions of upper management, those below feel forced to play "the numbers game." In this work, for the first time, we present their feelings, frustrations, and concerns. Our research is offered as an account of the dysfunctional deterioration of this kind of police performance management and a way to remedy the situation. Consequently, we hope the writing of this book will assist police globally.

This book is the culmination of years of collaborative research. Our extensive writings (in this area), including two previous books, center on the NYPD. Dr. Eterno's book, *Policing with the Law*, focuses on the legal parameters of policing. Dr. Silverman's book, *NYPD Battles Crime: Innovative Strategies in Policing*, is considered the first and one of the most preeminent works on the NYPD's Compstat managerial system. We are conversant with the NYPD's mores and internal workings. Dr. Eterno is a retired police captain who played a key role in policy development and research in the Police Commissioner's Office of Management Analysis and Planning. As managing editor of the peer-reviewed journal *Police Practice and Research: An International Journal*, he has collaborated closely with practitioners and academics globally. Dr. Silverman has extensive field research experience with police departments in the United States and around the world including seven years of in-depth study of the NYPD's managerial system.

This volume is important because police managers need to fully comprehend the ramifications of their supervisory actions and because the accuracy of crime statistics is paramount. Modern police departments make strategic decisions on officer deployment and tactics based on the frequency, type, and location of specific crimes, times of occurrence, developing crime patterns, and much more. If crime data is inaccurate, then police departments are less effective in fighting crime and even acts of terror, which are often preceded by so-called minor crimes. Many citizens' decisions are also based on the presumed accuracy of crime statistics. Choices often rest on the perceived safety of residential areas, community real estate values, neighborhood quality-of-life issues, and citywide urban planning needs. Many of these themes are explored throughout this book.

The consequences of myopic, short-term almost excusive focus on crime statistics has emerged as a worldwide phenomenon. This book's forewords offered by two internationally renowned and highly esteemed police leaders, Sir Hugh Orde of the United Kingdom and Commissioner Andrew Scipione of Australia, vividly speak to the hazards of blind faith in New York's numbers-oriented managerial system. American police leaders and scholars, resistant to change and the full ramifications of our study, sharply contrast with the advanced thinking of these two international leaders. Sir Hugh Orde and Commissioner Scipione recognize how our research illuminates the downside of slavish statistical fixation in pursuit of the dominant, virtually exclusive, crime control model.

In the words of one Australian academic and former police detective

... performance based led policing begins with the best of intentions ... but ends up as a cost benefit analysis of law and order that becomes totally politicized. Subsequently the social contract of policing is turned into a business with demands of continued growth and less accountability. The more sinister side of this is the manner in which critics are disposed of as if they are collateral damage. (Dr. Michael Kennedy, Head, Bachelor of Policing Programme, University of Western Sydney, personal e-mail, June 17, 2011)

Performance management systems, which have led to constrained police forces, focus on crime statistics thereby triggering many negative results including the manipulation of these very same crime statistics. The multifaceted negative effects are highly visible at the NYPD. In the words of one long-term observer of American policing, the NYPD's Compstat performance management system,

.... hit police executives from all over North America like a powerful narcotic. Within a few years, the numbers-driven Compstat concept had gone viral all over the nation. Yes, it has the short-term effect of distorting and driving crime statistics down, but it also has the long-term and deeply pernicious effect of driving a wedge between the police and the community. Great policing that contributes meaningfully to citizen satisfaction, enhanced quality of life in communities and the economic viability of our cities depends on partnership between the police and the community, not on numbers and relentless pressure on police commanders to deliver ever downward-trending crime statistics. (Terry O'Neill, Director, The Constantine Institute, Inc., personal e-mail, August 23, 2011).

As O'Neill notes, numbers-infected Compstat systems have spread widely. The September 2011 release of the U.S. Government's National Crime Victimization Survey (NCVS) and Uniform Crime Reports (UCR) show similar downward trends in nationwide crime rates. Our book agrees with and applauds this downward trend. Nevertheless, our research also raises significant concerns regarding the dimensions of this trend. For example, improper Compstat management customarily risks alienating communities through heavy handed police tactics. This concern is seen in the NCVS, which disturbingly reveals that for the past 10 years U.S police departments are aware of only half of violent crime. Compstat-like systems do not encourage this hidden 50 percent of victims of violence to come forward. How many assault, robbery, and rape victims are alienated and thus do not report crime to the police? How many are actively being turned away by police? Police knowledge of only 50 percent also creates an intelligence nightmare. Effective strategies can be better designed with a more complete picture. This enables police departments to work with local communities and their conditions and not rely on numbers-oriented bureaucrats driven by headquarters

The type of research we conduct in this book is unique. Police organizations are concerned about their image and members are anxious not to rock the organizational boat. Frequently, media and academics are resistant to this type of story or research because they are reluctant to risk access to the police. It is not comfortable to challenge political orthodoxy and its reigning narrative. This inhibits the likelihood of speaking truth to power. A paramount finding of this book is that distorted police performance systems become embedded in their managerial operations. As such while a useful first step, personnel replacements at the highest organizational levels can never suffice. Substantial reorientation and recasting of the organization is necessary. In addition, long abandoned police transparency and oversight must be restored.

Finally, we are proud to be a part of this international series of books entitled **Advances in Police Theory and Practices**. Our work offers a window into the interplay of theory and practices from the perspective of advancing policing beyond the limits of narrow-based performance management into a new era of collaboration and transparency.

The Unusual Suspects

1

We must not confuse dissent with disloyalty. … We will not be driven by fear
into an age of unreason, if we … remember that we are not descended from
fearful men—not from men who feared to write, to speak, to associate, and to
defend causes that were, for the moment, unpopular.

Edward R. Murrow

Police under Arrest

On October 31, 2009, New York City Police Department (NYPD) personnel, including a high-ranking Deputy Chief and a precinct commander,
forcibly entered the apartment of one of its officers, Adrian Schoolcraft, who
was thrown to the floor, handcuffed, dragged against his will, and held as a
patient in a hospital psychiatric ward for 6 days. He recently exposed NYPD's
manipulation of crime statistics.

Schoolcraft's whereabouts were not disclosed by the NYPD and therefore
unknown to friends and family even though NYPD procedure clearly indicates family must be notified (New York City Police Department, 2011). His
father called all New York hospitals until he finally located his son at Jamaica
Hospital. When Schoolcraft was released, it was "without a coherent explanation for his ordeal. Jamaica Hospital officials charged him $7,000 for his stay—
and another $86 to obtain his own medical records" (Rayman, 2010b, June 15).

According to reports, hospital records indicated that the NYPD

> … misled the medical staff about the events of that day, causing doctors to
> treat him as a psychiatric patient. The records show that a sergeant from the
> 81st Precinct told Dr. Khin Marlwin that Schoolcraft had "left his work early
> after getting agitated and cursing his supervisor." She also told Marlwin that
> police had "followed him home and he had barricaded himself, and the door
> had to be broken to get to him." None of these statements are true. Under
> New York State Law, a person cannot be committed against his will unless he
> is a threat to harm himself or harm others. A tape of that evening made by
> Schoolcraft clearly indicates he was neither a threat to himself or others. The
> discharge sheet included the relatively benign and vague diagnosis of "anxi-
> ety." After the hospital stay, he was suspended from the NYPD and moved to
> his father's home upstate. (Rayman, 2010b, June 15)

1

In December, the NYPD began sending supervisors to Schoolcraft's father's home on a repeated basis. According to Schoolcraft, "We didn't answer because we wanted to avoid a confrontation. There was a convention outside my door." The NYPD also sent people on December 13, January 12, 13, 14, 15, 21, 31, February 3, 12, and June 8—a campaign the Schoolcrafts describe as harassment. Lacking a paycheck, money was in short supply. "Ironically, Schoolcraft called the crime victims' hotline to obtain some sort of financial relief, but he was rejected because he had no complaint number for the Halloween incident" (Rayman, 2010b, June 15).

As of August 2011, a period of over 19 months, neither Police Commissioner Raymond Kelly nor Mayor Michael Bloomberg has uttered a word about the NYPD's alleged violation of Schoolcraft's civil rights in throwing him into the hospital's psychiatric ward. Nor, incredibly, has the Police Department released one report, document, or even a scrap of paper explaining the NYPD's handling of the episode.

Police Officer Adil Polanco apparently was subject to NYPD reprisal for going to the press. Similar to Officer Schoolcraft, Officer Polanco revealed the practice of ticket writing quotas and demands by management for stop and frisk reports. The department filed charges for misconduct against Polanco for filing false documents in issuing summonses. Polanco claims he was compelled to do these activities and furthermore he previously reported this (Rayman, 2011, August 4).

As bizarre as these strong-armed police events may seem, unfortunately they are not unique. For those who believe Schoolcraft's abduction and forced captivity was an over-reactive organizational anomaly, consider the case of the late Detective Sergeant Philip Arantz of Australia's New South Wales police force. In 1971, Arantz, a well-regarded detective, was ordered by the Police Commissioner to "undergo a psychiatric assessment and the police medical officer certified him mentally ill. He was kept for three days at Price Henry Hospital and it was later revealed that Allan (the NSW Police Commissioner) had rung the hospital psychiatrist who wrote in his report 'Possible political expediency is bringing pressure to bear on patient's admission'" (Five-Yeomans, 2011).

According to Arantz, the police surgeon

> … is alleged to have decided that I was paranoid and had to be disarmed because he feared I might shoot the commissioner. At the direction of Allan, I was then conveyed by two senior officers to a psychiatric ward at Prince Henry Hospital. I left the psychiatric ward with a certificate from a qualified psychiatrist attesting to my sanity. (Arantz, 1993, p. 7)

The psychiatric report said that there was "no evidence of psychosis … an intelligent man with some obsessional traits, but they are not out of control and in the interview he was at all times alert, rational and showed appropriate effort" (Arantz, 1993, p. 7). Suspended without pay on December 7, detective sergeant Arantz was charged with departmental misconduct and on January 20, 1972, he was dismissed from the police force with no pension.

Arantz had to wait 13 years, until 1985, to receive a pitiful government compensation award of $250,000. In return, Arantz had to agree not to engage in further public debate or in any court action. He also was denied what he most fervently desired—"notional" reinstatement, which, in Australia, would have cleared his name. It took another four years (1989) before he received this reinstatement. He died in 1998 at the age of 68 and was posthumously awarded the Police Commissioner's Commendation for Outstanding Service, the New South Wales (NSW) police's highest award (Brown, 1998).

The political and police treatment of Schoolcraft, Polanco, and Arantz certainly have disconcerting parallels. All three cases appear to be both startling and unconscionable. It is especially noteworthy that these organizations were not small, remote, non-professional, poorly trained police departments. Instead, two major police organizations were involved in what appears to be abusive and illegal actions. The NYPD of over 35,000 officers is the United States' largest police department. The NSW police department of approximately 16,000 is Australia's oldest and largest police force. These events, therefore, do not represent the aberrant deviations of obscure isolated police departments.

How does one explain such rash and overwhelming organizational handling of three relatively obscure police officers? Political and police organizational treatment of Schoolcraft, Polanco, and Arantz were astonishingly parallel because their challenges of official performance-based crime statistics were remarkably similar. Schoolcraft, Polanco, and Arantz apparently spoke truth to power. They shared a strong conviction that official crime statistics ought to be genuine. They believed that police effectiveness and public trust are both enhanced by accurate crime reports. In their own ways, Schoolcraft, Polanco, and Arantz were in positions to observe misclassifications and manipulations of crime data and statistics. Of course, they were not unique; however, they were three of a very select group willing to risk retaliation and being ostracized from the organizations for which they worked. They paid a very high price.

Regardless of the legal outcomes of the Schoolcraft and Polanco cases, their organizational experiences serve as vivid warnings to others who may be inclined to reveal the truth and risk not only their livelihood but also their very well-being. Their (and other) challenges of officialdom's version of crime throughout the world, as this book details (see Chapter 4), was and continues to be viewed as grave threats to the police and political establishments. It is necessary to review each case in order to fully grasp the dimensions of the organizational and political issues that affect official crime statistics.

Adrian Schoolcraft

Schoolcraft's "transgressions" first came to public light in February 2010 when the *Daily News* reported his claims of misleading and manipulated crime reports in Brooklyn's 81st police precinct (Parascandola, 2010). Concerned that his reports to the NYPD hierarchy were unheeded, Schoolcraft, beginning in March 2010, provided the *Village Voice* with previously undisclosed secret recordings of precinct roll calls and other police and citizen conversations that occurred during 2008 and 2009. The tapes provided accounts of precinct bosses telling officers, among other actions, to refuse certain robbery reports in order to manipulate and lower official crime statistics so that the neighborhood appeared safer. Command precinct personnel recount calling crime victims to discourage them from making complaints. Officers were encouraged to downgrade felony thefts to petty larcenies or (misdemeanors [for fuller discussion see Chapter 2]). Officers were instructed to convert robbery reports to the category of lost property (Rayman, 2010a, March 4). These recordings provided unprecedented tangible evidence of what many police and some reporters were revealing over many years—that precinct commanders were under increasing political and police leadership pressure to improve performance through lower crime statistics. These pressures frequently were manifested in headquarters crime strategy meetings (Compstat), which kept the fire under the feet of commanders for unending crime reductions. These recordings also confirmed the findings of our survey of retired police commanders (see especially Chapter 2).

Graham Rayman's multipart 2010 *Village Voice* series on Schoolcraft, "The NYPD Tapes," won the prestigious New York Press Club's Gold Keyboard award for investigative reporting—the top honor the press club gives each year. It is instructive to review excerpts from Rayman's June 2011 New York Press Club's acceptance.

> Adrian Schoolcraft also deserves a share of this award. Without his personal courage, none of this would have reached the public eye. And when we consider his motivation, it's very important to note that he spent two years trying to go through the NYPD chain of command. But he was repeatedly rebuffed and labeled a troublemaker.
>
> Finally, he went to department investigators. Three weeks after a three-hour meeting, in which he documented a dozen examples of downgrading of crimes, a deputy chief, a precinct commander and other supervising police officials ordered him handcuffed, dragged from his apartment and held against his will in Jamaica Hospital psychiatric ward for six days without explanation.

Even then he did not immediately go public. He tried to get Internal Affairs, the U.S. Attorney, the FBI, county prosecutors and local politicians interested in investigating what happened to him. No one wanted to get involved. Then, and only then, did he decide to reach out to the media.

Unfortunately in this case the department has been anything but responsive, ignoring or stonewalling numerous *Village Voice* inquiries and Freedom of Information requests over the past 13 months.

I was struck by the fact that reporters in Baltimore, Philadelphia, Nashville were each able to obtain thousands of crime records from their respective police departments of the type NYPD has never released.

Why do we allow this situation [at the NYPD] to continue? How is the New York City Police Department different from any other taxpayer-funded city police department? Why won't the NYPD release its complaint and arrest database? How many cases are closed without a full investigation? Why has the NYPD stopped reporting its clearance rate to the FBI? What is that clearance rate? Why won't the NYPD release all of its crime statistics, rather than the limited weekly Compstat charts? Why hasn't the NYPD updated and improved its inefficient and opaque Freedom of Information process? Is there any way to make DCPI [the department's public information office] more efficient and responsive? What happened in the Schoolcraft incident? Why won't the NYPD release the results of the various investigations ordered by Kelly? (Levitt, 2011, June 17)

As of this writing, Schoolcraft is still in limbo. He has filed a lawsuit against the City of New York and high-ranking members of the NYPD. "Basically, I'm trying to recover my reputation here," he says. "They assassinated my character in an effort to cover up what I was trying to report. I have no choice but to fight this battle" (Rayman, 2010b, June 15).

Philip Arantz

Philip Arantz's obituary appeared in the *Sydney Morning Herald* of March 5, 1998 under the banner "Philip Arantz, Whistleblowing Scourge of Officialdom, Dies at 68." The first sentence read, "He will go down in history as the archetypal whistleblower" (Brown, 1998). One Australian newspaper called him "Australia's answer to Frank Serpico" (Nason, 1998, p. 27).

Arantz's whistleblowing was no less threatening to the NSW Police Force than Schoolcraft was to the NYPD. Although Arantz's ordeals predate the age of Compstat crime strategy performance meetings, his experiences, in retrospect, foreshadowed Compstat's 1994 NYPD performance management's numerical frenzy. Arantz's assignment, vision, and triumph ushered in a Compstat-like system before the word Compstat was ever coined in police circles. Ironically, it was the initial development and ability of a new analytical computer system to accurately record crime that led to Arantz's forced psychiatric hospitalization, dismissal, and loss of income and pension.

The son of a police detective, his "only ambition was to be a policeman" (Arantz 1993, p. 9). His police service began in 1945 as a police cadet at the age of 15. His record was exemplary as he progressed to a Detective Sergeant. Arantz's 1993 book provides rich and detailed insights into the development of the NSW Police Force's analytical computer system and the benefits and hazards it generated. Arantz was invited to join the Police Research Bureau to introduce computer technology. When selected, he "unknowingly and unhesitatingly entered into the dying throes of my career" (Arantz, 1993, p. 45).

Arantz's approach was to assess the status of the Criminal Intelligence Bureau's (CIB) existing database and propose reforms necessary to provide accurate and timely information suitable for computer application. Consequently, detectives would be better informed, more successful, and the public would receive an accurate recording of crime in their communities. In reviewing the manner in which crime was recorded, Arantz and his colleagues recognized the inadequacies of the existing crime recording system. In effect, two reporting systems contributed to inaccurate crime reporting. The official detective reporting system was recorded on Criminal Offense forms and channeled to Central Headquarters' Modus Operandi Section. However, there was a second unofficial recording system through a separate set of books, which was called the paddy's system. This gave the impression of lower crime rates.

When Arantz and his colleagues examined this dual system, they found that the vast bulk of crime was recorded in the Paddy's Book and, therefore, only a small portion of crime information throughout New South Wales was centrally located and available to the police and the public. As Arantz noted,

> This was the essence and the purpose of the Paddy's System, to reduce the volume simply by not officially disclosing all the unsolved crimes and inflate the clear up rate by reporting officially every offence that was solved no matter how minor. This provided a false and misleading picture of police effectiveness to the public. (Arantz, 1993, p. 49).

At the outset, Arantz was made aware of the problems and fundamental dilemma inherent in a single reliable reporting system. Said one of his colleagues:

> Too many problems would have to be overcome by doing away with the Paddy's System and instituting a total and accurate crime reporting system throughout the state. *Not the least of these problems was the fact that the crime statistics derived from such a total system would create all sorts of problems for the commissioner of police.* (Arantz, 1993, p. 50, emphasis added)

This advice proved prophetic. The problems were difficult and Arantz paid a price for fixing them. For example, although the Paddy System was originally designed for "relatively minor crimes" with small expectation of clearance, Arantz found that it often expanded to include serious crimes. One Sydney detective told him that he

> ... had many an assault and rob in the Paddy's Book. Anyone with an American accent goes in the Paddy's even if he's got skin and flesh hanging off him. Even if we found an offender, we're not likely to have a complainant. So why load your book unnecessarily? (Arantz, 1993, p. 106)

Arantz was also well informed and aware that misleading crime statistics were not unique to NSW and were often linked to top-level police and political leadership pressure. In fact, his knowledge was not restricted to NSW or Australian police forces. Arantz remarkably cites President Johnson's 1967 Presidential Commission on Law Enforcement and the Administration of Justice study. Entitled *The Challenge of Crime in a Free Society*, this in-depth report referred to crime disparities dating as far back as the 1932 U.S. Wickersham Commission report. Johnson's Commission (p. 27, 1967, cited in Arantz, 1993, pp. 52–53) wrote:

> This tendency has apparently not yet been fully overcome. It sometimes arises from political pressure outside the police department and sometimes from the desire of the police to appear to be doing a good job of keeping the crime rate down. Defective or inefficient recording practices may also prevent crimes reported by citizens from becoming a part of the record.

Despite and perhaps because of his familiarity with statistical manipulation, Arantz vigorously pursued an upgraded computer system; in effect, a primitive version of a future crime-management system called Compstat, which maps and classifies crime according to type of crime, place, and time of occurrence. This timely and accurate data would supply more informed and effective police deployment supported by online retrieval of crime data from remote computer terminals throughout New South Wales.

Arantz was not naïve. He recognized the conflicting polarity of needs.

> The benefits to be derived for the members of the Police Force and the public far outweighed retention of the old system purely because a disclosure of the true crime situation could be an embarrassment to the commissioner. He was concerned only with statistics. My concern was with the victims of crime and the conviction that complete availability of all data on crime and criminals to police would prove to be of immense benefit regarding investigation and prevention of crime. (Arantz, 1993, p. 64)

His concern for victims prophesizes the treatment of victims today in similar police performance management systems.

It was only when Arantz finally acknowledged the stark reality, which his colleagues had long noted—that the Police Commissioner feared unfavorable performance publicity and would not release complete and accurate crime statistics—that Arantz finally provided accurate information to the press. So on November 26, 1971, the lead story of the *Sydney Morning Herald* read, "Hidden Crime Rate in NSW is Revealed." The story began:

> New South Wales suffers far more crime than Government and police have ever been prepared to admit. For the first time, reliable figures have become available to show this. They cover the 10 months to the end of October. They show that the total of reported crime this year is likely to be a staggering 75 percent above the official figures of last year." (Arantz, 1993, p. 103)

Later articles described Arantz as a "statistics pioneer, a key member of the police branch that collected the figures (Five-Yeomans, 2011). While some articles credited the Police Commissioner for implementing the new computer system to accurately record crime, he was, as demonstrated by his horrendous treatment of Arantz, defensive and only responded with punishing attacks.

Organizational treatment of Schoolcraft and Arantz's whistleblowing are very similar and emblematic of their highly pressurized and politicized police performance management systems. Their abusive treatment, regardless of guilt or innocence, makes it far less likely that others will come forward. Without offering immunity combined with fair treatment, such performance management systems will run amok.

The retribution and psychiatric branding of Schoolcraft and Arantz are only emblematic of the tactical responses of the NYPD, the NSW police, and other police forces that have adopted the statistical performance crime model of police effectiveness. Unofficial contradictions and revelations are perceived as massive threats to the organizations, their supportive political establishments, and those who benefit from their association with police departments. This book explores the nature of these threats as exposed in manipulated crime statistics in many countries, why they have arisen, how they are treated by the media, their defiance of official orthodoxy, their escalating calamitous consequences for the public and democratic policing, and a leadership path for reform.

In order to delve into this, we need to explore the manner in which crime statistics have become worldwide objects of manipulation. We note how this is not a new phenomenon. Yet with the development of performance management in policing, as typified by a management accountability system (called Compstat) and other similar crime management accountability systems, this practice has intensified in police departments around the world. Therefore, we briefly review Compstat's crime reduction origins in New York City (which were initially quite sound and beneficial) before unraveling into managerial bullying and numerical frenzy.

This is a story of police reform that has lost its way, gone astray, and succumbed to short-term numbers games. We will demonstrate how the misuse and subsequent deterioration of a system designed to fight crime became ossified and eventually skewered by its own success.

We offer insight into this process, much of which is informed by the participants' own voices. Our approach is that of social scientists who are "value neutral." We had no preconceived notions as to what our research would yield. We collected and analyzed data—both quantitative and qualitative. While there have been many valuable media reports of particular examples of manipulated crime statistics (see Chapter 6), our systematic findings, on the other hand, stem from and have been affirmed through a reputable academic peer review approval process. Although many of the distortions arise from numerical performance standards in policing, it is first necessary to review the generic pitfalls of measuring organizational performance by numerical standards.

Numerical Performance: Distortions and Displacement

Judging organizational performance by numbers is nothing new to the public and private sectors. A review of its historical development and misuse enables us to more fully grasp Compstat's performance management in New York City and elsewhere.

Public Sector

Since the early part of the 20th century, practitioners and scholars have sought to rationalize public services by measuring them. Interestingly as far back as 1938, an exhaustive scholarly analysis, *Measuring Municipal Activities,* concluded that public services do not lend themselves to measurement because their objectives are often multiple, sometimes conflicting, difficult to clearly define and therefore assign appropriate weights (Ridley and Simon, 1938).

This early study, however, has not deterred recurrent worldwide efforts to measure statistical performance for individuals and units within public organizations as well as the organizations themselves. These ventures have been virtually unbounded extending into the fields of public health, education, job training, criminal justice, and other public areas as well. Despite these repeated efforts, many analyses have documented dysfunctional consequences. In the words of the eminent social psychologist Donald T. Campbell,

> The more any quantitative social indicator is used for social decision-making, the more subject it will be to corruption pressures and the more apt it will be to distort and corrupt the social processes it is intended to monitor. (Campbell, 1976)

Campbell recognizes that attempts to reward institutional behavior should account for participants who tend to behave differently when they are being measured. This observation is very applicable to public education. Thus, Campbell draws a distinction between proper and improper use of education "achievement tests." They

> ... may well be valuable indicators of general school achievement under conditions of normal teaching aimed at general competence. But when test scores become the goal of the teaching process, they both lose their value as indicators of educational status and distort the educational process in undesirable ways. (Campbell, 1976)

This distinction has been played out on a national scale throughout the United States and elsewhere. Two early proponents of national educational testing, Chester Finn and Diane Ravitch, later acknowledged that they failed to foresee the inevitability of distortion when certain outcomes such as math and reading scores are measured. Inevitably, untested areas such as science, social studies, art, music, and physical education receive less emphasis.

> We should have seen this coming ... should have anticipated ... the "zero sum" problem ... more emphasis on some things would inevitably mean less attention to others. ... We were wrong. We didn't see how completely standards-based reform would turn into a basic-skills frenzy. (Finn and Ravitch, 2007)

There are other manifestations of distortion in education performance standards. The No Child Left Behind federal law requires states to establish proficiency cut-off levels on mathematics and reading standardized tests. Failure to increase the number of students above this cut-off level would trigger school sanctions. Studies have noted that this system "created incentives for teachers to focus their instruction on students just below the proficiency point" (Rothstein, 2008, p. 24).

Organizations employ myriad strategies to evade accountability sanctions. For example, in education, students are shifted among categories especially to subgroups such as second language learners or special education students where their unmeasured characteristics will be most helpful or least harmful (Figlio and Getlzer, 2002). Some schools suspend low-scoring

students for disciplinary infractions before testing begins (Figlio, 2005), encourage absence, or conduct field trips for low-scoring students on testing days (Kantrowitz and Springen, 1997).

Those assessing public health assessments have arrived at similar conclusions. The U.S. General Accounting Office summarized experts' assessments of U.S. healthcare report cards. "Administrators will place all their organizations' resources in areas that are being measured. Areas that are not highlighted in report cards will be ignored" (U.S. General Accounting Office, 1994).

Distortions in the form of focusing on the short run to the detriment of the long run also affect public sector performance management. A Department of Labor study of trainees' successful performance, as measured by employment and wage experiences 90 days after formal training completion, found that this created incentives for agencies to place workers in lower skilled and shorter-term jobs provided only that these jobs lasted at least 90 days (Courty, Heinrich, and Marschke, 2005, p. 338).

These distortions and so-called "cream skimming" have been summarized:

> The imprecise identification of relevant subgroups or, in other words, an inadequate risk adjustment for the comparison of performance, creates incentives for agents to meet accountability targets by taking advantage of imperfections in the subgroup definitions or risk adjustment categories. In human services, agents do so by disproportionately selecting those clients who are easier to serve because these clients have uncontrolled for characteristics. (Rothstein, 2008, p. 40)

Distortions in law enforcement performance management have also been exposed in the past. For example, false arrests have been identified as the result of arrests quotas or, for traffic officers, ticket quotas (Uhlig, 1987). Similarly, arrest quotas may encourage police to focus on less difficult and important arrests at the expense of more significant and arduous arrests as well as unmeasured activities such as patrol or community meetings (Deming, 1986). In 2005, New York's City's patrolmen's union reported that productivity arrest quotas resulted in the arrest of an 80-year-old man for feeding pigeons and pregnant women for sitting down to rest on a subway stairway (Murray, 2005). A study of federal law enforcement agents, who were measured by monthly cases completed, found that the agents focused on the easiest cases near the end of their monthly performance management period (Blau, 1955).

The impact of political pressures on crime recording practices is another example of the misuse of performance standards. This has been reported for many cities including Baltimore (Center and Smith, 1972–1973; Twigg, 1972). When President Nixon made crime reduction in the District of Columbia and other cities a priority, a pattern emerged of shifting reported crime among categories. For example, at that time, the largest reductions were in larcenies of $50 or more and the largest increases were in larcenies valued at $49. This enabled the District to reduce its Uniform Crime Reporting (UCR) index. Similarly, burglaries (which are a UCR crime defined as a forcible entirely with the intent of committing a theft or felony) were frequently reclassified as malicious mischief or vandalism, which are not UCR index crimes (Seidman and Couzens, 1974).

These and other examples led Campbell to conclude:

> It seems to be well documented that a well publicized effort at social change—Nixon's crackdown on crime—had as its main effect the corruption of crime-rate indicators, achieved through under recording and by downgrading the crimes to less serious classifications. (Campbell, 1976)

A 1998 *New York Times* article observed that American police worry that

> ... the sharp drop in crime in recent years has produced new pressure on police departments to show ever-decreasing crime statistics and might be behind incidents in several cities in which commanders have manipulated crime data. So far this year, there have been charges of falsely reporting crime statistics here, in New York, Atlanta and Boca Raton, Fla., resulting in the resignation or demotion of high-ranking police commanders. (Butterfield, 1998)

Private Sector Inspiration

Despite shortcomings in police and other public sector performance management systems, the guiding rationale has often been an idealized private sector model imbued with efficient performance standards. In American policing, enhancing accountability for performance by adopting business and professional practices has repeatedly emerged as the holy grail of management reform. Early 20th century police reformers such as O. W. Wilson sought to upgrade the quality of police performance through the introduction of sound business practices.

In recent years, the goal of refashioning police agencies so that they more closely mirror private organizations has been extended to entire police departments. Herman Goldstein's path-finding work advocated new managerial structures:

> A whole new dimension must be added to prior research and planning activities. *In a rough equivalent to the private sector. ... A centralized planning and research unit could contribute a great deal. ...* (Goldstein, 1990, p. 162, emphasis supplied)

The Government Performance and Results Act of 1993 provided overall impetus for federal agencies to follow a business model. By 1994, there was a clear trend within government to "reinvent" themselves. This all-embracing view was shared by many police scholars urging police adoption of "corporate strategies" and "entrepreneurial" approaches (Burns and Stalker, 1961; Moore and Trojanowicz, 1988).

Managers would be held accountable for results as well as these new practices. For police, as with other public organizations, performance measures were viewed as integral to adoption of and accountability for these business characteristics (Kravchuk and Schack, 1996; Wholey and Hatry, 1992). Osborne and Gaebler (1992) promoted the re-inventing government movement as the "public sector analogue to the corporate business process engineering movement, which has been described as one of the most influential management ideas of the nineties." (Case, 1999, p. 419; cited in O'Connell, 2002).

Performance measures are supported by concepts linked to the re-engineering process. "Benchmarking" and "best practices" cherish objectives and standards that are shared throughout the entire organization (Bowerman and Ball, 2000; Coe, 1999).

The introduction and spread of business performance management in American police departments is typified in the post-1993 changes in the NYPD. Modern business management provided the orchestral score for these changes; "re-engineering" was its name. Former Commissioner William Bratton insisted, "We re-engineered the NYPD into an organization capable of supporting our goals" (Bratton, 1996, p. 1). Reporters were captivated by the re-engineering motif and the "Management Secrets of Crime-Fighter Extraordinaire William Bratton" (Bratton and Knobler, 1998). The *New Yorker* described "the CEO cop" as "an avid consumer of the literature of corporate reorganization and motivation" (Lardner, 1995, p. 45). The *Economist* portrayed the commissioner as "a fan of the re-engineering rhetoric of Michael Hammer and James Champy" (*Economist*, 1995, p. 50). *Business Week* lauded the NYPD's "innovative turnaround artists" who used "private-sector" techniques (*Business Week*, 1995, p. 83).

In the parlance of business management, performance standards were set for the whole department and its subunits. Entrance to Bratton's higher echelon was restricted to commanders committed to double-digit crime reduction. Establishing a specific objective—a 10-percent reduction in crime for 1994—was the initial propellant for change. Lowering crime statistics was now to be considered analogous to increasing business profits. There are many problems with this analogy. We only mention a few. First, such a strategy ignores the fact that crime victims are not profits. There is a human element in dealing with victims. Second, Constitutional rights must be protected while fighting crime. Police managers operating in a performance management environment rarely attend to this important caveat. Third, clearly there is an incentive for police commanders to manipulate the crime statistics they themselves garner and record.

While statistical performance objectives served as mobilizers and an organizing framework for communicating changes, more was needed. Performance objectives required enforcement. This turned out to be a document and then a crime strategy meeting with the name of Compstat. (The word Compstat originally was short for a newly formed computer file named "compare stats.")

The commissioner and his top aides recognized that data needed to be gathered and analyzed in a timely manner if effective crime-reduction strategies were to be implemented. These statistics constituted the first Compstat book in February 1994.

Subsequently, periodic Compstat meetings were scheduled at headquarters whereby precinct commanders were required to report and react to newly created, accurate, and timely crime data generated from their areas of responsibility (i.e., their commands). Over time, these data-based informal discussions between department executives and field commanders developed into formal bi-weekly strategy meetings (known as Compstat meetings) whereby *all* levels of the department participated to identify precinct and city-wide crime trends, deploy resources, assess and are held accountable for crime control strategies and results. (For details, see Silverman, 2001.) The dramatic recorded crime drop in New York City since Compstat's inception has claimed so much attention that other jurisdictions and agencies throughout the world have undertaken similar systems.

Compstat Conversions

The swiftness of its conversions is amazing. It has been over 17 years since Compstat was first introduced in the NYPD in 1994. Five years later, a Police Foundation's 1999 survey for the National Institute of Justice (NIJ) revealed that one-third of the nation's 515 largest police departments would have implemented a Compstat-like program by 2001 and 20 percent were planning to do so. The same survey found that about 70 percent of police departments with Compstat programs reported attending an NYPD Compstat meeting (Weisburd, Mastrofski, McNally, and Greenspan, 2001).

The imitation of Compstat does not end here. Gootman (2000) reported that 219 police agency representatives visited NYPD Compstat meetings in 1998, 221 in 1999, and 235 in the first ten months of 2000. This includes law enforcement agencies from abroad that have adopted their own versions of Compstat-like police performance management systems.

Since its inception in 1994, Compstat systems have been adopted in other city agencies in New York and elsewhere. In 1996, New York City's

Corrections Department, for example, modeled its TEAMS (Total Efficiency Accountability Management System) program on Compstat with an examination of the department's "most fundamental practices and procedures" (O'Connell, 2001, p. 17; Anderson, 2001, p. 3).

Compstat accountability mechanisms, long a staple of the private sector and law enforcement, have become increasingly attractive to non-law enforcement public agencies as well. The New York City Department of Parks and Recreation developed its own version of Compstat, calling it Parkstat. When Parks officials visited NYPD Compstat meetings in 1997, they realized that they could utilize this system to develop and refine their Parks Inspection Program (PIP), which overseas the maintenance and operation of over 28,000 acres of property throughout New York City (O'Connell, 2001, p. 20).

Concerning the expansion of programs similar to Compstat, the *Gotham Gazette* published a piece describing the numerous agencies Compstat has influenced. The article states:

> In August 2001, the Giuliani administration announced the Citywide Accountability Program, which asked all city agencies to develop programs that implement the essential elements of Compstat.
>
> More "children of Compstat" appear every day. For example, the Mayor's Office of Health Insurance has been re-focusing Healthstat, a program designed to help uninsured New Yorkers enroll in publicly funded health insurance programs. In the first 18 months, participating agencies enrolled about 340,000 eligible New Yorkers. There are still 1.6 million uninsured New Yorkers, about 900,000 of whom are eligible for public insurance programs.
>
> The Department of Education's new Office of School Safety and Planning will use elements of Compstat for SchoolSafe, a program that will identify schools with the highest crime rates and implement action plans. (Webber and Robinson, 2003, p. 2)

Perhaps the most ambitious extension of Compstat's managerial accountability and informational exchange processes began in Baltimore, Maryland in mid-2000 when its mayor was delighted with the results of the Baltimore Police Department's first year with Compstat. Baltimore's program, called CitiStat (first developed by Compstat architect, the late Jack Maple), is an attempt to evaluate and coordinate performance on a citywide basis whereby supervisors report every two weeks (as opposed to the previous quarterly basis) on their departments' performance. CitiStat's timely data permits the assessment and coordination of diverse social services dealing with graffiti, abandoned vehicles, vacant housing, lead paint abatement, urban blight, drugs, and drug treatment. Discussions are based on up-to-date information. CitiStat meetings are similar to those of Compstat whereby data, graphs, and maps are projected to track and display department performance.

The prestigious *Innovations in American Government Award* was presented to Baltimore's CitiStat 10 years after NYPD's Compstat received the same award. This fact speaks to the enduring concepts embedded in this managerial and organizational approach. CitiStat, like most Compstat-type programs, seeks to lower the informational barriers that generally hinder intra- and inter-agency collaboration. Baltimore's experience has prompted similar approaches in numerous other cities—such as Atlanta (ATLStat); San Francisco (SFStat); St. Louis, Missouri (Citiview); Palm Bay, Florida (PalmStat); Somerville, Massachusetts (SomerStat); Providence, Rhode Island (ProvStat); Syracuse, New York (SyraStat); and King County, Washington (KingStat) (Behn, 2006, pp. 332–340). As Perlman (2007, p. 6) declared, "'Stat' Fever … really got hot."

Overseas, several cities in Scotland, including Aberdeen, Edinburgh, and Sterling, have experimented with CitiStat. All of these adaptations of the original Compstat innovation are based on the same premise: advanced governmental performance can be achieved by overcoming fragmentation and lack of accountability. This management approach, however, is not uniquely applicable to municipal government. In 2002, the Ohio Department of Job and Family Services created its "Performance Center." In 2005 in Washington, Governor Christine Gregoire developed GMAP (for Government Management Accountability and Performance). In 2007, when Baltimore's mayor became governor of Maryland, he created StateStat. Moreover, at least one unit of the federal government, the San Diego district of the U.S. Border Patrol, has created its own version of this approach, which it labeled BorderStat. Such innovation, however, is not the panacea initially envisioned.

Private Sector Performance Shortcomings

Despite widespread police and other public sector mimicking private sector performance approaches, the public sector has failed to acknowledge the private sector's diverse experiences with performance standards. The public sector has reified the private sector without actually examining its track record.

For example, when Mayor Bloomberg first announced a teacher's union agreement to pay teachers cash bonuses at schools where test scores increase, he said, "In the private sector, case incentives are proven motivators for producing results. The most successful employees work harder, and everyone else tries to figure out how they can improve as well" (Gootman, 2007). The foundation head promoting incentive pay plans for teachers added, "Virtually every other industry compensates employees based on how well they perform. … We know from experience across other industries and sectors that linking performance and pay is a powerful incentive" (Bloomberg, 2007).

Four years later, the *New York Times* reported that, based on a new Rand Corporation study, the "Teacher Bonus Program Is Abandoned by the City."

> A New York City program that distributed $56 million in performance bonuses to teachers and other school staff members over the last three years will be permanently discontinued, the city Department of Education said on Sunday. The decision was made in light of a study that found the bonuses had no positive effect on either student performance or teachers' attitudes toward their jobs. It compared the performance of the approximately 200 city schools that participated in the bonus program with that of a control group of schools. The results add to a growing body of evidence nationally that so-called pay-for-performance bonuses for teachers that consist only of financial incentives have no effect on student achievement, the researchers wrote. (Otterman, 2011)

Why did it take over three years for New York City to realize the futility of its ways? For years, education and other (including policing) public sector functions have studiously misrepresented private sector experiences. While performance incentive pay systems and performance goals are often stipulated in the private sector, they are almost never based exclusively or even primarily on quantitative measures of performance. One study found that over a quarter of full time private sector workers received performance pay in 2000, an increase from 21 percent in 1988. Yet there was a substantial increase of employees evaluated on subjective supervisory evaluations (Adams and Hayrood, 2007).

Since many of the distortions and corruptions of quantitative measures in the private sector parallel those in public activities, "business management literature nowadays is filled with warnings about incentives that rely heavily on quantitative rather than qualitative measures" (Rothstein, 2008, p. 60). These warnings are based on evidence. The respected business analyst, Chris Argyris, for example, observed how headquarters' quotas triggered factory workers expediting easy jobs through the line at the end of reporting periods (Argyris, 1993). This gaming also applied to managers such as H. J. Heinz company managers whose bonuses were based on continuous earnings growth. They maximized compensation by manipulating the timing of shipment or billing for services from one year to a previous or future year (Baker, Gibbons, and Murphy, 1994, p. 1125). (As noted in Chapter 2, this closely parallels examples from the NYPD.) A thorough review of management accounting concluded, "The behavioral literature on management accounting and control is replete with reports of subordinates who game performance indicators, strategically manipulate information flows, and falsify information" (Jaworski and Young, 1992, p. 17).

Private sector experiences also mirror the short-term versus long-term public sector quandary. A major bank concluded that rewarding managers for short-term branch financials worked to the detriment of long-term profitability as measured by customer satisfaction (Rothstein, 2000). As a result, despite its many flaws, subjective evaluations are increasingly used in the private sector, leading one personnel management review to conclude, "It is better to imperfectly measure relevant dimensions than to perfectly measure irrelevant ones" (Bommer et al., 1995, p. 602).

Years ago, the noted business analyst W. Edwards Deming warned against quota work standards, management by numerical objectives, and performance standards as they inevitably stress short-term goals. *"Management by numerical goals is an attempt to manage without knowledge of what to do, and in fact is usually management by fear.* Only good subjective leadership not restricted to mechanical and quantitative judgment can maximize long term goals" (Deming, 1986, pp. 76, 101, 102; emphasis added). A thorough review concisely summarized the literature:

> Policy makers who promote performance incentives and accountability seem mostly oblivious to the extensive literature in economics and management theory, documenting the inevitable corruption of quantitative indicators and the perverse consequences of performance incentives which rely on such indicators. (Rothstein, 2008, p. 79)

In a recent penetrating review of the automobile industry, Bob Lutz explains how the MBA numerical approach overshadowed the traditional engineer-customer oriented approach to building cars. As a result, the myopic "number crunchers" or "bean counters" dragged the American car industry into a downward spiral (Lutz, 2011).

Unraveling the Puzzle

Despite the massive evidence of dysfunctional components of Compstat and other performance management systems, it has, as indicated previously, spread throughout the world. This book addresses the distortions of an ossified crime fighting system, how and why the distortions have expanded and, at times, their disastrous consequences for the public and the police at home and abroad. We also examine Compstat's current leadership style skewered by its own "success" and offer viable alternatives. We explore the connection among those in the NYPD hierarchy, the media, and others who consider our findings threatening and devise barriers to shield themselves from any critiques or alternative non-official narratives. We also delve into the theories that underpin Compstat and their ramifications.

Chapter 2 documents and analyzes in detail a wide array of data that we have collected, which, for the first time, definitively demonstrates the range of manipulation reflected in official New York City crime statistics. Chapter 3 explores how the consequences of unreliable and non-trustworthy crime statistics ripple throughout police organizations affecting police, citizens, and victims. Chapter 4 documents the widening spell of police performance management throughout the world. Chapter 5 reviews current NYPD leadership approaches and offers alternatives. Chapter 6 analyzes the significance of the synchronicity of the media's and the NYPD's responses to our findings. Chapter 7 explores the implications of various theoretical approaches to Compstat. Chapter 8 offers an exit from a closed police department—an exit primarily fueled by a newfound organizational transparency.

Our work exposes imminent threats to democratic and transparent policing as it has spread throughout the world. We provide detailed scientific evidence of these phenomena. This volume for the first time unveils the inner workings of a police department surrounded by barriers and lacking transparency. These themes are woven throughout this volume and first emerge in an examination of the department's distorted crime statistics. These crime statistics are the subject of the next chapter.

References

Adams, S. and Heywood, J. (2007). "Performance Pay in the US; Concepts Measurement and Trends," November 19, Economic Policy Institute.

Anderson, D.C. (2001). "Crime Control by the Numbers: Compstat Yields New Lessons for the Police and the Replication of a Good Idea," *Ford Foundation Report.*

Arantz, P. (1993). *A Collusion of Powers.* Dunedoo, Australia: Philip Arantz.

Argyris, C. (1993). *Knowledge for Action. A Guide to Overcoming Barriers to Organizational Change.* New York: Jossey-Bass Wiley.

Baker, G., Gibbons, R., and Murphy, K.J. (1994). "Subjective Performance Measure in Optimal Incentive Contracts," *The Quarterly Journal of Economics* 109(4): 1125–1156.

Behn, R. D. (2006). "The Varieties of CitiStat." *Public Administration Review*, 66 (3): 332-340, May-June.

Blau, P. (1955). *The Dynamics of Bureaucracy.* Chicago: University of Chicago Press.

Bloomberg, M. (2007) "Mayor's Press Release," No. 375, October 17, www.nyc.gov.

Bommer, W., Johnson, J.L., Rich, G.A., Podsakoff, P.M., and Mackenize, S.B (1995). "On the Interchangeability of Objective and Subjective Measures of Employee Performance: A Meta-Analysis," *Personnel Psychology,* 48(3): 587–605.

Bowerman, N. and Ball, A. (2000). "Great Expectations: Benchmarking for Best Value," *Public Money and Management,* 20(2): 21–26.

Bratton, W. (1996). "Management Secrets of a Crime Fighter Extraordinaire," *Bottom Line*, August.

Bratton, W. with Knobler, P. (1998). *Turnaround.* New York: Random House.

Brown, M. (1998). "Philip Arantz, Whisteblowing Scourge of Officialdom, Dies at 68," *Sydney Morning Herald*, March 5, 4. The Whistle, Whistleblowers Australia Inc., University of Wollongong, Wollongong, NSW, http://www.bmartin .cc/dissent/contacts /au_wba/whistle19980 5.html#Heading2.

Burns, T. and Stalker, G.M. (1961). *The Management of Innovation*, London: Tavistock.

Business Week (1995). "A Safer New York City," December 11.

Butterfield, F. (1998). "As Crime Falls, Pressure Rises to Alter Data," *New York Times,* August 3, http://www.nytimes.com/1998/08/03/us/as-crime-falls-pressure-to-alter-data.html.

Campbell, D.T. (1976). "Assessing the Impact of Planned Social Change," The Public Affairs Center, Dartmouth College, Hanover, NH. http://www.eric.ed.gov/PDFS/ED303512.pdf.

Case, P. (1999). "Remember Re-engineering: The Rhetorical Appeal of a Managerial Salvation Device," *Journal of Management,* 36(4): 419–441. July.

Center, L. and Smith T. (1972–1973). "Crime Statistics—Can They be Trusted?" *American Criminal Law Review,* 11: 1045–1086.

Coe, C. (1999). "Local Government Benchmarking: Lessons Learned from Two Major Multigovernment Efforts," *Public Administration Review*, 59(2): 110–130.

Courty, P., Heinrich, C., and Marschke, G. (2005). "Setting the Standard in Performance Measurement Systems," *International Public Management Journal,* I(3): 321–347.

Deming, W.E. (1986). *Out of the Crisis.* Cambridge: Massachusetts Institute of Technology.

Figlio, D. (2005). "Testing, Crime and Punishment," NBER Working Paper W11194, March.

Figlio, D. and Getzler, L. (2002). "Accountability, Ability and Disability: Gaming the System," NBER Working Paper W9307, November.

Finn, C. and Ravitch, D., Eds. (2007). *Beyond the Basics.* Washington, D.C.: Thomas B. Fordham Institute.

Five-Yeomans, J. (2011, June 18). "Top Cop Who Fell from Grace," *Daily Telegraph*, http://www.dailytelegraph.com.au/top-cop-overlands-fall-from-grace/story-fn6b 3v4f-1226077400141.

Goldstein, H. (1990). *Problem Oriented Policing.* New York: McGraw Hill.

Gootman, E. (2000). "A Police Department's Growing Allure: Crime Fighters from Around World Visit for Tips," *New York Times,* B1, October 24.

Gootman, E. (2007). "Teachers Agree to Bonus Pay Tied to Scores," *The New York Times,* October 18.

Jaworski, B. and Young, S.M. (1992). "Dysfunctional Behavior and Management Control: An Empirical Study of Marketing Managers," *Accounting, Organizations and Society,* 17(1): 17–35.

Kantrowitz, B. and Springern, K. (1997). "Why Johnny Stayed Home," *Newsweek*, 60, October 6.

Kravchuk, R.S. and Schack, R.W. (1996). "Designing Effective Performance Measurement Systems Under the Government Performance and Results Act of 1993," *Public Administration Review*, (4): 348–358.

Lardner, J. (1995). "The CEO Cop," *New Yorker,* 45–56, February 6.

Levitt, L. (2011) "The Press Club Steps Up," http://nypdconfid ential.com/print/2011p/110627p.html, June 27.

Lutz, B. (2011). *Car Guys vs. Bean Counters: The Battle for the Soul of American Business*. New York: Portfolio.

Moore, M.H. and Trojanwicz, R.C. (1988). "Corporate Strategies for Policing" *Perspectives on Policing*, 5, National Institute of Justice.

Moore, S. (2007). "In California Deputies Held Competition on Arrests," *The New York Times*, http://www.nytimes.com/2007/10/05/us/05sheriff.html?scp=1&sq=in%20california,%20deputies%20held%20competition%20on%20arrests&st=cse, October 5.

Murray, M. (2005). "Why Arrests Quotas Are Wrong," *PBA Magazine*, Spring.

Murrow, E.R. "Edward R. Murrow Quotes," http://www.goodreads.com/quotes/show/222611. Retrieved on August 29, 2011.

Nason, D. (1998). "Wood Forces the Issue," *The Weekend Australian*, 27, February 10.

New York City Police Department. (2011). Patrol Guide, New York City Government Document. Guide for patrol officers including rules and regulations.

NYPD, Inc., 336(7925) 50. *Economist*. (1995, July 29).

O'Connell, P.E. (2001). *Using Performance Data for Accountability*. Arlington, VA: PricewaterhouseCoopers.

O'Connell, P. (2002). "An Intellectual History of the Compstat Model of Police Management," Ph.D. dissertation, City University of New York.

Osborne, D. and Gaebler, T. (1992). *Reinventing Government: How the Entrepreneurial Spirit Is Transforming the Public Sector*. Reading, MA: Addison Wesley.

Otterman, S. (2011). "Teacher Bonus Program Is Abandoned by the City," *New York Times*, http://www.nytimes.com/2011/07/18/education/18rand.html?sq=teacher%20bonus%20program%20is%20abandoned%20by%20the%20city&st=cs e&scp=1&pagewant ed=print, July 18.

Parascandola, R. (2010). "Brooklyn's 81st Precinct Probed by NYPD for Fudging Stats; Felonies Allegedly Marked as Misdemeanors," *Daily News*, http://www.nydailynews.com/news/ny_crime/2010/02/02/2010-02-02_precinct_probed_for_fudging_stats_li_say_bklyns_81st_wanted_to_improve_its_crime.html, February 2.

Perlman, E. (2007). "Stat Fever," *Governing*, January.

Rayman, G. (2010a, March 4). "The NYPD Tapes: Inside Bed-Stuy's 81st Precinct," *Village Voice*, http://www.villa gevoice.com/content/printVersion/1797847/.

Rayman, G. (2010b, June 15). "NYPD Tapes 4: The WhistleBlower, Adrian Schoolcraft," *Village Voice*, http://www.villagevoice.com/content/printVersion/1864848/.

Rayman, G. (2011, August 4). "Adil Polanco Case: NYPD Files New Charges Against Whistleblower for, Yes, Blowing Whistle." *Village Voice*, from http://blogs.village voicc.com/runninscared/2011/08/adil_polanco_ca.php, August 4. Retrieved on August 11, 2011.

Ridley, C. and Simon, H. (1938, 1943). *Measuring Municipal Activities*. Chicago: The International City Managers' Association.

Rothstein, R. (2000). "Making a Case against Performance Pay," *The New York Times*, April 26.

Rothstein, R. (2008). *Holding Accountability to Account*. Nashville, TN: National Center on Performance Incentives.

Seidman, D. and Couzens, M. (1974). "Getting the Crime Rate Down: Political Pressures and Crime Reporting," *Law and Society Review*, 8(3): 457–494.

Simon, H.A. (1978) "Rational Decision-Making in Business Organizations," Nobel Memorial Lecture, December 8.

Twigg, R. (1972). "Downgrading of Crimes Verified in Baltimore," *Justice Magazine,* 5/6: 15–18.

Uhlig, M.A. (1987). "Transit Police Remove Officer for Quota Plan," *The New York Times,* http://www.nytimes.com/1987/12/21/nyregion/transit-police-remove-officer-for-quota-plan.html?scp=1&sq=transit%20%20police%20remove%20officer%2 0for%20quota%20pl an&st=cse, December 21.

U.S. General Accounting Office. (1994). *Health Care Reform.* GAO/HEHS 94-219, Washington, D.C.: General Accounting Office.

Webber, R. and Robinson, G. (2003). "Compstamania," *Gotham Gazette.* New York: Citizens Union, July 7.

Weisburd, D., Mastrofski, S.D., McNally, A.M., and Greenspan, R. (2001). *Compstat and Organizational Change: Findings from a National Survey.* Report submitted to the National Institute of Justice by the Police Foundation.

Wholey, J. and Hatry, H. (1992). "The Case for Performance Monitoring," *Public Administration Review,* 62(6): 41–64.

Suggested Reading

Boivard, T. (2000). "Role of Competition and Competiveness in Best Value in England and Wales," *Public Policy and Administration,* 15(4): 82–89.

Campbell, D.T. (1969). "Reforms as Experiment," *American Psychologist,* 24(4): 409–429.

Jackman, T. (2004). "Falls Church Police Must Meet Quota for Tickets," *The Washington Post,* C01, August 8.

Punch, M. (1983). *Control in Police Organizations.* Cambridge, MA: MIT Press.

Ridgway, V.F. (1956). "Dysfunctional Consequences of Performance Measurement," *Administrative Science Quarterly,* 1(2): 240–247.

Silverman, E.B. (2001). *NYPD Battles Crime: Innovative Strategies in Policing.* Boston: Northeastern University Press.

Smith, P. (1995). "On the Unintended Consequences of Publishing Performance Data in the Public Sector," *International Journal of Public Administration,* 18(2 and 3): 277–310.

Stecher, B. and Kirby, S.N., Eds. (2004). *Organizational Improvement and Accountability, Lessons for Education from Other Sectors.* Washington, D.C.: Rand.

The NYPD's Untold Story

2

Crime Report Manipulation

There is no doubt that crime has gone down in New York City. While the police department year in and year out boasts about this success, there is a lesser-known underside to their crime numbers. Just as we are sure that crime has decreased, we are equally sure that the crime report numbers are being manipulated, making them look better than they actually are. Because of this, we question the *scope* of the decrease (not the decrease itself). We are concerned for city residents, victims of crime, the rank and file police, detectives, supervisors, police commanders, and many others who have suffered under the unrelenting, top-down management style that is now practiced in the NYPD. We also inform readers that this is not merely a NYPD phenomenon, but has infected policing both nationally and internationally as well as other occupations (e.g., education). In this chapter, we focus on the manipulation of crime statistics due to the pressures of the management system known as Compstat.

We begin by asking the reader, what do you think is the toughest aspect of being a police officer? Many might think it is wrestling with a suspect; perhaps making split second decisions about shooting or not shooting; some might even think it is concern about being shot or seeing a fellow officer hurt; perhaps dealing with an unsympathetic member of the public. Based on our detailed conversations with officers, their worries rarely touch on these critical aspects of their job. These important concerns pale in comparison to their most common complaint and worry; most officers find that dealing with upper management is the most challenging part of their job. Due to the pressures of upper management, officers worry if they can meet their quotas of tickets and arrests. They worry about whether their commanding officer will return to the precinct after experiencing a bad Compstat meeting at headquarters. One officer who spoke to us advised, "My job is to make sure we don't take a hit on a number unless we have to." What he is referring to is making sure the numbers of reports for serious crimes are down. Unfortunately, actual crime has become a secondary issue. As long as the *numbers* of crime reports appear to be decreasing, the upper echelon is kept satiated. Officers are keenly aware that they somehow need to keep these numbers down so the commander will not be exposed to the wrath of the high-ranking officials running Compstat meetings. While this may not be the intent of Compstat, it is how the message has filtered down to the street officer. Thus, the words of those running Compstat meetings may say one thing, yet that is not the message that is heard. Rather, it is the fear generated in commanders that resonates through the job. Regardless of the verbiage used by the upper echelon, the message being sent is one of fear—not reason, not crime fighting, not teamwork, not helping victims, but fear, leading to pressure to make the numbers look "right."

Most police officers of any rank are dedicated and filled with altruistic ideas of doing good, especially when they begin their careers. By the time most of them are on the street for a few years, their enthusiasm has dampened and they are relegated to the most common mantra in the department (with the exception of those in managerial positions)—"twenty and out" (when one is eligible for full retirement). Compstat robs them of their idealistic notions. They become sheep relegated to the hopeless routine of getting and watching numbers. They are no longer problem solvers, but automatons dedicated to making sure the figures look good. How does this demoralizing transformation take place? Why are crime reports and not actual criminal activity so important to officers? Why do numbers mean everything? To understand the NYPD, one must understand Compstat.

Compstat

What is Compstat? How can it have such an influence over officers of nearly every rank? Compstat, short for compare statistics, is a managerial system aimed at holding commanding officers accountable. Its basis is seen in its four-part mantra: accurate and timely intelligence, effective tactics, rapid deployment, and relentless follow-up and assessment. The first part is the key—accurate and timely intelligence. Without accurate crime data and information, the rest of the system is useless. This is because tactics, deployment, and follow-up will be formulated by examining and using the inaccurate statistics at the outset. Therefore, any plan developed from them will ultimately be doomed to failure. Therefore, at its foundation, Compstat relies on accurate and timely statistics.

Compstat involves weekly meetings at police headquarters (1 Police Plaza). At these meetings, charts and maps compare index crime (i.e., murder, rape, robbery, felony assault, burglary, grand larceny auto, and grand larceny) numbers to the same period last year at three levels: weekly, 28 days, and year to date. Thus, commanders are held strictly accountable. The numbers in their precincts are constantly being compared to last years' numbers.

Always being compared to last year's numbers can be a real burden, especially if your previous year was exceptional.

We can try to understand this by examining a hypothetical situation. Say you are working for a company with 40,000-plus workers at your disposal. Your production is very efficient leading to a high-quality product. For many years, the product is excellent and getting better. Now management takes away 6,000 of your employees and adds numerous other tasks to your schedule. You are forced to reshuffle thousands of the relatively few who are left. These workers must be reassigned to the new tasks, which are just as demanding as the initial task. Further, management demands that you keep up the same production and quality as before, even though you have far fewer workers at your disposal. Heads will roll unless the same quantity and quality are maintained or improved. Is management's demand reasonable or even possible? What will workers resort to in order to try to meet the unreasonable expectations? As we will soon see, this is exactly the situation at the NYPD.

In the NYPD, Compstat is where upper management pressures line workers. During Compstat meetings, commanders must present information about shootings and other information generally related to crimes with respect to their precincts, transit districts, or housing police service areas to the upper echelon of the department. The upper echelon, including but not limited to the police commissioner, first deputy commissioner, chief of department, and deputy commissioner of operations, among others, sit comfortably in chairs and desks that are in a U-shape format. There is a podium or table at the open part of the U. At the podium or table is a commander with a few others from his or her command. Hundreds of officers pack the operations center at headquarters where the meetings take place. They are there to watch and sometimes participate in the spectacle. Those known as the "inquisitors" generally run the meeting. The upper echelon's personalities generally shape the tone of the meetings. The commander, essentially powerless against a determined inquisitor, stands at the podium (or sits at a table) and presents information about how the precinct is doing with a focus on crime control. The commander is held strictly accountable for what is happening in the command. At times, commanders are berated and embarrassed in front of their peers because the numbers do not look "correct." Indeed, even the most dedicated NYPD commanders and former commanders that we interviewed indicated that they were aware of and witnessed their brother and sister commanders often being unnecessarily berated because they were not articulate or savvy enough to have an immediate response to a question.

It should also be noted that the inquisitors have vast troves of resources that are not made available to commanders. For example, the inquisitors have detectives and others working behind the scenes (rather than with the commander of the precinct) trying to find stolen items at pawnshops or other places. When the inquisitors so order, their detectives would check pawn-shops. At the shop, they might find stolen goods. At this point, rather than confront commanders privately, inquisitors make a great spectacle at the Compstat meetings. Photographs of the stolen items might be shown behind the commander. The commander's "failure" is displayed for all to see. The commander is left shamefaced and helpless in front of all present.

Clearly, the pressure is on the commander to show results (i.e., crime reports going down). Essentially, the unwritten message of Compstat is that if the numbers of crimes are going up, say "good-bye" to your career. However, if the numbers of crime reports are going down, you will be promoted and will have a great career. Given that commanders are in control of the crime numbers, they are led into enormous temptation to examine the reports closely and even manipulate them.

Thus, we believe it possible, even probable, that these pressures often become intolerable. Commanders feel an overwhelming need to do something, anything, to make the crime statistics look good for Compstat. The logic of this is impeccable and unquestionable. However, criminologist's logic is not enough. Rather, scientific investigation and evidence is required before we reach a conclusion. What evidence, other than a basic logical hypothesis, is there of such manipulation?

Evidence

New York City's gargantuan crime reduction is itself something at which to marvel. It has been hailed as the single most important aspect showing the success of the NYPD. Every year, for 16 straight years, crime has gone down in every index crime category, rarely an increase, rarely a statistical adjustment, rarely anything but down. In fact, the size of the reduction itself is amazing. The police department reports an astounding decrease in crime of 77.75 percent from 1990 to 2009. That, in itself, leads anyone with even a working knowledge of statistics to question them. From 1994 to 2009 (the last full year before our report went public), there is not a single year or a single category of index crime where crime numbers show an appreciable increase at year end. Normal statistical fluctuations would dictate that crime should increase somewhere. That assumes, however, that the books are not being cooked.

We further note that this "miraculous" drop was done while the department was bleeding out officers. Department head count went down—not by just a few officers, but by thousands of officers. Further, additional thousands were assigned to commands that did not exist until after 9/11, such as new units under the Deputy Commissioner of Intelligence and the Deputy Commissioner of Counterterrorism. This is like the company we talked about earlier. The NYPD had 40,000-plus officers at the height of its strength. The crime rate, its self-proclaimed product, was decreasing greatly. However, department strength went down over 6,000 officers and new tasks were added. Yet, vociferously, energetically, and overwhelmingly, management demanded the same product—decreases in crime numbers—year in and year out as before. Overall, roughly 20 percent (one-fifth) of the department was no longer available (6,000 to attrition and others reassigned). These facts alone make it difficult to swallow the NYPD party line that the entire drop in crime was accomplished with little or no manipulation.

Evidence from within the police department adds to our already tortured beliefs. The New York City Police Department's own Patrolmen's Benevolent Association (PBA; police union) has been quite vocal about their concerns. The Recording Secretary of the PBA Robert Zink (2004) writes,

> It was a great idea that has been corrupted by human nature. The Compstat program that made NYPD commanders accountable for controlling crime has degenerated into a situation where the police leadership presses subordinates to keep numbers low by any means necessary. The department's middle managers will do anything to avoid being dragged onto the carpet at the weekly Compstat meetings. They are, by nature, ambitious people who lust for promotions, and rising crime rates won't help anybody's career. ...

He goes into detail explaining how the crime drop was accomplished.

> ... So how do you fake a crime decrease? It's pretty simple. Don't file reports, misclassify crimes from felonies to misdemeanors, under-value the property lost to crime so it's not a felony, and report a series of crimes as a single event. A particularly insidious way to fudge the numbers is to make it difficult or impossible for people to report crimes—in other words, make the victims feel like criminals so they walk away just to spare themselves further pain and suffering. Some commanders even persecute the victims so they stop reporting crimes. In one case, it is alleged that a precinct commander shut down a fast food joint because the manager reported a grand larceny—someone stole a pocketbook. The precinct commander shut the place down for "an investigation" during lunch hour. Do you think the manager of that establishment, who relies on his lunchtime income, will ever report a crime again?
>
> The truth is, there are over 5,000 fewer police officers on our streets than there were in 1999. And there is a lot more work to do because of the threat of terrorism. And all along, the bosses have been peddling phony numbers to make everybody feel safe. Our mayor likes to say that the NYPD has been doing more with less. Perception becomes reality. But when people are being put at risk and victimized due to ambitious managers, that's unacceptable.

Here the PBA clearly outlines in detail how downgrading is accomplished. This is not a media account. This is not an enemy of the police department. This is not a radical fringe group. These are the police officers themselves speaking.

Similarly, the Sergeants Benevolent Association (SBA) joined the PBA in a joint press release on March 23, 2004. In the release by both unions, Patrick Lynch, the PBA president, discusses downgrading of crime reports. He states in the release, "It [downgrading] is a truth that is widely known by members of the department and now we have to see if the police commissioner has the courage to face the truth and do what is right for the city of New York" ("Unions Call," 2004).

Recently, others in the union have echoed this statement. Joseph Alejandro (2009), the PBA treasurer, further writes about pressures leading to a numbers game:

> Those numbers include the arrest and summons quotas ("managerial targets," the NYPD calls them) that this union has long complained of, the proliferation of stop-and-frisk incidents that the media have highlighted, and the increasing press coverage accusing precinct commanders of fostering a culture of knee-jerk felony-to-misdemeanor downgrades in an effort to improve their showing at those famously stressful Compstat meetings at One Police Plaza. Those numbers represent the dark side of Compstat. (Alejandro, 2009)

Anecdotal evidence for manipulation of the crime statistics is, therefore, very strong. Clearly, there has been a need for a more scientific study of the NYPD. Given that the police department will not voluntarily open its doors to outside inquiry (and even stymied a Mayoral Commission to investigate these practices headed by former federal prosecutor Mark F. Pomerantz), we needed an innovative method to study their behaviors with respect to Compstat and crime reporting. Our method of studying the department is based on both quantitative and qualitative scientific inquiry.

Survey of Retirees

Quantitative inquiry involved a sophisticated questionnaire that was distributed with the help of the Captain's Endowment Association (CEA). We sent a questionnaire via United States Postal Service to all retirees in the CEA's database. Retirees have the advantage of less fear from retaliation than current working members have and, therefore, are more likely to tell the truth. Further, we specifically chose to give our respondents anonymity. This means we cannot identify a particular respondent with a questionnaire. That is, we do not know how any particular person answered or indeed if a particular person responded. This is a very important feature of our survey in that providing anonymity is more likely to result in truthful responses (see, for example, Babbie, 1989; Bradburn, 1983; Dillman, 1983; Neuman, 2000).

Respondents were instructed not to put any identifying information on the questionnaire. Furthermore, respondents were not required to respond to the questionnaire. All responses were voluntary. Additionally, there were no repercussions for not filling one out. We simply wanted to learn about the NYPD management style and asked respondents for their assistance. The questionnaire took only a few minutes to fill out, which helped to increase the response rate (i.e., made it more likely that those sent the questionnaire would fill it out and return it). We also had our contact information on the questionnaire in case someone did not understand a question, needed clarification, or had any other questions.

On September 10, 2008, we sent the survey to 1,197 retired members of the CEA with the ranks of Captain and above. There were 491 returned, indicating a response rate of 41 percent Of these, 323 (66 percent) respondents retired in 1995 or later and 166 (34 percent) retired before 1995—the first full year of Compstat.

The survey itself (see Appendix B) consisted of four sides of 8½-by-11-inch paper and included 23 questions. It was purposely kept short as lengthy questionnaires often discourage respondents from filling out the instrument (Neuman, 2000). Question wording was tested extensively in development. Focus groups with retired and current members of the NYPD, as well as a separate focus group comprised of other researchers, reviewed the instrument carefully. Wording was extensively revised to ensure that respondents clearly understood the meaning of the questions. Most of the survey questions were closed ended except for the last question, which gave respondents an opportunity to share any crucial points that they wished to add.

A few points about the survey are necessary before discussing the results. The survey was sent out with a letter on CEA stationery asking for retirees' assistance (see Appendix A). The CEA president and the authors signed the letter. The researchers paid for postage. The CEA incurred no expenses whatsoever as the funding for the research came entirely from a grant from Molloy College. Thus, the CEA only gave us access. We did include three questions on the questionnaire that were CEA related. Other than that, the CEA had nothing to do with the survey, analysis, or results. We met with the CEA on January 29, 2010. We supplied them with a full report. We disclosed to them the results on every question including all the open-ended responses. We were later informed that this was shared with the police commissioner. We have heard nothing from the police department except through the media.

A second aspect of our method is the use of in-depth interviews. These cannot be anonymous because we know who the respondents are. Nevertheless, all respondents were promised that their answers would be kept confidential and their names not revealed. While these interviews are not a representative sample of the entire department, they do include various ranks from police officer through deputy chief. All worked during the Compstat era. Two worked regularly with Compstat in headquarters. All were in good standing and remain so today. None of them had serious disciplinary problems. These interviewees agreed to help us by contacting us after seeing news reports or advising us that they would help. We have conducted over 30 of these in-depth interviews. These unstructured interviews are similar to what is called an "informal conversational interview." As Maxfield and Babbie (2009, p. 205) state, "... the interviewer establishes a general direction for the conversations and pursues specific topics raised by the respondent. Ideally, the respondent does most of the talking." Interviews generally lasted about an hour to an hour and a half. They were casual and took place either through a conference call or in an office atmosphere. Both authors were present for every interview. This allowed us to clarify what was being said to each witness, to add reliability to what was being said, to compare notes regarding the discussion, and to clarify with follow-up calls any issues of which we were unsure.

Beyond this, both authors know numerous working and retired NYPD personnel. We are continually asked about our research and often, spontaneous comments are offered about the NYPD. These current and former police personnel have been supportive. While we cannot reveal names, we can say that exceedingly high-ranking officials have talked to us and confirmed nearly every aspect of our study.

Our intent is the same as it has been since the beginning—to conduct unbiased, scientific research. Any criticism of the NYPD is meant to be taken as constructive and helpful. While both authors have been supportive of the police department, the data speaks for itself.

We first examine the closed-ended survey data. Our first look at the data is an examination of those who worked before Compstat began versus those who worked during the Compstat era. We assess the level of pressure on retired Captains and above to decrease the level of index crime. Index crimes (murder/non-negligent manslaughter, forcible rape, burglary, robbery, felonious assault, grand larceny auto, and grand larceny) are the focus of Compstat meetings. We note that the FBI classifies Arson as a major crime while the NYPD does not in Compstat reports. Therefore, if our hypothesis is correct, there should be some differences in the level of pressure. The question we are examining is called a matrix question. That is, we ask a basic question and it is followed by a list of items on the left going down in a column. The respondents then answer that question for the items listed in the column. In this case, the question reads, "With respect to the following criteria and based on your personal experience, on a scale of 1 to 10 (with 1 being the least and 10 the most), how much pressure was there from management/supervisors to decrease index crime?" (see Retiree Survey in Appendix B). For this first question, note that we use the words "based on your personal experience." Our focus groups indicated it is clear that all questions following are to be answered in this way.

This question shows the largest single difference in responses in the entire study. The average response from commanders who worked pre-Compstat was 5.66. The average response from those commanders who worked post-Compstat was 8.26. This is a large mean difference of 2.6. For those with statistical knowledge, this is a large size effect ($r = .557$) and the probability of a result of this size occurring by chance is slim ($p<.001$). Essentially, what this means is that those commanders who worked in the Compstat era felt much more pressure from management/supervisors to reduce the level of index crime. This confirms Compstat's enormous pressures to reduce index crime.

The next comparison is based on question 9, which reads, "To what extent did management demand integrity in crime statistics?" This question is also on a scale of 1 to 10, with 1 being slight demand and 10 being high demand. We expect that demand for integrity in statistics would be about the same, or perhaps even more during the Compstat era, because of the new focus on crime statistics. The results from the survey, however, surprisingly indicate that demand for integrity in crime statistics was significantly greater in the pre-Compstat era. The average response was 7.18 for pre-Compstat commanders and 6.52 for Compstat commanders. The mean difference is .66 and this difference is statistically significant ($p<.01$). In addition, of the 82 respondents who stated there was slight demand for integrity in the crime statistics, nearly 80 percent were working in the Compstat era. This reveals that Compstat-era commanders felt much less demand from management for integrity in the statistics compared to their counterparts who did not work during the Compstat era.

This is a major concern. It is our contention that the combination of an enormous increase in pressure to decrease index crime mixed with decreased demand for integrity in the crime statistics is a recipe for manipulation of the numbers. The NYPD has argued that it has created a new Data Integrity Unit and that its Quality Assurance Division is ensuring proper preparation of crime reports. This is all well and good, and we have no doubt that these units review written complaint reports and perform other audit responsibilities. Regardless of what the department did up to the time of this survey, it is irrelevant. This is because our survey question does not address bureaucratic practices but addresses the *perceptions* of commanders. Indeed, NYPD practices may be aimed at deterrence, but, if this is the case, our research indicates the NYPD's management practices regarding integrity in crime statistics is simply not effective. In this survey, our data clearly indicate that the current NYPD units are ineffective at changing the perception of commanders. Regardless of the units, auditing, or other NYPD practices, the *perception* of commanders based on their experiences is that management in the Compstat era is not as demanding of integrity in crime statistics compared to earlier pre-Compstat era commanders.

We also asked a question regarding managerial pressure to downgrade index crime to non-index crime. This is different from pressure to decrease index crime. Pressure to decrease index crime is something we might normally expect of a police department. That is, crime should be low and such pressures might be considered normal. However, pressure to downgrade index crime to non-index crime is a specific practice requiring commanders to find ways to move crime from one category (index) to another category (non-index). An example of this activity is a commander feeling pressure to move grand larceny to lost property. We expect this pressure to be low because, by its nature, downgrading is suspect activity.

This is a very important distinction. When we see pressure to downgrade index crimes to non-index crimes, it means that commanders are not thinking about actual criminal activity but about the numbers of reports in each category. They are feeling pressure to make sure that the numbers are not too high in the index crime category. It specifically means that they feel pressure to play the numbers game.

Importantly, pressures to downgrade index crime were significantly higher in the Compstat era. The average response of commanders in the Compstat era was 3.88 and the average response of commanders in the non-Compstat era was 2.51. The difference is 1.37. This was a statistically significant difference ($p<.001$) and a small size effect ($r = .077$). What this means is that once again the pressures are higher for Compstat-era commanders, in this case, to downgrade index crime to non-index crime.

Another area of concern is promotion being based on crime statistics. While this may not be as critical as other pressures, we do note that of the 206 participants who responded that promotion is highly based on crime statistics, 76 percent worked during the Compstat era. This is more evidence indicating the overwhelming pressures of Compstat to show statistics are going in the "proper direction."

Given the previous analyses, our concern turns to actual manipulation of crime data. We use a contingency question to test this. That is, commanders are asked whether they are aware of any instances in which crime reports were changed due to Compstat. If they answer yes to that question, they are then asked questions that are more specific about that awareness. The use of a contingency question is very important. First, it establishes awareness. Those who are unaware of changes will answer "no" and move on to other questions.

We note here that if respondents as a whole were answering based on their general knowledge (e.g., news reports, rumors, and the like) and not personal information, nearly every commander would have answered "yes." This was not the case. Of the 309 commanders who worked in the Compstat era, roughly half (160) indicated they were aware of changes. Indeed, one respondent wrote this unsolicited remark:

> I think everyone in NYPD is "aware" of instances in which crime reports were changed due to Compstat. However, I marked "no" for my answer because the

instances that I heard of could have been only rumors and I have no factual information of such occurrences.

Thus, all respondents were likely aware of changes, but many answered "no" indicating they had no direct knowledge. We further note that if respondents based answers on general knowledge, they were unable to respond to the questions below. This is one reason for using the contingency question. It eliminates those who do not have basic information and clearly establishes personal knowledge through other questions.

We also point out that this question and the way it is worded protects respondents and gauges the existence of manipulated crime reports. The other questions below the initial one also gauge whether the manipulation is proper. However, we did not get precise counts of manipulation because that was not our research goal. If one is interested in prosecuting individual members of the NYPD, such numbers are appropriate. Our aim, however, is not prosecution but scientific research. We deemed the need for such stick counts minimal. This question met our needs and protected respondents. Importantly, we note for the purposes of accuracy that our gauge *under-counts* the level of report manipulation because we allow for multiple events. Therefore, our results must be read keeping in mind that crime manipulation is likely much higher than what we report.

We have established that 160 commanders indicated they were aware of manipulation of crime reports due to Compstat. Changes of reports due to Compstat are commonplace. Many of these changes are completely ethical and appropriate. For example, one interviewee, who was a commanding officer (CO) of a precinct, advised:

> Respondent: I actively sent out an officer to fix the numbers. If a car was reported stolen but was actually parked in a spot that the person could not find the car, well that had to be corrected. It was a matter of accuracy to be reflected in the Compstat figures.

Here there are two issues. First, the pressures on commanders force them to use officers to do such tasks as finding cars that were reported stolen but, in fact, were not actually stolen. This is a waste of scarce labor. Officers are being sent out not to fight crime but to fix the crime reports.

Second, this is one indication that changes to complaint reports are exceedingly common. It means that nearly anyone who has worked in a precinct is aware of changes being made to crime reports. This is important because it means that those respondents who were completely unaware of any changes, even ethical ones, clearly were not in a position (i.e., work assignment) to observe much of anything with respect to crime complaints. Based on our survey's contingency question (a preliminary question that is answered and only those who respond in a certain way go to the next question [see question 4 on the questionnaire in Appendix B]), we are able to expose those who did not work in precincts. That is, those who answered they were not aware of any changes to complaint reports must have had a work assignment in Headquarters, the Police Academy, or something similar. Therefore, one advantage of the contingency question is exposing those respondents who were in positions to observe changes without having them reveal information about their assignments, helping us to maintain anonymity (and, consequently, validity or truthfulness) while at the same time collecting important information. We therefore separate out the 160 respondents who were aware of changes, eliminating those who had no awareness at all. Thus, we examine the responses to the follow-up questions for those who were aware of changes to reports.

A follow up question asks respondents the "extent to which change(s) were ethically inappropriate." The scale is 1 to 10 with 1 being least inappropriate and 10 being most inappropriate. To examine this, we grouped responses into low (1–3), medium (4–7), and high (8–10) categories.

Of the 160 respondents who were aware of any changes, over half (53.8 percent) indicated that the changes observed were highly unethical. An additional 23.8 percent indicated the changes were moderately unethical. The remainder indicated the changes were ethical. With over half of those aware of changes indicating that those changes were highly unethical, there can be no doubt that unethical manipulation was taking place.

Overall, the obvious pattern throughout these data is that there are pressures generated by the leadership of the NYPD emanating from Compstat, which lead to unethical manipulation of crime reports. That is, the combination of pressures—much higher pressure to decrease index crime, less pressure to maintain integrity in crime statistics, and more pressure to downgrade index crime to non-index crime—has led to unethical manipulation of crime statistics in New York City. Those interested in more statistical analyses can see our peer reviewed scientific study on this topic (Eterno and Silverman, 2010).

Interviews

As if this were not enough, we have other data based on our in-depth interviews and other comments in the survey confirming the statistical analysis. These statements include common practices of which interviewees were personally aware. Some interviewees noted that commanders not only downgraded, but also resorted to going to the scene to attempt to sway victims of index crimes. For example,

> JE/ES: Can you explain some of the pressures you speak of?
> Respondent: One CO would check book and catalog to look up depreciated value to make it a misdemeanor, same with car parts. That's how desperate

COs would get. [They would] go to [the] scene where index crime occurred, assess, try to get [the] complainant to change story.

To understand this, you must have the knowledge that crimes become more serious based on the amount stolen. Here we see that some COs would look up values of stolen property in a frantic attempt to make the crime drop from a felony to a misdemeanor (misdemeanors are lesser crimes not reflected in the index crime figures). We note here that the NYPD has now incorporated this practice into its everyday operations. That is, they have department-approved Web sites that crime analysts may access in an attempt to reclassify a crime. We have several issues with this practice. First, it is different way of counting compared to the past. Such accounting practices were rare. Second, we have concerns when officers are spending time attempting to identify the cost of items rather than working the streets. How many officers are dedicated to this practice? Certainly, valuable time is being wasted to make the numbers look more favorable.

Even more disturbing is the CO going to the scene or an officer on the scene talking to the victim in an attempt to get the complainant to change a story. One of our interviewees spoke of an incident he witnessed after he retired. He was sitting at lunch with several other retired members when he witnessed the following exchange.

> Respondent: Right next to me was a gentleman with a laptop. ... Next thing I know police show up and the guy is telling them that he was working on his laptop when someone came over and ran off with it. The officer told him it was lost property and would not take it as a crime. The officer kept refusing to take it as a crime.
> JE/ES: Do you think this is typical behavior?
> Respondent: Perhaps it is a lack of training, perhaps they want a promotion, maybe a lack of interest, but everything you guys have said is accurate ... the message [of Compstat] is being relayed incorrectly to officers in the street.

Other respondents had similar comments,

> Respondent: There was full adherence to penal law, very literal interpretations. They would surf the Internet to find a bicycle price, question victims to ensure it was an index offense ... COs were driven to reading the letter of the law.
> Respondent: It was a matter of spiking [a sharp increase in crime] then apply the letter of the law ... try to find something to "legitimately" knock down crimes. ... As crime went down, the pressure to maintain it was great. Crime drop was real but after a while even an obvious homicide would be put in as "investigate death." Anything questionable was not a number.

Comments like these are so prevalent that we are confident that you can talk to anyone you know on the NYPD and he or she will certainly relay to you similar observations. In addition, if interested, there is a Web site where

NYPD officers regularly air their views on this and many other topics called "THEE Rant." It is an open site; feel free to visit and see their comments. Our particular favorite is "The Fudge Factory" for NYPD crime statistics.

Crime Victims Coming Forward

Victims have come forward to talk of their experiences when going to the NYPD for help. We believe that the NYPD is a professional organization, but the overwhelming pressures of Compstat have created a problematic culture where it becomes normal to attempt to minimize the number of index crime reports. The first victim we discuss is a victim of a recent identity theft. He went into his local precinct to report the crime. He was immediately presented with a letter on official department stationary and summarily told to leave the precinct—no report, no advice, nothing. The copy of the letter reads as follows (see Appendix C):

To Whom It May Concern:

The New York City Police Department requires specific documentation be submitted before a police report for Identity Theft or fraud-related crimes can be taken. The documentation is needed to aid in the proper investigation of the crime.

The documents that are need [sic] are as follows:

1. A letter on the company, bank or institutions [sic] letterhead, that states the person is disputing opening the account and/or the charges being billed; it should include:
   a. Account Holder's Name and Account Number
   b. Amount(s) or Services being disputed
   c. Name and address of person who opened the account (if available)
   d. Where merchandise was sent (if available)
2. A company affidavit, that is notarized, that states the complainant had no prior knowledge or involvement in the transaction of fraud or identity theft; this should include amount(s), account names, account numbers, services and/or any other item(s) being disputed.
3. A copy of your credit report from: Experian, TransUnion and Equifax, the credit reporting bureaus, to see if any other fraudulent transactions have occurred.
4. Any supporting documentation that can aid in your claim of fraud or identity theft.

Once the above documentation has been submitted and verified by our investigators, a police report can be taken. Please allow 24 to 48 hours after you file your report, [sic] for a complaint number to be generated and be made available.

Sincerely,

Police Administrative Aide
Complaint Room

As in this case, some victims are left helpless by the NYPD. The difficulty they have reporting identity theft is obvious. The NYPD placed numerous barriers in front of this victim preventing him from reporting the crime. Compounding that problem this individual was offered no help, no guidance, nothing but this letter. Rather discouraging for victims. Perhaps victims and city residents are not going to the police to make reports because of such behaviors. Are other victims treated this way?

A community leader, Joseph Bolanos, has contacted us numerous times since our report first went public. He has reported many incidents of police failing to record or, at times, respond to citizens' complaints of crimes. He writes to us about a typical incident:

> Last month a burglar climbed into a window from a brownstone stoop while the tenant was at home. She screamed and the perp ran out of the apartment. The police arrived and failed to take a report of the incident! My neighbor and her husband were stunned by it. It does not get more fundamental than that.

This is yet another example of types of police behaviors about which we are talking.

In an even more distressing report, the case of attempted rape victim Debbie Nathan (author of *Sybil Exposed*) represents the type of horror that victims can experience due to police behavior. Her account has now been publicized in the *Village Voice* and the *New York Times* among other outlets. She contacted us after our research went public early in 2010. This is her story in her own words:

> I am a freelance journalist, formerly an editor at *City Limits* magazine, who was sexually assaulted in February of this year [2010] in Inwood Hill Park. I was overpowered by a man and pushed/dragged into a wooded area. The man told me he wanted to have sex with me. Continuing to push me, he masturbated against me until he made a noise as though he was having an orgasm. Only then did he let me go, and he ran off into the woods.
>
> As soon as I was free, I called the police. It took them two hours to respond. When they did, six officers came to my home. They spent almost two hours talking with me about what had happened. Toward the end of that period, some of them stepped out into the hall of my apartment building and called SVU, the Special Victims Unit, the NYPD police unit that specializes in identifying and investigating sex crimes. After relaying questions from SVU to

me, and my answers to SVU, the officers told me that—at the behest of SVU—they were classifying the crime as misdemeanor "forcible touching." As far as I was concerned, it was clear that what had happened to me was a felony attempted rape. I argued with the officers but they insisted on maintaining their classification.

Next morning I complained about what had happened to me on an online, community public safety site. The people running that site notified my state assembly member and by early afternoon, the misdemeanor classification had been upgraded to felony attempted rape. A community meeting was called to discuss what had happened to me, and at that meeting, I told the precinct commander for my neighborhood that I wanted to see my incident report. When I got the report several days later, I discovered that all the details I had given the officers about the perpetrator—the color of his clothing, what he'd said to me, how he touched me physically, and how he pushed me into the woods—were missing. Further, the report falsely stated that no sexual contact had occurred.

A few days after the assault against me, I contacted Harriet Lessel of NYC Against Rape. She told me that her organization had become aware during the past year and a half of systemic misclassification and downgrading, in all the boroughs of New York City. Subsequently I got a call from Lisa Friel, head of the sexual assault unit at the Manhattan DA's office. Before she learned from our conversation that I was a journalist, she, too, told me that the NYPD was deliberately or at least systematically downgrading sexual assault reports. She said she had repeatedly complained about this to higher ups in the NYPD.

She later told me that she called all six officers who were in my house into her office and questioned them about why they misreported my report. They all simply shrugged, she said.

I certainly can't prove this. But oddly, while I was embroiled in the controversy and it became a public issue among anti-rape activists, I got calls from people who volunteer as counselors at hospitals that provide rape crisis services to sexual assault victims. I was told that SVU agents are some of the worst minimizers at the hospitals, when they come to take reports.

… I am feeling increasingly troubled that the NYPD might be pulling a fast one on the press … (Nathan, 2010)

Her words are disheartening, discouraging, and debilitating. One can only imagine the horror that Ms. Nathan went through. However, she was clearly victimized again by those charged to help her. Forcible touching is the lowest criminal charge—a misdemeanor. Had she not been a journalist who is politically savvy, her report would be buried with, we fear, countless others. At a minimum, this case appears to be an attempted rape first degree and possibly sexual abuse first degree—both felonies. Why forcible touching and not attempted rape? Attempted rape is an index offense counted in Compstat figures. While we do not know for sure, a plausible explanation for this downgrading is due to fear of Compstat. Are there others?

Commissioner Kelly appointed a committee called the Sex Crimes Working Group to examine reporting of sex crimes. He did this in response to an outcry from victims groups and rape counselors in April 2010. They claimed that reports of sex crimes were not being taken. Our report on downgrading went public in February 2010. After these groups confronted Mr. Kelly, he quietly formed this Working Group. This lends enormous credibility to Ms. Nathan's communication. Further, it strongly supports our position of downgrading. Gardiner (2010, December 22) reports on the key changes as a result of the Working Group. One of the most important is that, "… all sexual-assault complaints be assigned to Special Victims Division (SVD) detectives who are specially trained in sex-crime investigations. Currently, sexual-assault complaints are handled by patrol officers." While this may seem appropriate, it is merely window dressing—a superficial change. Our position is that Compstat has been used as the driving engine that leads to downgrading. Any changes must address top down management pressures reflected in Compstat meetings. Rape and other index crimes are downgraded due to this pressure. Further, as Ms. Nathan advises, SVD detectives may not be appropriate for determining the classification, as they apparently misclassified her case, and may be equally likely to downgrade. How many more victims will go unheard?

Detective Harold Hernandez

Village Voice reporter Graham Rayman exposed another egregious sex crimes case that appears to be downgrading as well. Retired first grade detective Harold Hernandez came forward to talk about a case he was working on in the 33rd precinct. The case involved a serial rapist. It was solved after someone spotted the perpetrator pushing a victim into an apartment. Police came and made an arrest. During interrogation of the perpetrator, Detective Hernandez became aware of six other forcible rapes committed by the suspect. He then searched the complaint file and found that all of them were recorded as lesser crimes, most being criminal trespass. These were sexual assaults apparently downgraded to criminal trespass. Detective Hernandez reported that the patrol supervisors were apparently downgrading. In Hernandez's own words, "They look to eliminate certain elements in the narrative. One word or two words can make the change to a misdemeanor" (Rayman, 2010c, June 8).

This is a tragedy. Had these reports been properly taken, a pattern could have been developed and a rapist stopped before he struck seven times. Further, with each sexual assault the perpetrator become more violent. Recently, the perpetrator was convicted and is now serving a 50-year sentence (Rayman, 2010c, June 8). There are several issues here confirming our research. First, the downgrading is apparent. Second, regardless of the level of oversight from headquarters, the paperwork is sufficiently doctored to prevent other units from properly classifying the report. For example, the Data Integrity Unit will read the report at headquarters as will Quality Assurance, but the report is not properly classified because the wording was changed. It is unlikely that a department accounting or audit will capture this. It requires methods of detection that are more intrusive. Third, and most important, how many others are out there? How many more victims must suffer? We return to our theme—without timely and accurate intelligence, the police department is hampered from doing its job.

Interestingly, reporter Leonard Levitt in his column pens that four members of the Shomrim volunteer patrol were shot chasing a suspect who allegedly exposed himself to children in the area. The week before the shooting, a man matching the newly caught suspect was seen exposing himself. At the time, a police officer was notified, as well as the Shomrim patrol. A witness gave key information to police including a detailed description and a license plate number. After the shooting, a search for the report apparently indicated that no police report was filed (Levitt, 2010). This incident occurred in Brooklyn. This is yet another indication that this is a citywide phenomenon.

Hospital Data

As if this were not enough, there are even more indicators of manipulation. The New York City Department of Health and Mental Hygiene maintains detailed statistics on patients who come to the hospital. Their data are publicly available and, while not directly comparable to NYPD data, they do give insight into important trends in the city. If NYPD numbers are accurate, they should show trends similar to the hospital data.

The trends are anything but similar. This strongly suggests manipulation of crime statistics by the NYPD. This is seen throughout the data. We examine four separate indicators in data collected by hospitals. None is consistent with NYPD records.

The hospital data for emergency department visits for assaults are completely at variance with NYPD figures. While NYPD data show a huge decrease approaching 50 percent, hospital records show an enormous *increase*. Figure 2.1 indicates a steady rise in emergency room visits for assault in every year that statistics are available. In 1999, there were 25,181 visits for assault. In 2006, there are 47,779 visits. This represents a whopping 90-percent *increase* in emergency room visits for assaults. These numbers are not even close! This is a very strong indicator of manipulation by the NYPD, possibly even turning victims away.

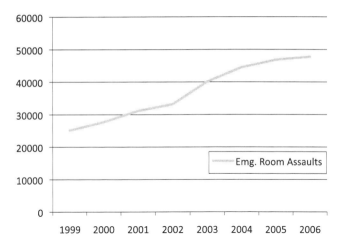

Figure 2.1 New York City Hospitals: Emergency Room Assaults. (*Source*: New York City Department of Health and Mental Hygiene.)

Second, emergency room visits for firearms have also skyrocketed. Figure 2.2 shows a steady increase in emergency room visits for firearms assaults. In 1999, there were 224 visits. In 2006, there were 514 visits. This represents a huge 129-percent increase in visits. This is yet another indicator completely in the opposite direction of NYPD's crime report data. We note that, by law, firearms assaults *must* be reported to the police by hospital authorities (see New York State Penal Law Section 265.25)! We have no indication that medical personnel are not following the law. Indeed, the NYPD

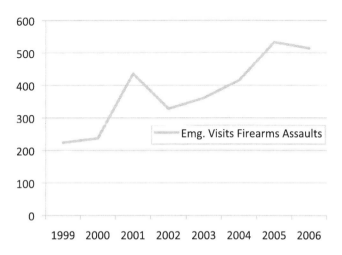

Figure 2.2 New York City Hospitals: Firearms Assaults. (*Source*: New York City Department of Health and Mental Hygiene.)

has strongly enforced this law in the past. The case of football player Plaxico Buress is an example (see Baker, 2008). So, where are the police reports?

Two other hospital indicators are also available supporting the position of manipulation by the NYPD. Intentional injury hospitalization statistics show an increasing trend as well. From 1999 until 2006, there is a percentage increase of hospitalizations for assault of 15 percent. While not as pronounced, again the trend is nothing close to the NYPD data. Yet another indicator, firearms assault hospitalizations, was unchanged from 1999 to 2006. What does all this mean? Absolutely none of the hospital data (New York City Health and Hospitals Corporation, 2011) showed the marked decrease in assaults that the NYPD claims. These data are in stark contrast to the NYPD's and clearly are evidence of manipulation.

New York State Division of Criminal Justice Services Data

Surely, the hospital data are enough to convince even the most stubborn of individuals. However, there is even more. Information available from the New York State Division of Criminal Justice Services (DCJS) on non-index crimes also shows a trend inconsistent with NYPD statistics. Data are available from 1993 through 2002 (see Figure 2.3). The trend is a decrease in crime from 1994 to 1996. This is what we expect. Index and non-index crime should parallel one another. Recall index crime is simply that—an index (or gauge) for all of crime. However, from 1997 to 2001, non-index crime steadily creeps up. In 2002, the last year available from DCJS, non-index crime goes down again (probably due to 9/11). The NYPD argues that crime has dropped steadily and precipitously during this entire period. Yet, DCJS data for non-index crime do not parallel that decrease. This is yet another indicator that

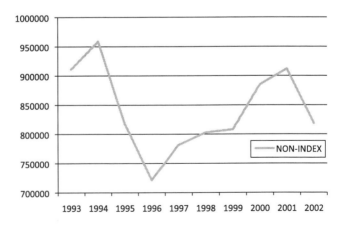

Figure 2.3 Non-Index Crime: New York City. (*Source*: New York State Division of Criminal Justice Services.)

there is a problem with NYPD manipulation of data. We note that the data from DCJS are not available after 2002. The NYPD was one of only two jurisdictions in New York State not to report this data. The NYPD has claimed that this is due to a computer software issue (Rivera and Baker, 2010).

Recently Released Historical Data

In December 2010, the *New York Times* announced a lawsuit against the NYPD to get the hidden misdemeanor data. Miraculously, almost immediately after the *New York Times* sued the NYPD for the data, the NYPD released what they call "historical data." This information has not been released since 2002 and appeared suddenly in 2010 after the *Times* lawsuit. In addition, as noted by Professor Andrew Karmen (2011) of John Jay College of Criminal Justice, other generally released data were no longer publicly available in full after 2001 (e.g., Statistical Report: Complaints and Arrests). While not directly comparable to the DCJS data, it is worth mentioning here because we see more evidence of manipulation even in this vetted data reluctantly released by the department.

The trends in these data are clearly compatible with manipulation. We examine here assault, sex crimes, and criminal trespass. Available Compstat data for felony assaults show an enormous drop since 1990. From 1998 to 2009, the percentage decrease is 41.9 percent. Further, recently released misdemeanor assault data show a decreasing trend from 2000 to 2009 of 9.1 percent. The concern here is that the trend in misdemeanor assault is clearly far less pronounced compared to felony assault. This is yet another indicator of manipulation in that the trends should be similar. It suggests that some felony assaults may be downgraded to ensure a larger downward trend in this area, which is closely scrutinized at Compstat (NYPD Web Site, 2011).

Examining burglary (an index crime) from 2001 until 2009, we see a decrease from 32,694 to 19,430 (−40.6 percent). This is a tremendous decrease. Downgrading a burglary can most easily be accomplished by reporting it as a criminal trespass. The trend in criminal trespass is in the complete opposite direction and then some. In 2001, there were 12,230 criminal trespasses. In 2009, there were 20,873—a whopping 70.7-percent increase (see Figure 2.4). Recall in our previous discussion of the serial rapist interrogated by Detective Hernandez, most of the forcible rapes were downgraded to criminal trespass as well. There is ample evidence here to make a case for downgrading.

Two other crimes we will look at are rape and felony assault. Rapes decreased 37.5 percent from 2001 to 2009. Misdemeanor sex crimes (we cannot parse out various crimes that are included here such as forcible touching, which appears to be a popular alternative to rape, e.g., Debbie Nathan) went

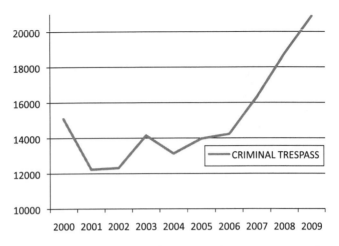

Figure 2.4 New York City: Criminal Trespass. (*Source*: New York City Police Department.)

down a mere 5.1 percent during the same period. This decrease is more than seven times less than the decrease in rape. Again, more evidence for downgrading. Felony assault went down 27.3 percent from 2001 to 2009. However, misdemeanor assault went down only half that much (13.2 percent).

We also point out that "offenses against public administration" (impeding an officer from doing his or her job) have skyrocketed—a real concern especially given the high number of stop and frisks (over one-half million—a huge number in comparison to previous years). We discuss this in more detail in other chapters. Importantly, we note that this large number of stops is further evidence of pressure from headquarters. Recall, the NYPD is arguing that crime is drastically down. Yet, at the same time, they argue that one-half million forcible stops are necessary. If we accept the NYPD argument that crime is down, then there also should be less need for forcible stops. Most of the previous years' crime drop occurred without so many forcible stops! If crime is down, then stops should be down too, assuming there is no pressure from Compstat. The one plausible explanation for such a large number of stops in a time of drastic decreases in crime is pressure from Compstat to conduct stop and frisks.

Furthermore, criminal possession of stolen property has doubled since 2000. Felony dangerous weapons have also skyrocketed during this period—adding more credibility to the hospital firearms data reported previously. Lastly, misdemeanors as a whole have trended up from 2005 until 2009. Again, this trend is completely at variance with NYPD reported index crime (NYPD Web Site, 2011).

Repeatedly, we see evidence of manipulation. For these newly released data, we simply confirm what we previously demonstrated. We see increases where we expect decreases and any decreases are usually less than expected. Overall, the fracture between index crimes and non-index crime trends remains even with these newly unleashed statistics. That is, there is still strong evidence for manipulation of crime reports.

We note here that the NYPD has consistently pointed to an internally supported study as suggesting their numbers are accurate. Contrary to the NYPD's assertion, that study has several fatal flaws. First, the study is not peer reviewed. It is simply the word of the authors without any neutral and detached judgment about its results or its methods. The methods are also highly questionable as seen in footnote 2 of that paper:

> ... Our conclusions are based on conversations with senior command staff and a review of written materials. We neither observed the actual sampling or auditing processes nor did we test the accuracy of the sampling procedures used by the Department in its audits. We can only infer how the written procedures were implemented in practice ... (Smith and Purtell, 2006, p. 5)

It is our contention that the people they rely on for their conclusions are the same upper echelon who are in charge of the system and have a stake in defending it. Therefore, the paper by these invited scholars is simply based on information fed from those expected to be favorable to the NYPD. Last, the paper compares trends of grand larceny to petit larceny. This is an inappropriate comparison. It assumes that the downgrading will be done that way. It does not examine, for example, the often-cited practice of downgrading grand larceny to lost property or consider victims who might be turned away.

The Letter of the Law

There are similar issues with work conducted by a second invited scholar, Franklin Zimring. Zimring (2011, p. 10) argues, "The best way to verify trends is with independent data." This means his research is essentially examining trends. We have no disagreement with crime trends in New York City. We have consistently stated that we believe crime is down. However, the extent of that decrease is open to serious question based on our work. Examining Zimring's evidence, however, we see various flawed and incomplete arguments making us even more skeptical of his conclusions. Zimring argues that he finds a near perfect correlation between health and police reports of murder and non-negligent homicide. This, he suggests, is clear evidence of police reports being accurate. What he fails to advise readers is that the police department is in continuous contact with the Medical Examiner (ME). They constantly check and verify homicides. Thus, the ME is not an independent source of confirmation because the police constantly change reports based on the ME's findings. Nothing could be further from independent. We also point out that homicides are most likely to be accurate. It is harder to fudge these. However, in our research we were told about how even these are gamed. One interviewee advised of a commanding officer who showed up at an obvious murder and ordered the complaint report to be written as "investigate aided." While at some point this will likely be listed as a homicide, it is clearly an attempt to hold down the count as long as possible. One commander was particularly innovative, explaining how he would hold back complaints on New Year's Eve until the next day. This would keep his numbers down for the year (see Naspretto, 2010, February 7).

The unrelenting pressures of Compstat clearly had an influence on how complaint reports were processed and handled. Without a doubt, a microscope was placed over reports (especially index crime reports) and they were examined as never before. We note that this, in and of itself, will have an enormous influence on crime numbers because it leads to a different way of counting compared to the past—enforcing the letter of the law on each report as it is carefully vetted through teams of officers and supervisors dedicated to trying to somehow, anyway they can, get the report reclassified as a non-index crime. Using the letter of the law is a completely different standard of counting compared to the past when the victim's word essentially would be accepted. We believe these citywide behaviors are at least partially responsible for some of the huge crime drop (see Eterno, 2003, p. 114). Indeed, Zimring's work essentially documents the phenomenon of victims being treated differently as we explain next.

Zimring also claims that auto theft is a second example because there are fewer claims. What he fails to advise readers is that around 1999 there was an enormous policy shift by the NYPD in which they began to require victims of auto theft to sign supporting depositions. Victims are now questioned much more extensively and are required to go back to the scene for a full investigation. This "biggest" decrease is at least partially due to how the NYPD treats victims differently. Not even mentioning this earth-shattering policy shift, which is documented in the NYPD Patrol Guide 207-11, is a major oversight, at best. He argues, "So the biggest decrease (auto theft) and the most important decrease (homicide) are both confirmed by independent sources" (Zimring, 2011, p. 11). We know, however, that neither of his key points is accurate.

He also asserts that there is no decrease in drug use based on hospital data. Yet, he says nothing of the incongruity of hospital data with NYPD data, which show large *decreases* in complaints for drugs. There is no correlation of NYPD complaint data with hospital drug data. On the one hand, he claims that independent data is the key, yet he ignores his own independent hospital data that refutes his main theme. It is clear that Zimring's work is open to question. We do note that even if he is accurate (we are adamant he is not with respect to report manipulation), we agree that there is a decrease in crime, but its extent, based on our published peer reviewed research, is also very questionable. If other critiques of Zimring (2011) are necessary for the reader, we suggest Selby (2011, March 25).

We also note that in our efforts to be value neutral and fair we mention the works of Smith and Purtell as well as Zimring. However, these studies, in turn, fail to acknowledge a colossal number of highly respected criminological studies that show major flaws in police reporting of crimes throughout the United States (see, for example, Mosher, Miethe, and Phillips, 2002). Our theme is completely in sync with this plethora of well-known and documented research. Furthermore, recent research on NYPD's influence on crime rates has been inconclusive, at best (see, for example, Bowling, 1999; Conklin, 2003; Harcourt, 2001; Karmen, 2000; Messner et al., 2007; Rosenfeld, Forango, and Rengifo, 2007). Even research favorable to NYPD may be fatally flawed since they tend to rely on official NYPD data (e.g., Kelling and Sousa, 2001).

NYPD Complaint Reports for Illegal Drug Use

NYPD data show an enormous decline in illegal drug use in the city. The NYPD recorded 38,088 felony dangerous drug complaints in 2000 (the last year available on the NYPD Web site). In 2006, they recorded 29,516. (We use 2006 merely to compare with other data. The 2009-percentage decreases are in the last paragraph of this section.) This represents a 22.5-percent decrease. Misdemeanor dangerous drugs show a similar trend. In 2000, there were 96,590 misdemeanor complaints for dangerous drugs. In 2006, there were only 65,945 complaints. This represents a 31.7-percent decrease. The downward trend, however, is completely at odds with a recent report from the New York City Department of Health and Mental Hygiene.

The Heath and Mental Hygiene Report (HMHR) indicates "from 1999 to 2006, the proportion of hospitalizations that were drug-related increased by 14 percent" (New York City Department of Health and Mental Hygiene, 2010, p. 2). Hospitalizations for illicit drug use, therefore, increased during the period. The trend is completely at variance with NYPD data (and Zimring's report indicating that hospital data show no signs of increases in drug use). Additionally, based on self-reports of drug use, New York City shows a higher illicit use compared to the national average (New York City Department of Health and Mental Hygiene, 2010). According to the report (New York City Department of Health and Mental Hygiene, 2010, p. 1), "nearly one million New Yorkers report using illicit drugs in the past year (16 percent). The national rate is 14 percent." This is not only completely at odds with NYPD data, but it is also an indication that the spin that New York is the "safest large city in America" is mistaken.

We note that based on NYPD statistics, the trend down for illicit drug complaints continues through 2009 with a nearly 40-percent decrease in complaints for felony dangerous drugs compared to 2000. The trend for misdemeanors is also down from 2000 with a 17.3-percent decrease. One can only ponder future trends, but if these data are any indication and no changes are made at NYPD, we are not hopeful. Why? The incompatible trends are likely due to the mimicking of Compstat-like management throughout the department. Narco-stat or other pressures emanating from Headquarters are the likely cause of the lack of congruity between HMRH data and NYPD complaint reports.

Admitted Problems with Manipulation by the NYPD and Other Jurisdictions

We have not yet mentioned manipulation of crime statistics that the department knows and admits to. At least four commanders (with another one pending) and seven others (with three more pending) have been accused and convicted of manipulation of crime statistics. This, in itself, is disturbing. Given our evidence, how many others have escaped detection? From our reading of the data, it may be quite a large number. Even the NYPD's Data Integrity Unit (DIU) admits that it tends to upgrade written complaint reports rather than downgrade when it does make changes. That is, in correcting reports that have already passed precinct inspection, the DIU more frequently upgrades reports. A 2005 Quality Assurance Division memorandum advises that complaint reports from 1999 until the time of the memorandum were corrected upward for 2 percent of the corrections and down for only 0.4 percent (Smith and Purtell, 2006, p. 18). Further, DIU is making fewer changes than in the past (Mac Donald, 2010). Is this good or, as Detective Hernandez suggests, are a few words being changed to have the report pass muster both in the field and at DIU so it is not considered an index crime (Rayman, 2010c)?

As if this were not enough, other cities throughout the United States and, indeed, the world, have admitted to serious crime manipulation issues. Most, if not all, of these jurisdictions are, or were, using the same Compstat-type management style as used by the NYPD. Some have copied outright NYPD's model and were commanded by former NYPD higher echelon personnel. Just a short list of some of these other cities include: Atlanta, Baltimore, Dallas, New Orleans, Washington, Philadelphia, and Broward County, Florida (Eterno and Silverman 2010; Rashbaum, 2010).

Internationally, crime statistic manipulation is well documented in the United Kingdom and Australia (see Chapter 4). We find this fact particularly salient because many of these locales were modeled after New York

City's Compstat managerial style. This strongly buttresses our point that it is occurring in New York City as well. NYPD, as a flagship police department (Bayley, 1994), has exported its management style without fully comprehending the consequences. Indeed, we think this phenomenon so important that we dedicate an entire chapter to performance management (see Chapter 3).

Audiotapes

Even the most stubborn must agree at this point that the case for manipulation is overwhelming. Any reasonable person, especially if he or she remains neutral and detached, would agree there is sufficient evidence calling for an outside audit, further investigation, and perhaps more. However, there is even more substantiation. In fact, the strongest evidence to date that cannot be refuted is audiotapes made by police officers themselves. We know of the existence of at least three audiotapes. Two are in the 81st precinct in Brooklyn. Police officer Adrian Schoolcraft recorded them. Confirming Schoolcraft's account was a ranking officer's recording of a supervisors meeting in the precinct. Adil Polanco made a third recording in the 41st precinct in the Bronx.

The tapes are very disturbing and confirm every aspect of our research, including the manipulation of crime reports. The Schoolcraft tapes clearly contain verbiage from supervisors advising patrol officers how to handle complaints such that the number of reports will be minimized. One of the most egregious discussions involves not taking complaint reports (i.e., 61's) if a victim of robbery does not go back to the station house to talk to the detective squad. This is heard in roll calls. At the roll call of October 12, 2009, for example, the supervisor is heard stating, "You know we been popping up with those robberies, whatever. The best thing I can say … if the complainant does not want to go back to the squad [detectives], then there is no 61 taken. That's it…" (Schoolcraft, 2009b). At this roll call, the supervisor is telling the officers *not* to take a report for robbery unless the victim goes back to the station house to talk to the precinct detectives. The concern is that the victim may be making up a story. Certainly, a preliminary investigation is necessary on the street. Requiring a complainant to go to the station house, however, is not only discouraging the complainant from making a report, but also is clearly contrary to proper police behavior. A few examples of what officers could do include the following:

- A description of the perpetrator could immediately be put over the police radio in an attempt to capture the suspect.
- The complainant could be placed in the back of the radio car to try to find the suspect.
- A canvass of the area could be done to find witnesses.

- Detectives could be called out to the scene, rather than requiring complainants to go to the station house.
- If detectives could not come to the complainant and the complainant was not willing to go to the station house, the report could be taken immediately in the field. Detectives could question a person later. Further, even if a complainant was uncooperative or did not wish to prosecute, this never means a report is not taken.

These are just a few examples of more appropriate conduct by police. Indeed, the NYPD Patrol Guide even advises that if the complaint is in another precinct, the report still must be taken (see NYPD Patrol Guide 207-04). Officers are supposed to take the reports at the scene and not refer complainants to go to a precinct. The basic rule is an officer should "refer the complaint, not the complainant." That is, the paper report is recorded and referred to the appropriate investigating body. The complainant should never be sent elsewhere. The police department has turned police science on its head. Clearly, this basic mantra of police academy training is simply being ignored.

On the tapes we hear officers being instructed not to take the complaint report (for robberies no less) unless the complainant is willing to go to the station house to talk to detectives. Not taking the report has serious consequences including preventing detectives from doing their jobs properly. For example, detectives will lack information necessary to establish a possible pattern (as was seen previously by statements made by Detective Harold Hernandez). Thus, many people may be being robbed yet may not be willing to visit the station house. In these cases, no report will be taken resulting in the police being left in the dark about numerous robberies.

Another audiotape reveals other unethical practices. The roll call of October 4, 2009 is particularly revealing. At this roll call, officers are instructed to question victims, that callbacks are being made by supervisors, and that officers should not take reports if they think the district attorney will not prosecute.

> Supervisor: … If you got a robbery and the squad's working, which they're usually working the day tour, the squad should be notified and they should do the complaint report. If you [have] any problems with that, talk to a [boss]. …

> Supervisor 2: Yeah, we had a robbery. Guy sounded totally believable. He said he got yoked up at Myrtle and Lewis. And he was yoked up from behind by a couple of guys who took his wallet and some money, and went to the squad for a debrief, and they were questioning him, where was this, where was that, and he finally admitted he was full of shit. I didn't get the rest of the story…It's a common tale. … Commercial guys … stole it himself, sold it or whatever the case is and he's trying to cover his tracks. Don't be afraid to question a robbery suspect. If it's a little old lady and I got my bag stolen, then she's probably

telling the truth, alright. If it's some young guy who looks strong and healthy and can maybe defend himself and he got yoked up, and he's not injured, he's perfectly fine, question that. It's not about squashing numbers. You all know if it is what it is, if it smells like a rotten fish, then that's what it is. But question it. On the burglaries as well.

Other supervisor: On that note too, because, uh, whether it's CO, [or other lieutenants (their names were removed)], they always do callbacks. So, a lot of time we get early information and they do callbacks.

Sgt: And then we look silly …. a domestic violence victim, woman, says, "Hey my boyfriend stole my phone." He didn't really steal the phone. It's his phone, and he was taking it. Did he snatch it out of her hand? Yeah. Is it a grand larceny? No, because I'm telling you right now the DA [District Attorney] is not going to entertain that.

Other supervisor: Exactly. (Schoolcraft, 2009a).

Why do the supervisors instruct police officers to question the veracity of robbery victims? It is not because they are interested in fighting crime but because robbery is a number that will be reflected at Compstat meetings. It will make the commander look bad. When we hear it's "not about squashing numbers," unfortunately, it comes across as exactly that, squashing numbers. Callbacks by the CO and lieutenants are among the most disturbing issues here. Victims are not being called back in an attempt to find a suspect. These are not detectives contacting victims, but relatively high-ranking personnel at the precinct level. Why? Clearly, they are doing everything possible, everything, to lower the index crime numbers. The supervisor states it is not a grand larceny because the "DA is not going to entertain that." This is highly unethical behavior. Precinct personnel are not in a position to decide what the district attorney will "entertain." District attorneys often lower charges made by police for many reasons. Police should not be taking initial reports based on what they think the district attorney will do. Again, why is this done? It should be clear at this point—to lower index crime numbers due to Compstat pressures.

These behaviors are, at a minimum, unethical. The audiotapes reveal how lower-level precinct supervisors and even precinct commanders have interpreted Compstat. Compstat's extreme pressure is translated into not taking reports, questioning the veracity of victims, downgrading reports, haranguing officers about callbacks by supervisors, attempting to figure out what a district attorney will do, and, in general, keeping the numbers of index crimes down in any way possible, regardless of consequences.

Is this localized to the 81st precinct? Other audiotapes from a precinct in the Bronx also show the extreme pressures officers are under to make their numbers. In a report aired by ABC News, investigative reporter Jim Hoffer (2010) states,

Officer Polanco says One Police Plaza's obsession with keeping crime stats down has gotten out of control. He advises that Precinct Commanders relentlessly pressure cops on the street to make more arrests, and give out more summonses, all to show headquarters they have a tight grip on their neighborhoods.

Again, we see the relentless pressures from Compstat translated to pressure at the precinct level. Audiotapes from two separate precincts, in two completely different boroughs, offer very strong evidence supporting our thesis.

Our Report Goes Public

Our report went public in the Sunday *New York Times* on February 7, 2010. Numerous other publications have covered our research including television news outlets in New York City. We find it notable that for the first time since Compstat began in 1994, we have seen an increase in the four categories of violent crime—murder, rape, robbery, and felony assault—the same year that our study went public. This is substantial. These violent crimes are more difficult to manipulate. Index crime report numbers did go down in 2010, but this is completely due to property crimes. Property crimes are much more easily manipulated because you can play with the cost of an item or even list it as lost property or other hidden non-index crimes.

We note here that lost property figures were recently released after many years of stalling by NYPD. They were released with great fanfare as an NYPD friendly newspaper was given a scoop (see Gardiner, 2011, January 28). Interestingly, we also note for our readers that as of this writing the NYPD has once again mysteriously removed them from their Web site. There was no publicity over this—just there one day and gone the next. This is typical of the NYPD crisis de jour mentality (see Chapter 6). In the case of lost property statistics, there were major concerns. Once released, we find it highly disturbing that the lost property numbers go directly down every single year since Paul Moses penned a critical report showing the numbers drastically increasing as burglary and other crimes were going down (see Moses, 2005; and Chapter 6). One must be suspicious of such a linear decrease year after year. Why? Did people suddenly stop losing property? Did the NYPD do a lost property initiative? Why do the numbers go down without any normal statistical fluctuations? Perhaps the NYPD focused enormous time and effort into making sure the lost property numbers went in a direction favorable to them after the embarrassment exposed in Moses' story. One can only ponder. However, when numbers decrease like this for no apparent reason, it is very strong evidence, yet again, of manipulation.

While not proof positive of manipulation, we do believe it quite possible, and logical, that our research has actually made a difference and caused those in the NYPD to be more aware of the issue. While there is no way for us to prove this, the fact that all categories of violent crime went up the same year our research was released has not gone unnoticed by us—particularly because every year for the past 15 years there has been, overall, a steady and clear decline. Is it possible that rock bottom was hit the same year as our study came out? Perhaps, but, given the previous evidence, how likely is that explanation?

Conclusion

The evidence is overwhelming. We started with anecdotal evidence in the form of comments from the NYPD's own PBA. We examined a scientifically designed questionnaire sent to retirees with over 400 respondents. Pressure to decrease index crime was far greater for those working during the Compstat era. Further, those working during this period felt *less* pressure to maintain integrity in the crime statistics and more pressure to downgrade index crime to non-index crime. Importantly, over half of survey respondents aware of any manipulation during the Compstat era indicated that the crime report manipulation they were aware of was highly unethical. In-depth interviews with respondents confirm the quantitative findings. A Web site of NYPD officers also regularly advises of manipulation. Victims of identity theft, rape, and other crimes have revealed their horrid experiences in trying to report crimes to the NYPD. A retired detective came forward reporting his experience of finding rapes downgraded to criminal trespass. Emergency department visits and other hospital data are completely at variance with NYPD data. Particularly disturbing is the staggering increase in emergency room visits due to firearms assaults. These must be reported to the police. Non-index crime data that are available from the New York State Division of Criminal Justice Services shows non-index crime increasing through 2001. Recently released historical data from the NYPD show disturbing trends. Criminal trespass, for example, went up 70.7 percent from 2001 to 2009, while the NYPD claims that burglary went down 40.6 percent during the same period. Alarmingly, misdemeanor sex crimes show a slight decrease of only 5.1 percent from 2001 to 2009 while rape shows a 37.5-percent decrease. National and international jurisdictions with similar management systems show marked evidence of statistical manipulation of the crime numbers. Audiotapes by officers and a supervisor at two separate precincts confirm our analysis as well.

This is a tremendous amount of evidence suggesting manipulation. At a minimum, there can be no doubt that further inquiry is necessary. As we have stated publicly, an impartial outside body needs to review the NYPD's practices. We note that Police Commissioner Raymond Kelly had appointed a panel of three former federal prosecutors in January 2011 to examine NYPD's crime statistics. They had a three- to six-month window to report. As of this writing, no report is available. The three members of the panel are Robert G. Morvillo, David N. Kelley, and Sharon L. McCarthy. All were appointed by the Police Commissioner to examine the crime reporting system. Questions have been posed recently about the police department forming its own investigatory team. We would feel far more confident if an independent analysis were conducted. Furthermore, an independent body should be authorized to grant immunity and have subpoena power. Without such power, any findings will likely be skewed in favor of the NYPD.

The importance of accurate and timely crime data should not be underestimated. It is not only important for Compstat to work properly, but it is also critical to policy formation. As Sullivan (2009, pp.10–11) writes,

> Crime prevention and crime control policies are often based on crime statistics. We've progressed regarding our data collection procedures, however, much work remains. Accordingly, crime related policies should be established only after policy makers are confident that the data used to make policy are valid and reliable. To rush to judgment and critically react, for instance by building more prisons, to the suggestion that crime is increasing seems premature. Time, advanced statistical analyses, due consideration of qualitative data, and the continued advancement in crime data collection will provide more effective guidance for crime-related policy.

To the extent possible, crime data need to be collected accurately. While we also have no doubt that crime has gone down, we strongly question the extent of this decrease. How many victims have gone unheard? How many detectives have been stymied by the system? How many past, present, and future crimes and terrorist activities could have been prevented if crime reports were properly taken? How many officers would have been hired had accurate data been available? In the next chapter, we demonstrate the consequences of statistical manipulation in malfunctioning performance management systems in vogue in New York and elsewhere.

References

Alejandro, J. (2009). "The Dark Side of Compstat," *PBA Magazine*, http://www.nycpba.org/publications/mag-10-09/alejandro.html. Retrieved on December 29, 2010.
Babbie, E. (1989). *The Practice of Social Research*, 5th ed. Belmont, CA: Wordsworth.
Baker, A. (2008, December 1). "Hospital Did Not Report Burress's Wound," *The New York Times*, Retrieved from http://www.nytimes.com/2008/12/02/sports/football/02hospital.html.
Bayley, D. (1994). *Police for the Future*. New York: Oxford University Press.
Bowling, B. (1999). The rise and fall of New York murder: Zero tolerance or crack's decline?, *British Journal of Criminology* 34(4), 531-554.
Bradburn, N.M. (1983). "Response Effects." In: P. Rossi, J. Wright, and A. Anderson, Eds., *Handbook of Survey Research*. New York: Academic Press, 289–328.

Bolanos, J. (2011). Personal communication. E-mail dated August 8, 2011.

Conklin, J. (2003). *Why Crime Rates Fell.* Boston: Allyn & Bacon.

Dillman, D.A. (1983). "Mail and Other Self-Administered Questionnaires." In: Rossi, P., Wright, J., and Anderson, A., Eds., *Handbook of Survey Research.* New York: Academic Press, 359–377.

Eterno, J.A. (2003). *Policing within the Law: A Case Study of the New York City Police Department.* Westport, CT: Praeger.

Eterno, J.A. and Silverman, E.B. (2010). "The NYPD's Compstat: Compare Statistics or Compose Statistics? *International Journal of Police Science & Management,* 12(3): 426–449.

Gardiner, S. (2011, January 26). "NYPD's Long War over Crime Stats," *The Wall Street Journal,* http://online.wsj.com/article/SB1000142405274870469800457610420 3869313630.html. Retrieved August 4, 2011.

Gardiner, S. (2010, December 22). "New Focus in Sex-Assault Cases," *The Wall Street Journal,* http://online.wsj.com/article/SB1000142405274870358120457603 3873467370478.html?mod=googlenews_wsj. Retrieved on January 14, 2011.

Harcourt, B.F. (2001). *Illusion of Order: The False Promise of Broken Windows Policing.* Cambridge, Mass.: Harvard University Press.

Hoffer, J. (2010, March 3). "NYPD Officer Claims Pressure to Make Arrests," Eyewitness News, http://abclocal.go.com/wabc/story?section=news/investigators&id=7 305356. Retrieved on January 3, 2011.

Karmen, A. (2000). *New York Murder Mystery: The True Story behind the Crime Crash of the 1990s.* New York: NYU Press.

Karmen, A. (2011, September 14). Unpublished personal communication.

Kelling, G.L. and Sousa, W.H. (2001). "Do police matter? An analysis of the impact of New York City's police reforms." (Civic Report No. 22) New York: Manhattan Institute.

Levett, L. (2010, September 27). "Police Crime Reporting Scandal: Now the 66th Precinct?" http://nypdconfidential.com/print/2010p/100927p.html. Retrieved on December 31, 2010.

Maxfield, M.G. and Babbie, E. (2009). *Basics of Research Methods for Criminal Justice and Criminology,* 2nd ed. Belmont, CA: Wadsworth/Cengage.

Mac Donald, H. (2010, February 17). "Compstat and Its Enemies," *City Journal,* np. http://www.city-journal.org/2010/eon0217hm.html.

Messner, S.F., Galea, S., Tardiff, K.J., Tracy, M., Bucciaelli, A., Piper, T. M., Frye, V., and Vlahov, D. (2007). "Policing, Drugs, and the Homicide Decline in New York City in the 1990s." *Criminology* 45: 385-413.

Moses, P. (2005, December 20), "Something's Missing." *Village Voice,* http://www.vil-lagevoice.com/2005-12-20/news/something-s-mnp.

Mosher, C.J., Miethe, T.D., and Phillips, D.M. (2002). *The Mismeasure of Crime.* Thousand Oaks, CA: Sage.

Naspretto, E. (2010, February 7). "Former NYPD Captain Didn't Fudge Crime Statistics in Past—He 'Delayed' in Reporting Them," *Daily News,* http://articles.nydailynews.com/2010-02-07/local/27055541_1_crime-statistics-index-crimes-crime-victims. Retrieved August 5, 2011.

Nathan, D. (2010). Personal communication. E-mail dated December 26, 2010.

Neuman, W.L. (2000). *Social Research Methods: Qualitative and Quantitative Approaches,* 4th ed. Boston: Allyn and Bacon.

New York City Department of Health and Mental Hygiene. (2010). "Illicit Drug Use in New York City," *NYC Vital Signs*, 9(1): 1–4. http://www.nyc.gov/html/doh/downloads/pdf/survey/survey-2009drugod.pdf.

New York City Health and Hospitals Corporation. (2011). http://www.nyc.gov/html/hhc/html/home/home.shtml. Retrieved on January 3, 2011.

NYPD Web Site. (2011). http://www.nyc.gov/html/nypd/html/crime_prevention/crime_statistics.shtml.

NYPD Patrol Guide. (2011). Unpublished New York City government document.

Rashbaum, W.K. (2010, February 6). "Retired Officers Raise Questions on Crime Data," *The New York Times*.

Rayman, G. (2010a, May 4). "NYPD Tapes: Inside Bed-Stuy's 81 Precinct," *The Village Voice,* http://www.villagevoice.com/2010-05-04/news/the-nypd-tapes-inside-bed-stuy-s-81st-precinct/. Retrieved on January 31, 2011.

Rayman G. (2010b, May 11). "NYPD Tapes, Part 2," *The Village Voice,* http://www.villagevoice.com/2010-05-11/news/nypd-tapes-part-2-bed-stuy/. Retrieved on January 31, 2011.

Rayman, G. (2010c, June 8). "NYPD Tapes 3: A Detective Comes Forward about Downgraded Sexual Assaults," *The Village Voice*, np. http://www.villagevoice.com/2010-06-08/news/nypd-tapes-3-detective-comes-forward-downgrading-rape/.

Rivera, R. and Baker, A. (2010, November 1). "Data Elusive on Low-Level Crime in New York City," *The New York Times*, np. http://www.nytimes.com/2010/11/02/nyregion/ 02secrecy.html?ref=rayrivera

Rosenfeld, R., Fornango, R., and Rengifo, A. (2007). "The Impact of Order-Maintenance Policing on New York City Homicide and Robbery Rates: 1988-2001." *Criminology* 45: 355-384.

Schoolcraft, A. (2009a). Schoolcraft tapes [Tape Recordings 81st Precinct Roll Call on October 4] from Rayman (2010, May 4). http://img.villagevoice.com/player/?i=4767708. Retrieved on January 3, 2011.

Schoolcraft, A. (2009b). Schoolcraft tapes [Tape Recordings 81st Precinct Roll Call on October 12] from Rayman (2010, May 4). http://img.villagevoice.com/player/?i=4767701. Retrieved on January 3, 2011.

Selby, N. (2011, March 25). "Metric of the Week: Zimring and the Prisoner:Patrolman Ratio," *Police Led Intelligence,* http://policeledintelligence.com/2011/03/25/metric-of-the-week/. Retrieved on August 4, 2011.

Smith, D.C. and Purtell, R. (2006, August). "Managing Crime Counts: An Assessment of the Quality Control of NYPD Crime Data." (Occasional paper). New York University School of Law.

Sullivan, W. (2009). "The New Math on Crime." Cited in Burns, R.G. (2009). *Critical Issues in Criminal Justice*. Upper Saddle River, NJ: Pearson Prentice-Hall.

Thee Rant. (2008, February 17). Retrieved from http://theerant.yuku.com/.

Unions call for crime stat audit and crime reporting policy change. (2004, March 23). Retrieved from http://nycpba.org/archive/releases/04/pr040323-stats.html on January 18, 2011.

Zimring, F.E. (2011). "The City That Became Safe: New York and the Future of Crime Control." Unpublished article retrieved on August 4, 2011 from http://www.scribd.com/doc/48102346/Zimring-Journal-Article.

Zink, R. (2004). "The Trouble with Compstat," *PBA Magazine*, http://www.nycpba.org/publications/mag-04-summer/compstat.html. Retrieved on December 29, 2010.

Performance Management

3

Pitfalls and Prospects

The consequences of unreliable and non-trustworthy crime statistics ripple throughout police organizations affecting police, citizens, and victims. On an organizational level, excessive top-level supervision not only contributes to misclassified police figures, it also affects internal organizational-managerial issues (hierarchical pressures, commander morale, and embarrassment; see Table 3.1). In addition, public reports of statistical manipulation frequently trigger further headquarters oversight and regulations. These tighter bureaucratic controls, however, not only fail to erase statistical legerdemain, they also aggravate dysfunctional management.

This chapter first examines organizational-managerial issues that stem from top-down centralized bureaucratic control. We then explore how these managerial issues cascade downward and negatively affect field operations, which, in turn, severely affect citizens, victims, and the community at large. Lastly, we assess the obstacles to reform and offer an alternative reform narrative.

Organizational–Managerial Consequences

The same excessive top-level supervision that insists on favorable crime statistics also affects the way police organizations operate. Headquarters' bureaucratic bullying (see Chapter 5) insists on crime reduction while imposing and strictly supervising procedures to meet these expectations. These restrictions are endemic in wayward police performance management systems.

A nationwide analysis of Compstat police departments (not including New York City) found that:

> Compstat departments are more reluctant to relinquish power that would decentralize some key elements of decision making geographically ... enhance flexibility, and risk going outside of the standard tool kit of police tactics and strategies. The combined effect overall, whether or not intended, is to reinforce a traditional bureaucratic model of command and control. (Weisburd et. al., 2003, p. 448)

Table 3.1   Descriptive Statistics

	N	Minimum	Maximum	Mean	Std. Deviation
Reducing crime	310	1	10	7.51	2.248
Improving teamwork among rank-and-file	311	1	10	5.18	2.553
Tension among management	311	2	10	8.78	1.484
Decrease index crime	315	1	10	8.26	2.053
Morale among rank-and-file	311	1	10	4.48	2.554
Improving teamwork within management	311	1	10	6.13	2.761
Improving management effectiveness	311	1	10	6.93	2.619
Valid N (listwise)	305				

Note: Response N differs because some respondents did not answer all questions. Minimum and Maximum indicate scores received. Valid N (listwise) refers to the number of respondents who answered all questions in this table. For reducing crime, improving teamwork among rank-and-file, improving teamwork within management, and improving management effectiveness, a score of 1 is very poor and a score of 10 is excellent. For tension among management and morale among rank-and-file, a score of 1 indicates greatly reduces and 10 indicates greatly increases. For decrease index crime, a score of 1 is least pressure and 10 is most pressure.

We can now confirm that this virus has also infected the NYPD. Many of our respondents focused on the top-down management style employed by the Compstat leadership at its meetings. One wrote, "Comstat (sic) has lost its original theme. C.O.'s were allowed to make their own decisions when it first started and then held accountable. Now all you do is follow."

Another respondent similarly writes,

> … the lack of management training to all ranks caused an Us vs. Them environment. Management training as the department was undergoing a sea change in how it was to accomplish its mission was left at the backdoor. The team concept from the Commissioners to the rank and file was not sought; the tools to accomplish the new tasks were not given. …

Hierarchical Pressure

Clearly, this respondent feels that at Compstat meetings you are told what to do and later held accountable for what someone else ordered. In other words, you are held responsible for doing what you are told whether it is successful or not. This is a "do as you are told" style of leadership lacking a team approach (see Chapter 5).

Many respondents refer to intense Compstat pressure emanating from higher ranks. One respondent observes:

The pressure placed on captains and above was just too much to live with on a long-term basis. It's a shame to leave a job you worked so hard for at the age of 44 because of the pressure and poor quality of life (days off, hours, vacation, etc).

Another respondent remarks,

For Captains and above, high pressure from supervisors to produce "impressive" results so that they (your supervisors) look good drives Captains out of the Department. Unrealistic given resources.

Respondents' comments regarding hierarchical pressure were confirmed in the statistical analysis of our survey. One survey question used to measure the extent of hierarchical pressure in the entire sample examines respondents' views about "the extent that Compstat reduces or increases tension among management."* Here, there can be no doubt that hierarchical pressure is very high. Indeed, no respondent chose "1" and the mean response clearly shows enormous tension felt by respondents with a very small standard deviation ($M = 8.78$; $SD = 1.484$). The mean difference between reducing crime and tension among management is large (mean difference 1.27). Univariate analysis indicates that 85.2 percent of the sample felt that Compstat greatly increases tension among management (see Table 3.2). This finding clearly confirms the comments about pressure at Compstat.

Respondents' references to top management pressures forcing retirement may also affect commander morale and embarrassment before one's peers.

Commander Morale and Embarrassment

The themes of poor morale and embarrassment repeatedly emerge from our survey. One respondent notes:

Compstat was a good Compstat but became very abusive to the very people that were expected to implement the problems, consequently turning people and depressing morale. There is still too much second-guessing, no other department goes through that. ...

Another respondent writes,

Compstat is a great concept and productive tool when used fairly. I have seen it become a personal vendetta by some commanders towards a variety of Captains and other Commanding Officers.

* A 1 is "reduces tension" and 10 is "increases tension."

Table 3.2   Tension within Management Categorized

		Frequency	Valid Percentage	Cumulative Percentage
Valid	Low	4	1.3	1.3
	Medium	42	13.5	14.8
	High	265	85.2	100.0
	Total	311	100.0	
Missing	System	12		
Total		323		

Note: Frequency refers to the number of responses in that category; low is a score of 1 to 3, medium is 4 to 7, and high is 8 to 10. Valid percentage refers to those responding.

Compstat abuse is frequently portrayed as a device for punishment and reprimand rather than as a mechanism to constructively fight crime. One respondent writes, "Compstat … was turned into a tool of petty vindictiveness to punish people who were thought not to be fully committed to the department policies." Another respondent writes, "Compstat … was a tool of 1 PP [1 Police Plaza–Headquarters] to elevate/end careers at will."

Respondents repeatedly framed managerial embarrassment in terms of their experiences at Compstat meetings. One respondent notes,

> Compstat the meeting is generally ineffective to those who work hard but aren't always successful. Compstat should do as it says; offer assistance, ideas, plans, etc. to managers. Not ridicule and embarrassment.

Another writes "Compstat was the most embarrassing moments [sic] in my career." Yet another, "Compstat = Embarrassment in front of peers. NYPD management style is to berate and embarrass subordinates publicly."

One survey question specifically focuses on morale, which is clearly related to reprimand and embarrassment discussed by our respondents. The low mean for morale stands out ($M = 4.48$; $SD = 2.554$). Compstat greatly reduces morale (40.8 percent) and only 13.3 percent indicated Compstat greatly increases morale (see Table 3.3).

Field Operations Restrictions

Compstat pressures filter down to the cops on the street. When Compstat was first introduced, it was linked to new auxiliary reforms that encouraged precinct commander crime fighting innovations. Precincts were encouraged to attack crime based on local conditions. However, as time progressed,

Table 3.3 Morale within Management Categorized

		Frequency	Valid Percentage	Cumulative Percentage
Valid	Low	127	40.8	40.8
	Medium	141	45.3	86.2
	High	43	13.8	100.0
	Total	311	100.0	
Missing	System	12		
Total		323		

Note: Frequency refers to the number of responses in that category; low is a score of 1 to 3, medium is 4 to 7, and high is 8 to 10. Valid percentage refers to those responding.

Compstat morphed into a mindless numbers game directed by top-down centralized control.

Centralization and Reduced Field Flexibility

Two years after Compstat's introduction, an increasingly heavy emphasis was placed on headquarters directives regarding arrests, summons, and citations in order to demonstrate an appearance of heightened police activity linked to successful crime fighting. Numbers, sometimes any numbers, rule the day. This system, in the words of one participant, is "wound up too tight." A Brooklyn detective, a 20-year veteran, put it this way, "Compstat is everything. People are tired of being harassed, searched and frisked, and run off the streets. People are fed up; the cops are, too" (Silverman, 2001, p. 212).

This decline in local level autonomy is quite ironic because Compstat was touted as a path to, and initially resulted in, greater discretion for street officers and mid-level police managers. Compstat supporters labeled this as "empowerment," whereby organizational power devolved from the top to lower levels. This centered on precinct autonomy whereby the long-sought goal of giving precinct commanders greater control over their personnel was attained. Strategies to reduce crime and disorder flowed from the precincts, whose commanders were held accountable through Compstat.

In addition, precinct and borough commands were provided with resources that formerly were the exclusive province of headquarters. For example, precinct commanders could have their crime units perform decoy operations, a function previously reserved for the citywide street crime unit requiring commanders to request help from specialty units to combat specific conditions. These reforms moved the NYPD away from using headquarters as the nerve center that conceived tactics on a citywide basis, often with little input from field commands. The department realized that citywide crime fighting decisions were not as effective as strategies tailored for particular communities. Since early 1996, however, these reforms have been blunted. Compstat is no longer what it was. The decentralization of authority and decision-making, which was fueled by the new Compstat process, has been reversed. This centralized hierarchical pressure lowers the morale of the street cop and widens the gulf between him or her and top management.

Upper Management–Street Cop Divisions

This top-down pressure is bound to affect street level morale and alienate the lower levels from higher police levels. This is certainly the view of the union that represents the rank-and-file of the NYPD, the Patrolman's Benevolent Association (PBA).

> *Our own members tell us that they have been conditioned to write crime complaints to misdemeanors rather than felonies because of the abuse they receive from superior officers worried about their careers.* The case of the 10th precinct where a 7 percent decrease became a 50 percent increase is a shocking example of what is occurring throughout the city in many station houses. *It is a truth that is widely known by members of the department and now we have to see if the police commissioner has the courage to face the truth and do what is right for the city of New York.* (PBA press release March 23, 2004; emphasis added)

The PBA also has commented on how this pressure is reflected in Compstat.

> It was a great idea that has been corrupted by human nature. The Compstat program that made NYPD commanders accountable for controlling crime has degenerated into a situation where the police leadership presses subordinates to keep numbers low by any means necessary. The department's middle managers will do anything to avoid being dragged onto the carpet at the weekly Compstat meetings. They are, by nature, ambitious people who lust for promotions, and rising crime rates won't help anybody's career. (Zink, 2004)

Our survey results provide further documentation of a stark differentiation among the ranks of the NYPD. Respondents had divergent opinions on the issue of teamwork at the different hierarchical levels. In contrast to their views on low-level teamwork, our high-level respondents expressed stronger support for the view that Compstat "improved teamwork within management."

It is our view that these contrasting views on teamwork are wholly consistent with our overall findings of Compstat as shoring up the bureaucratic top-down centralized style of police organization and management. When Compstat's top-down management promotes hierarchical pressure to immediately decrease index crime, it filters down to rank-and-file activities whether it is through increased use of quotas or discouraging crime reports.

Long-term goals, however, should be as important as short-term objectives. The complexity of crime, governed by local conditions, and the qualitative attributes of policing cannot always be captured by numbers. Today this distinction is scarcely recognized by NYPD's Compstat leadership and many other police performance management systems.

Headquarters' accretion of local autonomy was further compounded in a January 2009 policy change "that required the police commissioner to sign off on what used to be routine staff transfers."

According to the *Daily News*,

> The new edict requires borough commanders to seek approval from Police Commissioner Raymond Kelly's office before moving staff between precincts. "It brings micro-managing to a new high," a ranking member of the NYPD brass said. "In a department this size, it will bring transfers to a screeching halt." In the past if a borough commander wanted to move, for example, five cops from Harlem to Washington Heights, he or should could authorize the transfers. "It sends a message that no one is trusted to make the right decision, even on the most local level," another ranking member of the brass said. (Gendar, 2009, p. 29)

This new policy quickly followed another policy change that required precinct commanders to receive Chief of Patrol approval before changing cops' tours within a precinct (Gendar, 2009, p. 29).

This is not the first time that a distinct organizational fault line separating upper management from street-level New York City police has been observed. An in-depth study of two precincts in the late 1970s found deeply seated street cop resentment and alienation from what they perceived as the more educated, self-serving upper echelons motivated by efficiency criteria in order to appease politicians, the media, and the courts. The precinct cops viewed upper levels as impersonal and neither understanding nor sympathetic to the requirements of daily police activity (Reuss-Ianni, 1983).

With a glaring parallel to current day Compstat pressures, precinct-level cops were put off by the top-level constraints of the contemporary management fad (Management by Objectives) which, like Compstat, measured and held them accountable for their numerical production. Upper-level innovations were viewed as bureaucratically abstract and impersonal (Reuss-Ianni, 1983).

Today, in many distorted performance management systems, an even narrower range of options is available to line officers as they try to exercise their responsibilities. Describing the U.K. police managerial arrangements, one researcher noted that,

The managerial model in all this was a crude performance culture, where senior officers had to produce and hit the targets and the lower ranks were assembly line "grunts" with low discretion, had to fulfill their quotas without murmur. (Punch, 2007, p. 40)

The mindless headquarters' focus on numbers restricts the officer's discretionary abilities. In the words of one observer, this approach (sometimes labeled as zero tolerance policing)

tries to turn front line workers into assembly-like operatives who are evaluated on how productive they are and not on the quality of their interaction with citizens or their problem-solving skills. As such, these managerial movements distort policing and, at worse, undermine it by destroying competences and motivation. (Punch, 2007, p. 46)

This development also emerges from a study of U.S. Compstat programs:

Agencies that had adopted Compstat programs were much less likely to focus on improving the skills and morale of street level officers ... suggesting that Compstat represents a departure from the properties of "bubble up" community and problem-oriented policing programs that had been predominant in police innovation until Compstat arrived on the scene and had focused attention on the empower and training of street-level police officers. Indeed, Compstat appears in this sense to be modeled more closely on the traditional "bureaucratic" or "paramilitary" form of police organization. (Weisburd et al., 2006, p. 290)

When police officer activity is reduced to rote numbers, it not only affects morale and loyalty to upper management, but also it distorts police activity.

Distorted Police Activity

The domination of performance measures can also warp police performance in other ways. For example, if an organization perceives its performance evaluation to rest upon cost data amenable to performance measures, then it is not surprising that rewards and advancement are more likely to accrue to those who meet or exceed the numerical targets of summons and arrests (i.e., quotas). This spills over into training by producing technically developed professional experts skilled almost exclusively in the more quantifiable law-enforcement function. This parallels developments in education. For example, Diane Ravitch (2010a) writes, "NCLB [No Child Left Behind] assumes that accountability based solely on test scores will reform American education. This is a mistake. A good accountability system must include professional judgment, not simply a test score, and other measures ..." (p. 161).

At the same time, attributes such as interpersonal skills, creative thinking, experimentation, and risk taking are either ignored or undervalued when the police focus solely on the short run. The problem is that the members of an inward looking organization come to believe (and incorporate in their professional value set) that short-run efficiency skills are of paramount importance to the customers of the service offered. Measurements by upper echelon somehow magically transform into effective policing. NYPD measurement of commander performance has stark parallels in the field of education. As Ravitch writes,

> As the methodology gained adherents, education policy increasingly became the domain of statisticians and economists. With their sophisticated tools and their capacity to do multivariate longitudinal analysis, they did not need to enter the classroom, observe teachers, or review student work to know which teachers were the best and which were the worst, which were effective and which were ineffective. ... What mattered most in determining education quality was not curriculum or instruction, but data. (Ravitch, 2010a, p. 18)

An August 2011 independent review of the New York City school system noted a sharp rise in accusations of cheating by educators. "When you start giving money to the schools, that's another incentive to appear to do well if you are not doing well ... even in ways that are unacceptable," according to Richard J. Condon, the New York City Schools Special Commissioner of Investigation (Otterman, 2011, August 23, p. A17).

This dominance of the short run is reflected in "getting numbers." A former NYPD officer who served in the 2001–2004 Compstat era recalls the ascendancy of quotas in daily work. "I knew it was illegal for the job to push quotas on us; setting predetermined police activity levels was unconstitutional" (Bacon, 2009, p. 96). At the same time, the officer recalls his early police days:

> Inside, we were late for return roll call, an end of tour procedure inflicted on rookies for the official reason of a head count. The real reason for taking us off the streets thirty minutes early, leaving the neighborhood to fend for itself, was to count something else.
>
> "How many summonses you get, Bacon," said our patrol sergeant standing at a podium in front of a squad of tired-looking rookies. Hustling to the back of the formation, I said, "One, Sarge." (Bacon, 2009, p. 97)

Following this exchange, the precinct captain announced:

> Okay the good news is crime is down in the Impact Zone on the four to midnight tour, including robberies, so y'all are doing an excellent job. An excellent job. The bad news is that your summonses are also down. ... (Bacon, 2009, p. 97)

After stating that he does not have summons quotas, the Captain announced:

So I'll just let you know that the crime that was happening on your tour has been shifting to the midnight tour, and anyone that doesn't want to shift with it better bring up their numbers." (Bacon, 2009, p. 98)

Officer Bacon's book is replete with accounts of quotas and their negative impacts. When one of his fellow officers asked him his numbers for the month of February, Bacon responded that he had "three parkers." The response was, "So you need twenty-seven more by next week. Remember, February is a short month!" (Bacon, 2009, p. 100).

Officers were constantly subject to supervisory directives on shifting quotas. In the words of one sergeant,

Listen up. The borough's putting together a new rookie unit. It's some kind of mobile outfit, which may sound cool; but rumor is they'll only write summonses. They want ten bodies from our command, and since the flavor of the week is now collars, that's how we're making the cut. So, those with no collars, you better start humpin. Any questions? (Bacon, 2009, p. 101)

Shortly thereafter, the quota system shifted gears again.

The new flavor of the week was the Stop, Question, and Frisk Worksheet. Known by its shorthand clerical title, UF 250 or just two-fifty, this form was originally conceived to keep tabs on the many heated encounters between NYPD cops and the general public. The two-fifty wasn't a summons, but the two forms had a lot in common. ... And like a summons, the two-fifty wound up being as much a phony measure of police activity as a tool of law enforcement.

The standard of proof required for this kind of stop was reasonable suspicion, a very low bar floating somewhere between probable cause and "He just looked like a perp" and tending toward the latter. Given this wide latitude, I knew we'd be expected to bring in a slew of two-fifties every night exposing ourselves to more liability and strife than seemed prudent. ... (Bacon, 2009, p. 168)

When the latest directive was passed on down from the borough, it was labeled as the "borough's new flavor of the week." When Bacon inquired as to its name, the response was "Operation Pedestrian Safety." Commented one officer: "Jaywalking tickets. Fantastic community relations tool. Don't forget your pepper spray" (Bacon, 2009, p. 213).

Shackling the street cop is also operative in other police performance cultures. For some constables working the streets of the United Kingdom, the consequences of top-down targets and restrictions has been no less dysfunctional. One former police constable notes, "These days it's all numbers, action plans, strategies and partnership meetings" (Copperfield, 2006, p. 85). In a reference to:

> a government action plan aimed at replacing re-offending. It says it will do this "through greater strategic direction and joined-up working." Meaning "by having more people in charge and more forms to monitor things." (Copperfield, 2006, p. 211)

As a result, according to constable Copperfield, "police management is much more about the management of inactivity than it is about reducing crime" (Copperfield, 2006, p. 104). According to Copperfield, any way of minimizing risks and activities offers the path of least resistance.

> The easiest way of ensuring you get to retirement without having any complaints made about you is to join the ever-growing army of "vital" support staff performing "vital" work in offices, dealing with "crime prevention" or working on "best value" or "best practices" strategies. (Copperfield, 2006, p. 151)

Compounding the Problem

This dominant central control over field operations is subsequently compounded even more by warped performance management systems. These systems often redouble their control orientation when the public becomes aware of manipulation. For example, it was only after Compstat was installed that the NYPD instituted its data integrity unit. More recently, after our study became public and other revelations emerged confirming our research, Commissioner Kelly felt compelled to create a three-person committee to review the NYPD's crime reporting systems. Countless other examples exist at NYPD.

Similarly, when reports of British police forces' statistical manipulation emerged, the central government's Home Office responded with additional regulations and supervisory layers. Said one former Chief Superintendent:

> For the police service, the way to improve ethical recording, at significant cost, was the introduction of new bureaucratic controls. New protocols and rules were introduced to reduce officer discretion in crime recording and new rules introduced to audit and "gate keep" the system. Layers of audit at national and local levels have increased dramatically. The accretion in non-operational posts has been significant. (Marlow, 2010)

This mirrors a description of the U.K. police service as

> a servile agency of the state, performing to central demand—quite the opposite of Peel's intention. ... Indeed, there is a near-bewildering accountability

flow chart unlike the map of the London Underground, with multiple lines to and from the police. (Neyroud, 2004)

One chief officer observed, "It's even more complicated than that. There are an increasing number of players, a multitude of agencies and a confusing diversity of demands" (Punch, 2007, p. 38).

The cumulative effect of performance management's multiple review levels and obsessive demands and directives for crime reduction not only impact the police organizations and its members, it also spills over to the community at large.

Societal Consequences

Communities are affected in numerous ways. These include diminished quality and distorted delivery of police service, weakened crime fighting, unreliable crime statistics, increased public distrust of police, unfair police practices, and victims victimized by the police.

Diminished Quality and Distorted Delivery

The spillover for local communities is very significant (see Chapter 7). Community needs are ignored as Headquarters plays the numbers game. Mindless number counts to be reflected at Compstat meetings fail to acknowledge local conditions. Targets are met (quotas) without regard to the health of the community or the precinct. Exemplifying this is the huge number of summonses being dismissed at court as well as the high number of stop and frisks. There are countless other examples throughout this book. Additionally, this also applies in other countries.

In England and Wales, for example, the extensive array of police performance management numerical targets and standards (a la Compstat) has also exposed its communities to unremitting penalties. Over 15 years ago, a former police commander reported:

> The pressure of cost, together with rising crime, was being used to demand effective action from the police. Chief Constables and Police Authorities would need to have clear ideas on objectives and priorities Office. ... *Senior police officers have argued that these Home Office demands for effectiveness and efficiency have resulted in what has been empirically illustrated in this study— a reduction in the presence of uniform officers on the streets, a decline in the perceived services to the public. ...* (McManus, 1995, p. 119; emphasis added)

Not only has there been a decrease in the number of police serving their communities, but when Compstat-like targets and activities are directed from above, community needs can be easily ignored or downplayed. A recently retired chief superintendent succinctly expressed the tyranny of top-down numbers:

> Target setting was a "top-down" exercise and rather crude in the early days. The expression "what gets measured gets done" was the vogue expression. It has a converse "what does not get measured does not get done" and other matters, if not the subject of targets, did not "get done." (Marlow, 2010)

When police are assessed by numbers, they often police by the numbers. A recent U.K. government report acknowledged the distortion in police services, which flows from central government's definition of "nationally important" criminal issues.

> All too often targets have driven perverse incentives. For example the "Offences Brought to Justice" target incentivized officers to pursue easy to achieve low-level detections rather than focusing on more serious offences. Police officers and staff are overwhelmed by the sheer volume of central policing guidance being issued. … These manuals contained over 4000 new promises, covering duties such as policing international cricket matches and data collection for missing persons. (Home Office, 2010a, pp. 6, 7)

More recently, U.K. media identified local concerns beyond the range of the police's radar screen. One newspaper account, for example, revealed disturbing consequences of Compstat-like performance management quantitative target setting:

> The report warned that police forces are routinely ignoring thousands of repeat victims of harassment and thuggery. Forces often mark such calls as "low priority" because they do not qualify as crimes. The basic task of keeping the peace had been relegated to a "second-order consideration" for officers who were obsessed with meeting targets for recorded crimes, he added. "As a result, no action is taken." (Slack and Chapman, 2010)

Weakened Crime Fighting and Diminished Public Trust

The ability of the police to combat citizens' concerns is weakened not only by distorted police priorities, but also by downplaying or failing to accurately record or classify crime. As one government study noted:

> Part of the problem is that people feel they are reporting things that are wrong but they are not seeing any action. As a society we need to reclaim the streets,

and part of that is about police being on the streets and being visible. (Slack and Chapman, 2010)

When the police are not proactive in finding complainants and even turn some away with little or no help, the citizenry is alienated. For example, a confidential source was the victim of identity theft (see Chapter 2). He visited the local NYPD precinct to make a report of the theft. He was informed that the police could do nothing without a letter from the credit company indicating they want a police report. He was turned away by precinct staff and told, "it is a numbers game for us, sorry." This is unconscionable! Even if a report is not to be taken, the citizen should have been given information as to what he could do to prevent the crime's reoccurrence and to protect himself. This is another example of how the NYPD lost its focus from service oriented to counting numbers—a legalistic style (see Chapter 7). As a result, time-consuming police problem solving suffers when the Department is more concerned with numbers regardless of the long-term, overall effect.

In the United Kingdom, police downplaying of so-called antisocial behavior (ASB) has many similar ramifications. In 2010, Her Majesty's Inspectorate of Constabulary (HMIC, the national police review agency) released a report entitled "Anti-Social Behavior: Stop the Rot," in which it identified ASB as one of the public's top local concerns yet estimated that the public only report about a quarter of incidents of ASB to the police (HMIC, 2010).

According to the U.K.'s Home Office, ASB

covers a wide range of selfish and unacceptable activity that can blight the quality of community life. Terms such as "nuisance," "disorder," and "harassment" are also used to describe some of this behaviour.

Examples include: Nuisance neighbours; Yobbish behaviour and intimidating groups taking over public spaces; vandalism, graffiti and fly-posting; people dealing and buying drugs on the street; people dumping rubbish and abandoned cars; begging and anti-social drinking; the misuse of fireworks; reckless driving of mini-motorbikes. (Home Office, 2010b)

Another report notes:

ASB is a blight on the lives of millions who are directly affected, on the perceptions of millions more for whom it signals neglect in their neighbourhoods and the decline of whole towns and city areas, and the reputation of the police who are often thought to be unconcerned or ineffectual. ... ASB does not have the same status as crime for the police. There are consequences to this. The public dislikes ASB, *worry about reporting it*, and are intimidated in significant numbers when they do. A major study finds police treat ASB "differently" than crime. (Macmillan, 2010; emphasis added)

The report revealed a growing gap between what the public wanted, namely "boots on the ground," and what the police were delivering. The report noted that almost one-third of surveyed victims were unaware of any police action taken in response to their complaint regarding antisocial behavior.

This disparity between public needs and policing responses affects the way residents lead their lives. For example, the same U.K. study found heightened fear of crime leading to increased illness and diminished outdoor nighttime activities and use of public spaces (Macmillan, 2010).

The downplaying of citizen concerns inevitably diminishes public confidence in the police. In the words of one of the U.K.'s most senior police officers, the Commissioner of the London Metropolitan Police, "a psychological contract" between police and the public has been broken (Daily Mail, 2010). A retired U.K. Deputy Chief Constable writes, "The best that a complainant can expect is a 'crime number' for insurance purposes. There are rather too many horror stories from people who believe that there is little point in reporting crime" (Frost, 2010).

A leading British criminologist summarizes these U.K. developments. The "performance culture," he observes, generates "unintended but serious consequences which both undermine quality of service and questions its effectiveness" (Loveday, 2000b, p. 24).

When performance management is preoccupied with managing numbers rather than results, not only is crime downgraded or ignored, but also victims suffer. Officers may not aggressively seek victims (e.g., rape, domestic violence, and child abuse victims who are less likely to report to the police) for fear of creating another "number."

Prospects for Reform

Numerous police performance management systems have unfortunately proliferated in the footsteps of the NYPD's Compstat (see Chapters 1 and 4) and are consequently afflicted with similar top heavy, overburdened, warped, and distorted maladies. What started out as systems to improve performance have morphed into overly rigid cumbersome control schemes that diminish discretionary problem solving while encouraging revisionary crime reporting. Is there an escape route from this dysfunctional morass of wayward police performance management?

In order to address these issues, it is first necessary to explore the obstacles to reform. In other words, what helps explain police performance management's remarkable staying power over so many years despite its many shortcomings and critiques? Like a giant tree, there are both visible and hidden roots to the system's durability. We explore the first before discussing the second.

Visible Roots

Police performance management's business orientation (see Chapter 1) furnishes the most visible explanation of its widespread acceptance. For example, when the United Kingdom's chief spokesperson for policing (the Home Secretary) recently advocated a "radical" departure away from the country's long standing police performance management system (see Chapter 4), she also backed reductions in funding for police officers. The Home Secretary justified this reduction with the statement: "Look at the example of the New York Police Department where they have managed to cut crime at the same time as reducing the number of officers from 41,000 to 35,000" (Home Office, 2010c).

So on the one hand, the Home Secretary proposes moving away from an NYPD-like system and, on the other hand, justifies doing more with less based on the very same NYPD model. This dual assertion reveals inadequate understanding of the commonalities afflicting NYPD–U.K. performance-based policing systems (see Chapter 4). Perhaps more importantly, her statement reveals performance management's resistance to sound diagnosis and understanding.

This deep-seated allure of performance policing reflects the dominant cultural roots of business performance management. In justifying potentially drastic slashes in police budgets, the Home Secretary "Mrs. May said she wanted to see modern management practices in the police service. ..." (Slack, 2010). Mrs. May said:

> By bringing modern management practices to the police, this review will help ensure chief constables can deliver the front-line services people want, while providing the value for money that is so vital in the tough economic times we face. (Slack, 2010)

Blind faith in modern business management practices, however, dampens critical analyses of distorted performance management practices whether they appear in the criminal justice system, education, or some other arena (see Chapter 1). This overarching non-critical faith in the business model has contributed to widespread adoption in the law enforcement world. Part of this globalization is rooted in the desire of political and police officials to demonstrate that they are at the "cutting edge of international developments and return from (expensive) trips abroad with a 'new' conceptual vocabulary that is, in reality, old wine" (Punch, 2007, p. 9).

> Given the short term memory in policing circles, the new idea is often a reformulation of previous ideas. So that the police revisit ideas in "cyclical fashion." (Waddington, 2007, p 27)

This approach often promises magical managerial quick-fix techniques for doing more with less. This has been likened to the "McDonaldization" thesis (Ritzer, 2000) whereby powerful economic and political interests promote their common interests globally through the language of business management.

Performance Management in New York City: The Use of Symbolic Language

In addition to the enormous appeal of performance management as a business concept, there are deeper, less visible yet more powerful explanations for its resilience. This is vividly embodied in the symbolic uses of the New York City Crime Success Story and the Success Story of Compstat.

The Crime Success Story

The Crime Success Story has established itself as the dominant New York narrative. This narrative holds that until the early and mid-1990s, New York was the nation's epicenter of crime and disorder. Homicides, for example, peaked at 2,262 in 1990. According to this narrative, crime subsequently declined over 75 percent with homicides falling to 471 in 2009.

The Mayor and the Police Commissioner constantly recycle this narrative through numerous media outlets. According to one account:

> Among cities with a population exceeding 500,000 residents, New York City tops the list of safest cities in America. ... Mayor Michael Bloomberg touted the continuing downtrend in crime activity, declaring that New York City has had "43 fewer murders, 1,415 fewer robberies and 491 fewer cars stolen" in the first five months of 2009 compared to 2008." (Ott, 2009)

There are many duplicates of this story. See also, for example, http://www.theyeshivaworld.com/news/General+News/70187/NYC-Remains-Safest-City-In-America.html, and http://wireupdate.com/local/fbi-crime-report-says-new-york-city-is-the-safest-big-city-in-america/.

These and other media reports repeatedly regurgitated the Mayor's own press release:

> Mayor Michael R. Bloomberg and Police Commissioner Raymond W. Kelly today announced that New York City remains the safest big city in America, according to an analysis of crime data released by the FBI in its Crime in the United States, the Uniform Crime Report for 2009. The report shows that total crime decreased by 5.1 percent in New York City during 2009, outpacing national trends. (Bloomberg, 2010)

Mayors Michael Bloomberg and Rudy Giuliani repeatedly assert that the FBI ranks New York as the safest large city in America. This, however, is a dubious claim. First, the FBI abstains from ranking cities and specifically states that it is misleading to use its statistics that way. According to one NYPD observer:

When Bloomberg made the same claim during his mayoral run in 2005, a complaint from the FBI led his campaign to yank the FBI reference from the campaign's political ads, according to an FBI official. "They modified their ad," the official said. "But now they're doing it again." ... That's because Mayor Mike's "Safest City in America" claim relies on the FBI's 2008 Preliminary Uniform Crime Report, which lists major felonies for each city by such categories as murder, rape, burglary and grand larceny. But the report contains a "Please Note" section with cautionary language about rankings, saying, "Individuals using these tabulations are cautioned against drawing conclusions by making direct comparisons between cities." It also says, "The FBI discourages data users from ranking agencies and using the data as a measurement of law enforcement effectiveness."

In fact, back in 2004, the FBI cautioned that the crime index highlighted by the Bloomberg campaign "has not been a true indicator of the degree of criminality" because it gives the same weight to non-violent crimes as to violent ones. For example, the non-violent crimes of larceny—theft—comprised nearly 60 percent of all reported crime, and, as the FBI said then, "the sheer volume of those offenses overshadows more serious but less frequently committed offenses" such as rape, robbery or murder. Instead of totaling all these crimes together, says the FBI official, a more accurate gauge of safety in any city is totaling purely violent crime, which the FBI does not do. Reality, however, has not stopped the NYPD or New York's last two mayors from touting New York as "the safest large city in America," year after year. (Levitt, 2009)

Commanding Symbols

Despite these important cautionary warnings, the Crime Success Story is so commanding because it is infused with extraordinary symbolic implications.

The need for symbolization constitutes a basic need of man. ... The symbol making function is one of man's primary activities, like eating, looking or moving about. It is the fundamental process of his mind and goes on all the time. (Langer, 1957, pp. 32–33)

A symbol, as Murray Edelman eloquently posits,

Stands for something other than itself, and also evokes an attitude, a set of impressions, or a pattern of events associated through time, through space, through logic or through imagination with the symbol. Symbols evoke the emotions associated with the situation. ... It evokes a quiescent or an aroused mass response because it symbolizes a threat or reassurance. ... (Edelman, 1964, p. 6)

Symbols resonate with our needs for security as well as our fear of insecurity and ambiguity. A criminal episode, according to Edelman, is an "act that contributes to a pattern of ongoing events that spells threat or reassurance" (Edelman, 1964, pp. 6, 7, 13). As every TV and Hollywood producer knows, crime makes for great storytelling.

The long-standing advocates of this Success Story (particularly the NYPD's public information office—see Chapter 6) recognize the potency of symbols with its constant refrain that New York is now "the safest city in the United States." This success narrative is a story of reassurance that calms anxiety. But it is also a story of latent fear because any questioning of this narrative is reframed by its supporters as a challenge and threat to the city's well being, ushering a return to previously unacceptable high crime levels.

This is particularly the case because fear of crime does not run parallel with actual crime rates. Instead, personal fear is greatly influenced by media crime stories. When a college professor interviewed New York City women about their fears of crime,

They frequently responded with the phrase "I saw it in the news." The interviewees identified the news media as both the source of their fears and the reason they believe those fears were valid. Asked in a national poll why they believe the country has a serious crime problem, 76 percent of people cited stories they had seen in the media. Only 22 percent cited personal experience. (Glassner, 1999, p. xxi).

Based on this fear:

The purveyors of symbolic rhetoric craftily use language to support the meanings that they attach to particular symbols. The particular incidents in the news do not really matter so far as the creation of threat perceptions is concerned. No matter what incidents occur and which of these are reported, they will fit nicely as evidence to support people's preconceived hopes and fears. ... A continuing tension between threat and resurface is another central theme, explaining the reactions of general publics to political symbols. ... (Edelman, 1964, pp. 13, 15).

As Glassner notes, "symbolic substitutes" are offered for "moral insecurities" (Glassner, 1999, p. xxxviii).

The daily life stories . . . seem objective because they are confirmed time and again by self-fulfilling selection of documentation detail. Information that doesn't fit the symbolic mold can be ignored, denied or rationalized out of serious consideration. (Bennett and Edelman, 1985, pp. 158).

That is why the New York Success Story is constantly repeated in a tightly wrapped ironclad narrative that could unravel if any segment is discredited. Alternative approaches or facts are therefore ignored, thwarted, or rebuffed. This is especially the case when any critique may be possibly construed as a challenge to the validity of the conventional narrative. If Eterno and Silverman offer scientifically based peer-reviewed journal articles, the NYPD and its media supporters rely on what Glassner terms "poignant anecdotes in place of scientific evidence..." (Glassner, 1999, p. 208). If we maintain that the dimensions of the crime drop are less reliable than official NYPD crime statistics proclaim, then our critique is characterized as claiming that there has been no crime drop in New York and that we have maligned every police officer in New York. Consequently, their depiction of our narrative threatens to return the city to the "bad old days." While this characterization is a gross distortion of our findings, the NYPD and its uncritical supporters constantly regurgitate it. "What matters is remoteness not content. Thus can the subtle connotations of language freeze perception and conception. ..." (Edelman, 1964, p. 188).

Not only has the NYPD invoked the symbolic content of reassurance and safety of the Crime Success story, the media (see Chapter 6) has seized upon this symbolic issue as well.

The defenders of the faith offer a more familiar fare with greater appeal to security and certainty since it is novelty, uncertainty, and ambiguity that seem least tolerable. ... In place of presenting open and flexible analysis of situations, leaders tend to offer formulaic stories that dissolve ambiguity and resolve possible points of new understanding into black and white replays of the political dramas of the past. (Bennett and Edelman, 1985, p. 159)

The New York black and white replay is today's safer New York City as compared to the bad old days of high crime. When there is an uptick in crime, it raises anxieties. Therefore, the worst thing that can happen is to return to the "bad old days." For this would resurrect a crisis atmosphere that "heralds instability" (Edelman, 1988, p. 3). And instability induces uncertainty and anxiety.

The Compstat Success Story

Defenders of the realm utilize a second symbolic buffer zone in their response to our critiques. The NYPD Compstat Success Story asserts that the agency is the driving force behind this precipitous crime drop. In the words of a former commissioner, "crime is down in New York City, blame it on the police" (Bratton and Dennis, 1998; Silverman, 1997). This narrative began during the tenure of Mayor Giuliani, who proclaimed Compstat as his administration's "crown jewel" (Giuliani, 2002, p. 7). This view was echoed by Mayor Bloomberg:

> Using innovative policing strategies and a focus on keeping guns out of the hands of criminals, we are continuing to do more with less, in spite of the economic downturn. … "The men and women of the NYPD have found new ways to further drive down crime, even when faced with tough economic times and the threat of terrorism," said Mayor Bloomberg. "We will continue doing everything possible to keep making the safest big city in the country even safer … and reflects in no small measure the dedication and hard work of New York City police officers, and the Mayor's commitment to keeping New Yorkers safe, year after year," said Commissioner Kelly. (Bloomberg, 2010)

Compstat, this Success Narrative goes, has been New York's par excellence embodiment of performance management and the central mechanism in the NYPD's successful crime drive. Compstat is symbolically represented as modernity's most up-to-date full-throttled attack on crime. Catchy phrases such as "zero tolerance policing" promise a hard line against those who violate society's norms especially when crime-related stories take center stage. Zero tolerance, therefore, represents a rhetorical device that condenses thinking and reflection and appeals to a feeling of security and well-being. Compstat is portrayed as the embodiment and enforcer of this hard nose policing and security—it safeguards and institutionalizes the public's safety.

Despite our strong support of the concept and proper use of Compstat (Eterno, 2003; Silverman, 1999), critics constantly accuse us of attacking "successful crime reduction." Catchy phrases and labels, of course, handily short-circuit rational thinking. "Trite phrases may be used as incantations, serving to dull the critical faculties. …" Symbolic invocation "is a signal that discussion of the merits of the issue is out of place and profane. …" (Edelman, 1964, pp. 112, 116). Kenneth Burke designates political rhetoric as "secular prayer" intended "to sharpen up the pointless and blunt the too sharply pointed" (Burke, 1969, p. 393).

To contest a dominant narrative is to raise "ambiguity and uncertainty."

> contested issues … are quickly simplified and cast in mutually exclusive ideological terms. People become so accustomed to ideological formulations disguised and embedded in standard narratives that the "either or" policies of political debate seem natural and adequate characterizations of reality. (Bennett and Edelman, 1985, pp. 158, 159)

Milton Rokeach asserts, "Dogma serves the purpose of ensuring the continued existence of the institution and the belief-disbelief system for which it stands" (Rokeach, 1973, p. 68). Punch summarizes this well:

> To a certain extent, then, policy has become driven by personalities, incidents, media headlines, short term results, imported one liners and, in criminal justice in particular, by moral panics and populism. (Punch, 2007, p. 45)

Since all stories, by definition, must be selective in their details and narrative, the New York and Compstat Success Stories do not tolerate contradictory evidence. Therefore, questioning any story elements will be construed as challenging the integrity and authenticity of the entire narrative.

> In supplying these often unverifiable and unfalsifiable features of events, narratives create a particular kind of social world, with specified heroes and villains, deserving and undeserving people ... In other words, stock political narratives disguise and digest ideology for people... acceptance of a narrative involves a rejection of others ... (Bennett and Edelman, 1985, p. 159)

Consequently, inconsistent/contradictory information and dissenting critiques or commentary such as ours must be denigrated. The symbolic use of language serves to "immobilize opposition and mobilize support" (Edelman, 1988, p. 104). The authors and promulgators of New York's unalloyed success stories

> regard selected documentary detail as "facts" that substantiate their story. In this fashion, fragments of real-life situations become perceived as wholes, while the excluded aspects of situations are neglected, rationalized away or dismissed as the weak arguments of opponents who have failed to grasp the real issues at stake. Narratives drive out the stuff of critical thought and actions. ... (Bennett and Edelman, 1985, pp. 162, 164, 166)

The disingenuous narrative thwarts an informed citizenry. Is it any wonder that the City Council and other political actors have consistently failed to act in the face of widespread evidence of statistical manipulation? This failure includes an abdication of investigatory responsibilities.

Conclusion: The Narrative of Reform

Performance management's strongest sustaining force has been its reigning narrative. This narrative is so robust that it both conceals and props up dysfunctional police management. Ushering in reform requires a new narrative in order to dislodge a resilient malfunctioning system and reveal its shortcomings discussed in this and other chapters. This alternative narrative would evoke a different version of symbols, which may be more difficult to transmit and support. Yet, its outlines seem clear.

This new pathway, while continuing to embrace security and safety as powerful symbols, would redefine them in a more inclusive manner. This narrative would stress the connection between the rights and security of all citizens noting that police are there to protect all of us and not only a select few. In addition, when the rights of the most vulnerable are infringed through such actions as unjustified stops, quotas, and downgraded or non-recorded crime reports, these practices could easily seep into the whole body politic as the thin line protecting citizens from their government is easily breached. Security needs to be communicated in terms of safety for all; otherwise, security for anyone can easily be threatened.

Thus, a fresh narrative points out that when the rights and security of some are diminished, the rights and security of others are also threatened if police are unharnessed. Furthermore, a rupture in this wall of protection may be intensified by the contemporary narrative's narrow portrayal of the police role as almost exclusively crime control. An alternative narrative views undivided focus on crime control as diminishing due process rights and security for all (see Chapter 7). A new narrative's potential is boundless. It would liberate citizens and professionals alike from the restrictive constraints of dysfunctional performance management.

This new narrative could draw upon a staggering array of similar evidence from the world of performance management outside the realm of policing. For example, there is a plethora of evidence attesting to the misuse of statistical testing in education. Even long-time advocates of national testing, such as the prominent education historian Diane Ravitch, have experienced a radical conversion.

Ravitch recalls her initial support of the Federal No Child Left Behind (NCLB) "accountability regime" requiring annual testing of Grades 3 through 8 and recording scores separately by race, ethnicity, low income status, disability status, and limited English proficiency. "But over time, I became disillusioned with the strategies that once seemed so promising" (Ravitch, 2010b).

This disillusionment springs from the NCLB mandate of math and reading proficiency of all students by 2014 as measured by state tests.

> Since the law permitted every state to define "proficiency" as it chose, many states announced impressive gains. The states' claims of startling improvement were contradicted by the federally sponsored National Association of Educational Progress. Eighth grade students improved not at all on the federal test of reading even though they had been tested annually by their states. Meanwhile the states responded by dumbing down their standards so that they could claim to be making progress. Some states declared that between 80-90

percent of their students were proficient, but on the federal test only a third or less were. Because the law demanded progress only in reading and math, *schools were incentivized to show gains only on those subjects.* Meanwhile there was no incentive to teach the arts, science, history, literature, geography, civics, foreign languages or physical education. (Ravitch, 2010b; emphasis added)

These educational assessments have striking parallels with developments in police management. There is the same focus on units readily amenable to measurement to the exclusion of all other indicators of performance and customer satisfaction. In addition, in both education and policing, evaluations of success are typically rendered by the agency itself and so there are incentives to adjust success levels whether it is through the criteria of successful test proficiency or an index crime.

There is, however, one major distinction between the two worlds of education and policing. In education, there have been independent outside assessments of the validity of the states' testing scores. In U.S. policing, with only a few sporadic exceptions, there is no such external evaluation process, thus leaving it to police departments to produce and report on their own crime statistics "success." At NYPD, controlled access has meant few uninvited evaluations. The exceedingly few evaluations are severely limited in scope due to the NYPD's staunch resistance. Our study, using an innovative methodology, stands out as the only citywide independent assessment available since the arrival of Compstat nearly 20 years ago.

Wider dissemination of these widespread pitfalls of performance management would elevate the new narrative's status, enabling it to challenge the conventional narrative. Revelations of these dysfunctional commonalities could starkly link the negative impacts on schoolchildren and parents with residents victimized by crime and the police. It is no longer a question of a few dissenters challenging the dominant narrative; it is now the specter of this narrative and its management system threatening the safety, justice, and fairness of all citizens.

Chapter 7 offers a fuller exploration of these themes. First, however, it is important to sort out the global influence of this dominant narrative as exemplified through worldwide police performance management.

References

Bacon, P. (2009). *Bad Cop.* New York: Bloomsbury.

Bennett, W. L. and Edelman, M. (1985). "Toward a New Political Narrative," *Journal of Communication*, Autumn: 156–171.

Bloomberg, M. (2010). "New York City Still the Safest Big City in America, According to FBI Data," http://www.mikebloomberg.com/index.cfm?objectid=0C6D1A60-C29C-7CA2-F5C5A2DE775904C6.

Bratton, W. (1998). "Crime Is Down in New York City: Blame the Police." In: Bratton, W.J., Griffiths, W., Mallon, R., Orr, J., Pollard, C., and Dennis, N., Eds. *Zero Tolerance: Policing a Free Society*. London: IEA Health and Welfare Unit.

Burke, K. (1969). *A Grammar of Motives*. Berkeley, CA: University of California Press.

Copperfield, D. (2006). *Wasting Police Time*. Great Britain: Monday Books.

Daily Mail. (September 23, 2010). "Public Left to Fight Yobs Alone: Met Chief's Withering Verdict on Policing of Anti-Social Behaviour," http://www.dailymail.co.uk/news/article-1314600/Met-chief-Public-left-fight-yobs-alone.html#ixzz1Cs1FFHeo.

Edelman, M. (1964). *The Symbolic Uses of Politics*. Champaign, IL: University of Illinois Press.

Edelman, M. (1988). *Constructing the Political Spectacle*. Chicago: University of Chicago Press.

Eterno, J.A. (2003). *Policing Within the Law: A Case Study of the New York City Police Department*. Westport, CT: Praeger.

Frost, J. (2010). Personal email, December 23.

Gendar, A. (2009). "Cops see red over new NYPD edict on officers' transfers." *The New York Daily News*, January 23, 29.

Giuliani, R. (2002). *Leadership*. New York: Hyperion.

Glassner, B. (1999). *The Culture of Fear*. New York: Basic Books.

Her Majesty's Inspectorate of Constabulary (HMIC). (2010). "Anti-Social Behavior: Stop the Rot," http://www.hmic.gov.uk/media/stop-the-rot-20100923.pdf, September 23.

Home Office. (2010a). "Policing in the 21st Century: Reconnecting Police and People," July 26, http://www.homeoffice.gov.uk/publications/consultations/policing-21st-century/.

Home Office. (2010b). "Anti Social Behaviour," May 24, http://webarchive.nationalarchives.gov.uk/20100405140447/http://asb.homeoffice.gov.uk/default.aspx.

Home Office. (2010c). "Theresa May at Superintendent's Association Conference," September 15, http://www.homeoffice.gov.uk/media-centre/speeches/superintendents-conference.

Langer, S.K. (1957). *Philosophy in a New Key*. Cambridge: Harvard University Press.

Levitt, L. (2009). "Mike Bloomberg's Safest Largest City in America," One Police Plaza, July 6, http://nypdconfidential.com/print/2009p/090706p.html.

Loveday, B. (2000b). "Policing Performance: The Effects of Performance Targets on Police Culture," *Criminal Justice Matters*, 40: 23–24.

Macmillan, R. (2010). "Major Study Finds Police Treat ASB 'Differently' to Crime," September 27, http://www.24dash.com/news/housing/2010-09-27-major-study-finds-police-treat-asbs-differently-to-crime.

Marlow, A. (2010). April 6, http://unveilingnypdcompstat.blogspot.com/2010/04/turnaround-nypd-comes-around-on-crime.html#comments.

McManus, M. (1995). *From Fate to Choice: Private Bobbies, Public Beats*. Aldershot: Avebury.

Neyroud, P. (2004).

Ott, B. (2009). "America's Safest Cities," June 9, http://www.realclearpolitics.com/articles/2009/06/05/americas_safest_cities_96815.html.

Otterman, S. (2011, August 23). "Under Bloomberg, A Sharp Rise in Accusations of Cheating by Educators," *The New York Times*.

PBA. (2004). Press release, March 23, http://nycpba.org/archive/releases/04/pr040323-stats.html.

Punch, M. (2007). *Zero Tolerance Policing*. Bristol, U.K.: Policy Press.

Ravitch, D. (2010a). *The Death and Life of the Great American School System: How Testing and Choice are Undermining Education*. New York: Basic Books.

Ravitch, D. (2010b). "Why I Changed My Mind about School Reform," *The Wall Street Journal*, March 9, 21.

Reuss-Ianni, E. (1983). *Two Cultures of Policing*. New Brunswick, NJ: Transaction.

Ritzer, G. (2000). *The McDonaldization of Society*. Thousand Oaks, CA: Pine Forge Press.

Rokeach, M. (1973). *The Open and Closed Mind*. New York: Basic Books.

Silverman, E. (1997). "Crime in New York: A Success Story," *The Public Perspective*, 8(4).

Silverman, E. (1999). *NYPD Battles Crime*. Boston: Northeastern University Press.

Silverman, E. (2001). "Epilogue," *NYPD Battles Crime*. Boston: Northeastern University Press.

Slack, J. (2010). "Police to Demand Right to Strike in Return for Losing 'Jobs for Life' Protection," *Mail Online*, October 2, http://www.dailymail.co.uk/news/article-1317006/Tories-target-police-pay-perks.html.

Slack, J. and Chapman, J. (2010). "Victims of Anti-Social Behaviour Can Name and Shame Police Who Don't Help Them, Says Theresa May in Crackdown on Louts," *Daily Mail*, October 5, http://www.dailymail.co.uk/news/article-1317757/Theresa-May-Victims-anti-social-behaviour-police-dont-help.html#ixzz11U7k9p6X2010.

Waddington, D. (2007). *Policing Public Disorder*. Cullompton, U.K.: Willan.

Weisburd, D., Mastrofski, S., McNally, A., Greenspan, R., and Willis, J. J. (2003). "Reforming to Preserve: Compstat and Strategic Problem Solving in American Policing," *Criminology and Public Policy*, 2(3): 421–456.

Weisburd, D., Mastrofski, S., McNally, A., Greenspan, R., and Willis, J.J. (2006). "Changing Everything So That Everything Can Remain the Same." In: Weisburd, D. and Braga, A., Eds., *Police Innovation: Contrasting Perspectives*. Cambridge, UK: Cambridge University Press.

Zink, R. (2004). "The Trouble with Compstat," *PBA Magazine*, Summer, http://nycpba.org/archive/releases/04/pr040323-stats.html.

Suggested Reading

Bevan, G. and Hood, C. (2006). "What's Measured and What Matters: Targets and Gaming the English Public Health Care System," *Public Administration*, 84(3): 517–538.

Boivard, T. (2000). "Role of Competition and Competiveness in Best Value in England and Wales," *Public Policy and Administration*, 15(4): 82–89.

Bowerman, N. and Ball, A. (2000). "Great Expectations: Benchmarking for Best Value," *Public Money and Management*, 20(2): 21–26.

Case, P. (1999). "Remember Re-engineering: The Rhetorical Appeal of a Managerial Salvation Device," *Journal of Management Studies*, 36: 419–445.

Coleman, C. and Moynihan, J. (1996). *Understanding Crime Data: Haunted by the Dark Figure*. London: Open University Press.

Cowper, T.J. (2000). "The Myth of the Military Model of Leadership in Law Enforcement," *Police Quarterly,* 3(4): 226–246.

Jones, A. (2000). "Police Sick with Stress at NSW's Busiest Stations," *The Sunday Telegraph,* May 21, 25.

Jones, S. and Silverman, E. (1984). "What Price Efficiency," *Policing,* 1(1): 31–48.

Long, M. and Silverman, E. (2005). "The Anglo-American Measurement of Police Performance: Compstat and Best Value," *British Journal of Community Justice,* 3(3).

Loveday, B. (1999). "The Impact of Performance Culture on Criminal Justice Agencies," *International Journal of the Sociology of Law,* 27: 352–377.

Loveday, B. (2000a). "Managing Crime: Police Use of Crime Data As An Indicator of Effectiveness," *International Journal of the Sociology of Law,* 28: 215–237.

MacDonald, H. (2010). "Compstat and Its Enemies," *City Journal,* February 17, http://www.city-journal.org/2010/eon0217hm.htm.

New York Daily News. (2010a). "Mugging Compstat: Assault on NYPD Crime-Tracking Program Is Wrongheaded," February 11, http://www.nydailynews.com/opinions/2010/02/11/2010-02-11_mugging_compstat.html#ixzz19AYRSjwU.

New York Daily News. (2010b). "Arrest NYPD Bashing: Running a Numbers Racket with Crime-Fighting Statistics," October 3, http://www.nydailynews.com/opinions/2010/10/03/2010-10-03_arrest_nypd_bashing.html#ixzz19AY4XPwM.

New York Post. (2010). "Anti-Cop Idiocy," February 21, http://www.nypost.com/p/news/opinion/editorials/anti_cop_idiocy_hF4IkjAA0Zna2xm1KU0EXM#ixzz19AgNWXiD.

Ohlin, L. (1971). *The Challenge of Crime in a Free Society.* New York: Dacapo Press.

Pooley, E. (1996). "One Good Apple," *Time,* January.

Selznick, P. (1957). *Leadership and Administration.* New York: Harper and Row.

Shane, J. (2010). "The Myth of the American Police Quasi Military Model," paper presented at the Annual Meeting of the Academy of Criminal Justice Sciences, February 26, San Diego, CA.

Silverman, E. (2007). "With a Hunch and a Punch," *Journal of Law, Economics, and Policy,* 4(1).

Tink, A. (2000). Speech at New South Wales Police Association Biennial Conference, www.Pansw.asn.au.

Twain, M. (1960). *The Autobiography of Mark Twain.* London: Chatto and Windus.

Twain, M. (1885). *On the Decay of the Art of Lying.* Hartford, CT: Historical and Antiquarian Club.

Vitale, A.S. (2008). *City of Disorder.* New York: New York University Press.

Young, M. (1991). *An Inside Job. Policing and the Police Culture.* Oxford, UK: Clarendon Press.

Police Performance Management

4

The View from Abroad

On September 15, 2010, the U.K.'s chief spokesperson for policing addressed that nation's conference of police superintendents. Speaking before the Superintendents Association Conference, the new Coalition Government's Home Secretary* Theresa May outlined the government's proposed "reforms" that, in her words, "some people have called the most radical changes in policing for at least 50 years."

These "radical" reforms were offered as sweeping departures from the previous 13 years of Labour government policing performance statistical targets. Gone would be the central government's top-down restrictive mandates that focused on numerical police performance indicators rather than community tailored policing. Ms. May promised to enable police to mold crime programs to local conditions instead of constantly responding to top-down bureaucratic dictates. The Minister's speech encapsulated the new Government's Home Office approach.

> We will help you by getting out of the way and stopping interfering in policing. ... We won't impose national targets and one size fits all solutions to local problems. ... I like the phrase about too many officers chasing targets instead of chasing criminals. Well I want your officers chasing criminals. I want them to be crime fighters, not form writers. (Home Office, 2010c)

In her "Ministerial Foreword" to a document entitled, "Policing in the 21st Century: Reconnecting Police and People," (Home Office, 2010a), Ms. May noted that the police had become:

> responsive to government targets and bureaucracy rather than to people. They have become disconnected from the public they serve. We will do away with central targets. Frontline staffs will no longer be form writers but crime fighters. (pp. 2–3)

The body of the document stipulates "the challenge" facing the police, noting how in the past

---

* Due to devolved powers to Scotland and Northern Island, the Home Secretary's responsibility for policing is limited to England and Wales. Nevertheless, for brevity, the expression United Kingdom (UK) is commonly used as it includes rather than excludes.

> The Home Secretary has been given stronger and stronger powers to intervene, to set national objectives; publish data relating to performance; issues codes of practice and guidance; and direct police authorities. (p. 5)

What was the impetus for this grandiose, widely publicized reversal of previous governments' policing policies? Why did this major government paper come out so strongly for a new direction in policing? The performance policing status quo had been under attack for a number of years yet persisted due to its strong and familiar roots.

Performance policing in Britain arose, as in the United States, from a fear of crime, drive for greater police managerial accountability, and enhanced business-oriented police operations. In both countries, these developments had business, academic, and political roots. We first review these developments before analyzing their dysfunctional characteristics.

Performance Policing in the United Kingdom

Performance policing in the U.K. is the product of long and convoluted developments. The first far-ranging governmental performance proclamation was offered in 1983 with the Conservative Thatcher Government's Home Office Circular 114, which urged the police to pursue economy, efficiency, and effectiveness.

Home Office Circular 114 of 1983

As with New York and elsewhere, the U.K.'s call for change in "Manpower, Effectiveness and Efficiency in the Police Service" was activated by officialdom's criticism of a contemporary "crisis." The explicitly stated common denominator was the crime rate, which, in both cases, was deemed unacceptable. The circular refers to rising crime:

> Since 1971 ... the demands on the police have increased substantially. The number of serious crimes recorded by the police has practically doubled, while other commitments, such as the maintenance of public order, have also become more onerous. (Home Office, 1983, p. 1)

According to the Home Office, unacceptable crime rates, coupled with more police and funding, reflect ineffective performance and strategies.

> Since 1971 police strength (excluding civilians) has gone up by some 24,000 and on 31st March 1983 there were 121,003 police officers in England and Wales. Expenditure has also increased substantially and the cost of the police service in 1982-1983 was £2.4 billion as compared to £1.4 billion in 1970-1971 (estimated at current prices). (Home Office, 1983, pp. 1–2).

Again, as with New York's Mayor Giuliani, the Home Office spoke to the public's dwindling sense of security and confidence in the police. The Circular referred to consecutive British Crime Surveys revealing declining public assurance:

> If the police service is to deal with this situation and retain public confidence it is essential that it should make the most effective use possible of the substantial resources now available to it. (Home Office, 1983, p. 2)

Resembling U. S. developments, the private sector was proposed as the remedy for public sector malfunctioning. Police and other public organizations were viewed as "unaccountable" by "gurus" such as Peters and Waterman (1982), who urged closer customer connections. Employing a slogan similar to the U.S.'s "reengineering," (see Chapter 1), "reinvention" was offered as key to U.K. public sector creativity in solving problems of crime, as well those of as failing schools and inadequate health service.

Thus, the dual governmental and business condemnation of "outmoded," "outdated," and "illegitimate" practices in the name of "economy," "efficiency," "effectiveness," and "accountability" invigorated the police reform agenda. Nevertheless, this campaign was cushioned by the Conservative government's reliance on the police during workers' strikes in the turbulent 1980s.

By the 1990s, however, the reform agenda was reenergized as the police service lost its exemption from the Conservative government's drive for managerial reform. Successful anti-union legislation diminished organized labor's influence as well as the government's reliance on the police. With the simultaneous decline in urban unrest and the introduction of managerial reforms in the health and education sector, police claims for "special" exempt treatment lost their appeal. Police officers were also more dispensable in the context of a surge of available skilled labor.

The business basis for performance measures was articulated in a 1992 inquiry into police responsibilities and rewards established by a Conservative Home Secretary. Comprised of top non-police business managers, the inquiry highlighted performance indicators to assess labor and personnel issues. The unstated assumption, as in the NYPD, was that private sector management practices were precisely transferable to the public sector (see Chapter 1). The inquiry recommended flattening management structures, fixed-term appointments, and differential employee pay as instruments of enhanced police performance (Sheehy, 1993).

Enter the Labour Party

Concepts inherent in Prime Minister Margaret Thatcher's 1980s and early 1990s New Right Conservative government were incorporated in the Labour

Party's notion of "Best Value": when the Party swept into office in May 1997. Best Value reflects Prime Minister Tony Blair's public sector approach, a shift from a traditional, bureaucratic, "service-led" management orientation to a business "customer-led" basis.

Within a month in office, the Labour government enunciated Best Value principles: local governmental authorities would be held accountable to its customers and electorate for performance plans and economic, efficient, and effective services. The plans are set within a framework of central governmental national performance standards so that competitive local targets are compared, assessed, and reported in light of national targets and performance indicators established by the central Audit Commission. Inadequate progress toward measurable targets and failure of remedial action may be cause for central government intervention. In 1997, the government directed the police forces to achieve "best value" and crime reduction targets' through "league [comparative] tables, ranking and performance measures" (McLaughlin, 2007, p. 184).

The setting of performance standards, embedded in what is oftentimes termed as a "performance culture," was encapsulated in a barrage of additional government documents and edicts stipulating the process for police agencies. Her Majesty's Inspectorate of Constabulary (HMIC) released one such report in 1998. As an agency responsible for reviewing police force performance, HMIC stressed the need for activity costing and achievement of "value for money" (Long and Silverman, 2005).

The combination of New Labour's Best Value and its 1999-2000 Strategic Plan for Criminal Justice made national targets and objectives even more explicit. These targets were:

> highly prescriptive and based on the clear expectations that the agencies will be able to achieve them in a set period of time... [requiring] the police service to reduce the level of actual crime and disorder, to reduce the long run rate of the growth of crime, to reduce the level of disorder, to reduce the level of vehicle crime and to reduce the fear of crime. (Loveday, 2000a, p. 218)

This U.K. focus again parallels the experience in the United States and elsewhere. Efficient policing was equated with slim-down crime-oriented policing shorn of social work and an "officer friendly" outlook. After all, the major responsibility of police, it was asserted, was protection from the bad guys. Crime fighting should preoccupy police in order to achieve law and order. Police success would be measured by what turned out to be onerous crime reduction statistical targets while other items such as citizen confidence in the police were relegated to remote positions.

Government Revelations and Problem Intensification

Despite the proud police proclamations of pushing crime down, official inquiries raised numerous caveats. The collection and recording of crime statistics was questioned in a report entitled "Collection and Accuracy of Police Incident Data," commissioned by the Home Office in 1996, which stated:

> There appears to be some variation not only in the number and type of events being recorded by the police, but also in the way certain events are interpreted for statistical purposes. (Portas and Mason, 1996, p. 24)

A 2000 Home Office report revealed significant under-recording of crime by the police in its "Review of Crime Statistics."

Other evidence suggested that in some cases crimes were reclassified so that burglary was recorded as criminal damage or other type of theft (Loveday, 1996). In 1999, a Police Complaints Authority investigation into recording practices in one force found more than 9,000 crimes absent from official crime figures, indicating that the force's crime recording policy "was designed to have the effect of artificially reducing recorded crime to a more politically acceptable level" (Davies, 1999; for a fuller discussion, see Hallam, 2009).

Subsequent HMIC audits of regional forces were quite specific. One audit, for example, compared incident logs of citizen-reported crime with the police's crime recording system and found that "a high proportion of the sample had not been recorded as crime, which can lead to a significant under-reporting." In addition, the audit found that many officers who attended reported crime incidents were "too frequently finalizing incidents with the finding of 'no formal complaint, no action,' contrary to Home Office Guidelines that any notifiable offence coming to the attention of the police should be recorded" (HMIC, 1999/2000c, pp. 3, 17).

An HMIC audit of another force expressed "disappointment" in finding that 17 percent of the sample of crime records "which appeared to relate to a report of a crime was not recorded as such. This is likely to have a significant impact for effective analysis of crime patterns" (HMIC, 1999/2000b).

Another audit stressed the importance of accurate crime reporting.

> Within a 'performance culture' there is a need for integrity to enable the public to be confident that crime is being ethically recorded... Incident logs where initial reports are recorded were compared with the crime recording system. Some 15 percent of incidents that had sufficient detail to merit being recorded as crimes had not been 'crimed.' (HMIC, 1999/2000a; italics added)

Although the government recognized these dysfunctional consequences of managerial preoccupation with statistical crime performance measurement, the medicine unfortunately aggravated the disease. This can best be illustrated with a review of the government's November 2002 submission to Parliament of "The National Policing Plan, 2003-2006" (National Policing Plan, 2002).

The plan's introduction states that it

> provides the strategic national overview against which chief officers and police authorities should prepare their own [newly introduced] local three-year strategy plans and annual policing plans. (NPP, 2002, p. 3)

This plan takes performance measurement, planning, central government bureaucratic expansion, and review to new heights of absurdity. In order to compensate for what it perceives as too much reliance on crime-related performance measures, the government proposed a new "suite" of performance measures. These included a far wider array of standards and targets including some in the area of "reassurance policing." This is despite the fact that the British crime survey indicates a consistent downward trend while at the same time public surveys reveal that people do not feel safer. The government apparently believes that police preoccupation with crime statistics (which is a response to previous central government initiatives) can be overcome with more of the same—adding new measures to the existing array of measures instead of abandoning, substituting, or prioritizing some or all of them.

Just consider the wide range of performance measures proposed. The document lists six "performance indicators"

> to assess the extent to which police are able to reduce crime and the fear of crime, improve performance overall, including by reducing the gap between the highest crime areas and the best comparable areas; and reduce vehicle crime by 30 percent from 1998-99 to 2004, domestic burglary by 25 percent from 1998–99 to 2005, robbery in the ten Street Crime Initiatives areas by 14 percent from 1999–2000 to 2005 and maintain that level. (NPP, 2002, p. 36)

An additional seven "key performance indicators" are recorded in order to evaluate the extent to which forces have:

> Improved their performance and significantly reduced the performance gap between the best and worst performing forces; and significantly increased the proportion of time spent on frontline duties. (NPP, 2002, p. 37)

However, according to the planning document, much more was promised. Home Office monitoring would extend to six performance areas (domains): citizen focus, helping the public, reducing crime, investigating crime, promoting public safety, and resource usage.

The framework will require the development of additional performance indicators (to capture the breadth of policing responsibilities) including the development of more satisfactory indicators on race issues and compulsory collection of Activity Based Costing Data (to establish the link between the resources used and the outcomes delivered.) Regular comparative assessment of force performance will be conducted to assess the absolute and relative performance of forces, PPAF (Policing Performance Assessment Framework) will be introduced from April 2004. (NPP, 2002, pp. 37, 38)

To complicate matters further, the government discussed an undetermined "performance radar screen," which presumably injects a scientific analytical device to assess the performance of police forces. These screens would have represented whatever performance indicators are available at the time.

And who was to do the assessing? The number of central government units just kept on growing. In addition to the Home Office and the police review units of the HMIC and Audit Commission, the government established a new Police Standards Unit, which no one seemed to know how to fit into the existing units. Moreover, the government created a National Centre of Policing Excellence (NCPE) with the promise that it will "ensure that all forces are applying good practice and procedure for dealing with crime" (NPP, 2002, p. 13). In fact, the plan lumps all these units together:

A new framework is being developed to promote improved performance, backed by Her Majesty's Inspectorate of Constabulary (HIMIC) and the Police Standards Unit (PSU). (NPP, 2002, p. 3)

Moreover, NCPE was designed to work with ACPO (Association of Chief Police Officers), the APA (Association of Police Authorities), HMIC, and the PSU (Police Standards Unit) to identify, develop, and spread good practice throughout the service (NPP, 2002, p. 13).

Why still another unit was needed at the central level to do this is not explained. In the process of littering the central government landscape with multiple police review bodies, these new units soak up operative police personnel who otherwise would be occupied with their force police work.

To complicate matters more, the government imposed additional regulations, ironically, in the name of streamlining the police bureaucracy.

To tackle the administrative boarders and inefficient working practices which keep police officers off the street. ... *The Bureaucracy Taskforce* was commissioned to give the government a police service view of what could be done to achieve this. This Taskforce Report was published in September 2002 and *contained 52 recommendations* about how the presence of police officers in communities might be increased. The Government has published an action plan to implement most of the recommendations. *The onus is now on forces.* ... (NPP, 2002, p. 14; emphasis added)

The NPP was not content to rely solely on its directives. Police forces were also instructed to include directives from other sources in their planning.

Annual policing plans and three year strategies will not be the only planning processes that impact upon the police service. In the process of drafting local policing plans and strategies, forces and police authorities should take into account their own and others input to (and responsibilities flowing variously from) *the planning process of CDRPs (Crime and Disorder Reduction Partnerships), DATs (Drug Action Teams), Youth Offender Teams and Local Criminal Justice Boards. The Government has introduced secondary legislation to bring the cycle of three year policing strategies into line with the Development of Crime and Disorder Reduction Strategies.* (NPP, 2002, p. 41; emphasis added)

Strategies ran amok when guided by a plethora of directives, guidelines, and central government units. In developing their plans for the next three years, local forces were required to base their plans on the NPP and other central government directives but also on *forthcoming documents.*

Chief Officers and police authorities should include in their local plans a strategy for tackling youth nuisance and anti-social behavior taking account of the *forthcoming white paper and legislation.* (NPP, 2002, p. 6; emphasis added)

In discussing planning strategies "to tackle crime and anti-social behavior," forces are informed that:

The Home Office is establishing a multi-disciplined Anti-Social Behaviour Team to help achieve this. A White Paper will be published in the New Year, followed by a wide-ranging Anti-Social Behaviour Bill before summer 2003. (NPP, 2002, p. 9)

The fact that police force plans needed to be completed before this period was somehow disregarded. According to the document, police planning should be informed not only by local needs and performance measures but also by national standards and the performances of other forces as well.

Local plans must include local three year targets for reducing vehicle crime, burglary and robbery against which the contribution of each force to meeting the national targets in these areas can be measured. Local targets will need to be particularly challenging where forces (or individual unit) performance is demonstrably below that of comparable forces or units.

> For 2003-04, every police force must contribute effectively to their Local Criminal Justice Board (LCJB) target increasing the number of offences brought to justice by 5 percent. (NPP, 2002, pp. 7–8)

The cascade of government oversight and assistance agencies did not end there. In April 2007, the government established the National Police Improvement Agency (NIPA) "to make a unique contribution to improving public safety by providing critical rational services, building capability across the public service, providing professional expertise to police forces and authorities."

> Three short years later, the new Coalition Government decided to phase out NPIA by March 2012. "It is looking at which NPIA functions are still needed, and how these functions might best be delivered in a new, streamlined, landscape." (National Police Improvement Agency, 2010)

The culmination of these burdensome targets and oversight were highlighted by the Independent HMIC July 2010 study "Valuing the Police," which found that:

> In 2009 alone, there were 52 guidance documents produced by ACPO (Association of Chief Police Officers) and the NIPA comprising more than 2,600 pages and over 250 recommendations. ... Ideas, concepts and processes that started out as a simple checklist for doing business—such as "intelligence led policing"—have become cottage industries, generating doctrine, guidance and a plethora of supporting documentation. The National Intelligence Model (NNIM) is a "super-outputer" of documents; the guidance now runs to 213 pages with nine volumes of supporting documents that together comprises 816 pages ...
>
> The number of organizations and regulatory bodies that place requirements on the police has doubled since the early 1990s. Alongside HMIC, there are now 16 other organizations that can make regulatory demands on the police. Collectively, this has increased oversight and scrutiny of forces and has diverted police resources away from serving the public. (HMIC, 2010, pp. 17–18)

The study reports that central governmental bodies that impose requirements on the police doubled since the early 1990s with over 17 making regulatory demands. While centrally imposed targets were once "innovative," they have morphed into a "cluttered performance regime" (HMIC, 2010, p. 4).

Scholarly Analysis

These target-driven developments have heightened criticism of what some U.K. researchers have labeled the "emergence of U.S. style criminal justice policies in other industrial democracies" (Jones and Newburn, 1997, p. 123). They see similarities with the NYPD Compstat model in the almost exclusive focus on police results and outputs through the setting of explicit and measurable crime level indicators. As with our research, U.K. assessments indicate that crime statistical performance indicators often create "perverse incentives [that] compromise local innovation, efficiency and accountability" (Flanagan, 2008, p. 21).

It should be evident that in the United Kingdom, as elsewhere, the evidence of police misclassification and downgrading of crime statistics has been well documented by respected scholars (Loveday, 1999; Reiner, 1992; Maguire 2007). For example, 16 years after the government's first performance policing circular, Loveday asserted that performance target identification often resulted in more negative than positive impacts on police managers. This included "misclassification," "downgrading," "cuffing," and "prison visits" to describe unethical practices that have a long history within policing. Loveday refers to the HMIC's 1999 "Report on Police Integrity," which highlighted the way in which the "performance culture" was encouraging unhealthy arrest rate competition among officers (Loveday, 2000a, pp. 228, 230).

> Demand for police forces to reduce crime ... *must inevitably place pressure on them to deliver,* wherever possible such reductions. ... Cultural commitment within the police organization also had to accommodate massaging of crime figures to make these more acceptable to the public. Police monopoly of crime recording did mean that a mechanism was readily at hand to generate crime figures where they might reflect on the efficiency of the police force. (Loveday, 2000a, pp. 223–224; emphasis added)

An in-depth scholarly analysis of three U.K. performance management police forces concluded that "... the conflicting priorities brought about by managerial dictum and the bureaucratic rules governing the recording of crime are to 'define crime down.' It leads to a manipulation of data to provide pleasing results" (Hallam, 2009, p. iii). Another U.K. study referred to "repeated reports of the massaging of figures by the police" (Martin, 2003).

The United Kingdom's strong performance culture spawned a new interest in "ethical recording" of offenses.

> If performance is to be measured, there must be confidence in the data. ... As crime reduction has been identified for purposes of performance targeting, mis-classification of offences has become more salient. (Loveday, 2000a, pp. 228, 230)

Popular Press Revelations

Eventually this scrutiny filtered down to the public via the popular press. In October 2008, for example, the press reported that:

> Some police forces have been under-recording the most serious violent crimes, the Home Office said today, as it released figures showing a 22 percent increase. The category includes serious assault, murder, attempted murder and manslaughter. Officials admitted the under-counting could have been going on for more than 10 years. They said 13 forces were asked to re-examine their figures after they discovered some serious assaults were being recorded in a lower category of offence. (Metro.Co.UK, 2008)

Two months later, the head of the U.K. Statistics Authority (established to promote the ethical use of data) accused the Home Office of releasing "selective" knife crime figures in order to downplay the extent of knife stabbings (Booth, 2008). By April 2009, a respected Home Office adviser observed that the public had little confidence in the accuracy of the government's crime statistics (Whitehead, 2009).

Non-Official Police Confirmation

Governmental and scholarly analyses have been strongly supported by police on the ground. A former U.K. police commander provides a very detailed account of statistical manipulation.

> Nearly every crime department I encountered at the time was engaged in the practice commonly known as 'cuffing.' This, in effect, means hiding or eliminating the incidence of reported crime from public scrutiny by tried means. At many police stations the crime book was locked away and only detectives were allowed to record crime... Many of the run of the mill minor crimes were only collated on message pads or some other rough record and then only kept on the pad until it was suitable to ditch them. Once assessed as 'dead and unsolvable,' they were consigned to 'file 13' (the waste paper basket). ... The record of what was eventually recorded as crime was carefully controlled and there was little scope for anyone to deny or challenge the version of reality generated by the detectives, which proclaimed to all that crime figures were low and detections high. (Young, 1991, pp. 323, 324)

Other British police commanders and officers recall their first-hand experiences. One former commander commented:

> Manipulating crime stats—it has gone on for years—trouble now though is the pressure on managers from government and alike caused by our obsession with performance targets. ... If you do not achieve the targets now you are deemed a failure rather than looking at why and realizing perhaps that in the

surrounding circumstances one has actually achieved better than one would have expected even though targets not met. (MP, 2010)

Another former U.K. police commander commented:

The "New Public Management" was applied to public services in the U.K. from the 1980s onwards. ... Management becomes more effective, accountability is improved through the availability of information and identified problems are explicitly addressed. But like any innovation, problems often accompany mis-use and inadequate implementation.

The champions of New Public Management tended to underestimate the ingenuity of individuals to engage in statistical chicanery, particularly when contracts and careers could be at stake. Pleasing statistics make pleasing "sound-bites". One police force demonstrated an astonishing reduction in vehicle crime until it was discovered that marginal offences were reduced to non-recordable categories. (Marlow, 2010)

A former assistant chief constable noted:

Targets and performance measurement have to be used with great care and ... [r]ecent governments have been obsessed with these ... and quantity has triumphed over quality in many situations. In the police service ... we com-promised ourselves by always trying to comply with the latest fad. Any contra-diction was seen as reactionary and unwilling to change. (Frost, 2010)

A former senior commander makes a very useful distinction on how numerical data is utilized in performance management:

The smartest and best police commanders really understood the numbers, what they were and where the problems actually occurred or the links between different types of offending. The mediocre thought it was an internal organisational game and therefore all about the numbers. If they could crack the numbers then they would be seen in a good light and they would get the rewards they sought. It is in this environment that the numbers become the end rather than the means and the police performance yet again becomes detached from the reality of what the citizen experiences on the street. Huge amounts of time are invested in avoiding the need to record crime, or down-grade it from a crime to an "incident" or "intelligence" rather than deal with it. So a great deal rests on the quality of the commanders, the nature of their training and, perhaps *most importantly, the kind of organizational environ-ment which top management fosters.* (Robb, 2010; emphasis added)

Summary

The critical importance of top management and organizational environments cannot be underestimated. In the absence of proper political and police lead-ership, the single-minded focus on performance data leads to cumbersome bureaucratic dictates, extensive statistical selectivity, misclassification, down-grading, and failure to report crime. These factors are not only significant in the U.K. and U.S. police performance systems but in other nations as well.

Australia

In Australia, Compstat-like performance management systems were also modeled after New York's Compstat. The New South Wales police force, the largest in Australia, developed its Operations and Crimes Review (OCR) after visiting the NYPD's Compstat (Davis and Coleman, 2000). Similarly, the State of Victoria's Police Force adopted its own Compstat system with the stated "purpose—to evaluate and *improve performance against set measures*, identify strengths and share best practices, enhance intelligent policing and encourage effective use of resources" (Victorian Ombudsman, 2011, p. 9; emphasis added).

New South Wales Police Force

The New South Wales (NSW) Police Force's Operations and Crime Review (OCR), like New York and the United Kingdom, was also influenced by business-oriented police managerial reform themes accompanied with intense demand for crime reduction. During the late 1980s, the NSW Police Force Commissioner's Annual Reports and a Royal (Woods) Commission addressed the issue of police corruption. They urged an unremitting focus on police dishonesty to ensure enhanced police ethical conduct. This required radical surgery embracing an "uncompromising" style of internal zero tolerance policing policy (Miller, Blackler, and Alexander, 1997, pp. vii–xiii).

At the same time, however, crime increased in NSW eliciting a crisis environment similar to New York and the United Kingdom, prompting an appeal for more aggressive policing to counter drug addiction and street prostitution. Politicians and the media, in the words of one observer, created:

> a moral panic scenario; which built on the impression that "soft options" such as the mobile needle exchange and condom unit were playing a major role in creating drug addiction and allowing the proliferation of prostitution in the area—a crisis situation requiring extraordinary responses—just as martial law and conscription are made to appear acceptable in wartime. (Watney, 1987 cited in Kennedy, 2000, p. 38)

Assuming the role of a moral crusader disdainful of his own safety, one legislator was praised by the media—along with other "councilors and residents"—for their determination to "clear their street of drug addicts, prostitutes and men prowling in cars" (Warnock, 1996, p. 1).

The new Police Commissioner, Peter Ryan, attributed the surge in crime to the police service's preoccupation with corruption control. Using similar rhetoric as employed in other countries (such as William Bratton when he became NYPD's Commissioner, see Silverman, 2001), it was asserted that the police had "taken its eye off the ball" (Dixon, 1999, p. 176), straying from its core crime control mission.

Once again (see Chapter 1), private sector procedures were offered as the solution to these problems. The new policing was based on "new ideas, business principles and work practices" (New South Wales Police Service, 2000, p. 3). In 1998, the police service introduced its version of Compstat—the Operations and Crimes Review (OCR).

Like Compstat, OCR's data-led management strategy is performance-based (Davis and Coleman, 2000; New South Wales Police Service, 1999, pp. 4–5), quantifying crime reduction in victimization percentages. Competency is scientifically assessed in terms of empirical crime statistics and arrest rates (New South Wales Police Service, 1999) while measuring "individual productivity" and producing "cost effective policing" (New South Wales Police Service, 2000, p. 3; Kennedy, 2000, p. 27). This approach was enshrined in the NSW police document *Future Directions Policy*, which stated that the commissioner will improve the monitoring of individual productivity and organize a "dignified" exit for those officers who are no longer able to undertake the difficult and stressful work of "ethical cost effective policing" (New South Wales Police Service, 2000, p. 6).

As in other nations, the NSW's use and subsequent misuse of performance measurement spawned numerous consequences. Thus, police officers who were unable to accept the shift from serving as police officers in the community into the contradictory world of producing measurable cost-effective results for the shareholders were encouraged to leave the force as quickly as possible. Within this corporate framework, senior management is offered "perks" such as bonuses and lucrative retirement benefits, over and above their generous salaries. For senior police, any promotion prospects are directly aligned to whatever contribution they have been deemed to have made to their organization's "growth." This involves the use of performance contracts to measure the competency of senior police in terms of increased supervision and "productivity" demands on the rank-and-file to keep within the allocated budgetary constraints imposed from above (New South Wales Police Service, 2002). Once again, this reinforces the existing division of labor between administrative and operational police and separates the demands of management from the actual needs of the job.

Former NSW Commissioner Ryan acknowledged that OCR policing was data driven, "uncompromising, difficult and stressful" (New South Wales

Police Service, 2000, p. 3). Robinson reported that, while some crime levels dropped and arrest rates increased for the first time in more than a decade, this came at a considerable cost (Robinson, 1999, p. 3).

The NSW Police Annual Report (1999) indicated that assaults against police rose almost 10 percent, with an average of 31 officers being attacked every week. In addition, the stress on middle management and street level police to meet performance targets was reflected in the increasing rate of resignations and falling recruitment numbers. In the words of one legislator:

> ... why is it that out of a class of 403 in CEP 5 [Police Academy], only 340 were attested and what happened to the other 60 or 15 percent? ... Why is it that May's *Police News* shows that 20 percent of the resignations in February were probationary constables and a further 30 percent were constables—that is to say 50 percent of the resignations were by people new to the service? ... (Tink, 2000, p. 7)

The Police Association's research director issued a public statement to the print media stating that 5 percent of the State's police were on sick leave.

> I don't know any organisation which could sustain that. And what they are doing is speeding up the medical exit process—it's crazy. That's not solving the problem; the problem is much deeper than that. They need to start addressing the underlying problems, the lack of support and the way they treat people. (Jones, 2000, p. 25)

In spite of this, blame for individual or organizational stress is still conveniently moved from the executive and placed squarely at the feet of middle management (Kennedy, 2000, p. 47). In Australia, as elsewhere, the non-quantitative aspects of police discretion such as community awareness, officer discretion, service, protection of due process (as opposed to quantified arrests and crime statistics), tolerance, and warnings are less available options as they do not readily lend themselves to immediate measurement.

Like elsewhere, this Australian performance-based policing is controversial. On the one hand, for example, two Australian scholars' evaluation of the OCR found this process to be effective in reducing three of the four offense crime categories studied (Chilvers and Weatherburn, 2004). Yet a 2000 evaluation by an independent consulting group (Hay Group Consulting Consortium, 2000) found communication to be largely a one-way process with little feedback to commanders, "reinforcing the culture of fear and punishment." The following year, the Deputy Commissioner resigned after he announced that crime was falling when the independent NSW Bureau of Crime Statistics reported it was increasing (Williams, 2002, p. 297). In addition, Australia's National Uniform Crime Statistics Committee reported variations in crime statistics due to:

The extent of unreported crime; inadequacies in offence definitions, counting rules and offence classifications; procedural differences such as the offences under which an offender may be charged; differences in the way statistics are compiled. (Hallam, 2009)

Victoria Police Force

Australia's second most populous state of Victoria has a police force of almost 14,000 employees. For over two decades, the integrity of its crime statistics has been a public issue. Following earlier efforts in the 1980s, a 1991 Office of Police Integrity investigative report found that the "Victoria Police is unable to produce accurate clearance statistics to the Victorian Government, the Australian Bureau of Statistics and the Victorian community" and described the process "open to manipulation." The same year, a Victoria Parliamentary Committee recommended the establishment of an "independent Bureau of Crime Statistics," which would promote a "more rational and disinterested presentation and discussion of crime statistics" (Victorian Ombudsman, 2011, p. 8). (This is in sharp contrast to NSW's independent Bureau of Crime Statistics and Research, which issued a report contradicting the NSW police force's official crime statistics, contributing to a resignation of a deputy commissioner, see page 99.)

In 2002, another Victoria Parliamentary committee maintained that there was "continuing concerns about the quality and accuracy of Victoria Police crime statistics." Therefore, the committee recommended a Bureau of Crime Statistics and Research "as an independent statutory agency reporting directly to Parliament" (Victorian Ombudsman, 2011, p. 10). An extensive 2002 Australian Institute of Criminology study of Victoria Crime Statistics found that police benefit from "a degree of discretion" on how they recorded crime. They could use the "prima facie" method whereby police record all crime allegations. However, they were also permitted to use the "evidence" approach where the investigating officer who takes a crime report decides how that crime will be recorded. In an understatement, the study concludes, "Given this discretion, there is inconsistency in the way in which particular crimes are recorded" (Carcach and Makkai, 2002). Police leeway to employ either approach provides additional opportunity for statistical manipulation. Even the police force's own Corporate Management Review Division noted in February 2006 that there were "inaccuracies in the data presented to its Compstat forum" (Victorian Ombudsman, 2011, p. 9).

In 2009, another government body, the Victorian Ombudsman, recommended to the Victoria Parliament that "there needed to be an independent body separate to the Victoria Police to manage the release of crime statistics" (Victorian Ombudsman, 2011, p. 5). Two years later, the Victorian

Ombudsman bemoaned the continued failure to launch an independent body:

> Nothing appears to have changed. Crime Statistics are still managed and disseminated by Victoria Police, with known inefficiencies and other long standing concerns. There is still mistrust in the way crime statistics are used ... (Victorian Ombudsman, 2011, p. 5)

This absence of an independent oversight body likely provoked a whistleblower's February 2011 complaint to the Victorian Ombudsmen. The complaint alleged that the Victoria Police Force prematurely reported misleading and manipulated crime statistics on October 28, 2011, shortly before the November election in order to influence the outcome. The police press release highlighted a 27.5-percent reduction in assaults in Melbourne's Central Business District during the July–September 2010 quarter compared to the same period in 2009 and a 12.4-percent decrease in assaults across the state.

In June 2011, the Victorian Ombudsman issued his report, which stated that the release of the data

> ... without qualification, was based on yet to be validated data [and] therefore likely that the data ... could reasonably be perceived to be misrepresenting the fuller picture of the trends. The crime statistics were subsequently used for political purposes during a public debate by the then new Police Minister three days before the election. The release ... particularly so close to an election was likely to be used in a political context. (Victorian Ombudsman, 2011, p. 5)

The media and public furor that followed the Ombudsman's report led to the Commissioner's resignation only hours after the issuance of the report. One media source led with "The Victorian Ombudsman has found that Police Commissioner Simon Overland was solely responsible for the release of assault statistics he knew were bodgie [fudged] just before the Victorian election" (Simons, 2011, June 18).

Another source reported that the Ombudsman found the "statistics misleading, inconsistent and likely to be used for political means, which they were during the campaign" (McArthur, 2011, June 16). One newspaper headline read, "Victoria's Top Cop Simon Overland Quits over Misleading Statistics" (Vollmer, 2011, June 17).

Summary

These two Australian examples demonstrate two major points. The first point is that the Australian political climate, as in other countries, frequently fosters expectations of crime reductions that are habitually reflected in altered police statistics. The expectations of crime reduction are often transmitted from the top throughout the organization. As the police entity designed to deal with the outside world, the media-public information unit is therefore poised to present the best possible organizational face (see Chapter 6). In Victoria, the Ombudsman concluded that the "media saw its role as to put a positive story on information released by Victoria Police." The head of the unit was quoted as describing her "role as always to protect and enhance the reputation of Victoria Police but only through appropriate behavior." Despite claims of "appropriate behavior," the Ombudsmen recounted that the official police crime report of a 27.5-percent decline in CBD street assaults "was at odds with other assault data available to the Victoria Police at the time" (Victorian Ombudsman, 2011, p. 19).

Therefore, what constitutes "appropriate behavior" often emerges as a contentious issue. This brings us to our second point. There is a major difference in the two Australian states. New South Wales has an independent Bureau of Crime Statistics to assess police crime reports. The Bureau's findings contradicted and corrected official New South Wales police crime statistics and prompted a Deputy Commissioner's resignation.

The State of Victoria, on the other hand, despite long-standing appeals, does not have an independent police statistical review agency. Thus, the issue of the integrity of the police force's statistics has festered in Victoria for many years. This major distinction—our second point—provides another compelling reason for this volume's advocacy of police transparency and outside review by an independent body. At a minimum, this should entail regular audits of police crime reports by outside independent bodies.

France

Recent research of a Compstat-like police performance management in Paris reveals striking parallels with the manipulative components of the NYPD, U.S., U.K., and Australian experiences. The Compstat-like system was first imported to Paris in 1999 when the Socialist government under Prime Minister Lionel Jospin and his Minister of the Interior Jean Pierre Chevènement sought to ward off Conservative inroads. The government sought to transform the police through the introduction of the French version of community policing (police de proximité).

In securing a method to evaluate this new community policing, the French first considered auditing the "commissariats" (precinct units) but this was considered an excessively long and demanding process. Since the French police, as with most police forces, were aware of the NYPD's Compstat, Jean Paul Proust, then "Préfet de Police de Paris" (head of the Paris police, the leading French police force), visited a New York Compstat meeting and believed the system met his organizational evaluative needs.

When Nicolas Sarkozy became Minister of the Interior in May 2002, he provided added impetus for the full adoption of this American business-type police model. Some interpreted Sarkozy's efforts as an attempt to "bolster his tough image as crime fighter. This, in turn, helped to fuel his presidential ambitions" (Punch, 2007, p. 39).

The French approach valued this new police performance approach as a management system that would enable them to combat crime. The French labeled this approach as the "culture of results" with roots in the "New Public Management" (Didier, 2010). The process reshaped the way the Paris police force organized its data. Crime statistics were compared with police activity and resources. Upper echelons established quantitative objectives in order to motivate lower levels while a system of bonuses was fixed for different ranks. Each echelon requires reporting levels to produce statistical tables of activity, which form the bases of evaluation reports to higher ranks.

In the pithy words of a French sociologist:

> The fact is that from the moment delinquency figures are used for assessing the actions of each echelon, they become a strategic variable for each agent. Sociologists, initially English, have shown that statistics becomes the object of "gaming", that is to say it is organized in such a way as to produce positive results for the one producing them, who will be assessed by their yardstick. (Bevan and Hood, 2006)

In France, two authors specifically applied this analysis to police organizations as they employ various manipulative quantification techniques in order to minimize outside criticism. This is termed "the production of the right figures" (Matelly and Mouhanna, 2007).

> This means that the actors, on the basis of existing tools, use figures in a "right" way so as to serve a particular strategy: i.e., show that government policy is a success, that a particular police force is lacking in resources, that a particular Commissioner has excellent results, or a particular unit commander is effective. ... Each one seeks to optimize his situation. (Matelly and Mouhanna, 2007, p. 31)

The introduction of this hierarchically oriented business efficiency model yielded many of the same dysfunctional ingredients that have plagued the United States, United Kingdom, and Australian police forces. Researchers uncovered the setting of quotas and targets, which were never officially acknowledged but were definitely operative. Therefore, the French government, as in New York, could remain extremely ambivalent and unclear about the existence of targets.

The drive to demonstrate success and reductions in crime decline also generated similar damaging consequences. Explicit and implicit comparisons between peers and brigades resulted in tension among commanders while praise and punishments increased the distances among the different levels of the police. At many meetings, commanders were barraged with a cascade of statistical slides and charts with superficial analysis yet bedeviled with implicit praise and punishment.

Statistical recordings of criminal events became paramount. Different types of statistical distortions emerged. This included downgrading crime, making it difficult for victims to record complaints, postdating crime events, and failure to record an event so that it is not officially acknowledged as a crime. The fallout is distorted police objectives and focus on symbolic success as opposed to addressing citizen concerns with effective community policing problem solving.

A French observer provides "examples."

> The police always retain some leeway when recording facts. They can: deny facts reported to them, re-direct the complainant to other services so that his complaint is not recorded in their own statistics, or convert a written complaint into a simple oral notification (which does not enter the figures). Secondly, at the time of codification, they can: tone down the violence (establish a minor offence instead of a misdemeanor), play on the counting units by changing the penal classification (for example count the theft of a check book or count n thefts of n checks stolen, as it suits them), leave a procedure open for lack of information in such a way that it is not counted ... In our vocabulary it is called manipulation. (Didier, 2010, p. 7)

The importation of the Compstat model to Paris yielded remarkable parallels to other countries in its dysfunctional crime recording and management. Not only are statistics subject to similar manipulations, but also the public, the police organization, and its members are ill served by misleading and incomplete data.

Conclusion

Our review of the view from abroad of Compstat-like police performance exposes similar malfunctioning police organizations saddled with top-down political and police pressures to report favorable crime statistics. The consequences are disastrous for police and public alike.

In addition, regardless of the police force analyzed, scholars also arrive at the same fundamental rock-bottom conclusion: without independent analysis, the reliability and integrity of crime statistics are subject to reasonable doubt. As one U.K. scholar quoted an earlier U.S. conclusion,

> The interesting phenomenon of consistent under-recording of crime appears to be largely explained by the absence of any independent audit at the local level and the continued police monopoly over crime recording. ... In most other situations in our society when we wish to reach a reliable evaluation we search for or construct objective measures not subject to the control of those being assessed. Yet our judgment of police effectiveness depends in large part on the crime statistics they are urged to supply voluntarily. (Ohlin, 1971, p. 261 in Loveday, 2000a, p. 237)

Other independent assessments also arrive at the same conclusion. For example, 10 days after our survey results were reported in the *New York Times*, the New York non-partisan business group, the Citizens Crime Commission, cited our study and called for an independent analysis of the NYPD's crime statistics. The press release was entitled "Commission Urges NYPD to Release Audits on Precinct Crime Numbers: Call Comes on Heels of New Questions about Validity of Crime Statistics." The press release noted, "transparency is the best solution ... and the public is fully entitled to be assured that reported crime data is accurate" (Citizens Crime Commission of New York City, 2010).

An exhaustive review of crime statistics generated by American police forces strongly advocated independent analysis of police crime data.

> To insure complete impartiality, the auditor should be as far removed as possible from the police department he is checking. Audits ... by a police-appointed firm are not an effective check upon the police and do little to remove critics' distrust of police crime statistics. (Center and Smith, 1972–1973, p. 1045)

This stands in marked contrast to Commissioner Kelly's appointment of a three-person outside committee to review the NYPD's crime reporting system.

The lack of transparency not only obfuscates a candid portrait of the level and nature of crime, but also it raises even more disturbing and far-reaching issues. Without openness, there is only a scant reckoning of the critical consequences of crime misreporting, misclassification, and undercounting associated with police performance management. An open society and informed public deserve full disclosure of the impact of performance management on crime detection, police organizations, police personnel, the public, and victims of crime.

Without transparency, flawed police leadership can continue to misuse Compstat and other police performance management systems. The next chapter explores the type of leadership associated with this dysfunctional management system and offers viable alternatives.

References

Bevan, G. and Hood, C. (2006). "What's Measured and What Matters: Targets and Gaming the English Public Health Care System," *Public Administration*, 84(3): 517–538.

Booth, R. (2008). "Home Office Accused of Releasing Selective Knife Crime Figures," *The Guardian*, December 13.

Carach, C. and Makkai, T. (2002). *Review of Victoria Police Statistics*. Canberra: Australian Institute of Criminology.

Center, L. and Smith, T. (1972–1973). "Crime Statistics-Can They be Trusted?" *American Criminal Law Review*, 11: 1045.

Chilvers, M. and Weatherburn, D. (2004). "The New South Wales Compstat Process: Its Impact on Crime," *Australian and New Zealand Journal of Criminology*, 37(2): 22–48.

Citizens Crime Commission of New York City. (2010). Press release, February 16.

Davies, N. (1999). "Watching the Detectives: How the Police Cheat in Fight Against Crime," *The Guardian*, March 8.

Davis, E. and Coleman, C. (2000). "Getting Crime Down," *HR Monthly*, May, 22–23.

Didier, E. (2010). *Is the New Liberal State Lying*. GSPM, EHESS, CNRS.

Dixon, D. (1999). *A Culture of Corruption*. Sydney: Hawkins Press.

Flanagan, R. (2008). *The Review of Policing: Final Report*. Home Office. www.homeoffice.gov.uk/about-us/news/flanagan-report. Accessed February 7, 2008.

Frost, J. (2010). Personal e-mail, December 23.

Hallam, S. (2009). Policing in the Iron Cage, PhD Dissertation, University of Bedfordshire.

Hay Group Consulting Consortium. (2000). "Qualitative and Strategic Audit of the Report Process of the NSW Police Service," Sydney: Police Integrity Commission.

HMIC. (1999/ 2000b). Staffordshire, Inspection, London: Home Office.

HMIC. (1999/2000c). Suffolk, Inspection, London: Home Office.

HMIC. (2010). "Valuing the Policing: Policing in an Age of Austerity," www.hmic.gov.uk.

Home Office. (1983). *Manpower Effectiveness and Efficiency in the Police Service*. London: HMSO.

Home Office. (2010a). "Policing in the 21st Century: Reconnecting Police and People," July 26, http://www.homeoffice.gov.uk/publications/consultations/policing-21st-century/.

Home Office. (2010c). "Theresa May at Superintendent's Association Conference," September 15, http://www.homeoffice.gov.uk/media-centre/speeches/superintendents-conference.

Jones, A. (2000). "Police Sick with Stress at NSW's Busiest Stations," *The Sunday Telegraph*, May 21, 25.

Jones, T. and Newburn, T. (1997). *Policing After the Act: Police and Magistrates Court Act 1994*. London: Policy Studies Institute.

Kennedy, M.H. (October 2000). "Zero Tolerance Policing and Arabic Speaking Young People," Thesis, University of Western Sydney, Australia.

Long, M. and Silverman, E. (2005). "The Anglo-American Measurement of Police Performance: Compstat and Best Value," *British Journal of Community Justice*, 3(3).

Loveday, B. (1996). "Crime at the Core." In: Leishman, F., Loveday, B., and Savage, S., Eds., *Core Issues in Policing*. London: Longman.

Loveday, B. (1999). "The Impact of Performance Culture on Criminal Justice Agencies," *International Journal of the Sociology of Law*, 2: 352–377.

8

7

8

Loveday, B. (2000a). "Managing Crime: Police Use of Crime Data as an Indicator of Effectiveness," *International Journal of the Sociology of Law*, 28: 215–237.

Maguire, M. (2007). "Crime Data and Statistics." In: Maguire, M., Morgan, R., and Reiner, R., Eds., *The Oxford Handbook of Criminology*, 4th ed. Oxford: Oxford University Press.

Marlow, A. (2010, April 6). http://unveilingnypdcompstat.blogspot.com/2010/04/turnaround-nypd-comes-around-on-crime.html#comments.

Martin, D. (2003). "The Politics of Policing, Managerialism, Modernization and Performance." In: Mathews, R. and Yong, J., Eds., *New Politics of Crime and Punishment*. Devon: Willan Publishing, 227–240.

Mattelley, J.H. and Mouhanna, C. (2007). *Police des chiffres et des doutes*. Paris: Michalon.

McArthur, Grant, (June 16, 2011) "Victoria's Top Cop Simon Overland Resigns over Dodgy Crime Figures," Herald Sun http://www.news.com.au/national/decision-to-release-dodgy-crime-stats-was-overlands-alone-ombudsman/story-e6frfkvr-1226076239399 McLaughlin, E. (2007) The New Policing. London: Sage.

Metro.Co.UK. (2008). "Violent Crime Soars after Police Reporting 'Failures,'" October 23, www.metro.co.uk/news.

Miller, S., Blackler, J., and Alexander, A. (1997). *Police Ethics*. Sydney: Allen and Unwin.

MP. (2010). Retired Supt Police UK, Eterno, J.A. and Silverman, E.B. http://unveilingnypdcompstat.blogspot.com/.

National Police Improvement Agency. (2010). http://www.npia.police.uk/en/16761.htm.

National Policing Plan (NPP). (2002). Home Office, London, November.

New South Wales Police Service. (1999). New South Wales Police Service Annual Report 1998–1999, Sydney.

New South Wales Police Service. (2000). *Future Directions 20001–2005*. Sydney.

New South Wales Police Service. (2002). "Term of Office of Non-Executive Commissioned Police Officers: Fixed Term Appointments Policy," Sydney.

Ohlin, L. (1971). *The Challenge of Crime in a Free Society*. New York: Da Capo Press.

Peters, T. J. and Waterman Jr., R. H. (1982). What's Right with Big Business. *Washington Monthly*, December: 37. Criminal Justice Collection Web. Oct. 18, 2011.

Portas, D. and Mason, J. (1996). *Collection and Accuracy of Police Incident Data*. London: David Keith Consultants.

Punch, M. (2007). *Zero Tolerance Policing*. Bristol, UK: Policy Press.

Reiner, R. (1992). *Chief Constables: Bobbies, Bosses or Bureaucrats?* Oxford: Oxford University Press.

Robb, P. (2010). Personal e-mail, September 25.

Robinson, M. (1999). "Violence against Police on the Rise," *Sydney Morning Herald*, December 28, 3.

Sheehy, P. (1993). *Inquiry into Police Rewards and Responsibilities*. London: HMSO.

Silverman, E. (2001). *NYPD Battles Crime*. Boston: Northeastern University Press.

Simons, M. (2011, June 18). "Hands Up Who Failed Stats: Overland Resigns," *Crickey*, http://www.crikey.com.au/2011/06/16/ hands-up-who-failed-stats-overland-resigns/.

Tink, A. (2000). Speech at New South Wales Police Association Biennial Conference, www.pansw.asn.au.

Victorian Ombudsman. (2011). "Investigation into an Allegation about Victoria Police Crime Statistics," Victoria, Australia.

Warnock, S. (1996). "Street That Fought Back," *The Sun Herald*, April 14, 1.

Watney, S. (1987). *Policing Desire*. London: Methuen.

Whitehead, T. (2009). "Top Crime Adviser Admits Public Does Not Trust Crime Figures," *Daily Telegraph*, April 24, 4.

Williams, S. (2002). *Peter Ryan: The Inside Story*. Harmondsworth, Middlesex: Penguin.

Young, M. (1991). *An Inside Job. Policing and the Police Culture*. Oxford: Clarendon Press.

Suggested Reading

Bruno, I., Didier, E., and Prévieux, J. (2011). *Benchmarking*. Paris: La Découverte.

Boltanski, L. (1990). *L'Amour et la justice comme competences*. Paris: Metaillier.

Boivard, T. (2000). "Role of Competition and Competiveness in Best Value in England and Wales," *Public Policy and Administration*, 15(4): 82–89.

Bowerman, N. and Ball, A. (2000). "Great Expectations: Benchmarking for Best Value," *Public Money and Management*, 20(2): 21–26.

Case, P. (1999). "Remember Re-engineering: The Rhetorical Appeal of a Managerial Salvation Device," *Journal of Management Studies*, 36: 419–445.

Coleman, C. and Moynihan, J. (1996). *Understanding Crime Data: Haunted by the Dark Figure*. London: Open University Press.

Didier, E. (2005). Des statistiques pour un nouveau management de la police? Travau sur l'importation du Compstat new yorkasis par la Prefecture de police de Paris et sure s effects, enparticulier pour la secruite' routiere, Rapport de recherché, ACI SRS, Paris.

Didier, E. (2011). "L'Etat Néo-libéral ment-il? Le cas des statistiques de police," *Terrain*, à paraître.

HMIC. (1999/2000a). Cambridgeshire, London: Home Office.

Home Office. (2010b). "Anti-Social Behaviour," May 24, http://webarchive.nationalarchives.gov.uk/20100405140447/http://asb.homeoffice.gov.uk/default.aspx.

Kennedy, M.H. (2008). *The Police, Means, Ends and the Rule of Law*. Saarbrucken: VDM Publishing.

Long, M. (2002). "Naming, Shaming and the Politics of Blaming," PhD Thesis, University of East London.

Loveday, B. (2000b). "Policing Performance: The Effects of Performance Targets on Police Culture," *Criminal Justice Matters*, 40: 23–24.

MacDonald, H. (2010). "Compstat and Its Enemies," *City Journal*, February 17.

Vollmer, T. (2011, June 17). "Victoria's Top Cop Simon Overland Quits Over Misleading Statistics," *The Daily Telegraph*, http://www.news.com.au/victorias-top-cop-simon-overland-quits/story-e6freuzr-1226076701334.

Big Bad Bully Bosses

5

Leadership 101

For most in the law enforcement profession, policing is a brotherhood or what can best be described as a family. All are united as a team in a struggle against crime, terrorism, and deviance. Their common bond is a sense of doing good—of establishing and maintaining justice. We have observed this nationally and even internationally, as officers have an unspoken understanding of what they are up against. This phenomenon is especially seen when an officer dies in the line of duty. All ranks join in an understanding of the cost of battle. Compstat, as practiced by the NYPD upper echelon, can seriously hamper that sense of connection. It replaces team spirit with fear of management. No longer are all members of the NYPD joined as one, a family fighting the enemy together. Rather, management changes the dynamic to administration versus the rank-and-file. The lower ranks do come together but not primarily to battle crime, to save democracy, nor to help victims. They join in a task made necessary by the top-down management style practiced by the NYPD. Their efforts are focused on making sure the numbers of summonses, index crimes, and stop-and-frisk reports look good for Compstat; they play the numbers game.

In Chapter 2, we focused on manipulation of crime statistics. We demonstrated the main reason for this manipulation is pressure from upper management enforced at Compstat meetings. In this chapter, we focus on exposing and discussing the top-down leadership style based almost entirely on fear. This fear radiates from Compstat meetings. Commanders presenting at meetings are exposed to, at times, what can best be described as bullying behavior by senior officers. This may involve yelling, berating, and even embarrassing the commanders who were chosen for their command positions by the same upper echelon who later criticize and sometimes abuse them.

The Unrelenting Pressures of NYPD Compstat

We begin with an example from one of our interviewees. He talked about a visitor from another law enforcement agency who was also present at a Compstat meeting. The high-ranking law enforcement visitor left the meeting exclaiming to our interviewee, "I don't know how they [NYPD upper echelon] could treat their own people like this." What the visitor is referring to is the bullying behavior of the NYPD upper echelon.

In an article on zero tolerance policing, Eterno (2001, p.193) suggests that it is critical not to mindlessly emulate NYPD's Compstat strategies: "… departments and municipalities are willing to pay high prices to reduce crime, however, these same agencies seem much less attentive to programs aimed at reducing officer misconduct." Furthermore, John Timoney, former first deputy commissioner of NYPD, former Police Commissioner of Philadelphia, and former Miami Police Chief, notes,

> Unfortunately, early on, I think many departments looked at CompStat, went back to their cities and said, "I know how to do this. You just bring somebody up and yell at them." But that is not necessarily going to work in other cities. (Police Leaders, … 2011, p. 2)

We wholeheartedly agree. We also point out that these are his words about how others perceived Compstat. We further the point in this chapter and suggest that yelling at commanders is not only unprofessional but also poor leadership. This is not what Compstat is but what it has morphed into at the NYPD.

Fear Emanates through the Ranks

Commanders are well aware of incidents at Compstat where unprofessional behaviors were exhibited by higher ups. In fact, our interviewees would often speak of how fellow commanders were "beaten up" for one reason or another. Here, we cite some statements made in our interviews. We note that none of the commanders left under questionable circumstances. Each of the commanders presented or was present at Compstat meetings and directly observed the behaviors of which they speak. All of these particular respondents were generally favorable to the NYPD, did not have an "axe to grind," and had excellent careers. Only one retired as a captain; the others were inspectors or above.

> **JE/ES**: What was your overall impression of the police department?
> **Respondent**: There was efficiency, as good as most corporations. However, the way they treat people is not good. They do not practice good management. They drive some good people away. … Compstat is a great management tool but every tool can be misused. People were embarrassed in front of peers, often condescending. … A lot of people cannot present themselves. … It's all about numbers. … If you missed it, then you are dead. Compstat created a lot of pressure. … Most of the pressure is with crime numbers. … a lot of pressure on how things looked.

Another interviewee had similar comments about pressures of upper management at Compstat:

JE/ES: Was there pressure on commanders?
Respondent: Without a doubt. You were not trained to handle this. If they liked you, you lived a charmed life. Favoritism was a major part of life. Only a very small minority were assessed on competence. …As crime went down, the pressure to maintain it was great.

Similarly, another states,

Compstat was central to supervising. There was a lot of pressure to ensure the crime reduction. You were always compared to last year's numbers. The focus of Compstat was almost exclusively on crime control especially index crimes. Some CO's who were not prepared if they were politically well liked by inquisitors, they would not get hurt. I would say about 20 percent are favorites.

Another,

Compstat was the best thing that ever happened to the NYPD, when done right... Some beatings were warranted but they went too far. … You are out of your mind if you want to be a Captain. NYPD should not deny quotas. Cops losing discretion, that's what Hitler did, a very dangerous thing.

Yet another,

Compstat made everything. People's careers were made at the podium. … Numerous hardworking got screwed because they could not speak. Deputy Commissioner of Operations has a bigger squad than any around. Kind of a gotcha thing. … People in the Deputy Commissioner of Operations should not be checking on investigations. This destroyed morale in the detective bureau. A squad would come out of headquarters and find the one thing that could get a commander. … I observed one commander get bullied. They publicly embarrassed him. He was good with the community but could not get his point across at the podium.

Even another,

Eventually Compstat became just generate numbers. We even got pressure from City Hall … Upper echelon just wanted more and more … Chief had his heart in the right place but was a loose cannon.

We can fill the pages of this book with such comments. They were, frankly, commonplace among those we interviewed. The extreme pressure of Compstat at NYPD management emanates fear through the ranks. NYPD's key managerial style is fear based on a top-down approach. Indeed, three key themes emerge: (1) the top-down management style; (2) hierarchical pressure; and (3) commander morale, abuse, and embarrassment (see Chapter 3).

The results of the closed-ended questions in our survey also confirm this. For example, over 94 percent of commanders who worked during the Compstat era felt that Compstat increases tension among management. Further, over 74 percent felt that Compstat tends to reduce morale. In addition, over 73 percent felt that Compstat tends to increase tension among the rank-and-file. Pressure was also demonstrated in Chapter 3. These survey results could not be clearer. It is the perception of commanders that the upper echelon of the NYPD increases tension among management and the rank-and-file while at the same time reducing morale and adding to the pressures already there due to the nature of police work.

Management versus Street Cops

This top-down pressure widens the gulf between higher and lower levels of the police department. Importantly, this is not the first time that a distinct organizational division separating upper management from street level New York City police has been observed. An in-depth study of two precincts in the late 1970s found deeply seated street cop resentment and alienation from what they perceived as the self-serving upper echelons who are motivated by rationalistic efficiency criteria that appease politicians, the media, and the courts. Precinct officers view upper level management as impersonal and neither understanding nor sympathetic to the necessities of daily police activity (Reuss-Ianni, 1983). Without a doubt, this division between management and street cops is a deeply rooted aspect of the NYPD culture.

Much of Reuss-Ianni's study has applications to our work. Compstat greatly exacerbates the rift between management and street cops. For example, Reuss-Ianni (1983, p. 97) writes, "Management cop culture has to produce numbers to prove its accomplishments. The street cop does not see how any of it helps him do his job." Clearly, the numbers game is not new but it now plays a dominant role at the NYPD. A powerful tool has catapulted the numbers game to the forefront—Compstat. Street cops do what they have to do as the message filters down to them from Compstat meetings. Officers write summonses, do forcible stops, and make arrests; all to meet the demands of the upper echelon that often make little or no sense to street cops. In fact, retired Captain Costello spoke publicly about the mindless numbers game played by headquarters:

> Captain Costello's primary complaint was not pay, but what he viewed as the numbingly relentless demand to top his own arrest or summons numbers. "Nothing was good enough." ... In 1997, for example, his officers were

fortunate enough to stumble onto a large crowd of teenagers drinking in a plaza along Fifth Avenue and issued hundreds of summonses. The following year, though, the teenagers were not there. Still … he feared he would be chastised if his summons numbers dropped. So his plainclothes officers found themselves skulking in doorways. … "You are so desperate to get those summonses," Captain Costello said. (Flynn, 2000, p. A1)

One way in which this unrelenting pressure manifests itself is by intensifying the divide between the street cops and the management cops. Reuss-Ianni (1983, p. 124) writes,

Now there are two cultures which confront each other in the department: a street cop culture of the good old days, working class in origin and temperament, whose members see themselves as career cops; opposed to this is a management cop culture, more middle class, whose members' education and mobility have made them eligible for jobs totally outside of policing, which makes them less dependent on, and less loyal to, the street cop culture.

Peter Manning (1987, p. 11) similarly writes about the police culture, "Dependency, autonomy, authority, and uncertainty are key themes in the occupational culture." He also sees two subcultures in police departments. First is the subculture of officers, those who are working on the street. This subculture emphasizes dependency and uncertainty. The other subculture is the administrative cadre (paper pushers), which emphasizes centrality of authority and strives to preserve police autonomy.

Although street officers tend to be far more educated today (in fact, while working in the Personnel Bureau one of us helped do the research for the NYPD to raise its education requirements), the separation of cultures discussed by these scholars seems to be an offshoot whose growth is promoted by Compstat. Street cops view the pressures for numbers as mindless and, at times, destructive. Thus, the themes of dependency (on higher-ups) and uncertainty (actions by officers could be illegal) emerge as dominant among street officers. The administration stresses central authority (get the numbers, or else) and preserving autonomy (the lack of transparency by the NYPD is an example of this, which we discuss in more detail in Chapter 8).

In today's department, many officers complain of quotas, being forced to do unnecessary stops, and having to make arrests based on very little evidence. As stated earlier, the PBA has been very vocal on these matters. Two whistleblowers, NYPD officers Adrian Schoolcraft and Adil Polanco, also expose this phenomenon. We also note that both NYPD whistleblowers are being disciplined instead of embraced by management (see Chapter 1).

The Schoolcraft audiotapes expose what are known as "Mauriello specials." Deputy Inspector Mauriello was the commanding officer of the precinct where Officer Schoolcraft worked. "Mauriello specials" were apparently arrests that have little or no evidence supporting them. The commanding officer is holding someone (to be arrested) and an officer must go to the scene and take the arrest (commanders rarely, if ever, actually take the arrests through the system [i.e., do the paperwork, etc.]). As Rayman (2010, May 11) writes, "Mauriello would often roam the precinct in his car. When he saw groups on particular corners, he would call in officers to arrest the people on low-level charges. These collars came to be called 'Mauriello Specials.'" Officers were reluctant to take such arrests apparently because they were not the product of good police work; there might be legal issues, the collars were for minor crimes, and they were perceived as a waste of valuable time. Again, we note the Compstat-induced clash between management and street cop culture.

Officer Polanco relays similar concerns in a completely different borough and precinct when he speaks of pressures to make arrests, write summonses, and forcibly stop people. An Eyewitness News investigative reporter interviewed Police Officer Polanco. He reveals the pressure he and fellow officers were under to make quotas. Jim Hoffer (2010, March 3), a reporter for ABC News Investigations, writes,

> When Officer Adil Polanco dreamed of becoming a cop, it was out of a desire to help people not, he says, to harass them. "I'm not going to keep arresting innocent people, I'm not going to keep searching people for no reason, I'm not going to keep writing people for no reason, I'm tired of this," said Adil Polanco, an NYPD Officer. Officer Polanco says One Police Plaza's obsession with keeping crime stats down has gotten out of control. He claims Precinct Commanders relentlessly pressure cops on the street to make more arrests, and give out more summonses, all to show headquarters they have a tight grip on their neighborhoods. "Our primary job is not to help anybody, our primary job is not to assist anybody, our primary job is to get those numbers and come back with them?" said Officer Polanco. ...

We also questioned a new officer about his job. He said, "My job is to make sure the numbers look good." He was disappointed, even disillusioned, about his forced role. Beyond this, there is another audiotape from the 81st Precinct made by a supervisor, which clearly indicates the pressure officers are under. Baker and Rivera (2010, September 10, p. A1) write,

> Captain Perez offered a precise number and suggested a method. He said that officers on a particular shift should write—as a group—20 summonses a week: five each for double-parking, parking at a bus stop, driving without a seat belt and driving while using a cell phone.
> "You, as bosses, have to demand this and have to count it," Captain Perez said, *citing pressure from top police officials*. At another point, Captain Perez emphasized his willingness to punish officers who do not meet the targets, saying, "I really don't have a problem firing people." [italics added]

Again, we see the division between street cops who see their job as help-ing versus management who are looking to centralize control. One way in which management does this is by demanding more numbers. The fact that these data are citywide and the Captain in the 81st Precinct clearly talks about pressure from "top officials" are further indications that these are not isolated incidents but that the pressure emanates from management via Compstat at police headquarters. The key themes of centralization of author-ity and attempts to preserve autonomy by management culture are essential to understanding the NYPD today. The cultural norm for the NYPD has become "make the numbers look good." To ensure centrality and autonomy, management has developed behaviors over time that are accepted as normal, yet are clearly problematic. The next section examines these behaviors.

Bullying Behaviors by Management

The behaviors exhibited by management at Compstat tend to aggravate the separation between management and street officers. One example is man-agement berating street level commanders in front of their peers. These behaviors are part of management culture's efforts to control subordinates. Such behaviors can be classified by social scientists as bullying. Lee and Brotheridge (2006, p. 353) state,

> Workplace bullying is defined as a persistent pattern of negative acts directed at a worker. … It may incorporate actions falling within the domain of incivil-ity and aggression. As with incivility, the intentions of perpetrators to cause humiliation, offense, or distress are not always apparent and are of less impor-tance than the cumulative effects of the actions.

Such humiliation- and distress-causing behavior is familiar to Compstat attendees. For example, one respondent advises, "it was like a teacher who, instead of working with the kids just keep beating them down. … People were not treated fairly. … Chief beat people up. It just might be your turn to get flogged." Such comments are commonplace in our study.

Bullying Research

We examine this further by scrutinizing more closely the research on bul-lying and sharing some examples of bullying. Lee and Brotheridge (2006) discuss the most common behaviors of workplace bullying:

> … blaming targets for errors, making unreasonable demands, criticizing targets' work ability, inconsistently applying made-up rules, threatening job

loss, offering insults and put-downs, discounting targets' accomplishments, socially excluding targets, yelling and screaming, and stealing credit for targets' work. (Lee and Brotheridge, 2006, p. 354)

Many of these types of behaviors are what we have observed and what our respondents inform us occur regularly at Compstat and the NYPD. One respondent, for example, writes

… The NYPD management is based on negative discipline. The organization exists so we can blame others for our mistakes and reward bootlickers.

Another states,

Compstat equals embarrassment in front of peers. NYPD management style is to berate and embarrass subordinates publicly.

There are many more such comments, but these are more than enough to demonstrate the point.

Public Image
These and other statements certainly comport with bullying behaviors among the higher ranks of the NYPD. There is a trove of scientific research on supervisory and workplace bullying that is very informative. Hutchinson, Vickers, Wilkes, and Jackson (2009) offer pertinent insights regarding bullying in the Australian nursing workplace. Their research essentially uses a qualitative method in which they interview 26 nurses who experienced bullying including 14 who held senior positions. They examine the management culture that creates an environment of secrecy, hiding problems in the organization. The public image of the organization was always promoted while the inner workings were anything but healthy. For example, they write,

Senior management created a public image which concealed actual adverse internal circumstances and procedures [not enough hospital beds/rooms for patients]. The external façade of the organization was created in an image that coincided with industry standards and community expectations, while internally, contrary standards fostered unsafe practices. This behavior sent a clear signal about what was considered acceptable conduct—meeting performance targets and maintaining the public image of the organization regardless of the outcome. (Hutchinson et al. 2009, p. 229)

Similarly, the NYPD has been obsessed with a public image that crime is consistently going down, that no quotas exist, and that they are concerned about constitutional rights. They jealously guard data contrary to their public image. For example, there was a major drop in serious assaults, yet NYPD management did not inform the public that the number of misdemeanor assaults remains roughly the same. In addition, NYPD management reports that burglaries are down but fails to simultaneously report a sharp increase in criminal trespass (see Chapter 1). Indeed, every other jurisdiction except one in New York State was reporting this data regularly (Rivera and Baker, 2010). The NYPD has refused to give such data to academic researchers, journalists, and even a city investigative commission. Only recently after a lawsuit did the NYPD post vetted and selective data for the years 2001 to 2009. In addition, the NYPD did not release data on stop-and-frisks until they were sued. Note that the law required them to release this information, yet it was still not released (see New York City Administrative Code section 14-150, also called the Vallone Bill). When finally made available, we noticed that stop-and-frisks were skyrocketing in New York City to nearly 600,000 in 2009 from approximately 97,000 in 2002.

Other sources confirm these issues including abuse of authority complaints from the New York City Civilian Complaint Review Board (CCRB), which is a separate Mayoral agency, reporting on abuse of authority allegations against officers. These allegations have markedly increased. Indeed, in 2003 there were 7,488 allegations of abuse of authority while in 2009 there were 12,371 (CCRB, 2003, 2009). The number of abuse complaints essentially tracks with the number of stop-and-frisk reports. Most recently, the number of officers has decreased dramatically, yet the number of abuse complaints remains relatively stable and a concern for CCRB. In a recent press release from CCRB (2011, February 2), we see that while abuse complaints went down in the 6-month period, there are still major concerns about behaviors of officers at stops.

> … "stop, question and frisk" complaints still account for roughly 30 percent of the CCRB's total intake, and they have since 2005. This percentage stayed constant even though the actual number of "stop, question and frisk" complaints was 12 percent lower in the first half of 2010 than it was in the first half of 2009, or 1,076 compared to 1,222.

Quotas on officers that emanate from Compstat pressures are also regularly denied. Yet, audiotapes and commentary by whistleblowers Adil Polanco and Adrian Schoolcraft clearly reveal supervisors telling officers the specific numbers they must obtain. All this does not even address our discussion of manipulation of the crime numbers (see Chapter 2). The obsession with its public image is a major problem for NYPD, again demonstrating management's bullying behavior. Beyond public image and secrecy, the NYPD also is clearly illogical in its position. If crime is down to all time lows, why are summonses issued and stop-and-frisks conducted at very high rates? Regarding summonses, the Criminal Court of the City of New York reports that, "Summons filings are up 6.5 percent from 2008 to 2009, and up 28 percent from 1999. Petty offenses, which include misdemeanor violations, infractions and other low level online/DAT arraignments, also continue to rise with numbers 7 percent higher than 2008 and 24 percent higher than those in 2005" (New York City Criminal Court, 2009, p.11). Importantly, Hoffer (2010) concurrently reports that there has been a huge increase (500 percent) in summonses dismissed in the past 15 years.

The previously discussed data on stop-and-frisks also clearly show the illogical position in which the NYPD has placed itself. The Center for Constitutional Rights reports that 576,394 stops were made in 2009 and the NYPD has reported that over 600,000 were made in 2010. By way of comparison, there were 97,837 forcible stops recorded in 2002 when crime was also reportedly decreasing at an enormous rate. Most of the forcible stops are of innocent people. Why such huge increases in stops? Do these data make sense? The only logical explanation is pressure from the upper echelon through Compstat to demand numbers. If there is no pressure on police officers and crime is at an all time low, then there should be no need for so many summonses and stops. That is, since the NYPD states that index crime is down tremendously (80.08 percent in the last 20 years), then there should also be somewhat fewer summonses and forcible stops because the public is law abiding. Additionally, as discussed, the CCRB statistics indicate that abuse of authority complaints have skyrocketed (up 153.8 percent since 2002). The obsession that the NYPD has with public image can place field officers in a precarious position. That is, officers are being required to take actions that may be illegal (e.g., unconstitutional stops, illegal summonses, and downgrading of crime complaints).

These practices may also put the public at risk. Downgrading complaints or preventing crime reports from being written can be disastrous. Again, we point to the case of Detective Harold Hernandez who arrested a rapist. During interrogation, the rapist confessed to seven other rapes. When the Detective looked for the other rape crime reports to which the suspect had confessed, he found that they were listed not as rape, but as criminal trespass and other minor crimes (see Chapter 2). A rape pattern was not developed due to the downgrading of the previous rape reports. The serial rapist was not caught until he confessed. It is possible that he could have been arrested before he committed the large number of rapes.

Thus, the public image of a police department in control, with no quotas, and no bullying of its members appears to be a facade. Public image is just as all-important at the NYPD as it is in a study about the nursing profession. Such an organizational environment with the upper echelon overly focused on public image is, according to Hutchinson et al. (2009), tantamount to corruption and is undoubtedly bullying.

Reward and Promotional System

Hutchinson et al. (2009) also raise the issue of the organizational reward and promotional system. They point out how bullies can work together. This can influence opportunities nurses have with respect to their careers. Hutchinson et al. (2009, p. 221) write,

> The network of alliances between bullies provided extensive opportunities for co-operative, planned forms of bullying, as well as the mechanisms that rewarded the behavior. … Social relationships and ties of loyalty with "alliances" of bullies were an important vehicle for career progression.

One of their respondents stated, "And the interesting thing about [name of hospital] is that it seems, um, the worse you behave the more you seem to be rewarded …" (Hutchinson et al., 2009, p. 221).

We can also examine this issue using both quantitative (analysis of the closed-ended questions) and qualitative (analysis of the personal interviews) data from our study. Using the quantitative data, we find a significant difference between those who worked in the Compstat era versus those who did not. Officers who worked during the Compstat era believed that the promotion system was less fair. Of those who worked in the non-Compstat era, only 25.5 percent indicated that the promotion system was extremely unfair. Of those who worked in the Compstat era, 74.5 percent indicated the promotion system was extremely unfair.* The contrast in those figures clearly shows that those who worked during the Compstat era perceived the promotional system as markedly less fair.

The issue of promotion was also a common theme among our respondents. One respondent stated, "There was absolute favoritism. There were fair-haired people. Very small minority were assessed on competence." Another stated, "There was obvious favoritism. One can tell by the types of questions." Another said, "Compstat made everything. People's careers were made or broken at the podium. …" Yet another, "Why do they drive good people away?" Another, "There was favoritism." And another, "The system was a means of 'gotcha', not professionalism. Lots of favoritism." Another consequence is worker dissatisfaction. Those who are most talented will leave the NYPD for other jobs. A common saying on the NYPD is "twenty and out." That is, officers do the 20 years, which makes them eligible for retirement and then, if they have the talent and ability to find other jobs, they leave.

---

* This is based on collapsing responses to Question 8 into categories. Responses 1–3 were grouped together to obtain percentages in each category. This result was statistically significant ($p < .0001$). Throughout analyses, we collapse 1–3, 4–7, and 8–10. We remain consistent on this throughout the book.

According to Ngo (2010) generally around 80 percent of NYPD officers eligible to retire do so. However, the article also points out that in tough economic times, it is likely that fewer officers will retire. Who will remain? In many cases, the person cannot find another stable job. Those with talent and good job prospects, however, are more likely to leave the NYPD. Glendinning (2001) cites two research studies that indicate that it is not necessarily the work or pay that drives people away but the management. The first states,

> Compensation was not the primary motivation employees gave for choosing to quit their jobs. Nearly 95 percent of the respondents said the primary factor for deciding to leave was whether or not they will be able to develop a trusting relationship with their manager. (Anonymous, "Good Relationship with Boss Key to Retention," *HR Magazine*, 44, 10, 1999 cited in Glendinning, 2001, p. 270)

Similarly, a second study indicates,

> Empirical evidence broadcasts a consistent message: People reporting to more considerate bosses are less likely to suffer the ravages of burnout and more likely to experience work satisfaction than those reporting to less considerate bosses. ... Conversely, there is solid evidence that working for un-supportive bosses is associated with higher levels of anxiety, depression, and even heart disease. (Hornstien, H., *Brutal Bosses and Their Prey*. New York: Riverhead Books, 1996 cited in Glendinning, 2001, p. 270)

Again, our retirees voiced strong opinions about the promotion system. One wrote, "Promotion should be based on merit not 'who you know.' Too much attention paid to numbers and not members of the service." Our respondents clearly point out that lack of fairness in promotion and playing the numbers game as well as the lack of concern for workers are problems for the NYPD. Other respondents echo this: "Should have civil service testing from Deputy Inspector to Deputy Chief. Current policies of appointment are not objective nor fair." Another respondent speaks of younger people leaving the job because of dissatisfaction: "Promotion is usually not based on merit causing resentment among the high command. As a result, the NYPD is losing talent. Younger Captains leave the job and go on to private industry. No incentive to stay." Another writes, "Promotions: Discretionary promotions within the NYPD are easily the most unfairly biased example of cronyism as a tool for creating upper level management. ..." Yet another, "The promotion system above the rank of captain is a moral[e] killer." Another, "While crime statistics were important to promotion, they only mattered if whomever was in power didn't like you. If you were part of the group you could do no wrong; but, if not, you were the designated victim at Compstat."

Clearly, the promotion system in the NYPD in the Compstat era is perceived as not fair. The inquisitors could choose who would get the harassment and who would not. Many of our respondents point to the favoritism of the inquisitors. Apparently, this is a common theme and nearly everyone at the department seems to be aware of it. If you were a favorite of an inquisitor, you would benefit at the podium and enhance your career. Thus, favorites would be promoted and others would not. Just as Hutchinson et al. (2009) argue in their article on nursing, at the NYPD social relationships with the bullies is very beneficial to your career. This, in turn, perpetuates the conduct.

Protecting the Bullies

Hutchinson et al. (2009) also discuss how the organization will protect those bullies engaged in negative behaviors. They write,

> Within the organizational authority structures and systems of both work-places, mechanisms conducive to moral disengagement facilitated the abuse of institutional power for the purpose of protecting perpetrators in the alliances. (Hutchinson et al., 2009, p. 222)

The experiences of police officers Adrian Schoolcraft and Adil Polanco illustrate the organizational protections. Both whistleblowers were suspended from the NYPD. Polanco exposed pressures to write summonses, conduct forcible stops, make arrests, and, in general, make the numbers look proper. He discusses illegal quotas as part of this pressure. Further, he produced audiotapes confirming his allegations. According to Hoffer (2010, September 10), "Officer Polanco remains suspended with pay for a dispute he had with his supervisor about joining his suddenly-ill partner being taken by ambulance to the hospital." He is also being charged by the police department with filing a false official document based on questionable summonses that he was ordered to write (see Rayman, 2011, August 4).

Similarly, Schoolcraft was suspended after making allegations against management. He exposed illegal quotas, playing with the crime report numbers, and many other issues. His allegations are supported by a litany of audiotapes of precinct roll calls. His suspension, however, seems very sinister. Schoolcraft claims that he received permission to leave due to sickness. He states he went home after receiving the supervisor's verbal consent. The supervisor denies that she gave him that authorization. The department then sent a team of officers, including a high-ranking chief, to his house. Under very questionable circumstances, Schoolcraft was forcibly hospitalized as an emotionally disturbed person. One of the most troubling aspects of this suspension is that he was kept in the hospital without his permission for six days. Even after his release and suspension, officers of the NYPD were sent numerous times to his father's home upstate where he was staying. The forced hospitalization of an officer, the questionable circumstances in which he was hospitalized, and continuing to bother him while under suspension are all highly dubious. Further questions arise from the hospital records indicating that NYPD officials lied to admission staff. In addition, Schoolcraft possesses audiotapes of his forcible hospitalization and visits upstate, which apparently back him up as well (Rayman, 2010, June 15).

Both of these whistleblower officers appear to be victims of a vindictive system. They were simply exposing conduct that our research as well as numerous other sources—including statements by the police department's own PBA and SBA (see Chapter 2)—indicate is routine. Furthermore, the behaviors by NYPD lower-level supervisors exposed by the Schoolcraft and Polanco tapes show how pressures at Headquarters from Compstat meetings are operationalized at the precinct level. Lower-level supervisors take their cue from the upper echelon. When quotas need to be enforced, lower-level supervisors feel immune from repercussions. This is because higher-ups seem to be requiring them to enforce illegal quotas, downgrading of crimes, and other activities. Another recently released audiotape from Schoolcraft's precinct reveals a supervisor's meeting in which exact numbers of activity are discussed, further supporting Schoolcraft's assertions. Chief Michael Marino, who ordered police officer Adrian Schoolcraft forcibly hospitalized against the officer's wishes, was later found to be using steroids—a violation of NYPD rules. Chief Marino's punishment was a hand slap—probation for one year and loss of pay for one month. Of course, questions now arise as to whether Chief Marino had "roid rage" on the day he ordered Officer Schoolcraft hospitalized. Is the NYPD protecting its enforcers? Is this equal punishment? We note that this same Chief was caught using a department car for unauthorized purposes (Celona, 2011, February 23). We are also waiting to see what happens with Deputy Inspector Mauriello. Is NYPD protecting its bullies—the enforcers?

Abnormal Behavior Becomes Normal and Unhealthy

Hutchinson et al. (2009) discuss how higher-level management in the nursing profession made questionable behaviors routine. Similarly, in the NYPD, there have been hundreds of thousands of questionable forcible stops; summonses, many dismissed, go through the roof; complaint reports are downgraded or not written, withholding easily obtained data; and arrests for very minor offenses are examples of this bullying symptom. Hutchinson et al. (2009) also report the importance of association with more powerful actors allowing bullying to take place. They write,

> When corrupt behavior spreads through an organization it is more likely to diffuse or routinize through superior–subordinate relationships. ... Our study has shown that considerable individual power was gained through association with other more powerful actors in the networks. This "reflected power"... enabled lower level individuals to openly engage in bullying and corrupt acts

knowing themselves to be protected by others more senior. (Hutchinson et al., 2009, p. 225)

With respect to these questionable pressures and behaviors at the NYPD, they have recently tried to cover themselves by, for example, belatedly and grudgingly releasing data that have been and continue to be distributed will- ingly by nearly every police agency in New York State. In addition, the NYPD have recently released a directive from their lawyers with respect to stop- and-frisk practices (see Chief of Patrol's memo cited in Baker and Robbins, 2011, January 13). Regardless of these covering tactics, it is clear that wide- spread pressure on officers has led to huge increases in forcible stops and criminal court summonses. CCRB numbers are also questionable, especially with respect to stop-and-frisk.

Workplace bullying by management has led to many unforeseen issues. In this chapter alone, we have touched on abuse of authority, downgrading complaints, failure to develop criminal patterns, and treating victims and innocent New Yorkers illegally and without respect.

Other scientific articles on bullying by bosses show this pattern. Glendinning (2001, p. 273) writes, "Management by intimidation is not healthy, either for its victims or an organization. To be more specific, bosses who are mean to subordinates … are actually causing measurable injury to both their individual victims and to the institutions in which they and their victims work." Glendinning (2001) mentions specific consequences such as high turnover, employee health effects, reduced productivity, counterproduc- tive behavior, and legal countermeasures by employees. As far as NYPD turn- over, 80 percent leave when they are eligible to retire. However, this does not even come close to mentioning the entire turnover at NYPD. It is well known that the NYPD bleeds officers to neighboring jurisdictions where pay, work environment, and treatment by bosses is perceived as far more respectful. For example, Messing (2007) reports that half of the Nassau County Police class in 2007 was made up of officers who quit the NYPD. Indeed, we know of officers leaving for other law enforcement jobs throughout the United States. While pay is certainly part of the equation, we know many people who stay at jobs they perceive as excellent even though the pay is not as much as another job. Unfortunately, for some officers the NYPD is a job of last resort.

Another good indicator of bullying is to examine the extent to which lieutenants are taking the civil service test for promotion to captain. If so, it indicates that captain is an excellent job with career potential. If lieutenants do not take the captain's test, they cannot be promoted to higher ranks. This is because ranks above captain are no longer civil service test but appoint- ment. If lieutenants are not signing up to take the captain's test, it is a strong indicator of problems with the captain's rank particularly because there is a significant raise and your only chance for further promotion is to make it to captain. Given those incentives, if lieutenants are not signing up to take the captain's test, it is probable that they sense becoming captain, regardless of the pay raise, is not worth it because of the pressures of upper management particularly at Compstat. In early 2010, only about 30 percent (537 of 1753) of eligible lieutenants signed up for the captain's examination. Messing (2010, April 12) writes, "Once promoted, new captains are given commands of precincts where they face being raked over the coals by supervisors at ... Compstat, meetings for any crime spike that occurs on their watch. ..." He also cites a lieutenant as saying, "As a captain, you're at work at your command 24-7, and when you go to Compstat, they make you feel that you haven't done a thing, that you haven't accomplished anything."

Our respondents similarly state,

> The continual increase of responsibilities, demands and subsequent time constraints placed on those serving as Commanding Officers in patrol commands ... continue to have negative results relative to the individual management of his or her command. One simply does not have the time left in any given day to properly manage said command(s). Hence the situation exists where many highly qualified Lieutenants nearing or having reached retirement eligibility are declining to take the promotional exam to Captain. In their own words, "It's simply not worth it."

Yet another, "Demands on COs and Execs to be prepared for a possible grilling at Compstat took away from their time needed to pay attention to community needs, conditions on patrol and integrity issues."

Employee health is another concern. Alcoholism, suicide, divorce, and other such maladies are well-known issues with police. While the etiologies of these are very complex, having a top-down work environment is not helpful. Remember, all NYPD officers are screened psychologically before coming onto the job. Therefore, the likely cause of problems is something that is happening after being hired. Availability of the gun and the pressure of the street have been documented. We propose management style and lack of openness as problematic issues that need further study in the NYPD.

Glendinning (2001, p. 274) sums this up explaining,

> ... the management style of the bullying boss discourages dissent, openness, innovation, change, and risk-taking. It fosters a climate of covering oneself, carefulness, guardedness, and fear, in which doing only what is known to be accepted by the leader and obedience to the leader are the only way to earn rewards.

Secrecy, obedience, discouraging dissent, covering yourself—this reads as a description of our study on the NYPD. As we have already noted, the NYPD has issues with data not being released: fear of presenting at Compstat; over-concern about numbers; numerous FOIL requests being denied; not allowing law enforcement visitors to Compstat; not allowing outside research but only invited scholars; lower-level personnel rarely talking to the press (if at all); press needing permission to talk to precinct personnel; press credentials being removed (Leonard Levitt, see page 160), etc.

Glendinning continues with a particularly poignant description:

> The bottom line is that bullies love the power of office. They love displaying their power, and they use their bullying to remind everyone they are powerful. There is nothing secretive in their methods. One of the best ways to display power and ward off rivals is to bully with an audience. This is one of the favorite techniques of a bully boss. A researcher on the subject has the following telling conclusions in this regard: "The significance of the audience is that it is an effective means of spreading the word that the bully is powerful and thereby to enhance the reputation and power which the bully wishes to establish. The public humiliation is the second most popular form of workplace bullying and was reported to have taken place by no fewer than 70 percent of the sample." (Glendenning, 2001, pp. 276–277 citing Ellis, 1997)

Compstat meetings provide an arena for bullying bosses to display their authority. It is no longer a place of teamwork where all work together to bring down crime but a place to bully and ensure one's power is seen and maintained in front of key managers in the NYPD.

The evidence is clear and unequivocal. Compstat as a management system practiced by the NYPD often exemplifies bullying behavior. One respondent sums this up by stating that Compstat meetings made "people very nervous. It was totally unprofessional. Leadership was demeaning, unrealistic, unprofessional, and power hungry."

Related Research

As we have demonstrated, bullying behavior by management has had strong negative effects at the NYPD. The fact that people change their behaviors based on how they are treated is nothing new to social scientists. For example, direct observations of workers by social scientists are known to skew workers' behaviors. One of the first studies to document changes in behavior was conducted at the Westinghouse Electric factory in Hawthorne, Illinois. Researchers were testing behaviors of workers to determine if lighting and other changes to the environment would lead to increased productivity. What the scientists found was that every change they made to the environment led to increases. The workers were acting as the scientists who were observing them wanted them to. That is, it was not the change in the environment leading to changes in worker productivity; it was the fact that scientists were observing them (Neuman, 2000, p. 240; Hagan, 2006, p. 86).

Another social scientist who studied these issues is Max Weber. He examined bureaucracy. He discusses the bureaucratic "ideal" from a sociological perspective. Weber cautions against bureaucratic excess, "By it the performance of each individual worker is mathematically measured, each man becomes a little cog in the machine and aware of this, his one preoccupation is whether he can become a bigger cog." In the case of the NYPD, the numbers essentially include index crime numbers, summons numbers, and stop-and-frisk report numbers. Weber argues that there are both positive and negative aspects to such an approach (Weber as cited by Schaefer, 2001). However, due to the way in which the NYPD has operationalized this model, we argue that it fails to capitalize on the good aspects of bureaucracy and makes the negatives even worse.

One supposedly positive aspect is efficiency. For example, the NYPD has been efficient at reducing crime. While we do not disagree that crime has gone down, we argue that the complete focus on crime control has led to problems in protecting basic human rights of citizens. Symptoms of this include the enormous number of stop-and-frisks as well as increases in civilian complaints for abuse of authority and unnecessary force.

A second supposedly positive aspect according to Weber is that there is clarification of who is in charge. The upper echelon of the NYPD is clearly taking complete control of the organization from headquarters. While workers are aware of who is in charge, this can be organizationally dysfunctional when accompanied by excessively centralized micromanagement. For example, previously simple transfers for borough commanders, moving a police officer from one command to another within the same patrol borough, is no longer allowed until the police commissioner gives permission. Without some basic discretionary power, even previously important borough commanders are weak relative to their position and responsibilities.

Another positive aspect according to Weber, although this one also has an enormous negative side to it, is that workers are aware of expectations. Certainly, officers know how many arrests, stops, and summonses are needed for their commander to have a good Compstat meeting. While this can be a positive, it also has a downside that may even be illegal. What we are talking about is illegal quotas. Since commanders are compared to last year's numbers, these numbers must be seen as continually rising, regardless of the health of the organization. Therefore, such "expectations" can also devolve into illegal quotas by placing enormous pressures on officers to make their "expectation/quota."

A fourth positive aspect according to Weber is that there is a reduction in bias. That is, everyone is treated equally. Based on the negative comments about promotion, there is little evidence of this at the NYPD. However, to the extent that it is true, the downside of this is that everyone is treated equally, but "equally" does not mean "fairly." That is, everyone at the NYPD is treated in the same negative way—mindless robots following orders with little to no discretion.

We have not yet touched on Weber's negative aspects. First is depriving employees of a voice in decision-making. Only the highest-ranking officials have authority. Lower ranks have no discretion. They are automatons following directives from headquarters. Local conditions mean little or nothing. Every neighborhood is treated as if there were one community standard. This is similar to what is called the legalistic approach described by Wilson (1977). He discusses three types of police departments: service, watchman, and legalistic. Service is when a department takes all calls seriously but tends to handle the call informally. Watchman is when officers simply maintain order but do little else. However, the NYPD is taking a strict legalistic approach where formal sanctions tend to be taken regardless of the situation. That is, they write summonses and make arrests to be reflected in the Compstat figures. A recent incident in the borough of Queens is a good example of the negative influence this has. In this incident, an elderly woman and her husband were stopped for a no seatbelt violation. They did not have identification. While her husband walked to their home on a very cold night to secure identification, the woman was issued a summons using her prescription medicine as identification. When he returned, the elderly man had a heart attack and died (see Johnson, 2011, January 25 and Chapter 7 for more discussion on this). Why was the elderly couple not given a warning and sent on their way? Discretion would lead the officers to let the couple go. These are not criminals or even a threat. Why? Compstat pressure is the logical answer.

Weber's second negative aspect to this management style is concealment of mistakes. At a minimum, the NYPD has been nothing but secretive. Until recently under the pressure of lawsuits and media attention, basic data that were normally released on a regular basis were withheld for years. For example, from 2002 (coincidently the first year that Raymond Kelly returned to the NYPD for his second stint as police commissioner) until 2010 the NYPD did not release data on non-index crimes. As we have stated, they are only one of two jurisdictions not to release such data—Newburgh is the only other jurisdiction in the state (Rivera and Baker, 2010, November 1).

Beyond this, lower ranks will rarely admit mistakes for fear of retaliation by senior officers, which will have the effect of maintaining the non-working elements of the bureaucracy. Officers will maintain the blue wall of silence for fear of possible repercussions. Officer Schoolcraft, for example, was forcibly hospitalized presumably because he was mentally ill. However, his forced hospitalization coincidently occurred after he tried to reveal downgrading of crimes and quotas. His allegations were later confirmed by his tapes and the tapes made by a supervisor in the same precinct. While we do not know exactly what happened in this case, you can be sure every officer is aware of what happened when Officer Schoolcraft tried to expose these practices. Officer Polanco, another whistleblower, was also suspended after making similar allegations. The fact that both were suspended right after revealing these practices could have a chilling effect, making it less likely that other officers will come forward.

Weber believes bureaucratic management also discourages loyalty to the organization. The few lieutenants willing to take the captain's examination as well as many officers retiring or leaving the force are examples of this.

These are strong indicators of the lack of loyalty to the organization among the lower echelon. This leads to the last of Weber's negative aspects, which is feelings of alienation. Such feelings are common on the NYPD. For example, with respect to Compstat, our survey respondents indicated a very high mean score of 8.67 (on a scale of 1 to 10) with respect to increasing tension among management and a very low score for Compstat's influence on morale ($M = 4.49$). The large numbers of officers leaving for other jobs in the Fire Department or policing in the suburbs is also an indication of alienation.

The negative influence of this management style has been studied by social scientists. These independent studies support these ideas. Importantly, this body of research suggests that Compstat reinforces traditional bureaucratic policing with many of its negative consequences. Weisburd, Mastrofski, Willis, and Greenspan (2006, p. 290) write,

> [A]gencies that had adopted Compstat programs were much less likely to focus on improving the skills and morale of street level officers ... suggesting that Compstat represents a departure from the properties of "bubble up" community and problem-oriented policing programs that had been predominant in police innovation until Compstat arrived on the scene and had focused attention on the empowerment and training of street-level police officers. Indeed, Compstat appears in this sense to be modeled more closely on the traditional "bureaucratic" or "paramilitary" forms of police organization.

Similarly, Weisburd, Mastrofski, McNally, Greenspan, and Willis (2003, p. 448) write,

> Compstat departments are more reluctant to relinquish power that would decentralize some key elements of decision making geographically ... enhance flexibility, and risk going outside of the standard tool kit of police tactics and strategies. The combined effect overall, whether or not intended, is to reinforce a traditional bureaucratic model of command and control.

In another pertinent study by Cowper (2000), a former Marine officer and a captain in the New York State Police points out that the top-down model is not what the military currently practices. For example, Cowper (2000, p. 231) writes,

> The modern military is not the top-down, centrally controlled monolith that many traditional police managers cherish and forward-thinking police

progressives decry ... [it] has developed operational doctrine based on decentralization of decision making and action. The American police could be well served if they were to adopt the lessons of the real military experience ...

In New York City, this top-down style, supposedly based on the military, is exactly what is practiced. Compstat was originally designed as a decentralized management system giving power to local precinct commanders (Silverman, 2001). It has morphed, as one of our respondents put it, into "iron control." This top-down model is leadership failure. As Cowper (2000, p. 242) writes,

COMPSTAT is a highly simplified form of military operational planning that ... is comparatively elementary in that it fails to seek and understand the theories and concepts behind the method—the differences between tactical and strategic information/data; principles such as unity of command and combined arms operations; and the interaction and relationships between commanders, their staffs, and their operational units. It fails to address the organizational structures and operational practices ... COMPSTAT is an attempt to produce genuine results by treating organizational symptoms (lack of accountability, intradepartmental coordination, bottom-up information flow) in isolation from the wider systemic factors and issues in the department that actually drive operations.

This does not mean that we feel that Compstat is a poor innovation. Quite the opposite. We believe it can be an excellent tool, if used properly. However, the NYPD has failed to understand and institute policies that address the numerous problems we raise.

NYPD Management and Women Officers

As we have seen, Compstat focuses on the traditional aspects of policing—write summonses, make arrests. This legalistic approach tends to dismiss more recent developments in community policing and to reinforce traditional policing. That is, problem-solving approaches are not encouraged because they may not be reflected in the numbers. Indeed, not writing a summons or making an arrest may be more appropriate in certain situations (e.g., the elderly couple stopped for a seatbelt violation). Furthermore, bullying behaviors by supervisors do not create an environment of inclusiveness.

We also point out that some scientific studies suggest that women officers may be superior at non-traditional policing. For example, Sims, Scarborough, and Ahmad (2003, p. 281) state, "Officers in a community policing model are more likely to use the more feminine traits of fostering relationships with the citizenry ... and less likely to use the more traditional, masculine characteristics of detachment and authoritarianism." Another study by Bloch and

Anderson (1974) matched 86 men and women officers and studied them for a year. They found that women made fewer arrests, appeared to calm possible hostile situations better than men did, had a less aggressive style, and were less likely to be charged with misconduct. Generally, women do the job equally well, but some differences in style are noted in the research (Roberg, Crank, and Kuykendall, 2000).

While these studies are open to debate, there is enough evidence to suggest the possibility that women officers are alienated by this traditional, rigid bureaucratic environment (see Eterno, 2006). Indeed, the very small number of women in the higher echelon of the NYPD makes us more suspicious. Overall, our sample comports well with the characteristics of the NYPD. One concern for us is that our sample included only 14 women respondents in the higher ranks who retired after 1994. This means there is a pitifully small number of women at the ranks of Captain and above. Approximately 20 percent of the officers in the NYPD are women. However, they are clearly not represented in the higher ranks. Thus, the top-level management style that fosters bullying behaviors may have another negative side effect—alienating women officers. The aggressive crime fighting style that does not incorporate non-traditional approaches, bullying behaviors by the upper echelon, and the small number of women to reach the upper ranks are signs of a problem. Certainly, further research needs to examine this; however, the NYPD's closed-door policy makes this difficult, at best.

All of the research and other materials suggest a major issue in the NYPD and perhaps in many other Compstat-like jurisdictions. Key symptoms of the problem have been mentioned in this chapter: top-down pressure from management, the mindless numbers game, bullying behaviors, reinforcing traditional policing, and possible alienation of women. This strongly suggests a crisis of leadership.

Leadership

Leadership can help bridge the gap between the management and street cop cultures rather than exacerbate it. Unfortunately, NYPD managerial bullying behavior has clearly made matters worse. As we have seen, upper management, at least at its heralded Compstat meetings, has exhibited anything but leadership. We also believe they are too enamored with their program to see the truth. It sometimes takes uninvited outsiders (something the NYPD has not allowed in recent years), who are more neutral and detached, to see and understand what mountains of evidence say. As we reveal throughout this work, the system will benefit from change.

The issue of leadership is one on which the NYPD needs to work. As one of our interviewees states,

The lack of management training to all ranks caused an Us versus Them environment. Management training as the department was undergoing a sea change in how it was to accomplish its mission was left at the backdoor. The team concept from the Commissioners to the rank-and-file was not sought; the tools to accomplish the new tasks were not given.

Various leadership styles that have been noted by scholars help us to better understand this issue. Five basic leadership styles are consistent in the literature (see, for example, O'Moore and Lynch, 2007; Cordner and Scarborough, 2007). The first can be called autocratic. This is an authoritarian method of leadership. Generally, this person will make a decision and expect it to be carried out without question. While this style is generally not desirable, it can be effective especially if a speedy decision is needed and if others are trying to avoid responsibility (Cordner and Scarborough, 2007). When Compstat first began, this was the dominant style. At the time, it may have been more appropriate because NYPD commanders may have become comfortable with their positions and needed to take on more responsibility and accountability. However, we note that William Bratton, who founded Compstat in New York City, maintained that he would have ended this practice had he remained after 1996 (Henry, 2000).

A second style of leadership is called the bureaucratic style. Essentially subordinates follow the rules and procedures of the police agency. In the NYPD, this is the Patrol Guide and copious other materials such as Interim Orders (periodic changes in the Patrol Guide), Legal Bureau Bulletins, and other assorted memos and guidelines. One problem with always going by the "Guide" is that it may not be correct for a particular circumstance. The NYPD even teaches that the "Guide" is flexible. The third style is generally termed participative or democratic, in which subordinates are given a say in the decision. At a minimum, the leader consults with other personnel before making the decision.

A fourth style is what Cordner and Scarborough (2007) term the diplomatic style. The leader makes a decision and later tries to get others to "buy into" the decision. This may be beneficial if a leader is showing respect for others and distractive if the leader is simply going through the motions. The fifth and final style is allowing subordinates maximum freedom and essentially the leader either avoids making a decision or simply lets another have the authority to make the decision. This is often termed the *Laissez-faire* style.

While all styles have strengths and weaknesses, Compstat as currently practiced in New York City is clearly authoritarian. Although this method can be appropriate, it should not be the defining command style within an organization.

As several of our respondents indicate when asked about the department managerial style,

> Compstat has lost its original theme. C.O.'s were allowed to make their own decisions when it first started and then held accountable. Now all you do is follow someone else's orders and decisions and still you're held accountable.

Giddens (1993) (as cited by O'Moore and Lynch, 2007, p. 99) argues that, "authoritarianism is not a characteristic of personality [as some studies suggest], but rather reflects the values and norms of particular subcultures within the wider society." Here lies a key issue with Compstat. The management/headquarters subculture is authoritarian. It is at odds with the norms of both the street cop culture and even wider democratic society. Bullying their own members, management culture demands numbers, sometimes any numbers. These numbers are a centralizing force, a control mechanism. The authoritarian style of leadership feeds on this. Compstat is the mechanism by which it is accomplished. Thus, inadequate leadership is forced to use this approach to maintain iron control.

While there is no single preferred way of leading, examining the current literature on police supervision indicates some possible areas of weakness with the NYPD leadership. One such area is discussed by Iannone, Iannone, and Bernstein (2009), who examine the issue of reprimanding subordinates:

> The supervisor should never lose his temper and become angry or hostile when reprimanding subordinates, nor should he exaggerate and overstate the reason for the criticism. Indeed, effective communication skills, combined with effective interpersonal skills, will allow him to "punish without drawing blood." ... The employee should be given an opportunity to make a positive response concerning the issue and to save face. ... A "soft," intelligent approach rather than a "hard" one tends to reduce antagonism and resistance to criticism, the object of which is to bring about improvement, not to produce resentment and hostility. (Iannone et al., 2009, p. 41)

Furthermore, Iannone et al. (2009, p. 41) explicitly discuss basic supervisory behavior: "There are much more effective tools of leadership than condemnation, criticism, or punitive action. The supervisor should follow the adage, 'Commend in public but criticize in private.'" Conversely, Compstat has led to public punishment—certainly not exemplifying good leadership.

Our survey also demonstrates that NYPD Compstat meetings have not followed such basic leadership principles. Exceedingly common comments from our respondents such as, "People were embarrassed in front of peers" and "Some beatings were warranted but they went too far. ... You are out of your mind if you want to be a Captain" exemplify Compstat's leadership style.

Another issue is that the main motivator at NYPD is fear. As Iannone et al. (2009, p. 35) state,

Fear, as a negative motivator, involves threat, direct or implied, and a degree of intimidation, but because human beings can shield themselves by developing a tolerance of stress, fear soon loses its value … it will produce resentment, frustration, hostility, bitterness, and marginal performance, with low morale that accompanies these reactions.

Punishment is generally not considered an effective way to change behavior (see, for example, DiCaprio, 1983, p. 464). Other motivators are far more effective. Basic leadership principles indicate that rewards are far better at motivating and changing behaviors (see, for example, Iannone et al., 2009, p. 188). Further, Iannone et al. (2009, p. 35) state, "Negative motivators such as fear, coercion, intimidation, and punishment should be avoided except when more constructive, positive means have been tried and have failed."

Without a doubt, the use of fear as a motivator is weak, at best. Iannone et al. (2009, p. 35) clearly state, "The supervisor should utilize every positive motivator at his disposal to stimulate his subordinates toward the highest productivity. … He can assist them by establishing an atmosphere of cooperation in which each member of the organization strives of his own volition to assist others. …" We also note here that money as a motivator is not as effective as many think. This does not mean we advocate paying minimum wage. Officers need to be properly remunerated for a variety of reasons such as attracting high-quality recruits, helping to minimize temptations for corruption, and assisting in maintaining a professional force. However, what this does mean is that officers who are paid decent wages will not be swayed that easily by monetary motivators. Iannone et al. (2009, p. 34) write,

Money and other material incentives are vastly overrated … because they become weaker and weaker as physical human needs are progressively satisfied. The employee hungry for the satisfaction derived from such motivators as praise, recognition, and the like is usually a good producer, but when he becomes disinterested in his job and satisfactions available from it, he sometimes loses his drive to produce. Motivation through the process of inspiration is unquestionably the most difficult yet the most powerful and lasting force to forming attitudes that will induce workers to make fuller use of their potential.

Consequently, Compstat, which uses fear as its main motivator, is not a recommended supervisory method.

In addition, supervisors should gain trust by setting an example. Much of Compstat, however, is "do as I say, not as I do." Inquisitors berate subordinates at Compstat but sometimes fail to provide necessary resources, advice, labor, money, training, and investigators. Do more with less is the mantra as the NYPD has cut thousands of officers yet expects the same product. Ultimately, this is doomed to failure as subordinates motivated by fear create their own set of norms and values informally to deal with the overwhelming pressures placed upon them. Rather than resolve problems, commanders seek to avoid the punishment of Compstat. The number of commanders caught manipulating crime reports are examples of this behavior. In February 2010, the NYPD stated that during Mr. Kelly's tenure there were four precinct commanders and seven others who were disciplined for crime report manipulation (Rashbaum, 2010, February 6). We can add the commander as well as several other lower ranking supervisors in the 81st Precinct. The NYPD admits to having unearthed these cases on its own. Our research indicates this is only the tip of the iceberg and that many more are engaged in such avoidance behavior.

Another issue of leadership is "over-managing." In particular, what is termed the span of control should be limited. That is, the upper echelon should have very few subordinates under their direct control. Iannone et al. (2009, p. 20) recommend from three to five individuals. However, as one respondent put it, "Compstat morphed into iron control." Iannone et al. (2009, p. 20) point out that, "The tendency in modern police operations is to exceed the bounds of effective control. Chiefs of police and other high administrative officers too frequently attempt to exert direct control over too many subordinates. ..." This is the case in the NYPD. As we have mentioned, we are aware that even the most innocuous of actions by borough commanders (usually high-ranking 2-star chiefs) such as a transfer of a police officer from one command to another within the same borough is not allowed without first being approved by Headquarters. Compstat no longer effectively delegates control to local commanders; rather, it now looks to rigidly control their behaviors through fear and an overwhelming focus on numbers such as index crimes, summonses, and stop-and-frisk reports. Commanders are rigorously held up to last year's numbers. Such a focus is not necessarily accurate and will often depend on local conditions. Some commands may have had demographic changes, drug sale/use changes, or economic changes in their commands, which (if the numbers are accurate) will preclude consistent yearly drops in crime. In the real world, such fluctuations are common and should be reflected in the statistics. We note that the lack of any sustained, appreciable fluctuation in any precinct or in any index crime from 1995 to 2009 is also an indication of crime report manipulation (see Chapter 2 for more information).

Another problem with Compstat lies with delegation of authority. All commanders were chosen for their assignments by the upper echelon of the NYPD. Those chosen are theoretically the most competent, motivated individuals in the department. That being the case, the department needs to give them the authority and resources to do what they are asked. Iannone et al. (2009, pp. 22, 51) state, "When a task is delegated to an employee who is competent to perform it, enough authority to complete it must also be delegated. ... Traditional bureaucratic structure needs to accommodate by providing more decision-making authority to officers at the level where the work is being done." Screaming and yelling at Compstat meetings does not help solve a problem or complete a task. Rather than yell, the upper echelon can assist. They have large staffs available for their personal use. However, such luxuries are not available to commanders. In addition, respondents informed us about how commanders and executive officers (second in command at the precinct) fought for resources. The commander is responsible for Compstat and the executive officer is responsible for Trafficstat (a version of Compstat applied to traffic accidents). The respondent wrote,

> In addition TrafficStat is a complete waste of a Command's resources. It forces the XO to go against the overall mission of the Dept and the Pct Commander. Both the XO and CO are competing for very limited resources.

Another writes,

> I was embarrassed by a chief at TrafficStat, thought to be not writing the right type of summons & code, not engaging my officers appropriately. Fact was I was detailed for 4 months down at the 9/11 site and couldn't keep up with all the memos, the C.O. didn't care about TrafficStat and thus the cops weren't paying attention either. So when it came time for TrafficStat our accident #'s were up the boro called on me to appear and represent the command. With only 24 hrs knowledge the C.O. showed me the memos, I knew I was set up. … Exceptional performance was on occasion rewarded. However, it has never been the norm …

We note that other "stats" evolved and now occur regularly at the NYPD such as "DomStat" for domestic violence. This, too, is problematic. For example, one respondent writes,

> I would also argue that over time, applying the "Comstat process" to the myriad of other roles of the police (Trafficstat, Narcostat, etc.) weakened executives' ability to effectively do their jobs.

As previously discussed, promotion based on familiarity rather than merit is also symptomatic of leadership issues in the NYPD. Leaders need to assess the skills and abilities of those in the organization in a fair and impartial manner. Compstat is clearly a time where skills and abilities are assessed. However, familiarity should not play the overwhelming role that it apparently has. That is, if you know the "right person," you will have an easy time at Compstat; those who do not know the "right person" are more likely to be grilled. These perceptions of our respondents were very clear and indicate issues of favoritism, lack of impartiality, and, at times, bullying behaviors that contribute to leadership problems.

Experts on leadership principles point out that supervisors need to assist those who have obstacles. At the NYPD, this was rarely the case as those placed in positions of power by the upper echelon were berated but often not given the necessary tools to complete the tasks assigned. Iannone et al. (2009, p. 22) write, "Assistance should be given to overcome obstacles the employee is not equipped to handle ..." Embarrassment will lead to informal norms by lower ranks such as fudging crime reports, badgering subordinates for summonses, enforcing illegal quotas, and the like. Over one-half million stop-and-frisk reports in one year has become the norm to satisfy Compstat inquisitors. This is but one example of this phenomenon. Iannone et al. (2009, p. 28) put it succinctly:

When men obey another because of fear, they are *yielding*. Their obedience is given grudgingly. There is little loyalty or teamwork, and no desire to give their all for a common cause. But when men *follow*, they do so willingly— because they *want to do* what the leader wishes. Herein lies the distinction between being an authority and being a leader. The leader stimulates, motivates, and inspires the group to follow willingly, even eagerly. The authority pushes and drives his men who yield and obey because they fear the consequences of disobedience.

As Iannone et al. (2009, p. 7) advise,

He must stand by his convictions in spite of adversity and must adhere to those high moral standards of his profession regardless of a departure from them by others. He should adopt new principles when the need for higher or better ones becomes evident.

Originally a revolutionary management system, we are convinced that Compstat at the NYPD needs to regain its initial creativity.

In conclusion, research has suggested that inadequate leadership and a poor working environment is a recipe for bullying behavior (O'Moore and Lynch, 2007). The evidence we have gathered suggests that this is the case at the NYPD. Additionally, Compstat-like jurisdictions that carelessly emulate the NYPD's program are also in danger of developing similar problems. Law enforcement is already ripe for bullying behavior due to the quasi-military structure that has been the model for police since the time of Sir Robert Peel. Our study illuminates the dangers of these behaviors to policing organizations, to the rank-and-file, to victims of crime, and to democracy. The signs and symptoms of a dysfunctional organization, including but not limited to inadequate leadership, have been revealed in this chapter and in this book. We need to treat the disease by providing a comprehensive treatment plan. The influence of the media can be instrumental in making this change. The next chapter discusses the relationship between the media and the NYPD.

References

Baker, A. and Rivera, R. (2010). "Secret Tape Has New York Police Pressing Ticket Quotas." *The New York Times*. Retrieved October 20, 2011 from http://www.nytimes.com/2010/09/10/nyregion/10quotas.html?pagewanted=all

Baker, A. and Robbins, L. (2011, January 13). "A Quota by Any Other Name," *New York Times,* http://cityroom.blogs.nytimes.com/2011/01/13/a-quota-by-any-other-name/. Retrieved on May 18, 2011.

Block, P. B. and Anderson, D. (1974). *Policewomen on Patrol: Final Report.* Washington, DC: Police Foundation.

Celona, L. (2011, February 23). "'Roid Cops New Dumbbell Rap," *New York Post*, http://www.nypost.com/p/news/local/roid_cop_new_dumbbell_rap_zrqKXk-s1uZg1TJ9iU4JuNM. Retrieved August 23, 2011.

Center for Constitutional Rights. (n.d.). "NYPD Stop-and-Frisk Statistics 2009 and 2010," http://ccrjustice.org/files/CCR_Stop_and_Frisk_Fact_Sheet_0.pdf. Retrieved on January 14, 2011.

Cordner, G.W. and Scarborough, K.E. (2007). *Police Administration,* 6th ed. Newark, NJ: LexisNexus.

Cowper, T.J. (2000). "The Myth of the 'Military Model' of Leadership in Law Enforcement," *Police Quarterly*, 3(3): 228–246.

DiCaprio, N.S. (1983). *Personality Theories: A Guide to Human Nature*, 2nd ed. New York: Holt Rinehart and Winston.

Eterno, J.A. (2001). "Zero Tolerance Policing in Democracies: The Dilemma of Controlling Crime without Increasing Police Abuse of Power," *Police Practice and Research: An International Journal*, 2(3): 189–217.

Eterno, J.A. (2006). "Gender and Policing: Do Women Accept Legal Restrictions More than Their Male Counterparts?" *Women and Criminal Justice*, 18(1/2): 49–78.

Flynn, K. (2000). "Behind the Success Story, A Vulnerable Police Force," *The New York Times*, Nov. 25, A1.

Glendinning, P.M. (2001). "Workplace Bullying: Curing the Cancer of the American Workplace," *Public Personnel Management*, 30(3): 269–286.

Hagan, F.E. (2006). *Research Methods in Criminal Justice,* 7th ed. Boston: Allyn and Bacon.

Henry, V.E. (2000). "Interview with William J. Bratton," *Police Practice and Research: An International Journal*, 2(4): 559–580.

Hoffer, J. (2010, March 3). "NYPD Officer Claims Pressure to Make Arrests," Eyewitness News Investigations, television broadcast. New York: American Broadcasting Company (ABC), http://abclocal.go.com/wabc/story?section=news/investigators&id=7305356. Retrieved on January 7, 2011.

Hoffer, J. (2010, September 10). "Quota Questions and the NYPD," Eyewitness News Investigations, television broadcast. New York: American Broadcasting Company (ABC), http://abclocal.go.com/wabc/story?section=news/investigators&id=7661260. Retrieved on January 14, 2011.

Hoffer, J. (2010, n.d.). "Are NYPD Quotas Chipping Away at Public Trust?" Eyewitness News Investigations, television broadcast. New York: American Broadcasting Company (ABC), http://abclocal.go.com/wabc/video?id=7460267. Retrieved on January 14, 2011.

Hutchinson, M., Vickers, M.H., Wilkes, L., and Jackson, D. (2009). "The Worse You Behave, The More You Seem to be Rewarded; Bullying to Nursing as Organizational Corruption," *Employee Responsibilities and Rights Journal*, 21: 213–229.

Iannone, N.F., Iannone, M.D., and Bernstein, J. (2009). *Supervision of Police*, 7th ed. Upper Saddle River, NJ: Pearson/Prentice Hall.

Johnson, N. (2011, January 25). "Queens Woman: Husband Died after NYPD Stop," MyFOX New York, http://www.myfoxny.com/dpp/news/local_news/queens/queens-woman-husband-died-after-nypd-stop-20110124?obref=obinsite. Retrieved on February 3, 2011.

Lee, R.T. and Brotheridge, C.M. (2006). "When Prey Turns Predatory: Workplace Bullying as a Predictor of Counteraggression/Bullying, Coping, and Well-Being," *European Journal of Work and Organizational Psychology*, 15(3): 352–377.

Manning, P.K. (1987). "The Police Occupational Culture in Anglo-American Societies." Draft, March 3. Intended for W.G. Bailey, Ed. (1989). *Encyclopedia of Police Science*. Dallas: Garland.

Messing, P. (2007). "NYPD Officers Quit for County Jobs," *New York Post*, cited by forums.officer.com. Retrieved January 17, 2011 from http://forums.officer.com/forums/archive/index.php/t-76856.html.

Messing, P. (2010, April 12). "Capt. Badge Losing Its Lu$Ter for Cops," *New York Post*, http://www.nypost.com/p/news/local/capt_badge_losing_its_lu_ter_for_Zr2PxjBVieL8RAqphD9y2I. Retrieved on January 18, 2011.

Neuman, W.L. (2000). Social Research Methods: Qualitative and Quantitative Approaches, 4th ed. Boston: Allyn and Bacon.

New York City Civilian Complaint Review Board (CCRB). (2003). New York City Civilian Complaint Review Board Status Report January-December, 2003. X239I(2). New York City Government Publication.

New York City Civilian Complaint Review Board (CCRB). (2009). New York City Civilian Complaint Review Board Status Report January–December, 2009 *XVII*(2). New York City Government Publication.

New York City Civilian Complaint Review Board (CCRB). (2011, February 2). Press release. http://www.nyc.gov/html/ccrb/pdf/CCRB_Press_Release_20110202.pdf. Retrieved on August 5, 2011.

New York City Criminal Court. (2009). *Criminal Court of the City of New York Annual Report*. Published by the Office of the Deputy Chief Administrative Judge.

Ngo, E. (2010, February 2). "Budget Cuts Retirements Ahead Could Thin NYPD Ranks to New Lows," *AM New York*, http://www.amny.com/urbanite-1.812039/budget-cuts-retirements-ahead-could-thin-nypd-ranks-to-new-lows-1.1737680. Retrieved on January 14, 2011.

O'Moore, M. and Lynch, J. (2007). "Leadership, Working Environment and Workplace Bullying," *International Journal of Organization Theory and Behavior*, 10(1): 95–117.

"Police Leaders at PERF/BJA Meeting Discuss CompStat: Best Practices and Future Outlook." (2011). *Subject to Debate: A Newsletter of the Police Executive Research Forum*, 25(2), from http://www.policeforum.org/library/subject-to-debate-archives/2011/Debate_Mar-Apr2011_web.pdf. Retrieved on August 5, 2011.

Rashbaum, W. (2010, February 6). "Retired Officers Raise Questions on Crime Data," *The New York Times,* http://www.nytimes.com/2010/02/07/nyregion/07crime.html?pagewanted=1.

Rayman, G. (2010, May 11). "The NYPD Tapes, Part 2," *The Village Voice,* http://www.villagevoice.com/2010-05-11/news/nypd-tapes-part-2-bed-stuy/. Retrieved on January 7, 2011.

Rayman, G. (2010, June 15). "The NYPD Tapes, Part 4, The Whistleblower, Adrian Schoolcraft," *The Village Voice,* http://www.villagevoice.com/2010-06-15/news/adrian-school-craft-nypd-tapes-whistleblower/. Retrieved January 7, 2011.

Rayman, G. (2011, August 4). "Adil Polanco Case: NYPD Files New Charges on Whistleblower, Yes, for Blowing Whistle," *Village Voice,* http://blogs.villagevoice.com/runninscared/2011/08/adil_polanco_ca.php. Retrieved on August 5, 2011.

Reuss-Ianni, E. (1983). *Two Cultures of Policing.* New Brunswick, NJ: Transaction Books.

Rivera, R. and Baker, A. (2010, November 1). "Data Elusive on Low-Level Crime in New York City," *The New York Times,* http://www.nytimes.com/2010/11/02/nyregion/02secrecy.html?_r=1&pagewanted=1. Retrieved January 13, 2011.

Roberg, R., Crank, J., and Kuykendall, J. (2000). *Police and Society,* 2nd ed. Los Angeles, CA: Roxbury.

Schaefer, R.T. (2001). *Sociology*, 7th ed. New York: McGraw-Hill.

Silverman, E. B. (2001). *NYPD Battles Crime.* Boston: Northeastern University Press.

Sims, B., Scarborough, K.E., and Ahmad, J. (2003). "The Relationship between Police Officers' Attitudes toward Women and Perception of Police Models," *Police Quarterly,* 6(3): 278–297.

Weisburd, D., Mastrofski, S., McNally, A., Greenspan, R., and Willis, J.J. (2003). "Reforming to Preserve: Compstat and Strategic Problem Solving in American Policing," *Criminology and Public Policy,* 2(3): 421–456.

Weisburd, D., Mastrofski, S., Willis, J.F., and Greenspan, R. (2006). "Changing Everything So That Everything Can Remain the Same: Compstat and American Policing." In: Weisburd, D.W. and Braga, A., Eds. *Police Innovation: Contrasting Perspectives*. Cambridge, MA: Cambridge University Press, 284–301.

Wilson, J.Q. (1977). *Varieties of Police Behavior.* Cambridge, MA: Harvard University Press.

NYPD and the Media

6

Curbing Criticism

Our research first attracted media attention on Sunday, February 7, 2010 with a *New York Times* front-page article entitled "Retired Officers Raise Questions on Crime Data." The story highlighted Compstat's unyielding demand for crime reduction and its bearing on unethical crime reporting. The article triggered a rapid and furious response from the NYPD, its political allies (including two of New York's major newspapers, the *Daily News* and the *Post*), and its academic supporters. Unfortunately, the leadership of the Police Department and its allies willfully refused to take seriously what the department's own retired commanders said, and launched a public relations offensive based on many false claims: that we are opposed to Compstat, that the retired police we surveyed from the rank of captain and higher were tools of their union, and that the use of an anonymous survey is tainted.

The lightning-fast pace of these attacks was astonishing. The first official NYPD response appeared in the original February 7, 2010 *New York Times* article. The second attack occurred two days later when Mayor Bloomberg weighed in on February 9. Two days after that, the *Daily News* unleashed a February 11 editorial attack. It took another three days before the Police Commissioner criticized our study in a *Daily News* op ed on February 14. Three days later, a double-barreled attack was launched. The first was a full-scaled assault, which appeared in the conservative Manhattan Institute's *City Journal* February 17 Web site. The second was former police commissioner William Bratton's op ed in the *New York Times*. It only took another four days for the *New York Post* to weigh in with a critical editorial entitled "Anti Cop Idiocy" on February 21.

The Condemnations

The remarkably consistent and congruent condemnations (within a span of only 14 days) were quite striking. The critics echoed three major themes: our methodology was flawed, the funding for the study was tainted, and studies with contradictory findings were superior to our study.

In the original February 7, 2010 *New York Times* article, the NYPD first criticized the methodology results while offering its own sources as far more reliable than our study. According to the *Times*:

> The Police Department disputed the survey's findings, questioned its methodology and pointed to other reviews of the CompStat process that it said supported its position. … [A Department spokesperson] said that two other significant, independent and more comprehensive studies had been done in recent years analyzing the integrity of the city's crime statistics—one in 2006 by a New York University (NYU) professor and another by the state comptroller's office—and that he had found them to be reliable and sound. (Rashbaum, 2010, February 7)

Yet the NYU study (sponsored by the NYPD) was not subject to the academic peer review process, which assigns credibility to scholarly articles. Furthermore, the 2006 NYU study critiqued the 2000 New York State Comptrollers audit as "limited in its scope and completed more than four years ago. It is time for another, more probing assessment" (Smith and Purtell, 2006). The NYU study then immediately follows with a very telling footnote:

> Our review, while more comprehensive, of course was also limited in scope. Our conclusions are based on conversations with senior command staff and a review of written materials. We neither observed the actual sampling or auditing processes nor did we test the accuracy of the sampling procedures used by the Department in its audits. We can only infer how the written procedures were implemented in practice beyond a general comparison of these standards to accepted auditing practice. … (Smith and Purtell, 2006, p. 5, footnote no. 2)

In other words, the NYU study, contrary to the NYPD's assertion, was neither "significant" nor "comprehensive." Moreover, it was not even "independent" as it was conducted at the behest and under the supervision of the Department.

The limitations of the Comptroller and NYU studies, however, did not preclude the Police Commissioner and his allies from praising their so-called reliability and authenticity. The Police Commissioner's *Daily News* opinion piece asserted, "Comprehensive studies … found NYPD crime data collection to be accurate, complete and reliable and our auditing 'robust'" (Kelly, 2010, February 14).

The same line of reasoning reoccurs in Heather MacDonald's *City Journal* diatribe, "Compstat and its Enemies" (2010, February 17). MacDonald conveniently ignores the limitations that the NYU study footnote so graphically acknowledged. Instead, she regurgitates the Police Commissioner's and NYU study's statements, which are solely based on interviews with NYPD personnel. MacDonald simply asserts:

The NYPD, however, does not merely sample among its reporting units; it audits each command twice a year and samples every crime category within that command, observed New York University professor Dennis Smith and SUNY Albany Professor Robert Purtell in their 2005 study. (MacDonald, 2010)

Ignoring contradictory evidence is endemic to our media and other critics. Detractors, including the Police Commissioner and MacDonald, failed to acknowledge the fact that the one previous independent attempt to assess the authenticity of NYPD crime statistics was steadfastly rebuffed by the Department. In 2005, a Mayoral agency, the Commission to Combat Police Corruption, acting on police officers' anecdotal reports of altered crime documents, sought to examine the integrity of the Department's statistics. The Department refused and the Mayor did not support his own Commission; this led its chairman, Mark F. Pomerantz, a respected former federal prosecutor, to resign. Since then, this Commission has steadily lost steam in the frequency of its reports and its actual funding for personal service. For example, in 2004, the year before the NYPD successfully repelled the Commission's requests, the Commission's personal services expenditures were $422,000. The following year it was reduced to $369,000. By 2009, the spending amount had shrunk to $305,000 (Financial Management System, 2011). Police Department transparency on this issue has been and continues to be totally lacking.

The Mayor also tried to undermine our study by stating in a February 9, 2010 *Daily News* article that, "This is a study that you're referring to that was paid for by one of the unions. So, you've got to start wondering whether it was an independent study" (Parascandola and Lisberg, 2010, February 9, p. 7). The mayor's comments were offered despite the fact that the original *New York Times* article noted that we were responsible for the design and analysis of the survey, which was funded by Molloy College. The Union had nothing whatsoever to do with the funding or the results. The Union simply granted us access to its retired membership.

The attempt to discredit our study by intimating guilt by association did not end with the Mayor's effort. Two days later, on February 11, 2010, a *Daily News* editorial, "Mugging Compstat: Assault on NYPD Crime-Tracking Program is Wrongheaded," repeated the same inaccurate assertion: "What they have are the results of a mail survey conducted in cooperation with— alarm bells, alarm bells—the police captains union" ("Mugging Compstat," 2010, February 11). *This assertion was repeated despite the fact that the Daily News article (two days earlier) corrected Bloomberg's previous recounting of this falsehood when it said, "In fact, the survey was funded by Molloy College in Rockville Center, L.I."* ("Mugging Compstat," 2010, February 11).

MacDonald, living up to her reputation as an unalloyed long-standing NYPD defender, parroted the Mayor's erroneous claim about the survey's funding. In her *City Journal* article she states, "It is no coincidence that the Captain's Union funded the Silverman–Eterno study; the radical fringe in all the department's unions wants Compstat thrown out" (MacDonald, 2010, February 17). *MacDonald perpetuated this inaccurate criticism despite the Daily News' corrective article eight days earlier.*

The critics' attacks are also based on an erroneous depiction of our research as having a "flawed methodology." But how is the methodology "flawed"? Our research has been published in two peer-reviewed journals where our methodology was scrupulously examined. Furthermore, we used accepted social science methods including anonymity and focus groups, spent months in the questionnaire development process, and much more. Our critics fail to acknowledge the possibility that we may be correct or even partially correct. Indeed, the record thus far is overwhelmingly in our favor. While all research contains some limitations (see Chapter 8), this does not detract from the significance of our findings.

The media's excessive condemnation, *without having even read our report* since it had not been released at that point, is reflected in their editorials. A *Daily News* editorial said we "libeled the NYPD and every police officer ..." ("Mugging Compstat," 2010, February 11). Not to be outdone, the *New York Post* duplicated the allegations of the *Daily News* by accusing us of "Anti-Cop Idiocy," in its February 21, 2010 editorial ("Anti-Cop Idiocy," 2010, February 21).

The media and other critics main accusation is that we attacked the police by impugning their anti-crime efforts and denying the legitimacy of New York City's declining crime rate. This depiction of our research as condemning cops and denying New York's crime decline is not only contrary to our findings, but diametrically opposed to our previous writings, which were, ironically, applauded by our critics. The author of the *City Journal* article, entitled "The Enemies of Compstat," is the same Heather MacDonald who penned a *Wall Street Journal* review of Silverman's previous book. MacDonald wrote:

> In *NYPD Battles Crime*, Eli B. Silverman analyzes the managerial underpinnings of the Giuliani revolution, epitomized in his view, by the innovative crime-tracking system known as Compstat. ... It is a delight to read about a wildly successful—if, in retrospect, self-evident—idea: that policing is helpless without both data and the means to hold officers accountable for acting on it. (MacDonald, 1999)

Now, however, Silverman apparently was somehow transformed from hero to heretic. Heretics are outcasts whose voices do not warrant a hearing. Thus, our attempts to respond to our critics were not worthy of publication. On the evening of February 16, 2010, we submitted an op ed to the *New York Times* whose reporters were responsive to our research. In this case, we were dealing with the editorial unit of the *Times*. On February 17, the *Times* editorial section published a critical op ed by William Bratton. That same day, David Shipley, the former op ed editor for the *Times*, responded to our e-mail saying, "Thank you Mr. Silverman, but I'm afraid I'm going to have to decline." We responded, the same day, in an e-mail saying:

> Thank you for your prompt response. Naturally we are disappointed. Our sub-mission was written the day before Mr. Bratton's op ed appeared. Would you entertain a different submission from us addressing the issues he raised as a means of providing all views?

Mr. Shipley responded the next day, February 18, by simply stating, "Thanks for this, Mr. Silverman, but I'm not sure we're going to be able to do much more on this issue for a bit" (Shipley, 2010). It turns out "a bit" has an extended run. Mr. Shipley also rebuffed another inquiry.

Subsequent revelations regarding Mr. Shipley are quite intriguing. New York's interconnected political, business, and media worlds are viv-idly embodied in Mr. Shipley's January 2011 decision to leave the *Times* and join "the ever ambitious" Mayor Bloomberg's new venture "to dominate a new sphere—the world of opinion after conquering Wall Street in the 1970s, crushing competitors in the e-information technology industry in the '80s and reigning over New York City politics for the past decade" (Barbaro, 2011). According to the *New York Times*, Shipley will lead the Mayor's new venture "Bloomberg View," which seeks to extend his "influence into the opinion sphere" (Barbaro, 2011).

> This move reflects a broader frustration by the mayor and his company that, despite hiring binges, acquisitions and $7 billion a year in revenue, Bloomberg's content is consumed mainly by stock and bond traders and does not dominate conversations in the corner offices of America. (Barbaro, 2011)

Bloomberg's company "made no secret of its ambition to become one of the most—if not the most—influential media companies in the world" (Barbaro, 2011). In pursuit of this goal, the Mayor and his representatives "over the last year have quietly reached out to a handful of the country's top journalists with an intriguing job offer … for an annual salary of close to $500,000" (Barbaro, 2011). Was Mr. Shipley in discussion with Bloomberg the Mayor in terms of his future with Bloomberg the Company while the issue of our op ed was under consideration? Given the Mayor's antipathy to our study, is this another example of the incestuous world of New York City politics, media, and business? The timing of these "hiring opportunities" certainly raises questions.

The editorial section of the *Times* was not alone in ignoring us. Our letter to the *New York Post,* in response to its critical editorial, also did not see the light of day. The *Daily News,* while publishing two of our opinion pieces, continued its editorial assault with two additional attacks that especially named Eterno and Silverman. The titles capture the intensity of their assaults— "Arrest NYPD Bashing: Running a Numbers Racket with Crime Fighting Statistics" and "Crime Numbers Disprove Police Bashers' Cockamamie Compstat Theory."

We remained, and continue to remain, rigorous scholars despite these outlandish attacks by media critics who had not even read our detailed research studies as reflected in academic journals—the first of which was not accepted for publication until April 2010. Our public responses demonstrate that we remain as committed today to revealing the truth despite the flurry of NYPD–media spin. In the remainder of this chapter, we explore the reasons for this assault on our scientific work.

Understanding NYPD–Media Spin

The staggering parallels in the ferocity of the critics' attacks can hardly be ascribed to coincidence. They reveal a great deal not only about the media, but also, and perhaps more importantly for our purposes, the NYPD itself and its relationship with the media. The corresponding police–media reactions reside in factors that are: (1) unique to the nature of our threatening findings and (2) inherent in the long-standing relationships between the NYPD and the media.

Threatening Findings

Although we have never denied the reality of New York City's multi-year reduction in crime, we have questioned the proportions of that decline. As discussed in Chapter 2, numerous sources have provided corroborating evidence of statistical downgrading and manipulation of data. Although our critics have been reluctant to acknowledge reality as demonstrated in our study, the evidence is so compelling that, without question, it raises serious concerns regarding the magnitude of the crime decline.

Prior to the 1990s, when crime rates fluctuated, our and others' related findings would have posed far less of a threat. During the last two decades of unprecedented steadily declining crime rates, however, the NYPD and the political leadership have claimed credit for this "success." The repetitive political and police self-congratulatory public pronouncements have recast the law enforcement and political landscape with a powerful narrative (see Chapter 4).

Today, public and political expectation is that official crime reports, if not continually declining, must at least not increase and remain stable. Consequently, the expectations placed upon the police have been turned on their head. Since citizens are now wary of returning to the "bad old days," the police believe their crime statistics are under media and political scrutiny especially given the years of mayors and police commissioners trumpeting the crime decline. Therefore, no political or police leader can afford to be the first to have crime increase on his or her watch.

The NYPD rightly concludes that if crime reports creep upward, it may be automatically and unfairly blamed by the press and the public (due to its own foolhardy spin). These factors place added pressure on the NYPD to cast its crime fighting operations in the most favorable public light. This means even more consideration must be given to strategies designed to convince the public and the media that they are effective, just, and considerate. Consequently, any suggestion (such as ours) that the crime decline may be less than meets the public eye is considered threatening to the political and law enforcement establishments, and needs to be repelled and stifled if it cannot be ignored.

Research criticizing NYPD crime data also evoked a deeper layer of resistance. The administration of Mayor Michael R. Bloomberg has rested its reputation on a reliance on accurate and accountable information. As the *New York Times* noted in a February 9, 2010 article:

> Mayor Michael R. Bloomberg, an engineering major in college, has never been shy about proclaiming an unerring faith in statistics.
>
> He created 311 as a way to collate data, and improve the lives of New Yorkers. He has whipped out education data to justify extending mayoral control, reward star employees and close laggard schools. Rarely does a month go by without Mr. Bloomberg citing data analysis as the marrow not just of his administration, but also of his private-sector career and his philanthropic foundation.
>
> "I'm a great believer in the wisdom I learned in my first Wall Street job: In God we trust," he said at a philanthropy conference in Atlanta last May. "Everyone else, bring data." (Chen, 2010, February 9)

The Mayor's confidence in statistics explains why this *New York Times* article was entitled "Crime Survey Raises Questions about Data-Driven Policy." Referring to our study, the article continued:

> But what if the data were somehow skewed? … The results have made critics and admirers of Mr. Bloomberg wonder about—if not necessarily doubt—the reliability of data underpinning policy decisions on the budget, education, transportation, health and other issues. (Chen, 2010, February 9)

Therefore, it is no wonder that our survey has incurred the wrath of a mayor "who is obsessed with receiving up-to-the-minute data" (Barbaro, 2008, August 18).

Not only has data become so highly esteemed, the mechanism to collect and record the data has taken on the status of a venerated religion. The name of that religion is Compstat and it has made numerous converts throughout the United States and abroad.

As Chapter 3 demonstrates, Compstat has been reified. What started as a law enforcement crime management and accountability mechanism has morphed into a sacred institution, the centerpiece of the political and economic establishment. Any disapproval, regardless of how constructive, strikes at the heart of those in positions of authority and those aligned with their views, including intellectual hired hands and other acolytes. Criticism is, therefore, heretical and must be either ignored or repelled.

Consequently, our critique of Compstat's crime data has not only been viewed as an attack on the validity of the city's crime, education, and other performance data and results, but also as an assault on the central mechanism for achieving these "miraculous" statistical achievements. Nonbelievers are not welcome in Compstat's house of worship. They are either antireligious or heretical.

In addition to the factors discussed previously, other dynamics are at play that help explain the intensity of the NYPD and media's response to our findings. Many of these factors are inherent in the symbiotic relationship of the media and law enforcement in all major American cities. Other factors are unique to the NYPD and its relationships with the media. We address both sets of factors.

The Nature of Police–Media Interactions

Big city police organizations recognize that the public derives its opinion about crime, fear of crime, public safety, and even the police department itself from the media. This reliance on the media is likely because "most people have little direct experience with the types of crime that are presented in the news" (Gordon and Heath, 1981, p. 28). Despite incomplete and contradictory studies, experience instructs police on certain connections between crime and fear of crime. They are aware of the "if it bleeds, it leads" syndrome; namely, that violent crimes that lend themselves to media circulation can distort the public's fear of crime regardless of the crime rate. In addition, media is dependent on the police for such violent stories.

Most urban areas can chronicle this phenomenon. A two-year study in Chicago, San Francisco, and Philadelphia found that residents whose newspapers allocated most space to crime stories were more fearful than those reading papers with lower crime coverage (Gordon and Heath, 1981). Serious personal offenses, such as murder, rape, and robbery, are far more likely than less serious crime to be reported by the media. A study on how media presents large city crime documents this trend:

> Violent offenses accounted for nearly half of the crime stories presented. Conversely, misdemeanors and property offense stories accounted only for approximately 10 percent of the total. Nearly one fourth of all crimes mentioned in crime stories were murders. Media in the largest cities concentrate on selecting the most newsworthy murder. (Chermak, 1994, pp. 570, 578)

From this, and similar studies, it appears that media coverage in larger cities focuses on more serious crimes. Directly connected to this finding, numerous additional studies demonstrate that residents of inner neighborhoods of larger cities are more likely to fear crime than are people who live in smaller towns, rural areas, or the suburbs (Fisher, 1981; Finley, 1983; Krahn, 1984).

Given police dependence on the impact of media stories, it is often noted that there is a symbiotic relationship between the two. The police and the media have both a friendly *and* an adversarial relationship. Police recognize this reality. There is a need to cooperate closely because each benefits from a cordial relationship. News organizations can present large numbers of crime stories easily and cost efficiently. Police departments recognize that they need the media because

> … reporting of proactive police activity creates an image of the police as effective and efficient investigators of crime. Accordingly a positive police portrayal reinforces traditional approaches to law and order that involve increased police presence, harsher penalties and increasing police power. (Dowler, 2003, p. 111)

Police also realize that negative coverage of police conduct feeds negative police images. This can pertain to anything from inefficient crime control, corruption, and brutality to discourtesies and ineffective interactions with the public.

Given the media's critical role in influencing public opinion on issues of crime, law enforcement agencies have become increasingly sophisticated in their efforts to shape their environment through a proactive strategy of selectively disclosing knowledge about their activities. Police recognize that professional departmental public relations units can be effective in dealing with the media (Ericson, 1989).

In this effort to sway the media and the public, the police employ numerous levers of influence. This includes classifying what constitutes crime, crimes rates, and clearances of cases. The police provide crime news information and critique the media's depiction of crime and crime stories (Skolnick and McCoy, 1984).

Police recognize that in all of their communications, knowledge is power. In relation to the news media, power entails offensive and defensive strategies that maximize helpful news and minimize hurtful news. Viewed as a strategic commodity, news as knowledge is not considered for its truth value, but rather for its value in promoting the policing mandate. In the eyes of the police information officers, news is but another commodity in the social control business (Ericson, 1989).

As the police seek to maximize their ability to sell the media and therefore the public in pursuit of police occupational goals, they view the media as a resource for handling emergencies, investigations, and crime prevention, and enhancing police resources. The media also serve the police at the level of organizational and occupational ideology, helping to create a positive image of the police and thereby mobilizing popular support (Kasinsky, 1994, pp. 207, 208).

One study found that police were primarily preoccupied with the media's positive portrayal of their organizational image as opposed to accurate explanations of crime and the department. The police did not object to disproportionately heavily weighted media focus on the police's crime fighting role because it furthered their organizational image (Ericson, 1989).

The balance of power has increasingly tipped in the favor of the police as the dominant partner in this relationship. Media reporters are dependent on the police for factual details on crime and even access to officers and detectives involved in investigations. This is especially heightened, as reporters must quickly respond to media demands for immediate reports of crime stories and police activities. Therefore, reporters often rely on police public relations professionals, especially because crime stories sell newspapers, mainstream and cable television, and radio. All of which place reporters in a subordinate position (Chibnall, 1977; Fishman, 1981).

In major cities, the number of mainstream newspapers has drastically declined. The public is far less likely to be exposed to traditional police and crime news. On the other hand, cable television news has expanded. Its bourgeoning 24-hour news cycle, however, has only intensified the demand for rapid news regardless of its accuracy, thereby enhancing the influence of the professional police information units.

More fundamentally, mainstream media is frequently predisposed to be supportive of law enforcement. It is not unusual for media ownership and editors to be politically and economically aligned with a law and order outlook philosophy. The media is often portrayed as "uncritical, 'don't rock the boat'" in their approach (Kasinsky, 1994, p. 210). Studies, such as Herman and Chomsky (1988), demonstrate these close linkages, which enable the media to act as "propaganda" arms of the law enforcement establishment, which is "official" and, therefore, possesses the assumption of credibility.

Some have argued, moreover, that the police and media share similar instrumental and symbolic interests in the control of conflicts by defining and identifying deviance and promoting the "common good" (Van Outrive and Fijnaut, 1983, pp. 53–54). Other commentators extend this line of reasoning by observing that:

> ... social institutions ... are the purveyors of its cultural myths, values and legitimating viewpoints, and to the extent that news producers—from publishers to reporters—are immersed in that culture, they may not be fully aware of how they misrepresent, evade and suppress the news. ... *Devoid of the supportive background of the dominant belief system, the deviant sounds just too improbable and controversial to be treated as news, while the orthodox views appear as an objective representation of reality itself.* (Parenti, 1992, p. 240, emphasis added)

Any suggestion that crime statistics may be less than meets the eye may easily fall under the category of "unorthodox and deviant."

The NYPD and the Media: Political Ramifications

The NYPD's disproportionate influence on the media can be attributed to widely publicized law and order events. Two of the most significant of these events occurred in 1990 and 1991. They were the Korean Boycott and Crown Height's incidents (see Silverman, 2001). These events rose to the level of political campaigns particularly in Mayor Giuliani's election in 1993. From this point on, law and order has become prominent in New York City politics. We begin our discussion with Mayor Bloomberg's election in 2001.

2001

Giuliani trumpeted the city's tumbling crime reduction. Under his administration, 1,946 murders in 1993 dropped to 714 when he left office at the end of 2001. Giuliani's "reassuring calm" in the 9/11 terrorist attack greatly enhanced his crime control popularity.

Since barred from running for a third term by New York's two-term mayoral limit (Mayor Bloomberg's third term in 2009 was an exception), Giuliani embraced and campaigned vigorously for Republican Michael Bloomberg in 2001. His "endorsement gave Mr. Bloomberg a well-timed boost over his Democratic opponent, Mark Green" (Barry, 2001), contributing to Bloomberg's narrow victory of approximately 30,000 votes.

In addition, Bloomberg's record spending of over $75 million was also a major issue in the campaign.

The contest offered a measure of the extent to which Giuliani ... could designate his successor. The Mayor endorsed Mr. Bloomberg, appeared in a series of television advertisements for him ... Giuliani remains an extremely popular figure in New York, according to a survey of voters leaving the polls, and about one quarter said they had been influenced by his recommendation that they vote for Mr. Bloomberg. (Nagourney, 2001, November 7)

2005

Four years later, crime reduction and law and order punctuated Mayor Bloomberg's 2005 reelection campaign. Contrary to many expectations, crime statistics tumbled over 20 percent during the mayor's first term. The *New York Times* reported:

New York City's police force has fewer officers, less money and more work than it did four years ago. Yet, by almost any measure, the city is safer today than it was before Michael R. Bloomberg became mayor in January 2002. If that sounds like grist for a campaign commercial, it is. Public safety has emerged as Mr. Bloomberg's not-so-secret weapon as he goes about pressing his case for re-election

Mr. Bloomberg aggressively wields statistics showing that he not only continued the efforts of Rudolph W. Giuliani, who made crime-fighting a signature issue, but also did so while putting 1,000 officers on antiterrorism duty and avoiding the racial tensions that bedeviled his predecessor. "We are," Mr. Bloomberg said in a campaign speech in Brooklyn last week, "the safest big city in America." (McIntire, 2005, October 5)

The Mayor's achievements, coupled with his lopsided campaign spending, resulted in a 20-point victory margin, which exceeded fellow Republican Giuliani's 16-point victory in 1997.

2009

Four years later, in 2009, the Mayor was able to overturn the city's term limits law and run for reelection. Bloomberg was reelected, but voter resentment of his "maneuver to undo the city's term law and his extravagant spending ..." of a record $90 million resulted in a narrow victory of only 5 percent compared to a 20-percent margin four years earlier (Chen and Barbaro, 2009, November 4).

It is instructive to note that the Mayor's campaign continued to stress crime reduction. As crime statistics continued to drop during his second term, Bloomberg increasingly tied himself to his popular Police Commissioner Raymond Kelly. "In radio spots and direct mailings, the mayor's campaign warned voters that the Democratic candidate Comptroller William C. Thompson Jr. would replace Commissioner Kelly if he were elected"

(Schmidt, 2009, November 9). Crime control in 2009 became personified and identified with a particular police commissioner. According to this reasoning, any replacement would necessarily jeopardize the city's successful crime record. If Bloomberg's political opposition considered an alternative police commissioner, the public should question their election victory, the Bloomberg campaign suggested.

Thus, law and order acquired an indispensable and identifiable public face in the person of Raymond Kelly as the embodiment of successful crime control policies as embedded in the crime success narrative (see Chapter 3). Criticisms of the public face and any of his specific police strategies, for example, stop-and-frisk, are cast as defamation of NYPD crime control strategies best left unfettered. Upticks in crime, therefore, are, by definition, attributable to criticisms or restrictions placed on the department or its crime control strategies. One way to counter criticism is to promote favorable media coverage of the NYPD.

Promoting Favorable Stories

Media competition for crime news enhances the NYPD's ability to shape the news by monitoring the amount and type of information it makes available, limiting access to certain parts of the department, and relying on spokespersons to provide data and respond to questions. In most cases, reporters must first gain the clearance of the department's primary spokesperson before they can communicate with *any* member of the department.

Thus, this spokesperson serves as a "gatekeeper" in order to best portray the department's image. In the NYPD, the gatekeeper has the title of Deputy Commissioner for Public Information. He is responsible for an office of more than 35 people who serve the department around the clock. Deputy Commissioner Paul Browne has been associated with Police Commissioner Kelly for many years during his high-level positions with federal law enforcement agencies and is considered his closest and most trusted aide.

These gatekeeper officers, found in most large police departments throughout the world, are story selection gatekeepers. They are "experts in producing positive images of their police department, knowing the types of crime information that is newsworthy and understanding how to provide it in a way that captures public attention" (Chermak, 1995, p. 27). This is particularly applicable because the media primarily depend on a police department spokesperson to clarify the newsworthiness of events they have selected from other sources. Police are now considered experts who can comment about an event immediately after it is disclosed. The police play an important role in story production and presentation when deciding what aspects of an incident to downplay or emphasize. In addition, the police department can eliminate a story from media consideration by not releasing information about a crime and promote a favorable view of the department's activities (Chermak, 1995).

Two Examples

There are numerous instances of the NYPD shaping media presentations and public opinion images through the granting of exclusive and extensive interviews for newspapers or magazines widely circulated among opinion makers. One was a far-reaching, comprehensive article in the July 25, 2005 issue of *The New Yorker* written by William Finnegan, which received wide circulation including television and subsequent complementary coverage. This lengthy article was entitled "Defending the City." The subtitle reads, "William Finnegan Reports from Inside the Nation's Most Innovative Counterterrorist Unit—the NYPD" (Finnegan, 2005). Since the magazine was considered a "defining" publication (Browne, 2007), the NYPD considered it a worthwhile gamble to grant this access in order to achieve a positive NYPD image.

Another article based on an exclusive interview was entitled "On the Front Line in the War on Terrorism," by Judith Miller in the summer 2007 issue of the conservative *City Journal*. This article also praised the various facets of the NYPD's antiterrorist efforts. In this case, the favorable view of the NYPD, while more predictable than the other article, gained currency among many opinion makers.

Interestingly enough, the same Judith Miller a few months earlier was given rare access to the department's top officials and important intelligence files in order to counter a series of critical articles by *New York Times* reporter-columnist Jim Dwyer. From August 2004 through April 2007, Dwyer devoted no less than 13 of his pieces to NYPD tactics during the August-September 2004 Republican Convention in New York City. By their titles alone, to say nothing of their virtual exclusive treatment of this subject, these articles stand out from the vast majority of uncritical NYPD media accounts. For example, titles include "Another Convention Arrest Is Undercut by a Videotape" (2005a, May 3), "Police Infiltrate Protests, Videotapes Show" (2005b, December 22), and "Police Surveillance before Convention Was Larger Than Previously Disclosed" (2007b, April 2).

In sharp contrast to Dwyer's pieces, Miller's *Wall Street Journal* article was titled "When Activists Are Terrorists." Miller juxtaposes her analysis with:

... a front-page, 2,500-word article that led the *New York Times* in late March. Based partly on his review of more than 600 pages of the NYPD's still-secret "raw intelligence documents" and "summary digests of observations from both the field and the department's cyberintelligence unit," reporter Jim Dwyer concluded that the NYPD's "R.N.C. Intelligence Squad" had chronicled the views and plans of people who had "no apparent intention of breaking the law". (Miller, 2007)

Miller candidly acknowledges the NYPD eagerness to offer a counter-vailing view:

> Stung by the criticism, Police Commissioner Raymond W. Kelly, David Cohen, the deputy police commissioner for intelligence, and Paul J. Browne, the NYPD press spokesman, outlined in interviews last week the nature of the police's concerns, its conduct, and the goals of its intelligence surveillance effort that they told the *Times* and still argue enabled some 800,000 people to protest peacefully and helped keep New York safe. "The department was indifferent to the political views of the attendees," said Mr. Cohen, a former senior official at the Central Intelligence Agency. "The pre-convention surveillance was aimed solely at maintaining civil order." (Miller, 2007)

Miller contends that part of her analysis rests on exclusive access to top-secret information:

> The 600-plus pages of still-secret intelligence documents that this reporter has also reviewed do list numerous peaceful organizations and individuals planning to attend the protests, including as the *Times* accurately noted, three New York City elected officials, street theater companies, church groups and antiwar organizations, environmentalists, and people opposed to the death penalty and other Republican policies. ... But the material this reporter read does *not* show that the police monitored such peaceful groups and individuals because they opposed their political views, and the police say groups like "Billionaires for Bush" were never infiltrated. Rather, the intelligence documents appear focused mainly on estimating the number and motivations of people who were planning to attend the convention, as well as potential threats to the gathering, its delegates and the police. (Miller, 2007, italics in original)

Suppressing Dissent

Despite its best efforts, the NYPD sometimes confronts negative or potentially negative media coverage. The department often considers the media's reporting of crime at variance with the actual crime rate. According to the department's chief spokesperson, the Deputy Commissioner for Public Information Paul Browne, certain media, particularly the *New York Times,* currently report serious crimes more frequently than in previous years when the crime rate was higher. This strikes the NYPD as irresponsible and counterintuitive—on a logical basis, it does not make sense (Browne, 2007). In the words of the Deputy Commissioner, "The fact is that the incidence of crime remains relatively low. But the way it's covered you wouldn't necessarily know that" (Robertson, 2004, June 24). On the other hand, from the perspective of some of the media (which features "newsworthy" items), because murders are currently rarer events they are more "newsworthy" than in the past when they were more common.

Shaping the public's view of the NYPD takes on sharp edges when the Department identifies reporters, stories, or media that it considers unfair and unfavorable. If criticism is considered unacceptable or sometimes intolerable, then strategic NYPD obstruction is the operative dynamic. For example, with New York City's multiple media outlets and competition for information (despite the decline in traditional newspapers), the NYPD has considerable flexibility to play off one outlet against another.

An in-depth story on the NYPD's chief spokesman Paul Browne relates his notable personal accomplishments. Nevertheless,

The stories told about Mr. Browne among reporters who cover the department are not as favorable but equally compelling. For instance, they like to talk about an incident that occurred last year between *Daily News* reporter Wil Cruz and Sgt. Kevin Hayes at DCPI, the office of public information that Mr. Browne heads. According to reporters, Mr. Cruz was trying to learn the details of a subway stabbing when Sergeant Hayes said something along the lines of "I don't care what you do. Get the fuck out. I'll kick your fucking ass." According to fellow reporters, Mr. Cruz left Mr. Browne messages to complain about the sergeant, but Mr. Browne never got back to him; the matter was allegedly dealt with privately, between Mr. Browne and the *Daily News*. (Mr. Cruz declined to comment about the incident.)

"He knows how to do his job and he does it well," said a former One Police Plaza reporter. "But he's a little bit of a tyrant up there. He keeps the cops upstairs running scared, and the way they treat reporters is a little bit due to the tone he sets. They're just very dismissive and confrontational."

When asked whether Mr. Browne is good at his job, another crime reporter at a daily paper said, "I guess it depends. If you're the police commissioner and you can't stand any negative stories, then I guess he's good at his job. If you're the public and you want to know exactly how the Police Department is reacting to crime, then he's bad at his job."

"Wil is like the teddy bear of cop reporters," said a police reporter who has been covering the department for over a decade. "All he was doing was asking follow-up questions. It just seems like that office is completely unaccountable. I think it's now just Kelly's public-relations arm. ... Browne's job is to protect Kelly. It's not to provide public information."

According to other sources, if the department suspects officers of talking to reporters, they may order what is called a GO-15 (General Order 15)—an interview during which officers must tell the truth or they face termination of employment.

"He would feed stories to one reporter and not another when he was mad at you," said a former shack reporter about Mr. Browne. "And he would not call back if he was mad at a reporter." (Aleksander, 2010)

This pattern was evident in early 2010, when Browne gently reminded a mainstream newspaper reporter, who was writing a story on the NYPD, that the *Wall Street Journal* would soon begin reporting on local crime issues in the newspaper's forthcoming New York City section. This reminder could be interpreted as suggesting greater comparative NYPD access for the *Journal*—a not so subtle nudge toward more favorable mainstream reporting (Personal communication, 2010).

Sure enough, privileged *Wall Street Journal* access emerged during the next two years. For example, for at least seven years commentators have noted the conspicuous absence of an array of non-index crime data from the NYPD's crime reports. These observers have offered evidence of the linkage between the missing data and the downgrading of index crime to non-index crime (Parascandola and Levitt, 2004a, 2004b, 2004c, 2004d; Moses, 2005a, 2005b, 2005c).

Not surprisingly, when the NYPD haltingly responded to these criticisms in 2010, it singled out its latest media ally—the *Wall Street Journal*—to carry its messages. The first *Wall Street Journal* carrier pigeon arrived on the heels of two revelatory *New York Times* articles. The first *Times* article, which appeared on November 1, 2010, provided high visibility to what we and other commentators have noted for years—that the NYPD ceased reporting low-level crime data to New York State since 2002 when Commissioner Kelly took office for the second time despite the fact that this information had been reported to the State Division of Criminal Justice Services since 1978, "long before data analysis was so heavy a staple of crime fighting. ..." (Rivera and Baker, 2010). The NYPD was only one of two of the more than 500 police agencies in New York State that did not report the data.

The article also noted that the NYPD

... for years failed to abide by a city law requiring it to turn over quarterly data on its controversial stop, question and frisk policy. From 2003 to 2007, the department provided stop data to the Council only sporadically and often in incomplete chunks. Not until February 2007 did it begin to comply on a steady basis—but it still did not turn over the raw data which social scientists and others said was necessary to understand. (Rivera and Baker, 2010)

The second *Times* article followed the next month in December with the headline, "Times Sues City Police, Saying Information Has Been Illegally Withheld." The lawsuit claimed that the NYPD "routinely violated" a state law requiring the provision of information to the press and the public. The

Times asserted, "We've become increasingly concerned over the last two years about a growing lack of transparency at the NYPD (Barron, 2010). Among the data requested and denied, the *Times* noted, was

> ... statistics for minor crimes—offenses like misdemeanor thefts and assaults, marijuana possession and sex offenses other than rape. The department acknowledged last month that it has not forwarded the data to the state since 2002. (Barron, 2010)

It took only six days for the NYPD to respond by providing a scoop to the *Wall Street Journal* with a story announcing that the department will soon begin "posting data on citywide misdemeanor crime complaints dating back to 10 years, partly in response to claims that withholding such statistics indicated it had something to hide, officials said" (Gardiner, 2010).

Echoing the party line, a *Wall Street Journal* reporter noted, "NYPD officials have said that the statistics were not forwarded to the State because a new computer system was not compatible with the Department of Criminal Justice Services system" (Gardiner, 2010). No questions were asked as to the reliability of this explanation especially since the department has prided itself as being in the vanguard of computer technology. In addition, had the value of paper reports now escaped the Department's memory bank?

The NYPD–*Wall Street Journal* exclusive pipeline was refueled the following month (January 2011) with the scoop that the NYPD was about to release its statistics for lost property reports (Gardiner, 2011a). Conspicuously absent from this article was any reference to the fact that lost property statistics had not been reported since 2005. Strangely enough, the NYPD embargo on these statistics swiftly followed revelations of the soaring increases in lost property reports between 1997 and 2004 (Moses, 2005c, December 20; Murphy, 2005, December 10). The category of lost property serves as a convenient receptacle for reports that could otherwise be categorized as grand larceny (one of the seven index crimes).

The *Journal* story not only exemplified the NYPD's belated response to long-standing critiques of its lack of transparency but also sought to turn the tables on its critics (particularly Eterno and Silverman). When the *Wall Street Journal* reporter first received these lost property statistics, he contacted us and requested our quick reaction. In a long, protracted conversation, we informed him that the lost property report numbers the NYPD provided him decline every year without any normal statistical fluctuation. Not only does this defy the cyclical nature of crime statistics, but such a decrease directly following the 2005 revelations on lost property reports strongly indicates manipulation. Did people stop losing property immediately after the 2005 revelation? If so, what police intervention against lost property was used? What is the mechanism of this loss if not manipulation?

Clearly, manipulation emerges again as the likely cause. We also noted that while the department did publicly report non-index crime assaults staying flat, the skyrocketing of criminal trespass—another indication of manipulation—was ignored by the NYPD and the *Journal* reporter. Notably, criminal trespass was the crime that Detective Harold Hernandez identified to which rapes were downgraded (see Chapter 2). Beyond all this, we also inquired why nearly half of NYPD written summonses are thrown out of court out of a record number of more than half a million. Why, we asked, are so many summonses increasing when crime is decreasing and yet half of them are discarded? In fact, we also referred to the numerous police tapes documenting suppression and downgrading of crime statistics and the Department's failure to open its books even to Mayor Bloomberg's Commission to Combat Police Corruption.

The *Wall Street Journal* story not only failed to include any of these points but instead concluded that "statistics reviewed by the *Wall Street Journal* don't appear to support the theory" of downgrading (Gardiner, 2011a). Is this a news report or an editorial? In addition, the article implied that Eterno and Silverman were constantly changing the goalposts for NYPD reporting. Quoting the NYPD's chief spokesman, Paul Browne, the *Journal* reporter writes, "There's no reasoning with some chronic critics. I expect next they'll say, Aha the department hasn't disclosed the number of oil changes for police cars" (Gardiner, 2011a).

This is despite the fact that our position has been rock solid from the beginning, also not reported. Further, numerous other sources clearly support our findings that the NYPD manipulated its crime numbers and, more importantly, that there is an urgent need for NYPD transparency. The lack of transparency has permitted a selective NYPD leak of favorable data and claims that our position has changed. Who is really moving the goalposts? By selective release of favorable data, the NYPD seeks to fool an uninformed public.

We communicated our concerns to the reporter regarding the omissions and distortions in his article. His e-mail response was equally unresponsive:

> The editors thought the story I gave them about lost property was too inside baseball and they wanted a story more on the NYPD's stat skeptics dating back in history and now. So points if (sic) yours I had included like Paul's story got edited out so too did references to NYT lawsuits. A lot of stuff did. It's part of the process. I gave them 1,800. I ended up with 800. ... There's no way to include everything we talked about in one newspaper article. (Gardiner, 2011b)

Sadly, no subsequent article presented our position. They remained hidden from *Journal* readers.

Catering to favored reporters is one NYPD tactic. Even more drastic media control measures have been exercised to tame reporters and critics considered less than friendly. Three non-mainstream critical "gadfly" blog-gers sued the NYPD in November 2008 asserting that they were denied press credentials in 2007 "with little explanation or opportunity for appeal." They asserted that the system for issuing press credentials was "inconsistent and constitutionally flawed" (City Room, 2009, January 9). All three bloggers, with prior journalistic practices, previously possessed working press cards but their applications to obtain or renew credentials were denied. In January 2009, the NYPD "relented" and the bloggers were "issued credentials" (City Room, 2009, January 9).

Another example is *Newsday* reporter Leonard Levitt, who for years wrote a weekly column entitled "One Police Plaza" in which he would focus on "inside" NYPD activities and relationships. His columns, based on con-fidential information, often aroused the ire of the NYPD leadership. Former Commissioner Bratton commented on his previous relationship with Levitt:

> He's been in the doghouse from time to time when I was there, but we called it the penalty box. We wouldn't talk to him for a while but then we'd let him out. With the press, you can't control what they write but you try to influence it as best you can. (Kilgannon, 2009, November 8)

Years later, Commissioner Kelly "traveled to *Newsday's* Long Island offices to complain about critical coverage" from Levitt.

> "The New York City police commissioner taking a day off from crime and ter-rorism to spend an afternoon on the Long Island Expressway to drive 60 miles to complain about a reporter?" Mr. Levitt said by phone. "It's unprecedented!" (Aleksander, 2010)

After Levitt left *Newsday* in 2005, he continued his column online. During this period his press pass was rescinded and Levitt "needed the help of civil rights lawyers to regain his press pass after being barred from the building" (Kilgannon, 2009, November 8).

Yet another media control contrivance was attempted in April 2009 when Police Commissioner Kelly informed news organizations that they must leave their working offices at police headquarters by July 31 "in order to make room for a new Joint Operations Center" (Koblin, 2009). This office, known as "the shack," has been occupied by news organizations since the Police Department's headquarters buildings opened in 1973 and has served as the "site of many informal briefings and the traditional base of operations for journalists covering crime and the police" (Chan and Baker, 2009, April 14; Associated Press, 2009, April 14; Weiss, 2009, April 15).

Proximity to police sources is critical to serious and responsible report-ing. This is in sharp contrast to the view of the Deputy Commissioner for

Public Information. "While Mr. Browne said the absence of space for journalists in the building might make the flow of information 'less convenient' for news gathering, he said, 'It will not impede the flow of information'" (Chan and Baker, 2009, April 14). However, this flow would be unidirectional and emanate from only one source: Mr. Browne. The reaction to this clumsy silencing was vociferous and included complaints to Mayor Bloomberg. The typically sympathetic *New York Post* editorialized, "This isn't about special treatment for reporters; if anything it's in the NYPD's best interest to have them on at all times to cover breaking stories and have immediate access to police officials" (Levitt, 2009, April 20). The *Daily News* chimed in: "There is a reason why the Police Department's storied history is so well known. It's because police beat reporters were there to tell the stories" (Levitt, 2009, April 20). The NYPD rescinded its displacement message hours later.

Based on numerous interviews, it is clear that members of the department well understand that they must secure the permission of the Public Information Division before engaging in any communication with the media. Reporters who have worked in other cities have remarked how this policy is at variance with other departments.

This occasional police–media divergence is heightened by the NYPD's belief that public opinion is influenced by the media's recasting of public expectations of acceptable crime rates. The old conventional wisdom, which held police could do little about crime rates, has been turned on its head. Today crime is no longer considered an inevitable result of a host of societal, cultural, racial, ethnic, demographic, and economic issues—the so-called "root causes"—with crime increasing as conditions deteriorate. The fact that the political and police establishment has long claimed credit for New York City's crime decline has somehow escaped the NYPD.

This new "reality" of intensified public expectations places added pressure on the NYPD to discourage dissent in order to cast its crime-fighting operations in the most favorable public light. This translates to enhanced strategies aimed at convincing the public and the media that the police are effective, just, and considerate. Therefore, an important mediating factor between media reports of crime and the public's perception of safety is the public's confidence in the NYPD's ability to combat crime in a respectful manner.

Issues of NYPD credibility periodically emerge as to how well the police handle themselves. In general, the media have historically scrutinized "police promptness, friendliness and fairness" (Dowler, 2003, p. 113). In other words, what have been the civil liberties costs of NYPD strategies used to drive down crime? Even when the media assign the police credit for driving crime down, periodic (albeit diminished), media controversy envelops the manner in which this has been accomplished. This debate centers on such issues as alleged police abuse, stop-and-frisk activities, and civilian complaints. This issue is manifested in media discussions of high-profile cases of alleged police misconduct. Media reports of these events are very important since studies, including those in Los Angeles and New York, have shown that "attitudes toward police dropped considerably following police misconduct incidents, especially among African Americans" (Chermack, McGarrell, and Gruenwald, 2006, p. 263).

Marginalizing Criticism

Although media reports of manipulation and distortion in NYPD crime statistics have periodically emerged in the last several years, they have attracted only sporadic media attention. This includes reports documented below and our previous discussion of this topic (see Silverman, 2001; Eterno, 2003; Eterno and Silverman, 2006). *These accounts have never been subject to any follow-up or systematic, thorough exploration by the NYPD, the media, or the political establishment. Instead, their responses ignored, discounted, or repelled any "offensive" disclosure.*

Reports of Manipulation 2004

Although accounts of misclassification surfaced earlier, 2004 marked a year in which significant reporting first emerged. Ten years after Compstat was introduced in 1994, *Newsday* offered a series of articles depicting alterations in crime reports. The first article, published on March 21, 2004, examined a three-year, 26-percent crime decline in the 50th Precinct.

> Some cops who worked in the 50th precinct, though, say numbers don't tell the whole story. They say the dip, and subsequent 11 percent rise in crime in the first 10 weeks after the precinct commander's departure raises questions about the way crimes were reported under his command. Many in the department, officers as well as supervisors, point to an atmosphere of apprehension in the NYPD since the advent of Compstat, the computerized system used to track crime trends. *Although even the most ardent critics agree Compstat has helped reduce serious crime to levels not seen in four decades, some say that there is such pressure on precinct commanders to keep crime down that some look for ways to reclassify major crimes so rates appears lower.* (Parascandola and Levitt, 2004a, March 21, emphasis added)

The article recounts specific instances of questionable crime reporting. Several of the cases refer to police refusing to take reports, constantly questioning complainants, and downgrading crimes. The former precinct commander was described by his subordinates as "an aggressive commander whose scrutiny sometimes took the form of personally reviewing crime complaints two and three times to determine whether they were felonies, or could be downgraded" (Parascandola and Levitt, 2004a, March 21). Our research has uncovered current occurrences of similar practices.

The day after this article was published, the head of the PBA said he had warned Police Commissioner Kelly that, "officers feared crime statistics at a Bronx precinct were being downgraded" (Parascandola and Levitt, 2004b, March 22). The following day, March 23, the PBA head, Patrick Lynch, called on Kelly to conduct a "thorough, complete and honest" investigation into allegations that precinct commanders were underreporting crime statistics. Lynch said,

> It [downgrading crime] is a truth that is widely known by members of the department and now we have to see if the police commissioner has the courage to face the truth and do what is right for the City of New York. (Parascandola and Levitt, 2004c, March 23)

The NYPD's response to these stories is emblematic of its dual track strategy of obstruction and obfuscation. Instead of addressing the assertion that the pressure for downgrading crime emanates from the top to precinct commanders via the Compstat process, the Deputy Commissioner for Public Information focused on the street officers represented by the PBA. Deputy Commissioner Paul Browne termed the *Newsday* report "inventions" and said it was "baffling that a police union would assert that its own members are failing to suppress crime as effectively as we know they are" (Parascandola and Levitt, 2004c, March 23).

Eight days later, *Newsday* reported an NYPD investigation of the reliability and integrity of a Queens's precinct's crime statistics. Both the head of the PBA and the Sergeants Benevolent Association claimed that these accusations were arising in numerous precincts (Parascandola and Levitt, 2004d, March 31).

Three months later, *Newsday* continued its investigative reporting. A June 18 article dealt with allegations of downgrading criminal complaints in the 105th Precinct (Gardiner and Levitt, 2004, June 18). This was followed by an article on precinct categorization of stolen commercial merchandise by its wholesale cost instead of its retail cost in order to reduce the value of the item and lower the crime rate (Parascandola, 2004, June 27). While these *Newsday* stories are quite revealing, they barely made a ripple throughout the media and political worlds. The *New York Times* published only two stories in 2004 remotely related to the *Newsday* accounts. The first one simply recounts the *Newsday* report of questionable statistics in the 50th Precinct adding that "about a half dozen precinct commanders have been accused of cooking their books since 1994, when the department introduced new accountability measures" (Dewan, 2004, March 24).

The other *Times* 2004 article, reporting on the 2003 FBI crime statistics for New York City, noted the Mayor's and the police union's disagreement on the authenticity of the statistics.

> The PBA has charged that precinct commanders feel such intense pressure to drive down crime that they "cook the books," reducing the severity of crimes on paper to avoid recording them among the seven index crimes reported to the FBI. (Rashbaum, 2004, May 25)

Once again, Mayor Bloomberg offered a disingenuous response: "Let's get serious; it's an insult to the people in this city. These are FBI numbers; do you really think someone is going to falsify these numbers?" (Rashbaum, 2004, May 25). This response, of course, ignores the fact that the FBI receives its statistics from the reporting cities—in this case, New York City.

Throughout the remainder of 2004, the *Daily News* offered only one article devoted to the controversy raised by the *Newsday* articles. The article repeats the union leader's contention that commanders "are forced to falsify stats in order to maintain the appearance of a drastic reduction in crime." Similarly, the article duplicates the NYPD official characterization of the allegations—"invented stories of crime data suppression." However, the article did add an attack that was employed against our findings six years later. "Our police officers have made New York the safest city in America. Only the PBA disagrees," said Paul Browne, the NYPD's top spokesman (McPhee, 2004). Who would know better whether the numbers are accurate, the person sitting in his office working to protect the department's image or the people in the field who actually generate those numbers?

The *New York Post* followed the same path as the *Daily News* in its single 2004 story on the *Newsday* revelations. Repeating the union's call for a city-wide investigation, the *Post* quoted Paul Browne's response: "It is baffling that a police union would assert that its own members are failing to suppress crime as effectively as we know they are" (Messing, 2004, March 24). Not only does this resurrect the Eterno–Silverman analogy, but also it is comparable to Bratton's 2010 op ed criticism of us.

> I have a hard time understanding why the Captain's Endowment is defending the findings of a study that compromises their own membership's accomplishments by casting aspersions on both their integrity and their crime statistics. (Messing, 2004, March 24)

It is worth noting that Paul Browne served as Deputy Commissioner for Public Information in 2004 and 2010. It is not surprising to hear the same refrain from the same conductor. This line of reasoning from Browne and Bratton fails to acknowledge upper echelon directives guiding such practices, not the CEA or PBA who try to protect their membership.

As noted previously, the PBA was one of the few voices that entered the public domain in protest of Compstat. Its summer 2004 magazine included a brief article entitled "The Trouble with Compstat." This piece resonates with the opinions of our survey respondents and interviewees six years later.

> It was a great idea that has been corrupted by human nature. The Compstat program that made NYPD commanders accountable for controlling crime has degenerated into a situation where the police leadership presses subordinates to keep numbers low by any means necessary. The department's middle managers will do anything to avoid being dragged onto the carpet at the weekly Compstat meetings. They are, by nature, ambitious people who lust for promotions, and rising crime rates won't help anybody's career.
>
> So how do you fake a crime decrease? It's pretty simple. Don't file reports, misclassify crimes from felonies to misdemeanors, under-value the property lost to crime so it's not a felony, and report a series of crimes as a single event.
>
> A particularly insidious way to fudge the numbers is to make it difficult or impossible for people to report crimes—in other words, make the victims feel like criminals so they walk away just to spare themselves further pain and suffering. (Zink, 2004)

Despite these allegations, the isolated *Newsday* stories, and the call for citywide investigations, none ensued and no political body called for an inquiry, nor did any other media outlet follow up on the *Newsday* stories.

Reports of Manipulation 2005

In 2005, a similar pattern of solid investigative reporting was either ignored or downplayed by the NYPD, the media, and the political establishment. The first significant 2005 article appeared in the *Village Voice* in March.

> It's been a year now since an extraordinary event occurred in local police annals: The heads of the Patrolmen's Benevolent Association and the Sergeants Benevolent Association charged publicly that the police department had cooked the books on crime statistics. Maybe you missed the news about the outcry that followed—the hasty audits, the City Council investigations, the criminal probes, the corruption commission hearings. But if you've missed all that, it's not your fault: There hasn't been any outcry. No comptroller audits. No City Council investigation. Nothing to date from the city's Commission to Combat Police Corruption. (Moses, 2005a, March 22)

In October 2005, Paul Moses, a Brooklyn College journalism professor, followed up with an in-depth analysis, which revealed that assault victims in New York City hospitals increased dramatically in four of the last five previous years in sharp contrast to the plunging number of assaults the NYPD reported. These findings again called into question the authenticity of the NYPD's crime statistics (Moses, 2005b, October 25).

Two months later, Moses analyzed the number of lost property reports filed with the NYPD from 1997 to 2004. He found an increase of 44 percent with half of that increase occurring in the last two years. This was additional substantiation of anecdotal reports—that police were converting traditional grand larceny or other property crime to the "lost property" category, which is not included as an index crime (Moses, 2005c, December 20).

In the same issue of the *Village Voice,* Jarrett Murphy recorded his laborious and time-consuming "Kafka"-like effort to overcome NYPD obstacles and file a complaint report for his stolen wallet. His experience mirrors the accounts of others who reported NYPD resistance to the filing of police complaint reports (Murphy, 2005, December 10). Our research confirms these reports.

These 2005 revelations once again failed to gain the attention of the mainstream media and the political establishment, no less the NYPD. Instead, the stories were ignored, cavalierly dismissed, or repelled. A search of the archives of the *New York Times, Daily News,* and the *Post* did not uncover a single article in which reporters raised issues or analyzed charges of crime misclassification.

The few 2005 news articles that touched upon this issue focus on the Mayor's Commission to Combat Police Corruption attempt to analyze the integrity of the NYPD statistics. The panel's chairman, Mark P. Pomerantz, a respected former federal prosecutor, testified before the City Council's Public Safety Committee that the NYPD was not responsive to its data requests on this issue and other issues, such as fraudulent claims for police overtime and sexual misconduct and domestic violence by officers. Since the Commission was stymied by the NYPD's withholding of information, Mr. Pomerantz requested City Council authorization for subpoena power, which the Mayor did not support. In discussing the NYPD, "Pomerantz said that such disputes had been common during his 18 months as chairman of the six-member panel. Mayor Michael R. Bloomberg appointed him to the post in August 2003" (Rashbaum, 2005, April 19). Neither the *News* nor the *Post* reported on Pomerantz's testimony before the City Council. The *News* did join the *Times* in reporting on Pomerantz's resignation three days after his testimony. All three newspapers very briefly reported on the appointment of Pomerantz's successor in June.

Taken as a composite, the mainstream daily newspapers paid scant attention to the issue of statistical manipulation during all of 2005. Furthermore, their avoidance of investigative reporting empowered the NYPD. Thus, it is no surprise that the Mayor and the City Council's Public Safety Committee Chair, in addition to the NYPD, were unsupportive of the Commission's request for subpoena power.

The NYPD's refusal to release information to a Mayoral agency parallels its resistance to honor Freedom of Information requests. In January 2002, Moses sought to assess the validity of allegations of crime statistics manipulation. In order to accomplish this, Moses filed a Freedom of Information request for:

> A precinct-by-precinct breakdown for complaints in all categories of crimes, both index and non-index. The goal was to spot precincts where crimes were being shifted into non-index categories—in broad terms, where misdemeanor complaints were rising even as felonies dropped. I had somehow gotten the idea that the Freedom of Information Law would get more respect in Michael Bloomberg's police department than in Giuliani's. (Moses, 2005a, March 22)

Moses encountered repeated resistance. Despite numerous phone calls, he finally received information three years later, but this incomplete information was "already publicly available in a NYPD report available in the Municipal Reference Library. Rather than appeal that decision, I filed a new and more specific request in 2005. No luck with that either" (Moses, 2011).

In his January 2005 letter to the NYPD, Moses wrote:

> The Police Department has responded to my FOIL request No. 2002-PL-0108 by sending a computer disk that did not have the information I requested. I've enclosed a copy of the original request.
>
> I asked for the total number of *each* reported offense, annually from 1993 to 2001, precinct by precinct. I noted in my request, by way of example, that this would include the number of attempted burglaries in each precinct.
>
> The data I was sent earlier this month does not provide numbers for *each* offense: It gives the seven index crimes, a broad category of "other felonies" and a single figure for all misdemeanors. There was no data for 1993-1994. All of the data the department released is already publicly available.
>
> After three years, I am yet unable to get access to statistical data that clearly should be disclosed under the statute. I ask that the department respond to me by Feb. 16 with either the data I've requested or a denial of my request. After that date, I will file an appeal. (Moses, 2005d, January 25, emphasis in original)

In June and August 2005, Moses filed his next FOIL requests which were "narrower, more specific requests" (Moses, 2005e, June 14). On September 9, Moses sent a copy of the request noting that he had not received a reply to this request which he "mailed out more than five weeks ago" (Moses, 2005f, September 9).

In 2010, Moses further pursued his quest for data with two requests:

> The first was aimed at reports of specific non-index crimes. (What I did was find out which NY statutes constituted each of the 7 index crimes, and then I asked for the lower-level, non-index versions of those offenses.) The second asked for the data on non-index offenses that was previously released to the

State Division of Criminal Justice Services, and included a list of those categories. Both requests were denied quickly. I appealed the second request, on the state-related data.

The NYPD did not respond to the appeal (in violation of the statute) until, many months later, it posted data for non-index crimes on its Web site (as a result of a *Times* lawsuit, apparently). Then, I got a brief e-mail referring me to the department's Web site. (Moses, 2011)

The NYPD's lack of transparency and the political establishment's resistance to oversight has a long history. Even when Mayor Giuliani first formed the Mayor's Commission to Combat Police Corruption in 1995, it was created as the lesser of oversight "evils." In 1993, the Mollen Commission raised serious questions about the NYPD's ability to monitor itself and recommended an independent body with subpoena power. At that time, the City Council Speaker, Peter Vallone, was far more independent of Giuliani than his counterpart was during Mayor Bloomberg's tenure. In 1995, the Council created an independent investigative monitoring body with subpoena power. Mayor Giuliani vetoed the bill on the grounds that it would have too much power, would duplicate the work of the district attorneys (who were also opposed), and would violate the separation of power.

When the City Council overrode his veto, the Mayor took the Council to court and set up his own agency—the Commission to Combat Police Corruption. This agency was a vastly stripped down, subpoena-less version of the Council's oversight agency. In June 1995, a State Supreme Court Justice ruled that the City Council had overstepped its authority by creating an independent body to monitor police corruption. The Mayor's Commission became the operative agency. It was his to create and his to render ineffective.

2010

Fast-forward to 2010. How much further has New York advanced toward greater oversight of the NYPD and transparency within the organization? We believe events since 2004 and culminating in 2011 have only fortified the NYPD's barricades. This view rests on the NYPD's virtually unmarred record of ignoring and deflecting mounting evidence of statistical manipulation. New York City's dormant and defensive mainstream media and political establishment has only reinforced the NYPD's stonewall.

Prior to 2010, the accounts of statistical adjustments are typically portrayed as sporadic and scattered and hence never linked or thoroughly investigated. In May 2006, the former commanding officer of the 105th Precinct was demoted after revelations of downgrading crime and "infiltrating the department's Compstat program to increase archived crime numbers for his precinct from before he arrived there" (Celona and Kadison, 2006, May 8).

This revelation of infiltrating Compstat's archived numbers is quite staggering and calls for disciplined inquiry. Unfortunately, this topic did not arise in any of the mainstream media papers.

The only follow up occurred a month later in a local Queens newspaper, which reported that the Community Board Chairwoman, Betty Braton, subsequently questioned the accuracy of the precinct's Compstat crime figures. "Braton explained that she had sent a letter to Police Commissioner Kelly expressing her concern over the manipulation of the statistics. She requested that Kelly offer new, accurate crime numbers for the precinct" (Geffon, 2006, June 8). This account was not followed up by any of the major newspapers. This conspiracy of silence makes it next to impossible for any inquiry to acquire traction and mobilize reform.

Enter Schoolcraft

Compared to previous years, the beginning of 2010 marked the outset of a decidedly more focused challenge to the integrity of the NYPD's crime statistics. Heavily documented accusations were first revealed in a series of *Daily News* articles, which disclosed charges of statistical manipulation to improve crime figures in Brooklyn's Bedford Stuyvesant's 81st Precinct. The articles reported on the allegations of police officer Adrian Schoolcraft as well as crime victims that the precinct recorded felonies as misdemeanors and sometimes refused to take crime complaints. The first two articles appeared on February 2, 2010 with nine additional articles in the period up to August 23, 2010 (Parascandola, 2010a–2010j).

At virtually the same time, the *New York Times* reported on our department-wide research on unethical statistical manipulation, which strongly paralleled reports from the 81st Precinct, which could hardly be labeled idiosyncratic (Rashbaum, 2010, February 7). The next day, the *New York Post* reported on a series of revisions in crime statistics. A 23-year veteran was "busted for reclassifying 23 grand larceny felonies as petite larceny misdemeanors in early 2008." The article cites other examples of "a growing chorus of complaints—including those from *Post* interviews with dozens of officers and a new survey of retired captains [our survey]—allege that the pressure of Compstat leads precinct bosses to downgrade major crimes to minor offenses" (Messing, Celona, and Fanelli, 2010, February 7).

Shortly thereafter, the *Daily News* articles were strongly reinforced with a series of well-documented *Village Voice* articles that were buttressed with excerpts from Schoolcraft's secretly recorded audiotapes of precinct roll calls and other police meetings. From May 4 to August 23, 2010, reporter Graham Rayman wrote 11 articles that explored, in detail, the issues of manipulated crime statistics and arrest and stop-and-frisk quotas (Rayman, 2010a–2010k)

As powerful as these *News* and *Voice* articles were, the overall media response was aimless, docile, and muted. The *Daily News* reported on the *Voice* tapes stories with one brief article. The *Post* (with the exception of its February 8 story noted previously) was remarkably silent. Only a brief July 31 article, while failing to mention the *Voice,* alluded to its revelations in a story of an Internal Affairs' sting of trumped up police charges against one individual.

> It's the latest black eye for the 81st Precinct in Bedford-Stuyvesant, which is under investigation for pushing cops to make arrests for petty crimes as well as fudging stats to downgrade the more serious ones.
>
> Internal Affairs began investigating the 81st Precinct after an officer there made allegations that bosses were telling cops to intentionally downgrade crimes to make their statistics look better. (Celona and Perone, 2010)

The *Times* treatment was amazingly low-key as it waited until June to report on the NYPD's downgrading of sexual assaults (Eligon, 2010). The article did not mention the *Voice,* Rayman, or the NYPD tapes series. The *Times* finally referenced the *Voice* articles in a story focusing on a clash between Commissioner Kelly and City Councilman Albert Vann.

> But behind the showdown, which was brief and vague, lies a months-long controversy involving charges of manipulated crime reports, quotas, the department's street-stop tactics and several instances of questionable police behavior—an array of provocative charges being met with a blanket response from a department that says it is broadly investigating.
>
> A tipping point for Mr. Vann came last month, after *The Village Voice* published transcripts of audio recordings of what it said were stationhouse conversations made by an officer in the 81st Precinct, in Bedford-Stuyvesant, Brooklyn, that laid bare what the newspaper's report characterized as a pattern of pressure exerted by commanders there onto the precinct's rank-and-file officers. (Baker, 2010)

On August 10, 2010, Schoolcraft filed a $50 million lawsuit against the City of New York and high-ranking members of the NYPD. This lawsuit details the NYPD's "illegal quota policy for the issuance of summonses and arrests and instructions to police officers to lie on police reports in order to distort COMPSTAT statistics" (Schoolcraft complaint, 2010).

The sweep and breadth of the charges embodied in the Schoolcraft lawsuit vis-à-vis the NYPD did not attract the media attention it surely warranted. While the *Village Voice* provided appropriate coverage of the lawsuit, neither the *Times* nor the *Post* devoted any attention to this newsworthy event. The *News* offered only a brief account of this event (Parascandola, 2010j, August 10). *New York Magazine* carried a two-paragraph account of the lawsuit (*Tiku,* 2010).

Interestingly enough, *The Chief/Civil Service Leader* offered a comprehensive presentation on the lawsuit and the allegations that lie behind it (Toor, 2010, August 20). While this article is admirable, an editorial in the same day's *Chief* also raised this major issue but at the same time regrettably missed sight of its implications.

> The biggest complaint about Compstat ... is that it leads some commanders to bend if not break the rules to ensure that they aren't giving bad news to department brass.
>
> There are worse things, however, than an upward tilt in crime figures, as should be obvious to Police Commissioner Ray Kelly and Mayor Bloomberg by the fact that jumps in several key felony categories this year have not provoked an avalanche of public criticism. ("NYPD Crime Story," 2010, August 20)

So far, so good. The editorial, however, then not only defers to the NYPD to sort things out, but urges the NYPD (instead of some independent agency) to determine if these practices are unique to the single precinct.

> The misconduct described by Mr. Schoolcraft, and in some key respects the corroborating evidence already available, amply fit the definition of "worse things." What matters now is that the department makes a genuine attempt at determining whether the problem extends beyond one precinct and then adjusts policy accordingly. ("NYPD Crime Story," 2010, August 20)

This editorial drops the ball when all the evidence points to the impact of Compstat throughout the whole department. It is illogical to assume that Compstat's underbelly resides in only one precinct. Furthermore, the typical NYPD defense of irregularities is that they are isolated and not widespread, aka the rotten apple theory. Only infrequently does a non-major newspaper raise this issue. In January 2011, the *Staten Island Advance*, citing our research, decried the NYPD's failure to release "precinct by precinct statistics on traffic deaths, injuries and summonses." The editorial concluded, "Honesty and transparency are what's required in the reporting of police statistics, not stonewalling" (Staten Island Advance, 2011, January 10). In sum, then, the combination of absent and deferential media only empowers the NYPD.

Quiescent Political Establishment

Rivaling the dormant press, the tranquility of the city's political leadership has been equally revealing. A day after the first *News* article on Schoolcraft appeared, Councilman and Public Safety Committee Chair Peter Vallone, Jr. (D-Queens) stated forcefully, "Crime numbers should never be manipulated. If there were credible allegations made by police officers who would testify, it would be something we would seriously consider holding hearings on" (Parascandola, 2010a, February 2).

Despite the subsequent *Times* report of our findings and the numerous *Voice* articles, Vallone never followed through on his expressed concern. This Vallone is the son of Peter Vallone, the former Speaker of the Council who fought for greater NYPD transparency and independent oversight despite Mayor Giuliani's objections.

In the case of Peter Vallone, Jr., the son, up to this point, has not lived up to his father's significant legacy. Further confirmation of the son's diminutive determination emerged in January 2011 after Commissioner Kelly announced the appointment of three former federal prosecutors to review the department's internal crime reporting system in the "face of questions over whether crime statistics have been manipulated to cast the New York Police Department in a positive light" (Baker and Rashbaum, 2011, January 5). Councilman Vallone's response to the formation of this new committee speaks volumes.

> However, Peter F. Vallone Jr., the chairman of the City Council's public safety committee, had been gathering evidence for months to hold his own hearing on the subject, and said he now would wait until the panel had reached its conclusions.
>
> "I believe that the statistics were in fact being manipulated," Mr. Vallone said. "I have spoken to many current and former police officers who unfortunately refused to go on the record but who have corroborated that fact. And I've spoken to many civilians whose valid complaints were not accepted by the Police Department." (Baker and Rashbaum, 2011, January 5)

So, almost a year after first publicly raising the possibility of hearings on the NYPD's crime statistics, the chair of the City Council's Public Safety Commission procrastinated with yet another meaningless declaration of possible exploration. Furthermore, since the Commissioner's Committee lacks subpoena power and its own independent staff, its ability to assess the reliability of the city's crime statistics is severely hampered. Therefore, given the likelihood of a favorable Committee report, there is scant possibility that Mr. Vallone will subsequently investigate this issue *even though he is apparently aware of manipulation*. Nor are there reasons to believe that other governmental bodies will provide an independent analysis of the crime statistics. The department's chief spokesman "Mr. Browne added that to his knowledge, no outside inquiry—such as by a prosecutor's office or other government agency—into the department's crime-reporting systems existed" (Baker and Rashbaum, 2011, January 5).

The ducking and weaving of governmental bodies has not been lost on the Department's rank-and-file. Responding to Mr. Vallone's continuous contemplation of hearings, many officers appended their comments to newspaper stories. One officer observed, "Anyone who can't bring the numbers we need will be replaced by someone who can" (Muessig, 2010, February 2). Another stated:

> Wait till they find out that cops arrest homeless people and charge them with whatever crime the precinct is low on for the month to make COMPSTAT numbers look good. The whole system is shit. This whole Vallone inquiry is bullshit. He is part of the reason why this thing occurs. The city has bullshit laws; the politicians pressure the Police Commissioner to enforce them. He then turns to the Precinct Commanding Officers to enforce these laws. They then turn to the Lieutenants and Sergeants to pressure cops into making arrests and writing summonses or else they get "punished." Shit rolls downhill. So glad I left all that bullshit. (Muessig, 2010, February 2)

Mr. Vallone's long-standing vacillation apparently has been less than surprising to police officers. When he first announced he was considering hearings a year earlier, his declarations were met astutely with disbelief by cops.

> Councilman Vallone wants to have hearings with the rest of the blowhards at city hall but he needs cops to come forward and testify before the city council. How honorable and noble of you to offer. This guy is an attorney. Hey Peter did you see what happened to Officer Schoolcraft? They forced him into the psych-ward for coming forward. Do you really expect us to think that you really care? The NYPD has been fudging numbers since you became the chair of the public safety committee eight years ago. You did nothing then and will do nothing now. (Parascandola, 2010c, February 3)

Another officer offered his reaction:

> Where there is smoke there is fire!!! Ever been to the NYPD's COMPSTAT meeting? There is reason for Police Precinct Commanders to get creative in JUKING the stats! (Parascandola, 2010c, February 3)

Cynicism was the prevailing reaction of all commentators.

> Wow, Should we be shocked? No ... Convenient the Mayor is now in his third term he has nothing to worry about crime is down and he rode that statement all the way through ... Cooking the books ain't nothing new at all ... Watch Season 3 of *The Wire* on HBO when the Commanding Officers get hammered about their numbers ... Let's see how far this goes before this story goes cold ... Politician has nothing else to sell the voters but to say crime is down..!!! (Parascandola, 2010c, February 3)

Similarly, another observer wrote:

> Peter Vallone is just like Bloomberg, out of touch with reality. So many cases of fudging numbers have occurred yet no one has done anything about it.

Vallone wants to grab headlines, but mark my word, he doesn't dare open that can of worms. Because, like the rest of the members of the city council, he doesn't want to draw any attention his way. (Parascandola, 2010c, February 3)

Conclusion—Conflicting Forces

At this writing (November 2011), the complex relationships among the NYPD, the media, and the political establishment remains unstable. Conflicting forces are at play and it is not clear which will triumph.

The NYPD Approach

The NYPD embraces positive news and repels unfavorable accounts. *NYPD media strategy is based on the premise that the public's view of safety is in large part based on their confidence in the department.* To ensure confidence in public safety and the police, the NYPD, like all law enforcement agencies, employs strategies that are tailored to the particular city and particular media.

New York City is unique. More than being the largest city in the United States, it is the media capital of the United States with its print, radio, and television outlets. This being the case, the NYPD receives extensive (primarily favorable) attention with reports featuring crime control, anti-terrorism efforts, and the department's role around the world because New York is central to so much of what happens in the United States. Furthermore, there are numerous sympathetic television and Hollywood movie portrayals of the NYPD. This extraordinary coverage is heightened by the fact that the NYPD is by far the largest municipal police force in the country (currently 34,000 sworn officers). Hence, the NYPD draws a great deal of interest not only for its location, but also by virtue of its sheer size, publicized crime reduction record, and its post September 11, 2001 role in combating terrorism.

The multiplicity of media outlets (although significantly fewer than decades ago) permits selective NYPD leaks to those who are more disposed to a favorable NYPD image. In addition, NYPD public spokespersons appear on radio and television programs, which may be politically at odds with the city's police force. Interviews and press conferences are an effective way for departments to announce innovative programs, accomplishments, and arrest statistics.

Recent events, however, sporadically challenge the NYPD's ascendancy in the management of its public relations and public perceptions. The cumulative effect of the numerous accounts of statistical manipulations discussed previously is unknown. In addition, the Schoolcraft case and lawsuit are still unfolding with many facets still unidentified. New stories are continually spilling out. An August 25, 2010 *Voice* article revealed, for example, another officer's secretly taped recordings of precinct crime downgrading (Rayman, 2010l).

In addition, a cascade of unfavorable and discrediting media revelations has recently emerged. These numerous media accounts include excessive stop and frisks, planting of drugs, gun smuggling, unlawful detentions, ticket fixing, excessive force, quotas and the manner in which the Occupy Wall Street protestors were removed from Zuccotti Park.

The media raised "profound, displeasure, disappointment and concern" regarding the manner in which the NYPD restricted coverage of the removal of OWS protestors. A November 21, 2011 *New York Times* letter (also signed by representatives of the *New York Post*, the *Daily News*, the Associated Press, WNBC TV, Dow Jones, Reporters Committee for Freedom of the Press, the National Press Photographers Association, Thomas Reuter, WABC TV, New York Press Photographers Association, WCBS TV and the New York Press Club) to Paul Browne, the NYPD Deputy Commissioner of Public Information) detailed specific incidents where "credentialed media were identified, segregated and kept away from viewing, reporting on and photographing vital manners of public concern." The letter documents "numerous instances where police officers struck or otherwise intentionally impeded photographers as they were taking photos, keeping them from doing their job and from documenting instances of seeming police aggression."(Freeman, G. 2011, November 21)

The Media

Will the media's legitimate protestations regarding the rights of a free press spill over into an equivalent concern for accurate crime statistics and the rights of victims victimized by the NYPD's statistical legerdemain? Will these accounts ever so slightly disturb the close association with the Mayor, the Police Department, and the media's business ownership? It is understandable that a great deal has been invested in the media's long heralded storyline of a glorious and uninterrupted run of tumbling crime rates. NYPD crime statistics constitute the uncontested foundation of this story and reporters have showcased these figures for many years. In addition, reporters are not usually trained to examine numbers and have shared with us the alliance between certain editors and the NYPD. Will editors drift away from their close allegiance to the NYPD and urge reporters to peek behind and examine official crime statistics instead of accepting them at face value?

Thus far, it is difficult to unearth any evidence of a significant shift in media attention. In fact, a *New York Daily News* editorial seized upon the Police Commissioner's appointment of a committee to examine its crime reporting as another opportunity to assail Eterno and Silverman (*Daily News*, 2011, January 8).

This *Daily News* mockery of our research does not even pretend to have an open mind. Its preordained conclusions that all is well with New York's crime statistics permeate all its editorials and offer little hope of subsequent in-depth *News* inquiries. Thus far, there is unfortunately little promise of full-scale coverage of crime statistics emanating from other sources.

How about the system the NYPD utilizes to drive its crime statistics? Will Compstat's veneration by outsiders also continue to go unchallenged? NYPD former transparency has clouded up since *Time* magazine's 1996 observation: "Compstat has become the Lourdes of policing, drawing pilgrim cops from around the world ... for a taste of New York's magic" (Pooley, 1996, pp. 5, 6). For the last several years, however, Compstat meetings have been virtually closed to anyone who is not a member of the NYPD. As a result, law enforcement officials, regardless of rank or city or country, are generally no longer welcome. Transparency has been dealt another blow.

The Political Establishment

The NYPD has been further empowered by a dormant political establishment. What will it take to embolden any member of the political establishment to challenge the NYPD's monopoly on all things crime? Of course, it is unreasonable to expect Mayor Bloomberg to address candidly the reliability of crime statistics because he has continually trumpeted the NYPD's crime reduction "success." At a minimum, the data-driven Mayor can politically ill afford to acknowledge the possibility of bogus crime statistics for reasons that extend beyond their frequent linkage with proclamations of New York as the "safest big city" and the resultant allure to tourism and business. As we noted earlier, questions of skewed crime data could easily raise strong doubts regarding "the reliability of data underpinning policy decisions on the budget, education, transportation, health and other issues" (Chen, 2010, February 9).

On the other hand, perhaps the Mayor can urge the NYPD, without admitting any past mischief, to now honor Compstat's first and most important step—accurate and timely information—in its four-step mantra. After all, without accurate and timely information, effective crime fighting is hampered. In other words, will the NYPD realize that, in their drive to deceptively distort crime reduction successes, they are hindering its attainment?

If the NYPD and the Mayor continue to remain inactive, will other political actors ever step up and fulfill their official roles? For example, there is the City Council, its Speaker, the Committee on Public Safety and its Chair, Peter Vallone, Jr. Thus far, only a handful of council members have called for any kind of hearing. The Speaker has been silent and Councilman Vallone, despite protestations to the contrary, has not exercised any oversight on this issue. In fact, he has been resolutely inconsistent on this issue.

What is quite clear, however, is Vallone's close affinity for the positions advanced by Commission Kelly, Mayor Bloomberg, the *News,* and the *Post.* Take, for example, the controversy surrounding a July 2010 New York State law that prohibited the NYPD from maintaining personal information in electronic databases on those stopped and frisked by police but not arrested with recent tallying approximately 94 percent of stops.

Kelly commented on this law saying,

> Albany has robbed us of a great crime-fighting tool, one that saved lives. Without it, there will be, inevitably, killers and other criminals who won't be captured as quickly or perhaps ever. They'll be free to threaten our neighborhoods longer than they would have been otherwise. (Dicker, 2010)

Mayor Bloomberg chimed in, "We didn't lose. The people who are going to lose are the victims" (Seidman and Sutherland, 2010, July 17). The *New York Post* editorial echoed, "One new state law forcing cops to ditch a database of suspects halted under stop-and-frisk is sure to send crime rates higher" ("Glimpse of Dodge City," 2010, August 11).

Not to be outdone, a *Daily News* editorial cited NYPD statistics:

> By barring the department from entering names and addresses into an electronic file, the new law will also prevent the police from using the information to identify witnesses to crimes, as well as potential perpetrators. In the last 18 months, police say, the data have contributed to 170 arrests, including for murders, robberies and burglaries. ("Does Not Compute," 2010, July 23)

Councilman Vallone's opinion was a mirror image: "Albany also cut an extremely useful NYPD database used to apprehend criminals quickly" (Vallone, 2010, August 5).

Perhaps this history explains Vallone's tepid reaction to Commissioner Kelly's appointment of a crime reporting committee. Of course, the fact that Kelly and Vallone, in the words of the press, "generally agree on law enforcement issues" may provide some explanation (DiStefano, 2011). This compatibility spilled over to the Commissioner's drum playing participation in an ensemble including Vallone in celebration of the latter's 50th birthday. Videos of this joint concert were shared with the public (Queens Campaigner, 2011).

City agencies with oversight responsibilities have also retreated into the woodwork. Based on history, one should not expect any District Attorney's office to get involved. The Mayoral Commission to Combat Police Corruption, created in 1995, has been defanged. Even when the Commission dares to critique the NYPD, its comments are couched in the most defensive of terms. For example, in its 2011 Annual Report, the Commission observes in a footnote:

> There were three other cases where the respondents were charged with caus-ing false entries to be made in Department records. Each respondent prepared between 17 and 20 summonses with fictitious information. For this mis-conduct, the respondents were placed on dismissal probation and forfeited between 60 and 80 penalty days. Although based on the changes, it appeared that more severe penalties were warranted, because the Commission had incomplete paperwork, it cannot evaluate the adequacy of the imposed penal-ties. (Commission, 2011, p. 22)

The Commission did not explain why it had "incomplete paperwork." Nor did it recount any Commission attempt to secure it from the NYPD and any possible response from the Department. Are we left to conclude that the Commission can only obtain information that the NYPD deems to grant it, even if this information is within the Commission's prescribed ambit?

In addition, the main body of the report omits one of its most important findings, which can only be found as a postscript to the report under the heading of "Future Projects."

> The Commission is in the process of compiling data for a report it expects to publish in 2011. Over the last two years, the Commission has observed an increase in false statement allegations against officers for perjuring them-selves in court, signing false documents under oath, or lying during their offi-cial Department interviews and interviews with other investigative bodies, including CCRB. (Commission, 2011, p, 29)

If the Commission has observed this increase in "false statement allega-tions" for the past two years, why is it only now preparing a report that "it expects to publish in 2011?" The Commission can scarcely be considered an oversight body of substance.

The Civilian Review Complaint Board offers no more hope for mean-ingful NYPD scrutiny of crime statistics although it has begun to look into stop-and-frisks. The Board restricts its focus to individual citizen complaints and so ignores the forest for the trees. The private nonprofit civic Citizens Crime Commission publicly requested that the NYPD release its semian-nual audits of precinct crime statistics after our survey was first publicized in the February 2010 *New York Times* article. The Commission's president, Richard Aborn, stated that our study "raises deeply troubling questions" (Edroso, 2010, February 16). Since this statement was issued, the Commission remained silent (including on its web site) on this matter for almost two years when in November 2011 it noted that "a repeated course of conduct dem-onstrating an unwillingness to comply with proper demands for data have once again brought into focus the question of sufficient independent oversight of the NYPD." (Citizens Crime Commission, 2011). The prospects for review on the state and federal levels are also dim, as no agency has publicly addressed this issue.

The Future

In the final analysis, the relationship between the NYPD and the media is often a guarded, cautious relationship because both parties need each other yet are wary of one another. It is interesting to note that the NYPD's Deputy Commissioner for Public Information, as with other law enforcement and government public information officials, is quite familiar with former U.K. Prime Minister Tony Blair's final speech in which he decried the media as "driven by impact" to the detriment of accurate reporting. With the advent of the Internet and cable news' 24-hour cycle, the media face such immense pressure and competition that they are no longer "masters of this change" but rather "in many ways the victims" (Blair, 2007). With competition as a dominant issue, truth and accuracy in reporting often take second place to making an "impact" in terms of their reporting. This approach to reporting is often referred to by the NYPD chief spokesperson as "gotcha reporting" whereby the media is most interested in making an impact by uncovering public wrongdoings (Browne, 2007, September 9).

This NYPD perspective appears to influence greatly the Department's dealing with the media. Thus far, it has been very effective in terms of protecting the Department's image. The media appears frozen on the issue of accurate crime statistics. The freeze is both self- and externally induced. One thing is certain: if the media eventually thaws on this and other issues we have raised, the resulting river of negative police behaviors will fill an ocean.

References

Aleksander, I. (2010, September 21). "Spinning the NYPD," *The New York Observer*, http://www.observer.com/2010/daily-transom/spinning-nypd-paul-browne-may-have-more-do-how-new-yorkers-view-their-city-anyone.

"Anti-Cop Idiocy." (2010, February 21). Editorial, *New York Post*, http://www.nypost.com/p/news/opinion/editorials/anti_cop_idiocy_hF4IkjAA0Zna2xm1KU0EXM.

"Arrest NYPD Bashing: Running Numbers Racket with Crime Fighting Statistics." (2010, October 3). Editorial, *Daily News*, http://www.nydailynews.com/opinions/2010/10/03/2010-10-03_arrest_nypd_bashing.html.

Associated Press. (2009, April 14). "NYPD Boots Reporters out of Headquarters," *New York Post*, http://www.nypost.com/p/news/regional/nypd_boots_reporters_out_of_headquarters_sRf7RJNx6IXEAqRjN4jWpL.

Baker, A. (2010, June 3). "City Police Commissioner and Councilman Clash," *New York Times,* http://www.nytimes.com/2010/06/04/nyregion/04precinct. html?ref=nyregion.

Baker, A. and Rashbaum, W. (2011, January 5). "New York City to Examine Reliability of its Crime Reports," *New York Times,* http://www.nytimes.com/2011/01/06/ nyregion/06crime.html.

Barbaro, M. (2011, March 1). "Bloomberg Testing the World of Opinion." *New York Times.* Retrieved Oct. 22, 2011 from http://www.nytimes.com/2011/03/01/ nyregion/01Bloomberg. .html?pagewanted=all

Barbaro, M. (2008, August 18). "Bloomberg Encourages Staff to Watch the Clock," *New York Times,* http://www.nytimes.com/2008/08/18/nyregion/18clocks. html?scp=1&sq=bloomberg%20encourages%20staff%20to%20watch%20 the%20clock&st=cse.

Barron, J. (2010, December 21). "Times Sues City Police, Saying Information Has Been Illegally Withheld," *New York Times,* http://www.nytimes. com/2010/12/22/nyregion/22nypd.html?_r=1&scp=1&sq=times%20sues%20 city%20police&st=cse.

Barry, D. (2001, November 7). "The 2001 Elections: News Analysis: An Election in a Shadow," *New York Times,* http://select.nytimes.com/gst/abstract.htm l?res=FB0914F63B5D0C748CDDA80994D9404482&scp=4&sq=The%20 2001%20elections:%20News%20analysis:%20an%20election%20in%20a%20 shadow&st=cse.

Blair, T. (2007, June 12). "Lecture on Public Life," London, http://news.bbc.co.uk/2/ hi/uk_news/politics/6744581.stm.

Bratton, W. (2010, February 17). "Crime by the Numbers," *New York Times,* http:// www.nytimes.com/2010/02/17/opinion/17bratton.html?_r=1&scp=2&sq=cri me+by+the+numbers&st=nyt.

Browne, P.J. (2007, September 9). Interview.

Celona, L. and Kadison, D. (2006, May 8). "Crime Stats Rigged," *New York Post,* http://webcache.googleusercontent.com/search?q=cache:0Fs9M95mkecJ:www. treatingyourself.com/vbulletin/showthread.php%3Ft%3D13038+%22crime+st ats+rigged%22&cd=1&hl=en&ct=clnk&gl=us&source=www.google.com.

Celona, L. and Perone, D. (2010, July 30). "Cops Sting Cops," *New York Post,* http:// www.nypost.com/p/news/local/brooklyn/cops_sting_cops_lyItuTeLedhKWtru JZYsdL#ixzz1HiVwaEkF.

Chan, S. and Baker, A. (2009, April 14). "Police Dept. Backs Off Plans to Remove Press Offices," *New York Times,* http://cityroom.blogs.nytimes.com/2009/04/14/ no-room-for-press-at-police-headquarters-officials-say/?scp=1&sq=police%20 deparment%20backs%20off%20plans%20to%20remove%20press%20 offices&st=cse.

Chen, D.W. (2010, February 9). "Crime Survey Raises Questions about Data-Driven Policy," *New York Times,* http://www.nytimes.com/2010/02/09/ nyregion/09mayor.html.

Chen, D. and Barbaro, M. (2009, November 4). "Bloomberg Wins 3rd Term as Mayor in Unexpectedly Close Race," *New York Times,* http://www.nytimes. com/2009/11/04/nyregion/04mayor.html?scp=1&sq=bloomberg+wins+third+ term+as+mayor&st=nyt.

Chermak, S.M. (1994). "Body Count News: How Crime Is Presented in the News Media," *Justice Quarterly*, 11(4).

Chermak, S. (1995). "Image Control: How Police Affect the Presentation of Crime News," *American Journal of Police*, 14(2).

Chermak, S., McGarrell, E., and Gruenwald, J. (2006). "Media Coverage of Police Misconduct and Attitudes toward Police," *Policing: An International Journal of Police Strategies and Management*, 29.

Chibnall, S. (1977). *Law and Order News*. London: Tavistock.

Citizens Crime Commission, 2011, Retrieved on November 29, 2011 from http://www.nycrimecommission.org/policeoversight.php)

City Room. (2009, January 9). *New York Times*.

Commission to Combat Police Corruption. (2011). Thirteenth Annual Report of the Commission, New York.

Daily News. (2011, January 8). "Police Commissioner Isn't Afraid to Have a Panel of Tough Prosecutors Examine Compstat," editorial, http://articles.nydailynews.com/2011-01-08/news/27086748_1_crime-statistics-crime-victims-crime-levels.

Dewan, S. (2004, March 24). "Union Leaders Allege Fudging of Statistics on City Crime," *New York Times*, http://www.nytimes.com/2004/03/24/nyregion/union-leaders-allege-fudging-of-statistics-on-city-crime.html?scp=1&sq=union +leaders+allege+fudging+of+statistics&st=nyt.

Dicker, F. (2010, July 16). "Mayor Bloomberg, Cops Fume As Gov Purges Frisk List," *New York Post*, http://www.nypost.com/p/news/local/mike_cops_fume_as_gov_purges_frisk_sY739RAjVUf0GGRY2qZfsI.

DiStefano, A. (2011, April 1). "NYPD Comm. Kelly: A Beat Cop from Way Back," *Newsday*, http://www.newsday.com/long-island/politics/spin-cycle-1.812042/nypd-comm-kelly-a-beat-cop-from-way-back-1.2795538.

"Does Not Compute: NYPD Database Law Not Worth Paper It's Printed On." (2010, July 23). *Daily News*, editorial, http://www.nydailynews.com/opinions/2010/07/22/2010-07-22_does_not_compute.html.

Dowler, K. (2003). "Media Consumption and Public Attitudes toward Crime and Justice," *Journal of Criminal Justice and Popular Culture*, 10: 2.

Dwyer, J. (2005a, May 3). "Another Convention Arrest Is Undercut by a Videotape," *New York Times*, http://www.nytimes.com/2005/05/03/nyregion/03video.html?scp=1&sq=another%20convention%20arrest%20is%20undercut%20by%20a%20videotape&st=cse.

Dwyer, J. (2005b, December 22). "Police Infiltrate Protests, Videotapes Show," *New York Times*, http://www.nytimes.com/2005/12/22/nyregion/22police.html?scp=1&sq=police+infiltrate+protests%2C+videotape+show&st=nyt.

Dwyer, J. (2007b, April 3). "Police Surveillance before Convention Was Larger Than Previously Disclosed," *New York Times*, http://query.nytimes.com/gst/fullpage.html?res=9A00EEDC1F30F930A35757C0A9619C8B63&scp=1&sq=police%20surveillance%20before%20convention%20was%20larger%20than%20previously%20disclosed&st=cse.

Edroso, R. (2010, February 16). "Richard Aborn, Former DA Candidate, Wants NYPD Crime Audit Figures Released, Checked," *Village Voice*, http://blogs.villagevoice.com/runninscared/2010/02/richard_aborn_f.php.

Eligon, J. (2010, June 2). "Panel Seeks More Training on Sex Crimes," *New York Times*, http://www.nytimes.com/2010/06/03/nyregion/03rape.html?_r=1&scp=1&sq=Panel%20seeks%20more%20police%20training%20on%20sex%20crimes&st=cse.

Ericson, R.V. (1989). "Patrolling the Facts: Secrecy and Publicity in Police Work," *British Journal of Sociology*, 40(2).

Ericson, R.V. (1955). *Crime and the Media*. Dartmouth, U.K.: Aldershot.

Eterno, J. (2003). *Policing within the Law*. Westport, Praeger.

Eterno J. and Silverman, E. (2006). "The New York City Police Department's Compstat: Dream or Nightmare?" *International Journal of Police Science and Management*, 8: 3.

Financial Management System. (2011). New York City, data provided by Independent Budget Office.

Finely, G.E. (1983). "Fear of Crime in the Elderly." In: Kosbert J.I., Ed., *Abuse and Mistreatment of the Elderly: Causes and Intervention*. Littlejohn, MA: John Wright.

Finnegan, W. (2005, July 25). "Defending the City," *The New Yorker*.

Fisher, C.S. (1981). "The Private and Public Worlds of City Life," *American Sociological Review*, 46, np.

Fishman, M. (1981). "Police News: Constructing an Image of Crime," *Urban Life*, 9(4): 371–394.

Freeman, G. 2011, November 21 Letter to NYPD Deputy Commissioner Paul Browne. Retrieved on November 29, 2011 from www.nyclu.org/files/releases/DCPI Letter - Signed 11-21-11.pdfb.

Gardiner, S. and Levitt, L. (2004, June 18). "Police Probing Alleged Fudged Crime Stats," *Newsday*.

Gardiner, S. (2010, December 27). "Police in About Face on City Crime Data," *Wall Street Journal*, http://online.wsj.com/article/SB10001424052970204527804576043741771362756.html.

Gardiner, S. (2011a, January 11). "NYPD's Long War over Crime Stats," *Wall Street Journal*, http://online.wsj.com/article/SB100014240527487046980045761042038693313630.html.

Gardiner, S. (2011b, January 31). Personal e-mail.

Geffon, S. (2006, June 8). "NYPD Statistics Questioned after Incidents Downgraded," *The Queens Chronicle*.

"Glimpse of Dodge City." (2010, August 11). *New York Post*, editorial, http://webcache.googleusercontent.com/search?q=cache:__u5J4ImjIYJ:www.nypost.com/p/news/opinion/editorials/glimpse_of_dodge_city_gu9J82oJreaqki5jmf63SO+glimpse+of+dodge+city&cd=1&hl=en&ct=clnk&gl=us&source=www.google.com.

Gordon, M. and Heath, L. (1981). "The News Business, Crime and Fear." In: Lewis, D.A., Ed., *Reactions to Crime*. London: Sage.

Giuliani, R. (1992, August 7). "Rumor and Justice in Washington Heights," *New York Times*, http://query.nytimes.com/gst/fullpage.html?res=9E0CE5DA1339F934A3575BC0A964958260&scp=2&sq=rumor%20and%20justice%20in%20washington%20%20heights&st=csep.

Herman, E. and Chomsky, N. (1988). "Propaganda Mill," *Progressive*, 52(6): 14.

Kasinsky, R. (1994). "Patrolling the Facts: Media Cops and Crime." In: Barak, G., Ed., *Media, Process and the Social Construction of Crime*. New York: Garland.

Kelly, R. (2010, February 14). "Why Crime Stats Can Be Trusted: Commissioner Raymond Kelly Defends the Numbers," *Daily News*.

Kilgannon, C. (2009, November 8). "Permitted Behind Police Lines, But Not Welcome," *New York Times*, http://www.nytimes.com/2009/11/08/nyregion/08levitt.html? scp=1&sq=permitted+behind+police+lines%2C+but+not+welcome&st=nyt.

Koblin, J. (2009, April 14). "Ray Kelly Whacks 'Police Shack," *New York Observer*, np.

Krahn, H. (1984). "Rural-Urban Origin and Fear of Crime," *Rural Sociology*, 49: 247–260.

Levitt, L. (2009, April 20). "Farewell to the Shack," *NYPD Confidential*, http://nypd-confidential.com/columns/2009/090420.html.

MacDonald, H. (1999, July 20). "How to Fight and Win," *Wall Street Journal*, p, 16.

MacDonald, H. (2010, February 17). "Compstat and Its Enemies," *City Journal*, http://www.city-journal.org/2010/eon0217hm.htmlnp.

McPhee, M. (2004, March 24). "PBA: Crime Stats False," *Daily News*.

McIntire, M. (2005, October 5). "New York's Falling Crime Rate Is a Potent Weapon for the Mayor," *New York Times*, http://www.nytimes.com/2005/10/05/nyregion/metrocampaigns/05crime.html?scp=1&sq=New+York%27s+falling+crime+rate+is+a+potent+weapon+for+the+mayor&st=nyt.

Messing, P. (2004, March 24). "Cop Unions: Brass Downplaying Crime Rise," *New York Post*.

Messing, P., Celona, L., and Fanelli, J. (2010, February 7). "NYPD Stats were Captain Cooked," *New York Post*, http://www.nypost.com/p/news/local/nypd_stats_were_captain_cooked_ykUWy6gXcPxYl87fGonQoO.

Miller, J. (2007, May 3). "On the Front Line in the War on Terrorism," *City Journal*.

Moses, P. (2005a, March 22). "Corruption? It Figures," *Village Voice*, http://www.villagevoice.com/2005-03-22/news/corruption-it-figures/.

Moses, P. (2005b, October 25). "These Stats Are a Crime," *Village Voice*, htt://www.villagevoice.com/2005-10-25/news/these-stats-are-a-crime/.

Moses, P. (2005c, December 20). "Something's Missing," *Village Voice*, http://www.villagevoice.com/2005-12-20/news/something-s-mnp.

Moses, P. (2005d, January 25). Letter to the New York City Police Department.

Moses, P. (2005e, June 14). Letter to the New York City Police Department.

Moses, P. (2005f, September 9). Letter to the New York City Police Department.

Moses, P. (2011, April 14). Personal e-mail.

Muessig, B. (2010, February 2). "Possible Hearing on Police Report Manipulation," *Gothamist*, http://gothamist.com/2010/02/03/councilman_investigate_whether_crim.php.

"Mugging Compstat: Assault on NYPD Crime-Tracking Program Is Wrongheaded." (2010, February 11). Editorial, *Daily News*, http://www.nydailynews.com/opinions/2010/02/11/2010-02-.

Murphy, J. (2005, December 10). "Larceny? Grand!" *Village Voice*, http://www.villagevoice.com/content/printVersion/199272/.

Nagourney, A. (2001, November 7). "The 2001 Elections: Bloomberg Edges Green in Race for Mayor,".*New York Times*, http://www.nytimes.com/2001/11/07/nyregion/2001-elections-mayor-bloomberg-edges-green-race-for-mayor-mcgreevey-easy-winner.html?scp=1&sq=the+2001++elections%3A++Bloomberg++edges+Green+in+race+for+mayor&st=nyt.

"NYPD Crime Numbers Disprove Police Bashers' Cockamamie Compstat Theory." (2010, December 29). *Daily News*, editorial, uhttp://www.nydailynews.com/opinions/2010/12/29/2010-12-29_crimes_and_misdemeanors.html.

NYPD crime story. (2010, August 20). Editorial, *The Chief*.

Parascandola, R. (2004, June 27). "A Number of Flaws," *Newsday*.

Parascandola, R. (2010a, February 2). "Brooklyn's 81st Precinct Probes by NYPD for Fudging Stats," *Daily News*.

Parascandola, R. (2010b, February 2), "Angel Gonzalez Robbers Stole $22,700 but 81st Precinct Found No Evidence," *Daily News*.

Parascandola, R. (2010c, February 3). "Report of Fudged Crime Stats from Brooklyn's 81st Precinct Deserves Hearing, Councilman Vallone Says," *Daily News*, http://www.nydailynews.com/news/ny_crime/2010/02/03/2010-02-03_fudged_crime_stats_report_deserves_hearing_sez_pol.html.

Parascandola , R. (2010d, February 12). "Police at 81st Precinct under the Gun in Crime-Stat Shenanigans," *Daily News*.

Parascandola, R. (2010e, May 26). "Crime up 13% in 81st Precinct," *Daily News*.

Parascandola, R. (2010f, May 29). "Enraged Pols, Activists Want Brooklyn Police Supervisor Booted," *Daily News*.

Parascandola, R. (2010g, July 4). "NYPD Officer in Midst of Brooklyn Stat Probe Transferred to Bronx," *Daily News*.

Parascandola, R. (2010h, July 30), "Brooklyn Cops Charged with Barging into Sting Operations," *Daily News*.

Parascandola, R. (2010i, August 10). "Whistleblowing Cop Slaps NYPD with $50 Million Suit for Locking Him Up in Psych Ward," *Daily News*, http://before-itsnews.com/story/132/711/Whistleblowing_cop_slaps_NYPD_with_50_million_suit_for_locking_him_up_in_psych_ward.html.

Parascandola, R. (2010j, August 22). "Cop Says Shrink Vouched for His Sanity Days before He Was Involuntarily Committed to a Psych Ward," *Daily News*.

Parascandola, R. and Levitt, L. (2004a, March 21). "Police Statistics: Numbers Scrutinized," *Newsday*, np.

Parascandola, R. and Levitt, L. (2004b, March 22). "Crime in the 50th Precinct: PBA Feared Fudging," *Newsday*, np.

Parascandola, R. and Levitt, L. (2004c, March 23). "Police Procedures: Crime Stat Probe Sought," *Newsday*, np.

Parascandola, R. and Levitt, L. (2004d, March 31). "Probe at 112th," *Newsday*, np.

Parascandola, R. and Lisberg, A. (2010, February 9). "Mike Doesn't Budge on Comp-Stat Fudge," *Daily News*, p. 7.

Parenti, M. (1992). *Inventing Reality: The Politics of New Media*. Belmont, CA: Wadsworth.

Personal communication. (2010). Unpublished confidential source.

Pooley, E. (1996, January 15). "One Good Apple," *Time*, pp. 55–56.

Queens Campaigner. (2011). "Vallones Rock Out with Ray Kelly—See the Video Here," http://www.queenscampaigner.com/2011/04/vallones-rock-out-with-ray-kelly-%E2%80%94%C2%A0see-the-video-here/.

Rashbaum, W. (2004, May 25). "Crime Declines, But Union and Mayor Spar over Data," *New York Times*, http://www.nytimes.com/2004/05/25/nyregion/crime-declines-but-union-and-mayor-spar-over-data.html?scp=1&sq=crime+declines%2C+but+union+and+mayor+spar+over+data&st=nyt.

Rashbaum, W. (2005, April 19). "Panel Wants to Obtain Police Data by Subpoena," *New York Times*, http://www.nytimes.com/2004/05/25/nyregion/crime-declines-but-union-and-mayor-spar-over-data.html?scp=1&sq=crime+declines+but+union+and+mayor+spar+over+data&st=nyt.

Rashbaum, W. (2010, February 7). "Retired Officers Raise Questions on Crime Data," *The New York Times*, http://www.nytimes.com/2010/02/07/nyregion/07crime.html?scp=1&sq=retired+officers+raise+questions+about+crime+&st=nyt.

Rayman, G. (2010a, May 4). "The NYPD Tapes: Inside Bed-Stuy's 81st Precinct," *Village Voice*, http://www.villagevoice.com/2010-05-04/news/the-nypd-tapes-inside-bed-stuy-s-81st-precinct/.

Rayman, G. (2010b, May 11). "The NYPD Tapes, Part 2. Bed-Stuy Street Cops Ordered: Turn This Place into a Ghost Town," *Village Voice*, http://www.village-voice.com/2010-05-04/news/the-nypd-tapes-inside-bed-stuy-s-81st-precinct/.

Rayman, G. (2010c, May 13). "The NYPD Tapes Series: The Cliffs Notes Version," *Village Voice*, http://www.villagevoice.com/2010-05-04/news/the-nypd-tapes-inside-bed-stuy-s-81st-precinct/.

Rayman, G. (2010d, May 17). "NYPD Officer Captured Talking about Cases Being Routinely Downgraded," *Village Voice*, http://www.villagevoice.com/2010-05-04/news/the-nypd-tapes-inside-bed-stuy-s-81st-precinct/.

Rayman, G. (2010e, May 19). "Tapes Show That Often, NYPD Treated Training as a Joke," *Village Voice*, http://www.villagevoice.com/2010-05-04/news/the-nypd-tapes-inside-bed-stuy-s-81st-precinct/.

Rayman, G. (2010f, June 8). "NYPD Tapes 3: A Detective Comes Forward about Downgraded Sexual; Assaults," *Village Voice*, http://www.villagevoice.com/2010-05-04/news/the-nypd-tapes-inside-bed-stuy-s-81st-precinct/.

Rayman, G. (2010g, June 15). "NYPD Tapes 4: The Whistleblower, Adrian Schoolcraft," *Village Voice*, http://www.villagevoice.com/2010-05-04/news/the-nypd-tapes-inside-bed-stuy-s-81st-precinct/.

Rayman, G. (2010h, June 21). "NYPD Confidential Offers Its Take on the Voice's NYPD Tapes Series," *Village Voice*, http://www.villagevoice.com/2010-05-04/news/the-nypd-tapes-inside-bed-stuy-s-81st-precinct/.

Rayman, G. (2010i, August 9). "Ray Kelly's Tom Spokesman Paul Brown Present When NYPD Whistleblower Hauled to Psych Ward, Lawsuit Says," *Village Voice*, http://www.villagevoice.com/2010-05-04/news/the-nypd-tapes-inside-bed-stuy-s-81st-precinct/.

Rayman, G. (2010j, August 10). "New York Mag and Other Media Offer Their Takes on NYPD Whistleblower's Lawsuit," *Village Voice*, http://www.villagevoice.com/2010-05-04/news/the-nypd-tapes-inside-bed-stuy-s-81st-precinct/.

Rayman, G. (2010k, August 23), "NYPD Tapes Fallout: Precinct Commander and Deputy Chief under Investigation," *Village Voice*, http://www.villagevoice.com/2010-05-04/news/the-nypd-tapes-inside-bed-stuy-s-81st-precinct/.

Rivera, A. and Baker, A. (2010, November 1). "Data Elusive on Low-Level Crime in New York City," *New York Times*, http://www.nytimes.com/2010/11/02/nyregion/02secrecy.html

Robertson, C. (2004, June 24). "Brazen Violence Shocks City, Even as Crime Rate Keeps Declining," *New York Times*, http://www.nytimes.com/2004/06/24/nyregion/brazen-violence-shocks-city-even-as-crime-rate-keeps-declining.html?scp=2&sq=brazen+violence+shocks++city+even+as+crime+rate+keeps+declining&st=nyt.

Schmidt, M. (2009, November 8). "For Kelly, a Chance to Add to his Legacy," *New York Times*, http://www.nytimes.com/2009/11/09/nyregion/09kelly.html?scp=1&sq=For+Kelly%2C+a+chance+to+add+to+his+legacy&st=nyt.

Schoolcraft Complaint. (2010, September 10). http://schoolcraftjustice.com/SchoolcraftAmended.pdf.

Seidman, D. and Sutherland, A. (2010, July 17). "Dave's Frisk-List Nix Imperils NYers: Mike," *New York Post*, http://webcache.googleusercontent.com/search?q=cache:dPPmfYpKCDEJ:www.nypost.com/f/print/news/local/dave_frisk_list_nix_imperils_nyers_Hpq2Leaz6FJWTLt05hNsCO+dave%27s+frisk+list+nix&cd=3&hl=en&ct=clnk&gl=us&source=www.google.com.

Shipley, D. (2010, February 17). E-mail to authors.

Silverman, E.B. (2001). *NYPD Battles Crime: Innovative Strategies in Policing.* Boston: Northeastern University Press.

Skolnick, J.H. and McCoy, C. (1984). "Police Accountability and the Media," *American Bar Foundation Research Journal*, 9(3): 521–547.

Smith, D. and Purtell, R. (2006). "Managing Crime Counts: An Assessment of the Quality Control of NYPD Crime Data," Center for Research in Crime and Justice, New York University School of Law, Occasional Paper, August.

Staten Island Advance. (2011, January 10). "Safety in Numbers," editorial.

Tiku, N. (2010, August 10). "NYPD Sent a Whistleblowing Cop to the Psych Ward, and Now He's Suing," *New York Magazine*.

Toor, M. (2010, August 20). "Cop Says Brass Leaned on Him to Hide Quotas," *The Chief/Civil Service Leader*.

Vallone, P., Jr., (2010, August 5). "Blame Albany for Crime Wave," *New York Post*, http://webcache.googleusercontent.com/search?q=cache:5uWBlUMQ7dUJ:www.nypost.com/p/news/opinion/opedcolumnists/blame_albany_for_crime_wave_dWFzEQ6faW0rnPST4r6HdN+%22albany+also+cut+an+extremely+NYPD+databased+used+to+apprehend&hl=en&gl=us&strip=0.

Van Outrive, L. and Fijnaut, F. (1983). "Police and the Organization of Prevention," in Punch, M., Ed., *Control in the Police Organization*. Cambridge, MA: MIT Press, 47–59.

Weiss, M. (2009, April 15). "Police HQ Reporters Get Boot," *New York Post*, http://www.nypost.com/p/news/regional/police_hq_reporters_get_boot_cfeLIhQf4tvNHpaSdJKu9L.

Zink, R. (2004). "The Trouble with Compstat," *PBA Magazine*, http://www.nycpba.org/publications/mag-04-summer/compstat.html.

Suggested Reading

Anderson, D.C. (2001). "Crime Control by the Numbers: Compstat Yields New Lessons for the Police and The Replication of a Good Idea," Ford Foundation Report.

Behn, R.D. (2006,). "The Varieties of CitiStat," *Public Administration Review*, May/June: 332–340.

Boung, J.J. et al. (1990). In the matter of, Respondents v. Brown et. al. Appellants Case No. 90-02710, Supreme Court of New York, Appellate Division, Second Department 161 A.D2nd 49, 560 N. Y. S.2d 307 N.Y, App. Civ 11339, Sept. 5.

Daly, M. (2010, August 8). "Former City Mayor Rudy Giuliani Is Quite the Hypocrite with Cry for Privacy after Daughter's Theft," *Daily News,* http://articles.nydailynews.com/2010-08-08/local/27072005_1_patrick-dorismond-altar-boy-press-charges.

Dao, J. (1993, October 11). "Dinkins and Giuliani Split on Public Safety Issues," *New York Times,* http://query.nytimes.com/gst/fullpage.html?res=9F0CE0D81F3BF932A25753C1A965958260&scp=1&sq=dinkins%20and%20guiliani%20split%20on%20public%20safety%20issues&st=cse.

Dinkins, D. (1990, October 3). "Mobilizing to Fight Crime," *New York Times,* http://www.nytimes.com/1990/10/03/nyregion/dinkins-on-crime-excerpts-from-dinkins-s-address-mobilizing-to-fight-crime.htmlnp.

Dwyer, J. (2004, September 17). "City Arrest Tactics, Used on Protesters, Face Test in Court," *New York Times,* http://www.nytimes.com/2004/09/17/nyregion/17detain.htmlnp.

Dwyer, J. (2006a, March 9). "Charges, But No Penalty, For a Chief's Role in a Convention Arrest," *New York Times,* region/09board.html?scp=1&sq=charges+but+no+penalty+for+a+chief's+role&st=nyt

Dwyer, J. (2006b, December 13). "City Fights Efforts to Release 2004 Convention Arrest Records," *New York Times,* http://www.nytimes.com/2006/12/13/nyregion/13convention.html?_r=1&scp=1&sq=city%20fights%20efforts%20to%20release%202004%20convention%20arrest%20records&st=cse.

Dwyer, J. (2007a, February 8). "Records Show Extra Scrutiny of Detainees of '04 Protests," *New York Times,* http://query.nytimes.com/gst/fullpage.html?res=9800E4DB113FF93BA35751C0A9619C8B63&scp=1&sq=records%20show%20extra%20scrutiny%20of%20detainees&st=csenp.

Eisenberg, C. (2007, August, 15). "NYPD: US Could Face Terror Threat at Home," *Newsday.* Retrieved from newsbank database.

Feuer, A. and Rashbaum, W.K. (2004, August 26). "Two Are Charged with Plotting to Bomb Train Station," *New York Times,* http://query.nytimes.com/gst/fullpage.html?res=9906E7DC1F3EF93AA1575BC0A9629C8B63&scp=1&sq=two%20are%20charged%20with%20plotting%20to%20bomb%20train%20station&st=cse.

Fox, R.L. and Van Sickel, R.W. (2001). *Tabloid Justice.* Boulder, CO: Lynee Riemer Publishers.

Garland, S. (2007). "NYPD Report Outlines Threat from Homegrown Terrorists," *New York Sun.* Retrieved August 16, from online database.

Gender, A. (2011, February 17). "Brooklyn's 77th Precinct Probed for Manipulating Crime Statistics," *Daily News,* http://www.nydailynews.com/ny_local/2011/02/17/2011-02-17_cop_stats_numbers_game_bklyns_77th_precinct_probed.html.

Gootman, E. (2000, October 24). "Police Department's Allure Is Growing," *New York Times,* http://www.nytimes.com/2000/10/24/nyregion/a-police-dept-s-growing-allure-crime-fighters-from-around-world-visit-for-tips.html?scp=1&sq=police%20department%20allure%20is%20growing&st=csep.

Grabosky, P. and Wilson, P. (1989). *Journalism and Justice: How Crime Is Reported.* Leichardt, Austria: Pluto.

Guffey, J.E. (1992). "The Police and the Media: Proposals for Managing Conflict Productively," *American Journal of Police*, 11(1).

Haberman, C. (2000, July 8). "NYC: Inviting an Invasion of Privacy," *New York Times*, http://www.nytimes.com/2000/07/08/nyregion/nyc-inviting-an-invasion-of-privacy.html?scp=1&sq=nyc+inviting+an+invasion+of+privacy&st=nyt.

Hayes, T. (2007, August 15). "NYPD Says Homegrown Terror Threat Mounting," *Associated Press*, retrieved October 22, 2011 from http://www.infowars.com/articles/terror/NYPD_mounting_homegrown_terror_threat.htm.

Heath, L. (1984). "Impact of Newspaper Crime Reports on Fear of Crime," *Journal of Personality and Social Psychology*, 47(2): np.

Hepinstall, S. (1990, June 11). "Korean Grocer in Brooklyn Struggles with the American Dream," *Reuters*.

Howitt, D. (1998). *Crime, the Media and the Law.* New York: John Wiley. & Sons.

Hughes, K. (1993, October 28). "Doubts about New York City's Future Colors Mayoral Race," *New York Times*.

Humm, A. (2007, October 9). "Policing the Police," *Gotham Gazette*.

Jacobson, D. (1990, September 12). "Lawyer Defends Mayoral Report on Korean Grocery Boycott," UPI New York Metro.

Jewkes, Y. (2004). *Media and Crime.* London: Sage.

Jordon, R. (1993) "Crown Heights Haunts NYC Race," *Boston Globe*, 3, October, A5.

Lubash, A. (1991, January 31). "Jury Acquits Korean Cited by Grocery Boycott," *New York Times*, http://query.nytimes.com/gst/fullpage.html?res=9F0CE0D81 F3BF932A25753C1A965958260&scp=1&sq=dinkins%20and%20guiliani%20 split%20on%20public%20safety%20issues&st=cse.

Manegold, C.S. (1993a, September 8). "Giuliani Takes a Strong Stand on Crown Heights and Arrests," *New York Times*, http://www.nytimes.com/1993/09/08/nyregion/giuliani-takes-a-strong-stand-on-crown-heights-and-arrests.html?sc p=1&sq=giuliani+takes+a+strong+stand+on+crown+heights&st=nyt.

Manegold, C.S. (1993b, October 13). "Giuliani on Stump, Hits Hard on Crime and How to Fight It," *New York Times*, http://www.nytimes.com/1993/09/08/nyre-gion/giuliani-takes-a-strong-stand-on-crown-heights-and-arrests.html?scp=1 &sq=giuliani+takes+a+strong+stand+on+crown+heights&st=nyt. (Retrieved December 22, 2005).

Mitchell, A. (2003, September 20). "Giuliani Zeroing in on Crime Issue," *New York Times*, http://www.nytimes.com/1993/09/20/nyregion/giuliani-zeroing-crime-issue-new-commercials-are-focusing-fears-new-yorkers.html?scp=1&sq=giuli ani+zeroing++in+on+crime++issue&st=nyt.

MSNBC. (2007, August 15). "NYPD Warns of Homegrown Terrorism Threat," http://www.msnbc.msn.com/id/20278590/ns/us_news-security/.

Muraskin, R. and Domash, S. (2007). *Crime and the Media.* Englewood Cliffs, NJ: Prentice Hall.

"Muslims Slam U.S. for Biased Claims," (2007, August 18). *Press TV*, np.

Nagourney, A. (1997, November 5). "The 1997 Elections: The Overview; Giuliani Sweeps to Second Term as Mayor; Whitman Holds on by a Razor-Thin Margin," *New York Times*, http://www.nytimes.com/1997/11/05/nyregion/1997-elec-

tions-overview-giuliani-sweeps-second-term-mayor-whitman-holds-razor.
html?scp=1&sq=the+1997++elections%3A+the+overview%3A+Giuliani+swe
eps+to+second+term&st=nyt.

New York City Police Department. (2007). Radicalization in the West: The
Homegrown Threat, http://www.nyc.gov/html/nypd/downloads/pdf/public_
information/NYPD_Report-Radicalization_in_the_West.pdf.

New York State Division of Criminal Justice Services. (1993). "A Report to the
Governor, on the Disturbances in Crown Heights," Albany, NY.

Noonan, P. (2007, August 17). "Hatred Begins at Home," *Wall Street Journal*.

O'Connell, P.E. (2001). *Using Performance Data for Accountability*. Arlington, VA:
PricewaterhouseCoopers.

On the Homegrown Threat. (2007, August 14). Editorial, *Dallas Morning News*.

O'Shaughnessy, P. (1999, February 13). "Red Flags on Two Cops," *Daily News*.

Parascandola R. (2011, January 5). "Police Commissioner Ray Kelly Announces New
Study of NYPD Crime Statistics to Combat Criticism," *Daily News*, http://www.
nydailynews.com/ny_local/2011/01/05/2011-01-05_police_commissioner_
ray_kelly_announces_new_study_of_nypd_crime_statistics_to_co.html.

Perlman, E. (2007). "Stat Fever," *Governing*, January.

Purdham, T. S. (1993, October 24). "Giuliani Campaign Theme: Dinkins Isn't Up to
the Job," *New York Times*, http://www.nytimes.com/1993/10/24/nyregion/giu-
liani-campaign-theme-dinkins-isn-t-up-to-the-job.html?scp=1&sq=giuliani+c
ampaign+theme%3A+Dinkins+isn%27t+up+to+the+job&st=nyt.

Pyle, R. (1992, March 23). "Crown Heights Ruling Reversed," *Bergen Record*.

Rayman, G. (2010l, August 25). "NYPD Tapes 5: The Corroboration," *Village Voice*, http://www.
villagevoice.com/2010-05-04/news/the-nypd-tapes-inside-bed-stuy-s-81st-precinct/np.

Rayman, G. (2010m, October 18). "NYPD Commanders Critique Compstat and the
Reviews Aren't Good," *Village Voice*, http://blogs.villagevoice.com/runnins-
cared/2010/10/nypd_commanders.php?print=true.

Rayman, G. (2010n, October 22). "NYPD Tapes Scandal: A 'Giant Oil Spill' Ray Kelly
Can't Contain, Criminologists Say," *Village Voice*, http://blogs.villagevoice.com/
runninscared/2010/10/nypd_tapes_scan.php.

Rayman, G. (2010o, December 23). "Ray Kelly Hounded by Voice Revelations, To
Revamp NYPD Handling of Sex Crime Complaints," *Village Voice*, http://blogs.
villagevoice.com/runninscared/2010/12/ray_kelly_hound.php.

Reddy, M. (2007, October 30). *NYPD Study Offers Insights to Counter Domestic
Islamic Terrorism*. Washington: Medill Reports.

Ripley, A. (2007, August 16). "How to Look at Homegrown Terror," *Time*.

Robinson, G. (2004, June 21). "Summer of Protest," *Gotham Gazette*, http://www.
gothamgazette.com/article/iotw/20040621/200/1012.

Rosen, M.S. (1999). "The Role of the Press in Police Reform." In: Lynch, G.W., Ed.,
Human Dignity and the Police, Springfield, IL: Charles C Thomas.

Rosenbaum, D.P. and Heath. S. (1988). "The Psycho Logic of Fear Reduction
and Crime Prevention Programs." In: Lab, S.P., Ed., *Crime Prevention*.
Cincinnati, OH: Anderson.

Silverman, E.B. and Della-Giustina, J. (2001). "Urban Policing and the Fear of Crime,"
Urban Studies, 38(5–6): 941–957.

Surette, R. (1992). Media, Crime and Criminal Justice. Pacific Grove, CA: Brooks.

"The Crown Heights Report." (1998, July 21). *Newsday*, 24.

UPI. (1990, May 10). "Judge and Dinkins Trade Barbs over Grocery Boycott," *Regional News*, 1.

Webber, R. and Robinson, G. (2003, July 7). "Compstatmania," *Gotham Gazette.*

Weisburd, D., Mastrofski, S., McNally, A., and Greenspan, R. (2001). "Compstat and Organizational Change: Findings from a National Survey," report submitted to the National Institute of Justice by the Police Foundation.

Compstat

7

Underpinnings and Implications

The blossoming field of criminal justice has become a very complex interdisciplinary area of study. Academics and practitioners must understand local, national, and even international trends. As such, scholars in this area are exposed to multifarious theories. Therefore, scientists must keep an open mind and not let personal bias enter their interpretations. Max Weber discusses the need for scientists to remain value neutral. Carefully examining evidence and making reasonable and logical conclusions based on that evidence are critical to the scientific method (see Weber, 1949 original 1904 as cited by Schaefer, 2001, 47). Exhortations about Compstat's successes and the lesser publicized weaknesses must be understood through the lens of scientific understanding. Additionally, this means being open to debate as well as criticism. Absent scientific results, human action will be the product of habit and convenience.

Consequently, readers need to keep an open mind regarding each of the theories discussed. Some can be quite radical. As scientists, you may disagree with a theory but you should base that disagreement on clear and convincing evidence, not rhetoric. Pertinent theories should never be discarded simply because one disagrees. Learning takes place through understanding and being open to all points of view. In this book, strong evidence is utilized as pillars to support our findings. It is necessary, therefore, to have an open mind, even to those who try to silence and disregard our work. Of course, we fully understand that the tactics used against us are typical and to be expected when the truth we expose hits home.

As a given, Compstat as a policing revolution has been very successful in terms of the number of police departments that have adopted it. Throughout the world, police leaders have been quick to implement Compstat-like systems in their jurisdictions (see Chapter 1). Clearly, the democratic world for better or worse has embraced this new police managerial program. Its success has been heralded in the media and elsewhere (Silverman, 2001). Few, however, are willing to suggest the sacred cow they worship is not perfect—that there is a deep, dark underside.

The sacred cow mentality has developed from the enormous record-breaking crime reductions, which give police and political leaders countless headlines and accolades. Police managers have been quick to jump on the

Compstat bandwagon because of these apparent crime control properties. To the extent that may be true, we applaud Compstat as an innovation; however, its adoption is often coupled with little or no understanding of its dysfunctional consequences. Other chapters outline many of the practical negative consequences of Compstat such as manipulating crime statistics, focusing on numbers, bullying behaviors by top-level management, disregard of leadership principles, and many others. In this chapter, we develop an understanding of Compstat based specifically on criminal justice theory. Theory can be used to show the positive aspects of Compstat that are already well explicated (see, for example, Kelling and Coles, 1996) as well as unveiling other less understood and unexpected negative side-effects. Understanding, studying, and learning both its positive and negative consequences are critical to advancing police managerial practices. In order to understand Compstat, we begin this chapter by expounding on Compstat's origins from a theoretical perspective.

Broken Windows Theory and Compstat

Compstat has been inextricably linked to Broken Windows theory (e.g., Henry, 2002; Kelling and Coles, 1996; Kelling and Bratton, 1998). Compstat was viewed as the managerial mechanism to enforce Broken Windows quality-of-life crime. It was argued that Compstat was linked to a managerial system to bring down crime. Wilson and Kelling (1983) as cited by Kelling and Bratton (1998, 1218–1219) first discussed this theory in *Atlantic Monthly* in 1982:

> just as a broken window left unattended was a sign that nobody cares and leads to more severe property damage, so disorderly conditions and behaviors left untended send a signal nobody cares and results in fear of crime, serious crime, and the "downward spiral of urban decay."

Based on this, Kelling and Bratton suggest that to influence crime rates, police need to be attentive to minor quality-of-life offenses and use assertive policing methods. It would seem then that Compstat was developed in conjunction with criminological theory to fight crime.

Such theoretical ideas, however, were not the origin of the Compstat managerial approach. It was only after the managerial process was developed that the founders realized how neatly it fit with Broken Windows. Although Bratton and Kelling's relationship was certainly established well before Compstat began in 1994, this relationship was not the key to Compstat's development. Bratton's role as Chief of the New York City Transit Police (a separate police agency from the NYPD at the time) did permit academic insight and innovation into the Transit Police especially by Kelling. In both of our experiences, Bratton was generally open, even transparent to scrutiny from outside the police department when he was with the NYPD. Outside agencies, scholars, and the press were given full access in 1994 and 1995.

Such access while laudable, and we even argue necessary in democratic society, does not mean these outsiders had a part in developing the program. Our experience and training coupled with a fair reading of the literature on Compstat penned by its founders indicates that the origins of Compstat are such that it was designed as an innovation essentially to fix what Bratton, Maple, and others in their company perceived as a dysfunctional organization (i.e., the NYPD). Jack Maple, one of the key figures to develop Compstat, sheds light on this issue. He is clearly not enamored with Broken Windows theory and directly points out that he feels the crime drop has little to do with the theory. Maple (1999, 154) succinctly writes the following about the New York City crime decrease:

> ... many people credited "Broken Windows" notion that crooks had suddenly taken to the straight and narrow because they had picked up on the prevailing civility vibe. That's not how it works. Rapists and killers don't head for another town when they see graffiti disappearing. ...

Broken Windows was clearly not on this Compstat architect's mind when he helped develop the innovative program. In fact, he likens quality-of-life tactics to "giving a facelift to a cancer patient. The patient may look better and even feel better but the killer disease has not been arrested" (Maple, 1999, 154).

Compstat was developed as a management tool essentially to bring down crime. It was a policy innovation of immense proportion but its origins have little to do with criminological theory. The fact that certain aspects of the program may fit with Broken Window's theory is merely happenstance. As Bratton (1996, 232) writes,

> Maple was not a master of tact. "I see that robberies in the Fifth Precinct are up fifty percent, chief," he said. "What's goin' on?" "Uh, the word is there's a lot of heroin out there." ... This happened a couple of times. Then Maple said, "These guys are full of shit." ... Maple understood, as I did that the biggest secret in law enforcement is that many police departments do not address crime. They are dysfunctional.

This dissatisfaction essentially gave birth to Compstat, not theory. We do point out that we are aware that Bratton was very familiar with management theory (see Silverman, 2001 and Chapter 3 for a discussion on performance management). However, the literature does not support those theories being critical to the development of Compstat either. Rather, it was essentially developed on an ad hoc basis to address an ineffectual bureaucracy. The NYPD was not operating in a way that focused on what they saw as the primary mission of police, namely, to fight crime. Importantly, all of the Police Commissioners who followed Bratton in New York City continued to use the system; however, it morphed over time.

The lack of a theoretical underpinning and input from outside the NYPD does not necessarily take away from the brilliant innovation that Compstat is. Indeed, had they been students of criminology, they probably never would have developed Compstat. In the early 1990s, the prevailing theoretical belief was that police have little or no influence on crime. For example, Bayley (1994, 3, 13) expounds on the state of criminology at the time:

> The police do not prevent crime. This is one of the best kept secrets of modern life. ... In democratic countries all over the world, then, there is a sense of crisis about public security. And at the center of this crisis are the police, who promise to protect us but do not appear to be able to do so.

Criminologists and others still debate the effect of police on crime. For example, Eck and McGuire (2000, abstract) argue that, "police were responsible for some portion of the crime drop of the 1990s, but the evidence does not support some of the most popular claims for the effects of police on crime." Conversely, Bratton emphatically argues that police are the source of the crime drop. Bratton (1996, 2) writes,

> Scholars are ready to attribute these declines [in crime rate] to demographics, social causes, to supposed changes in the drug market, and to unsubstantiated speculations about drug gangs making peace—in short, to any possible cause *except* to police work. I think most of these alternative explanations can be rather easily discounted. ... Better management, better strategies, higher expectations, and more effort on the part of police departments can do far more than just affect crime rates at the margins.

Assuming his argument is accurate (we do not fully accept it but do believe police play a role), this does not mean that the management tool is flawless. Certainly, Compstat is an ingenious innovation; however, its founders had little or no understanding of the full implications of the program's overall effect. While we fully support Compstat, it has well-developed side effects that can be harmful and even malignant. Understanding the full effects of the system put in place is critical to evaluating it and making appropriate changes. We now turn to criminal justice theory to help explain those side effects and point out that practical, negative side effects are seen throughout the book.

Crime Fighting Focus

With respect to Broken Windows theory, there appear to be two irreconcil-able views: one that Compstat is based on Broken Windows and the other that it is not. The common denominator among these ideas is, first, that crime reduction is the key to police work. Here there is no dispute among those who strongly support Compstat-like management. Crime control is seen as the central mission to police. Second, a focus on quality-of-life offenses is needed. The extent of this is subject to question by those who practice Compstat-like management. Third, it is apparent that the founders of Compstat did not use Broken Windows theory as a blueprint but as an afterthought; they use it as support for the program. As such, policymakers made little or no attempt to critically examine and evaluate Compstat—theoretically or otherwise—to possibly expose problematic areas. Just as there were problems implementing community policing such as the hours officers were allowed to work, Compstat too has concerns. Revealing those weaknesses is another step necessary to understanding, improving, and changing the managerial system.

Those who have been an integral part of Compstat often cite Broken Windows theory as the key to understanding Compstat. While there are certain aspects of Broken Windows that do fit well with Compstat, Broken Windows is a theory about crime, not management. Compstat is a manage-ment tool that may be utilized to fight crime, but its utility and worth are very different.

As discussed, the creators of Compstat may not agree nor fully com-prehend Broken Windows theory (at least during the development process). This is not a trivial point. Afterward, with crime decreasing at enormous unprecedented rates, they did see how neatly the theory fits. That is, they did not understand the theory that they now suggest is behind the crime fight-ing successes until after it was functioning. Broken Windows, then, is an afterthought but is important because it reveals the underlying philosophi-cal lynchpin that Compstat's founders now ultimately rely on to support the crime-fighting aspects of the Compstat innovation.

Unfortunately, however, their understanding of Broken Windows is lim-ited. It appears that Compstat is seen simply as a crime-fighting tool. In the fight against crime, Broken Windows has become a staple of the Compstat philosophy. For example, Police Superintendent of Chicago Gary McCarthy, who ran Compstat meetings for the NYPD as its Deputy Commissioner of Operations from 2000 to 2006, feels that Broken Windows is a key to fighting crime and Compstat. "I learned very early on in life that you have to stop the little things so that you can prevent the big things from happening" (As cited by Dougherty, 2011, June 1).

Academics too link Broken Windows to Compstat. For example, Henry (2002, 118) in writing about Compstat states, "At some level of awareness, both the police and the public knew all along that the principles Wilson and Kelling articulated in Broken Windows theory were accurate." Henry also suggests that police of the pre-Compstat era failed to develop a true understanding of the cause of the problems. Henry (2002, 118) writes, "To a large extent they treated the symptoms and ignored the cause." Again, the approach is clear. Fighting crime is suggested as the key mission of police.

The Crimefighter—Jack Maple

One of the founders of Compstat is so adamant about the crime-fighting mission of police that he outright rejects Broken Windows and goes so far as to suggest his own theory based on practical experience. He vehemently argues that the Broken Window's theory is patently incorrect with respect to crime fighting. He writes,

> The implication [of Broken Windows theory] is, if the police would take care of the little things, the big things would take care of themselves. How sad. That idea was tested in New York's subways in the late 1980s along with a strain of community policing. … The result was an 87 percent rise in subway robberies from 1987 to the middle of 1980..implementing quality-of-life tactics alone is like giving a facelift to a cancer patient: The patient may look better and even feel better, the killer disease hasn't been arrested. (Maple, 1999, 154)

Maple is the consummate practical crime fighter—a hardnosed street cop. His practical theory in his book takes issue with practices that the NYPD today takes for granted—quality-of-life enforcement, numerous stop-and-frisks, summonses—all to be reflected at Compstat. Such practice, however, is clearly not what Maple had in mind. Maple (1999, 155) argues that for "quality-of-life enforcement to make significant contributions to crime reduction, it has to be supported by a larger strategy." Importantly, his first piece of advice is to be "selective about who we were arresting." He argues that rules have to be designed to catch the "sharks," not the "dolphins." He points out how costly and inefficient it is to simply arrest anyone who commits minor violations. Today, very few have focused on his insights. Indeed, quality-of-life enforcement has run amok in New York City. Once again, the grueling number of forcible stops including over one-half million people—most of whom are completely innocent—is a simple example of this.

Maple understood practical policing and certainly was no fan of academics. Maple (1999, 131) writes, "The giveaway that community policing was hatched by academics is how the model devalues the role of supervisors. Everything is left to the individual cop, including the hours he or she is going to work." His stereotypical view of academics reflects street cop culture at the time. In this case, he erroneously blames academics for *horrible management decisions by the NYPD.* The NYPD hierarchy at the time made the awful decision to allow officers to make their own hours with minimal supervision. Delegating these decisions to officers without supervision is poor management. Indeed, permitting officers to make their own hours is not how community policing is taught by the Community Policing Consortium (a partnership of five leading police organizations in the United States: the International Association of Chiefs of Police, the National Organization of Black Law Enforcement Executives, the National Sheriffs' Association, the Police Executive Research Forum, and the Police Foundation). NYPD management at the time bears the brunt of this misinterpretation. Once again, we vehemently argue that policymakers need to understand fully the implications of their decisions by gaining knowledge in their areas of expertise (including theory) and then applying them properly. The NYPD did neither in the case of community policing. With Compstat, it appears NYPD management has yet again failed to appreciate constructive advice and criticism.

Maple's aim is certainly not to promote community policing; he is squarely advocating policies to aggressively address crime reduction. His book, *The Crime Fighter,* provides insights into his basic strategies to do just that. In short, his book is a brilliant exposé on how to fight crime. However, his understanding of criminological theory and the downsides of such a focus are not well delineated. It is essentially a powerful but limited view of what needs to be done. While such crime fighters often have their hearts in the right place, their zeal needs to be carefully checked and balanced by politicians, voters, community members, policymakers, the press, and others. All have an important role. For example, former NYPD Police Commissioner William Bratton reigned in Mr. Maple when it was necessary. Bratton writes in his book how he had to punish Maple for being overly zealous with respect to the well-known (among the NYPD of that era) Pinocchio incident. In this incident, Maple abused his position in an attempt to publicly embarrass a commander at a Compstat meeting by putting a picture of Pinocchio on the screen for all to see. The suggestion was that the high-ranking commander in question (who had a large nose) was lying. It was clearly wrong, an example of bullying, and even an act of outright prejudice. It is a good example of how Compstat sometimes got out of hand (see Bratton, 1998, 237).

A Better Understanding of Broken Windows—Kelling and Coles

The authors of the preeminent work on Broken Windows policing are George Kelling and Katherine Coles. In their book, *Fixing Broken Windows,* they carefully outline what they believe occurred in New York City. They suggest that attacking quality-of-life crimes will reduce overall crime (i.e., Broken Windows theory). While Jack Maple does take issue with some of this, Broken Windows theory has become folklore among Compstat supporters.

Contrary to Maple, Kelling and Coles suggest that the New York City subway experience, in particular, is a model that should be followed. Indeed, Kelling worked closely with Bratton when he was Chief of the Transit Police (prior to Bratton becoming the NYPD commissioner and prior to the birth of Compstat). We do not take issue with Broken Windows nor with who gets credit for crime dropping—Maple, Kelling, Bratton, others, or some combination thereof. We give them each credit; rather, our research focus is not on credit but consequences. Indeed, we agree that crime has dropped but take issue with the extent of that drop due to the consequences of specific behaviors by NYPD upper management, which has been documented in this book and elsewhere. Here, we point out that Kelling and Coles, the paramount supporters of this method of policing, also understand and note in their book an important caveat to their method. This may be because the two of them are more versed in criminological theory. Regardless, they directly point out that such proactive policing methods can lead to police trampling on basic rights. Kelling and Coles (1996) write,

> The shift to a community-based, problem-oriented approach [i.e., Broken Windows] to maintaining order and reducing crime, as promising as it is for cities contains real dangers. ... The community model is active and interventionist, involving police intimately in neighborhoods as they attempt to solve problems before they worsen, and to some degree justifying intervention by citizens, directed at crime prevention, as well. Such actions by police and citizens must arise out of a broader base of authority and wider network collaboration. How such use of authority is to be controlled so as to protect the fundamental rights of all citizens is a major issue in a democratic society.

When staunch supporters give such clear warnings, it is best to listen. It is a key point and something that most acolytes of Compstat rarely address. That is, there are various pressures on police leaders such as the politics of appearing to be tough on crime. Other pressures exert themselves on police leaders such as the pressures from within the organization (i.e., the police culture) to show toughness. Police leaders in particular are very susceptible to simply copying the NYPD's Compstat without fully understanding its ramifications because it is a highly prized crime-fighting managerial process. We will discuss more on this issue later in this chapter.

Limited versus Unlimited Government

In a democratic society, the police are an arm of the executive branch of government. Two other separate and equal branches share power with the executive branch and are called the judiciary and the legislature. Our government was founded on the idea that no one branch should have too much power. As one of our founding fathers, James Madison writes (*Federalist Papers,* No. 48),

> An *elective despotism* was not the government we fought for; but one which should not only be founded on free principles, but in which the powers of government should be so divided and balanced among several bodies of magistracy as that no one could transcend their legal limits without being effectually checked and restrained by the others. For this reason that convention which passes the ordinance of government laid its foundation on this basis, that the legislative, executive, and judiciary departments should be separate and distinct, so that no person should exercise the powers of more than one of them at the same time.

This system is designed to protect what we as Americans consider our most cherished possession—liberty. Clearly, concern over too much government power is a tradition in our society dating back to our founding fathers. They purposely developed a governmental system whereby no branch of government would be supreme. As Madison (*Federalist Papers*, No. 51) writes,

> It may be a reflection on human nature, that such devices [checks and balances] should be necessary to control the abuses of government. But what is government itself, but the greatest of all reflections on human nature? If men were angels, no government would be necessary. If angels were to govern men, neither external nor internal controls on government would be necessary. In framing a government which is to be administered by men over men, the great difficulty lies in this: you must first enable the government to control the governed and in the next place oblige it to control itself. A dependence upon the people is, no doubt, the primary control on the government, but experience has taught mankind the necessity of auxiliary precautions [checks and balances].

Additionally, this tripartite structure is mimicked at the federal, state, and local levels, making the American system of government somewhat complicated.

Police power, then, is theoretically checked and balanced by the other branches of government and, at times, by other levels of government. Local police such as the NYPD must conform to local, state, and federal laws. Importantly, they must also abide and protect the Constitution of the United States. This is particularly true after passage of the 14th Amendment following the Civil War. Subsequently, the United States Supreme Court has decided a large number of cases that used the 14th Amendment as a conduit to apply the Bill of Rights to the states and thereby local law enforcement. Court cases such as *Miranda v. Arizona* (1966) and *Mapp v. Ohio* (1961) are cornerstones of study in criminal justice.

To put it succinctly, in our society, we not only expect police to be limited in their behaviors toward the public, we demand it. It is the essential fabric of our government. While not perfect, and no human creation is (including Compstat), it is the best we have. Blemishes and difficulties must be worked out. They need to be admitted and discussed in an open forum. Citizens then vote on them. In our view, former Prime Minister of the United Kingdom Winston Churchill (1947, November 11) states it best: "It has been said that democracy is the worst form of government except all the others that have been tried."

Social Contract

The police are also expected to work under what is generally known as a social contract. With respect to this discussion, it essentially means that government power emanates from the people and that their consent is essential. Among many thinkers that influenced our founding fathers were Jean-Jacques Rousseau and John Locke. They discuss the essence of the social contract. Rousseau essentially argues that,

> When, however, people agreed for mutual protection to surrender individual freedom of action and establish laws and government, they then acquired a sense of moral and civic obligation. In order to retain its essentially moral character, government must thus rest on the consent of the governed, the volonte generale (general will). (Social contract, 2011, para. 6)

Similarly, Locke argues that the people are the key to government power. Nevins and Commager (1986, 68) write, "Locke maintained that the supreme function of the state is to protect life, liberty, and property, to which every man is entitled. Political authority, he said is held in trust for the benefit of the people. ..."

The key to this discussion is that police power and all government power is derived from the people. The police work under this social contract. That is, they are public servants and to the extent possible should not force the will of others onto people but work with them. They need to maximize liberty while at the same time enforce the laws—a difficult task, at best.

Police in a Democracy

Without a doubt, the police are the focal point of governmental operations. How they do their job is like a microscope examining the innards of a society. On the one hand, they can be transparent, properly checked and balanced, work with communities, and serve the public; on the other hand, they can become the defining aspect of the government as in a police state. Thus, we can picture a continuum that ranges from police being restricted or limited in their authority to police being supremely powerful or unlimited.

Examining police behavior, then, is critical to understanding the society in which one lives. Bouza (1990, 171–72), for example, discusses this issue:

> There is no doubt that making the state more efficient usually means making it more powerful. ... The push pull of individual freedoms and the power of the state form the central dilemma of political life in society. It's never more dramatically illustrated [than] surrounding the operating of police departments.

Law enforcement officers in democratic countries are theoretically constrained by the law and sworn to uphold the rights of all. They are, quite literally, public servants. Their power ultimately comes from the people. Local officers must also work within the mandates of the Bill of Rights. These are the first ten amendments to the United States Constitution. The United States Supreme Court interprets the Constitution and thereby theoretically limits officers' street behaviors. For example, in *Terry v. Ohio* (1968) the high court states that officers need a level of proof known as reasonable suspicion before making a forcible stop. Thus, by law, local police in the United States cannot forcibly stop anyone they wish; at a minimum, they must have reasonable suspicion.

As a country, we have made certain choices to limit the authority of government especially of our police. Contrary to what some police leaders, academics, and members of the media have claimed about the main mission of police being to fight crime (see, for example, numerous books on Compstat and fighting crime including Bratton, 1998; Maple, 1999; and Henry (2002), as well as articles by Compstat acolytes such as MacDonald, 2010, February 17), a major mission of the police is to protect the Constitution of the United States. This is what a *sworn officer* is—a protector of the Constitution.

Crime Control versus Due Process

Closely related to policing in democracies is the tension between crime control and due process. Herbert Packer (1966) discusses two models of the criminal justice system. He uses the terms crime control and due process models. He describes the former model as, "...the efficient, expeditious and reliable screening and disposition of persons suspected of crime as the central value to be served by the criminal process" (Packer, 1966, 238–239). To this end, he uses the analogy of an assembly line. Essentially this means making arrests and getting those arrested to prison as soon as possible. In this model, there is less regard for basic rights. Conversely, Packer explains the due process model, "sees that function [the criminal process] as limited by, and subordinate to the maintenance of the dignity and autonomy of the individual" (Packer, 1966, 238–239). He likens this model to an obstacle course that criminal justice practitioners must go through to eventually have the person arrested and sent to prison. *Miranda, Mapp,* and other cases would be seen as obstacles for law enforcement to overcome. While these models are extremes, they are useful for discussion.

Compstat is clearly a crime control policy and a successful one. Law enforcement rhetoric on reducing crime has become commonplace in policing. As stated in the NYPD publication *The Compstat Process* (NYPD, 1998, 1), "The success of this strategic control system and our Crime Control and Quality-of-Life strategies are evidenced by the tremendous declines in crime we have achieved since 1993." As far back as 1994 and earlier, the NYPD was declaring its overwhelming crime control successes. Initially, we believe the NYPD gave attention to balancing due process policies with crime control policies through programs such as *Courtesy, Professionalism and Respect* (see Eterno, 2001, 2003). However, few police departments who emulated Compstat bothered to examine such programs at the NYPD when they came to visit and bring back to their departments the NYPD model. Further, based on our findings, Compstat appears to have morphed into a numbers game over the years with little attention to due process programs. Repeatedly we hear trumpeting of NYPD crime numbers but little in the way of due process is mentioned. Thus, when a program like Compstat focuses almost exclusively on crime control, one can hypothesize that if the department is not careful, due process considerations will likely suffer. Civilian complaints for abuse of authority were skyrocketing (in 2003 there were 7,488 abuse complaints [CCRB, 2003, Table 1a], in 2009 there were 12,321 [CCRB, 2009, Table 1a]); forcible stops wildly increasing (97,837 in 2002 [Baker, 2007, November 21]) when crime was down enormously to over 601,055 in 2010 [DelSignore, 2011, February 23]); and increases in civil rights lawsuits for abuse of authority by police (see *Litigation and Settlement News*, 2011, June 23) are just some examples pointing to the dangers in this area.

Compstat is the driving engine of the crime control model in many police departments in modern democratic society. Other research has suggested that Compstat brings law enforcement back to a traditional model of policing (Weisburd, Mastrofski, McNally, Greenspan, and Willis, 2003). Yet many of those who claim its success and practice its policies have not attempted to grasp fully the mechanisms by which it works. This is because police managers and others essentially see the main mission of the police as reducing crime. For example, Henry (2002, 178) stresses the role of crime reduction and suggests community policing takes police away from its main mission:

> … police agencies should not attempt to venture too far from the provision of police services, despite the pressures put upon them by some Community Policing ideologies. Police agencies must recognize that their proper and legitimate role is the protection of life and property under the law, the maintenance of order in the community, and the reduction of crime and the fear of crime.

Notably omitted from the list is what should be considered one of the most important aspects of policing in a democracy—protecting the Constitution and people's rights. Crime reduction, arguably the main positive aspect of Compstat, is certainly important to policing. However, it is patently incomplete to suggest crime reduction is the central mission of democratic policing. Indeed, it is easy to bring crime down. Simply create a draconian law such that anyone who commits a larceny will have his or her hands chopped off. Of course, this law will have the effect of reducing crime. Clearly, however, this would violate the 8th Amendment's prohibition against cruel and unusual punishment. Alternatively, perhaps the police will forcibly stop nearly everyone walking in any part of the city. This would clearly violate *Terry* and the 4th Amendment's prohibitions against unreasonable search and seizure. As a society, we take this so seriously that officers are sworn to support the Constitution. A typical oath for a new officer is,

I swear (or affirm) that I will support the Constitution of the United States, and that I will be faithful and bear true allegiance to the State of Maryland and support the Constitution and laws thereof; and that I will, to the best of my skill and judgment diligently and faithfully, without partiality or prejudice, execute the office of police officer according to the Constitution and laws of this State. (City of Greenbelt, Maryland, 2011)

It should be noted that this oath of office was taken from a department that is accredited by the Commission on Accreditation for Law Enforcement Agencies (CALEA). CALEA describes itself as,

The Commission on Accreditation for Law Enforcement Agencies, Inc., (CALEA') was created in 1979 as a credentialing authority through the joint efforts of law enforcement's major executive associations:

- International Association of Chiefs of Police (IACP);
- National Organization of Black Law Enforcement Executives (NOBLE);
- National Sheriffs' Association (NSA); and the
- Police Executive Research Forum (PERF).

The purpose of CALEA's Accreditation Programs is to improve the delivery of public safety services, primarily by: maintaining a body of standards, developed by public safety practitioners, covering a wide range of up-to-date public safety initiatives; establishing and administering an accreditation process; and recognizing professional excellence. (CALEA, 2011)

While NYPD is a professional police organization and has acceptable standards based on New York State law, it has not been accredited—either by CALEA or by any other outside body. Many agencies voluntarily achieve the high standards required of accreditation. The NYPD continues to balk at this. It is yet another indication that the NYPD simply does not permit outside scrutiny, even from within the law enforcement community. The NYPD can certainly not be described as transparent.

What makes policing so difficult and such a high calling in democracies, however, is not crime reduction but *crime reduction while at the same time respecting basic human rights*. Here lies one of the key issues with Compstat as the department's leadership in the democratic world is currently practicing it. Finding a proper balance between civil liberties and crime control is the difficulty faced by modern law enforcement in a democratic society.

Note that the oath of office focuses on support of the Constitution. New officers do not swear to bring down crime, although that seems to be the prevailing thought of the current Compstat followers. Even the titles of the books authored by those who developed Compstat are revealing. For example, Jack Maple's book, *The Crime Fighter*, is especially revealing. William Bratton's book also suggests that crime fighting is the key—*Turnaround, How America's Top Cop Reversed the Crime Epidemic*. Favorable accounts of Compstat tend to focus on this crime-fighting aspect. As stated earlier in this chapter, even the most adamant supporter of Compstat argues for some selective enforcement (see Maple, 1999, 154). Additionally, Kelling and Coles, arguably the most vocal supporters of Broken Windows, recognize what is one of the most controversial aspects of this policing method, the possibility of violating citizens' basic human rights.

The Dilemma for Police: Balance Crime Fighting with Due Process

While not completely rejecting the NYPD Compstat model, we argue that in democratic society its nearly total focus on crime fighting for the police role is myopic—even malignant. More important than bringing down crime is following and supporting the Constitution of the United States and other applicable laws. Thus, while controlling crime, officers, at the same time, *must* follow the law. This is difficult to do and it is meant to be that way in a democracy. As a society, our rights are more important to us than controlling crime. While controlling crime is important to police, it is patently incorrect to state that it is their sole mission. Rather, police departments need to bring down crime while at the same time respecting basic rights. That is the dilemma, the difficulty for police in a democratic society. It is precisely what makes the police officers' job so important and challenging. By definition, police must work under restrictions in a democracy.

These are not trivial points. Many claim that police in the United States do not work under the restrictions they are required to, at least in some instances (Bittner, 1970; Chambliss, 1994; Manning, 1977; Skolnick, 1966;

Skolnick and Fyfe, 1993; Westley, 1970). That is, the police go beyond their powers to enforce the law and indeed may violate the law. For example, in their book on police, New York University professor Jerome Skolnick and a highly respected police expert, former lieutenant, professor, and the late former deputy commissioner of NYPD James Fyfe write,

> In the popular view, perhaps the most frequent check on day-to-day police operations is the criminal courts, which in theory see to it that police anti-crime efforts conform to the Constitution. The right to be free from unreasonable search, the right to remain silent, the right to an attorney. ... Neither practice and theory nor reality and perception always match, however, and the general conception of the courts' influence on police activity is exaggerated. The exclusionary rule, for example, is no bar to the search practices of officers. ... Popular overestimation or exaggeration of the court's effects on police effectiveness is a matter of more than academic interest. (Skolnick and Fyfe, 1993, 193–194)

Lundman (1998, 542) writes that legal factors play a secondary role in police arrest decisions, "What street cops call 'attitude' (... also see Bayley 1994, 30) had the largest effect in the present research, followed by race, class, and finally the legal variables." Other researchers suggest similar extralegal influences on police decision making especially the arrest decision (see, for example, Worden and Shepard, 1996; Linn, 2009).

Some have speculated that officers in the United States are working with very few checks on their behaviors. A few scholars go so far as to suggest some Americans live in a police state. While such views are quite radical, in the spirit of remaining value neutral, we convey the ideas. A police state can be defined as,

> a political unit characterized by repressive governmental control of political, economic, and social life usually by an arbitrary exercise of power by police and especially secret police in place of regular operation of administrative and judicial organs of the government according to publicly known legal procedures. (Police state, *Merriam Webster Dictionary*).

Chambliss (1994), for example, does research on rapid deployment units (RDUs). He writes,

> The RDU patrol the ghetto continuously looking for cars with young black men in them...There is a nod to legality in vehicular stops in that the officers look for a violation in order to justify the stop...The RDU does not patrol the predominantly white sections of Washington, D.C. Observations of policing in this area of the city reveal an entirely different approach by the police. There are no "rips" and no vehicular stops unless there is a clear violation. Officers

are not looking for cars with black drivers. If a car is stopped other cars are not called as backups, and the officer handles the infraction on his or her own. ... the United States will move towards a society divided by race and class into communities that are *quasi police states* patrolled by RDU-type police units in search of crime and communities where minor infractions of the law are treated, as they should be, as tolerable indiscretions. (Chambliss, 1994, 179–180, 192–193 [italics added])

Clearly, he is eliciting an image of uncontrolled police behavior especially in minority neighborhoods.

As Americans, we must be concerned about actions by police that even appear like uncontrolled police power. As former Chief Justice Earl Warren (1959, 89) writes, "Life and liberty can be as much endangered from illegal methods used to convict those thought to be criminals as from the actual criminals themselves." His dire warning certainly raises alarms when we compare it to police behavior when the Nazis came to power in Germany. Burleigh and Wipperman (1991, 63) write,

Not only the Gestapo could detain people in "protective custody," but also the regular and criminal police, who could now keep the "asocial" in "police preventive custody." This practice was retrospectively legalised on 14 December 1937 when Himmler issued a "decree for the *preventive fight against crime.*" [italics added]

Thus, as Americans we need to be extra vigilant especially when crime fighting becomes the key to police behavior.

Transparency

With respect to the New York City Police Department, we have observed a tendency toward closing its doors to scrutiny. Certainly, the agency has some prerogatives with regard to access. However, policing in democracies requires transparency. Visitors, even from other police departments, are no longer welcome at Compstat meetings unless carefully vetted. Reporters have talked to us about the lack of openness at the NYPD. One reporter went so far as to tell us that he had been all over the nation and this is the only department that does not allow access to precinct commanders. Police Commissioner Ray Kelly took away Leonard Levitt's press credentials. Mr. Kelly went so far as to travel to Long Island to talk to Mr. Levitt's bosses. Mr. Kelly's concern about this reporter's provocative column is highly unusual (see Chapter 6). Graham Rayman, who wrote the award-winning series of articles on Adrian Schoolcraft, is one of the few reporters willing to put in writing what is occurring in New York City. In one article, he talks about a small newspaper as being one of the few to challenge the NYPD on its lack of transparency. Rayman (2011, July 13) writes, "While much of the local media accept the NYPD's resistance to providing public information, the stalwart editors of the tiny *Norwood News* weekly in the Bronx are at least trying to do something about it." Similarly, in another recent article, Ortiz (2011, July 17) writes,

> The public's "right to know" has become the public's right to wait—and in some cases, getting information from government agencies is a process that can drag on for months without a reliable response. ... Over the years, the NYPD has routinely ignored or responded with the bare minimum to amNew-York's requests for information, from basic details on crimes and effectiveness of surveillance cameras to whether cops are assigned at specific landmarks.

Lawsuits such as those by the *New York Times* (see Barron, 2010, December 21) and the New York Civil Liberties Union (*NYCLU v. NYPD,* 2009) among others are indicative of the closed-door policy at the NYPD. The NYPD only seems to release vetted data and information and then only reluctantly.

In a democracy, the press needs a free reign to report. At times that will mean negative press, but this can assist a department in uncovering weaknesses and then making changes. A certain openness is required of the department to allow this. Reporters have consistently noted to us their concern about closed access because of a critical NYPD story. They told us that these concerns began under Mayor Giuliani and became more pronounced as the years went on. As of this writing, we would describe the NYPD as not in the least transparent or open (see Chapter 6 for a more detailed analysis of this topic).

Some police leaders in the free world have recognized this critical need for transparency. In an interview with Odd Berner Malme, the former second in command of Norway's police and currently one of Norway's key representatives to the United Nations, he discusses the need for transparency in democratic policing. Further, he talks about the need for police leaders to be part of the public discussion in democracies and they should freely express their views in the public arena. In a recent interview, Eterno (2008, 152) asked the police leader a very pertinent question:

JE: Do political considerations make it difficult for a police chief to speak his or her mind?

OB: In Norway, the government appoints the chief of police and they cannot fire you without raising a case against you. Additionally, you are a political person [as an individual] independent of your professional duty. But, professionalism is essential to a police chief. They need to be able to receive critics in an open way... You are generally free to discuss issues with the media and others. Police chiefs should take an active part in the public debate.

Policing expert David Bayley also feels that there is a need for the political will to be there before change can take place in policing. However, he was not talking about policing in the United States when he penned this. He was discussing democratizing the police abroad (see, for example, Bayley, 2001). Yet both of these individuals, one a former practitioner and the other an eminent scholar, touch upon the key missing element at the NYPD—transparency.

Democratic policing requires an open discussion with the public. However, the system currently at the NYPD stifles any communication with the public. At the NYPD, anyone above the rank of captain is appointed to that rank at the pleasure of the police commissioner who is also a political appointee who, essentially, serves at the pleasure of the mayor. The promotion system above captain is a source of great displeasure among our sample. Further, to be promoted one apparently must tow the company line. Because of this, there are very few who reach the upper echelon of the NYPD who are vocal critics or even critical at all in public. Such an unhealthy environment is a recipe for disaster. Transparency in democracy is necessary. Free flow of information allows for open discussion and positive change to take place. This helps police to maintain their legitimacy through the social contract.

Social Science Theory and NYPD Compstat

Rational Choice/Deterrence Theory

Another social science theory that helps explain Compstat as practiced by the NYPD is rational choice/deterrence theory. Using this theory as a guide suggests that Compstat is a program that tries to be proactive at preventing crime by focusing on those who want to do wrong. On a very basic level, those who practice Compstat generally believe it will deter those who may commit an illegal act by making the "would-be criminal" aware that the police will sanction a potential perpetrator.

During Compstat meetings at Headquarters (also, at each borough and each precinct), the police identify hotspots by mapping complaint reports of crimes—places where crime occurs more regularly—and essentially the police focus resources on those areas. Mapping software is used to identify these areas and computer-generated electronic pin maps display the places where various crimes have taken place. Colorful dots or points on a map indicate locations, times, places, types of crimes, etc. This helps the police to visualize what is occurring with respect to crime. Using this and other available data from crime complaint reports, the police try to identify patterns and areas of concern. Essentially, what this means is that police aim to "make the dots go away" (see Maple, 1999, 38; Figure 7.1). We note here that, in general, there is little or no attempt to understand why the dots got there in the first place (e.g., underlying social causes, economic depression in the area, etc.); nor do the police try to work with communities to determine whether their strategies will have an adverse impact. Rather, the police who practice NYPD-style policing are enforcing the law as if there were one community standard throughout the city. This is an important point and needs further explanation.

As discussed in Chapter 5, Wilson (1977) points out that there are three basic styles of police departments. Again, the three styles are service (police take all requests seriously but are less likely to make an arrest or summons); watchman (basically maintaining order and little else); and legalistic (police handle incidents formally by making many arrests and writing summonses). The NYPD practice of Compstat is unquestionably legalistic. Officers must make arrests and write summonses, regardless of their impact on the community, to be reflected at Compstat meetings. As such, NYPD's leadership tries to impose one legal standard on the entire city, regardless of neighborhood. Essentially, the department does not attempt to work with communities to establish or discuss any issues or costs (not just monetary) involved in whatever policing strategies are chosen. The police essentially choose to enforce the laws they feel need to be enforced with little community input. As such, the NYPD deems itself to know what is best for each community with limited, if any, consultation with those whom the strategies affect most.

Thus, regardless of neighborhood, the police engage in a strategy based on the assumption that focusing police resources on these areas, criminals

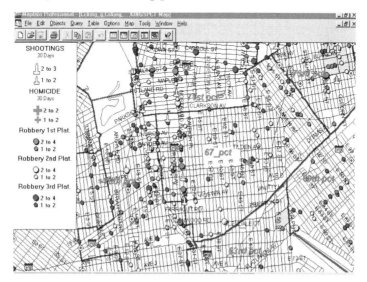

Figure 7.1 Example of Compstat Computerized Pin Map.

will change their behaviors. Such a system is fundamentally based on the idea that criminals are rational in their actions. That is, criminal behavior is the byproduct of the potential wrongdoer's rational assessment of the costs and benefits of conforming versus illegal behavior. If the costs outweigh the benefits, the potential criminal will remain law abiding. If the benefits outweigh the costs, a crime will occur.

Of course, the entire exercise of "making the dots go away" assumes that the police are actually taking complaint reports for the crimes they are trying to stop. Even Maple realizes the possibility that not taking reports may occur due to the pressures of Compstat meetings. Maple points out that he learned some of this from John Timoney (another NYPD veteran—former First Deputy Commissioner). Timoney's experiences in Philadelphia with respect to crime reporting clearly comports with our suggestions of downgrading in New York City. Commissioner Timoney went so far as to not report the crime statistics of Philadelphia to the FBI for a time because the numbers were so troubling. He had to crack down on the practice of downgrading crime complaints (see, for example, Maple, 1999, 180–182). Further, Maple writes that in New Orleans, as in Philadelphia, integrity tests were developed to promote honest behavior by officers. While the NYPD claims to have some devices to check the numbers, no integrity testing has been conducted to date. Based on our interviews, the monitoring that does exist is completely ineffectual.

Raymond Dussautt (1999) interviews Jack Maple on this issue. Maple states quite specifically what needs to be done by departments to protect their crime figures:

> You can do this by matching up the data they are giving with the CAD [Computer Aided Dispatch] printout every day. Also, the quality assurance team needs to regularly go out and do relentless audits, and chiefs of police should regularly call in a couple of phony radio runs and see how they show up in crime reports. (Dussault, 1999)

Responding to problems raised by our research and others, Commissioner Kelly set up a panel to examine the alleged manipulation of crime reports (see Chapter 2). The commissioner (see Bode, 2011, January 6) chose three former United States Attorneys for the task. When we were called before the Committee, we clearly stated that the absence of such an integrity system is an enormous weakness in the NYPD auditing system (that to our knowledge remains until this day). Officers we have talked with state they had little or no concern about being caught by Quality Assurance as practiced by the NYPD. We note again that not taking these reports undermines the entire Compstat process. Additionally, police management at the precinct level is keenly aware that upper management is bean counting as well as examining the electronic pin maps.

The NYPD has also been made aware of such issues by our research and other works clearly showing the problem. A few years after Compstat began, the NYPD concerns were evident as they created a Data Integrity Unit. The NYPD also suggests that it devotes enormous resources into attempting to make sure the numbers are reported accurately. Yet, they still have not instituted the key integrity mechanisms that we identify (see Chapter 8). Given the enormous pressures of Compstat meetings, it is exceedingly unlikely that crime numbers are entirely accurate. The NYPD itself has stated that four commanding officers have been disciplined from 2001 to 2009 for manipulating the crime reports (see Rashbaum, 2010, February 6). Why the NYPD does not incorporate such simple, low-cost devices is anyone's guess. Regardless, it leaves a gaping hole in their costly, generally ineffective system for monitoring crime report manipulation activities.

Labeling Theory

Contrary to deterrence theory, labeling theorists, sometimes called societal reaction theory, suggest that enforcing minor violations with formal sanctions will ultimately lead to *more serious deviant activity*. What are the mechanisms of this transition?

The labeling perspective (see, for example, Liska and Messner, 1999, 114–146) focuses on who is sanctioned by formal authority. The idea is that the formal sanctions carry with them strong negative social consequences. Labeling theorists argue that minor deviance is better handled informally— just the opposite of the NYPD's heavy-handed policies, which essentially require officers to make summonses and arrests so they can be reflected in the Compstat numbers.

Essentially, labeling theorists argue that a person who commits a minor deviant act, if not formally sanctioned, will terminate the unwanted behavior on his or her own accord. That is, minor deviant acts are ephemeral, fleeting, temporary actions. The person who does minor acts of deviance generally does not consider him or herself a deviant. However, when formal sanctions, especially the aggressive type in New York City, where minor violations such as beer drinking by youth in a park or marijuana possession are constantly enforced with summonses and arrests, it will ultimately lead to more illegal behavior on the part of the person sanctioned. Why? Labeling theorists suggest that the social stigma created by the formal action leads to deviance. That is, police sanctions lead to a formal citation or arrest which, in turn, makes it less likely that the person will obtain gainful employment, less likely that the person will have non-deviant peers, and, ultimately, the person will develop a deviant self-concept. Labeling theorists suggest that if police, as practiced in some untargeted neighborhoods (often white, middle-class areas), simply give a warning or something similar, the person interacting with the police is far less likely to become a deviant.

One way to understand labeling theory is through a process John Braithwaite calls reintegrative shaming. Braithwaite (1995) argues that the social context of the labeling is the key to understanding whether it will work. The idea is to shame a person into proper behavior. In some societies, such as Japan, shaming an individual is more likely to change behavior for the better. The society emphasizes reintegrating the person into the mainstream. In contrast, it can be argued that in a society like the United States, shaming does not work well. There is certainly an attempt to shame and punish the person (e.g., DWI walls of shame for those found guilty). However, that same person is not reintegrated into the society. Rather, the opposite occurs as American society continues to shun the person even after the punishment takes place. Thus, the cultural context in which shaming is done is very important. The correlates of this theory suggest to us that after punishment, American society should try its best to accept the person back.

How does this translate into law enforcement policy? The NYPD uses stop-and-frisk, arrest, and summonses in a nearly ubiquitous way. The numbers must look good for Compstat meetings. It has become a mindless numbers game. If police wish to use these tactics, theory suggests that they also need to ensure that such offenders are reintegrated into the society. Unfortunately, we know of no program sponsored by the NYPD to reintegrate offenders. Indeed, in the case of stop-and-frisk, the vast majority of those affected by the policy have done nothing wrong. They are completely innocent. While the numbers of police activity continue to rise, there is little or no follow up or concern about what the consequences are. The pressure to make sure the numbers look good overwhelms any logic or need for them in the first place. Further, it is simply assumed that such police activity including formal sanctions is appropriate for nearly every situation (i.e., a legalistic style). It is a policy based completely on formal sanctions by police with little thought or use of outside resources or community input.

Strain Theory

The NYPD concentrates its activity in those areas they identify as high crime. Inevitably using official numbers that the police themselves collect, the targeted areas tend to be lower class and minority. Even if we accept their numbers, the method used to attack crime in these areas may have unanticipated results. We have already discussed labeling theory. Other criminological theory, however, also leads us to, at a minimum, question the adequacy of the NYPD formula.

Robert Merton developed what is generally called strain theory (see Liska and Messner, 1999, 28–54). Essentially, Merton argues that there is a disjuncture between culturally accepted goals and the culturally accepted means to attain those goals. In the United States, he argues, hard work should eventually lead to the cultural goal of money. However, Merton argues that this is a misnomer. That is, very few can attain the goal of money using acceptable means. This leads some to deviate from the norm. Who are most likely to deviate? Cloward and Ohlin suggest it is those who have the opportunity to learn and use delinquent tactics. In the lower-class areas on which the NYPD concentrates, there is less opportunity to succeed in the non-delinquent world (see, for example, Liska and Messner, 1999). The NYPD exacerbates the difficulties of those children growing up in these neighborhoods by labeling them though formal sanctions. Police forcibly stop even those who are not delinquent in very high numbers. Compare this to the middle-class, white neighborhood where youth are often engaged in similar deviant activities such as smoking marijuana, drinking beer, and other quality-of-life violations. Since the NYPD concentrates its force on lower-class, minority areas, those youth in middle-class, white areas doing the same activities will not get a criminal record. In today's world of information, having a criminal record at a young age can be a life sentence. The NYPD need look no further than its own applicant processing where those applying for a job are weeded out in part based on their past summonses and arrests (see also Dwyer, 2011, June 16). Given that the NYPD concentrates its efforts in "high-crime" areas, those children who grow up in those neighborhoods are more likely to have a criminal record, more likely to get summonses, and more likely to be forcibly stopped. Essentially this occurs because the NYPD generally treats the entire city as if there is one community standard. There is little conversation with various communities about what they think is appropriate for the police. Rather, the police dictate the problems and the solutions. While this may be necessary to some extent, the overwhelming numbers of stops, summonses, and arrests especially of minorities is clearly a concern.

Of course, all of us want safe neighborhoods, but the police need not dictate from headquarters how it is done. Local commanders and officers need to have discretion to determine how best to handle neighborhoods and individual situations. Having the ever-increasing pressure of Compsat on officers (with what may be illegal quotas on them) is no way to police a city (see, for example, Murray, 2005).

The job of policing is difficult and it is meant to be in a democracy. Police are servants of the people and ultimately need to understand and deal with the entire array of the ramifications of policies that affect everyone.

Conflict Theory

While more radical, it must be acknowledged that some criminal justice theorists argue that the police are agents of the ruling classes. Theories that fall into this category, in general, are called conflict theory. The most relevant is racial conflict theory, although the largest school of thought in this area argues that the wealthy control the laws and police.

Racial conflict theory argues that the police, acting as an agent of the powerful majority, abuse their power and position to try to keep minorities from achieving full equality. For example, local police enforced former Jim Crow laws of the South. While such laws are unconstitutional today, behaviors by police such as racial profiling, driving while black, use of excessive force (e.g., Sean Bell, Amadou Diallo—discussed in more detail later in this chapter), enforcing laws only in minority areas, lack of fair hiring practices, and similar activities are indicative of racial conflict theory being alive and well today. John Jay College of Criminal Justice, for example, has The Center for Race, Crime and Justice, showing how important this area of study is.

The federal government's Justice Department is one of the most important agencies charged with ensuring fair practices of law enforcement officers. Recently, the New Jersey State Police, the Pittsburgh Police Department, the Los Angeles Police Department, and others have been under consent decree for practices targeting minorities. The most prominent example is the possibility of racial motivation of the NYPD's stop-and-frisk practices (e.g., Attorney General, State of New York, Eliot Spitzer, 1999; CCRB, 2001).

Specific Examples

For the purposes of this chapter, the ramifications of specific police behaviors are explicated from a theoretical view. That is, these behaviors by police have far more reaching consequences than the individuals involved. For example, if citizens are being issued summonses, either illegally or perhaps unnecessarily, then this may mean that:

1. the quality-of-life crime fighting focus has gone too far
2. police are acting without checks on their behaviors
3. police are losing their mandate under the social contract, that democratic policing is being minimized and police are, at a minimum, not respecting people's rights
4. police are not being transparent, informing the public of their behaviors
5. people who are targeted for police intervention (mostly minorities) are labeled and therefore find it more difficult to get suitable employment and may even resort to further deviant activity due to these behaviors by police

6. the communities police are supposed to serve are being victimized by police rather than assisted
7. the police department may be in violation of the law (e.g., Quota bill, illegal stops)

To illustrate the importance of a theoretical understanding of Compstat, we offer some pertinent examples. The key to understanding at least a portion of these incidents is pressure from Headquarters through the Compstat process. This pressure is passed down through the ranks and translated into these street behaviors by officers.

We have already discussed how officers are under enormous pressures to write summonses to be reflected in the Compstat numbers. The NYPD argues that it gives "targets" to officers on what is expected of them. However, when targets are combined with specific punishments for failure to meet them, it amounts to an illegal quota. This is not trivial, as violation of the law and the practical need to stop the behaviors and help the community must be paramount. Summonses should not be written merely to meet a mindless demand by management. We discuss and give other evidence for this pressure in more detail in Chapter 5. We now cite some examples of incidents that clearly demonstrate actions of the aforementioned theories. The fact that police officers engage in these behaviors is another indication of the overwhelming pressures they are under as well as their lack of discretion. Importantly, the enormous repercussions for democratic policing must also be kept in mind.

Overpowering Pressure to Write Summonses

One of the more bizarre examples is when officers issued summonses to two sets of women eating doughnuts in a park in Brooklyn. Essentially the story as reported by Johnston, (2011, June 8) is that there is a doughnut shop in the 76th Precinct in the Bedford-Stuyvesant area of Brooklyn. The doughnuts are very tasty and there is a playground across the street with benches. When the doughnut shop gets too crowded, some people like to go to the playground and eat. On one particular day, two very diligent officers found two women eating doughnuts in the park and wrote them summonses. They observed two other "violators" eating doughnuts and repeated the issuance of summonses to these other women. Neither of the two groups of women was threatening and, indeed, they were talking to the mothers in the park who had no problem with them. The officers most likely needed to fill their quota.

The reason for the law that no people without children are permitted in the park is ostensibly to protect children from perverts and other criminals. These women were no threat and even if there was an issue, the best way to handle such activity is simply for the police to ask them politely to leave. Our readers should note that the summons for the doughnut caper requires the "perpetrators" physically to go to court to plead their case and then pay a fine if found guilty. The officers too may have to waste their time going to court to testify. While we are not questioning their guilt, we do question how it was handled. These officers were overly concerned about numbers. If these women now try to get a job in law enforcement or elsewhere, these summonses will be on their records.

Officer discretion is important. When trained at the Police Academy, recruits are told about enforcing the spirit of the law as opposed to the letter of the law. In this case, as in many others, the spirit of the law is simply to tell these women to leave assuming they are a problem, which we tend to think they were not. Pressures to write summonses are great. We ask—is this just as likely to happen in a middle-class, white area where the women may have been lawyers, police officers, or politicians?

Another well-known playground incident with summonses involves some people playing chess in a park. In New York City, some tables in parks have, quite literally, chess boards built into them. For years people have used these obviously marked boards to, well, play chess. Again, New York's finest have determined that such chess-playing fiends must be removed from the park. On October 20, 2010, police officers gave summonses to seven people playing chess. This occurred in the Inwood area of upper Manhattan (see Zanoni, 2010, November 17). We note that this is a completely different borough compared to our last example. As with the previous incident, the area is predominantly minority. Again, officer discretion is missing. No warnings, no requests, just summonses. Why? The only apparent reason is mindless numbers.

A similar but far more tragic incident occurred to an elderly black couple in Queens—a third borough of New York City apparently infected by aggressive police (see CBS News, 2011, January 24). On a freezing cold January evening, Robert and Doris Hudson drove to a pharmacy to get Mrs. Hudson's prescription filled. The police stopped them outside the pharmacy for not having a seatbelt on. They did not have identification with them. On the cold evening, Mr. Hudson went on foot to get their identification in their home. When he returned, he found that the summons was already written using the prescription bottle for his wife's medication as identification. They drove away and he soon collapsed of a heart attack and later died. While the officers certainly enforced the letter of the law, the spirit of the law is once again cast aside. The pressure to write summonses is the only possible explanation for writing a summons to this elderly woman. This lack of discretion is, quite simply, lunacy. It is Compstat gone wild. How does this serve the ends of justice? If anything, these officers should have escorted the elderly couple home. Is this crime fighting in the sense that Jack Maple had in mind? Certainly, the officers could have handled this differently but the mindless pressures of Compstat have now filtered down to street officers and changed the playing field.

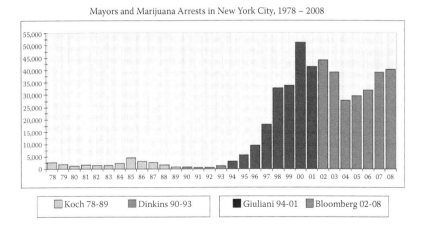

Figure 7.2 Mayors and Marijuana Arrests in New York City, 1978-2008. (*Source*: Dr. Harry Levine, Professor, Queens College, retrieved July 15, 2011 from http://dragon.soc.qc.cuny.edu/staff/levine)

Overzealous Marijuana Enforcement

Mere possession of marijuana has been decriminalized in New York State since 1977. What that means is that it is still illegal to possess marijuana but possession is merely a violation of the law—a lower-level infraction similar to a traffic violation. Those who are caught with concealed marijuana should generally face a fine of $100 and be released immediately. However, this law does not decriminalize open view marijuana, which is still a misdemeanor (a crime). The NYPD has been making overwhelmingly large numbers of arrests for marijuana in public view, which is still a crime (a B misdemeanor). Essentially, it comes down to this—in your pocket okay, outside your pocket you are in trouble.

The number of arrests for public view, however, is clearly the focus of NYPD targeted enforcement. In the case of New York City, marijuana arrests have truly skyrocketed from 1994 onward—the first full year of Compstat (see Figure 7.2). The first two years of Compstat under William Bratton (1994 and 1995) showed 3,400 and 6,000 arrests for possession inclusive (Levine, 2011). While higher than the past, arguably it was still within reason. During Bratton's tenure, he managed to bring down crime enormously without the corresponding arrests for possession of marijuana. Indeed, the NYPD was responsible for much of the crime drop in the United States in those two years (Silverman, 2001). However, in the following years, the numbers of arrests for marijuana doubled to a high of over 50,000 in 2000 and then dropped a bit. In 2010, the NYPD again made 50,383 arrests for minor marijuana possession charges. These arrests, we note, are going up while the NYPD claims that crime continues to go down.

More importantly, these arrests are targeting young Hispanics and Blacks. This is due completely to NYPD policy. As Levine writes,

> U.S. government surveys consistently find that young whites use marijuana at higher rates than young blacks and Latinos. But for many years, New York City has arrested African Americans at seven times the rate of whites, and Latinos at nearly four times the rate of whites. ... As *New York Times* columnist Jim Dwyer accurately titled his December 23, 2009 column, "*Whites Smoke Pot, But Blacks Are Arrested.*" (Levine, 2011, p. 2)

Examining criminal justice theory, we are aware that arresting people can have very damaging side effects (see discussion on labeling theory and Dwyer, 2011). Levine (2011, 3) puts it quite succinctly:

> Twenty years ago, misdemeanor arrest and conviction records were papers kept in court store ... often impossible to locate. Now they are computerized and instantly searchable on the Internet for $20 to $40 through commercial criminal-record database services. A simple Google search for the phrase "criminal database" or "criminal records" produces numerous links to firms. ...

Employers, landlords, credit agencies, licensing boards for nurses and beauticians, schools, and banks now routinely search these databases for background checks on applicants. A simple arrest for marijuana possession can show up on criminal databases as a "drug arrest" without specifying the substance, the charge, or even if the person was convicted. Employers and landlords, faced with an abundance of applicants, often eliminate those with criminal arrest records, especially for drugs. Nurses, security guards, and others licensed by the state can lose their licenses and their jobs from just one misdemeanor marijuana arrest.

The NYPD, whether intentional or not, is clearly targeting minorities who suffer far more and are doing the same activities as whites. As Levine (2011, 4) writes,

> In the 1980s Barack Obama was a college student in New York City, living on the border of Harlem. He used marijuana, walked around the city. ... If the current policing policies of New York and other cities were in effect at that time, he might well have been arrested and jailed. If that had happened Barack Obama would not be president today.

The reasoning behind this law in 1977 in the introduction to the law reads,

> The legislature finds that arrests, criminal prosecutions, and criminal penalties are inappropriate for people who possess small quantities of marijuana for

personal use. Every year, this process needlessly scars thousands of lives and wastes millions of dollars in law enforcement resources, while detracting from the prosecution of serious crime. (As cited by Levine, 2011)

Nothing could be clearer. The intent of the law was to stop overzealous law enforcement. Further, the legislature reveals its concerns for the underside of quality-of-life policing—labeling theory. Where is the police discretion? What about enforcing the spirit of the law? Under the pressures of Compstat, we expect little change. Some may argue it is for the better but they are probably not the poor young minority (doing the same acts as middle-class whites) struggling for a decent life.

The call to change police practices by those with an understanding of theory and practice are gaining voices. While Compstat sympathizers try to mute such calls, those who know what is just will not be silenced. Chambliss (1994, 192–193) writes,

Law enforcement agencies will have to change their reward system to emphasize community policing and rewarding officers who do not have to make arrests in their communities, rather than rewarding those who do. ... It is unlikely, however, that any of these changes will take place so long as we continue to criminalize drugs and provide an incentive for police officers and prosecutors to entrap and arrest people for the possession or sale of small amounts of drugs.

In New York City, Levine (2011) has been especially vocal. However, others too have strongly suggested that the NYPD change its policies; apparently, this wisdom is falling on policymakers' deaf ears. Golub, Johnson, and Dunlap (2007, 131) write,

... Arrest data indicate that during the 1990s the primary focus of QOL [Quality of Life] policing became smoking marijuana in public view (MPV) ... By 2000, MPV had become the most common misdemeanor arrest, accounting for 15 percent of all NYC adult arrests. ... Of note most MPV arrestees have been black or Hispanic. Furthermore, black and Hispanic MPV arrestees have been more likely to be detained prior to arraignment, convicted, and sentenced to jail than their white counterparts. ... In light of the disparities, we recommend that the NYPD consider scaling back on MPV enforcement and reducing the harshness of treatment by routinely issuing Desk Appearance Tickets when the person is not wanted on other charges, so that most MPV arrestees would not be detained. ...

It should also be noted that the cost of these marijuana arrests is $75 million per year to taxpayers. There are numerous other issues with this policy (Levine, 2011). One that we wish to discuss in more length is the stop-and-frisk policy of city officers.

The search-and-stop behaviors by officers seem to be an area of concern as well. Is the search for marijuana constitutionally valid? Hammond (2011, May 17) writes,

> The blitz is driven not by an epidemic of marijuana use but by the city's aggressive community policing tactics of the past two decades. ... If that many people were brazen enough to light up in front of the police the enforcement might be justifiable. But a lot of those being arrested tell a different story. They report that their pot was well concealed, and that the officer only found it by searching their clothing or handbags. In other words, the marijuana was not truly in public view until the police dragged it out of hiding. In other cases, arrestees say the officer threatened or cajoled them into turning over their contraband—and then slapped them with a misdemeanor charge. That this stuff happens is verified by groups such as the Drug Policy Alliance. ... Even some retired officers confirmed the use of such tactics to WNYC. A Bronx prosecutor also told the radio station that she throws out 10 to 15 cases a day because officers apparently confused about the law file reports describing the pot as being discovered in a pocket or a sock.

There are also concerns about how police may abuse stop-and-frisk powers to make an arrest. Both stop-and-frisk and arrests will then be reflected in the officers' activity as well as in the Compstat numbers. Gray (2011, June 13) writes,

> Advocates of drug and juvenile justice reform have launched a campaign against what they contend are the New York Police Department's illegal "stop and frisks" and the disproportionate number of arrests of black and brown young men for possessing allowable amounts of marijuana.

Stop-and-Frisk

The use of forcible stops by police is a legitimate law enforcement tool. When used properly, it is a valuable law enforcement mechanism for fighting crime. As we have explained, the legal justification for forcible stops is based on the United States Supreme Court case *Terry v. Ohio* (1968). Subsequently, New York State has codified police powers to forcibly stop suspects in the New York State Criminal Procedure Law section 140.50. Further, the NYPD has created guidelines for officers to follow that are publicly available in their Patrol Guide section 212-11 entitled Stop and Frisk. The law and the Patrol Guide are quite clear on when officers have the legal power to stop someone. The Patrol Guide, for example, mimics the law stating, "When a uniformed member of the service *reasonably suspects* a person has committed,

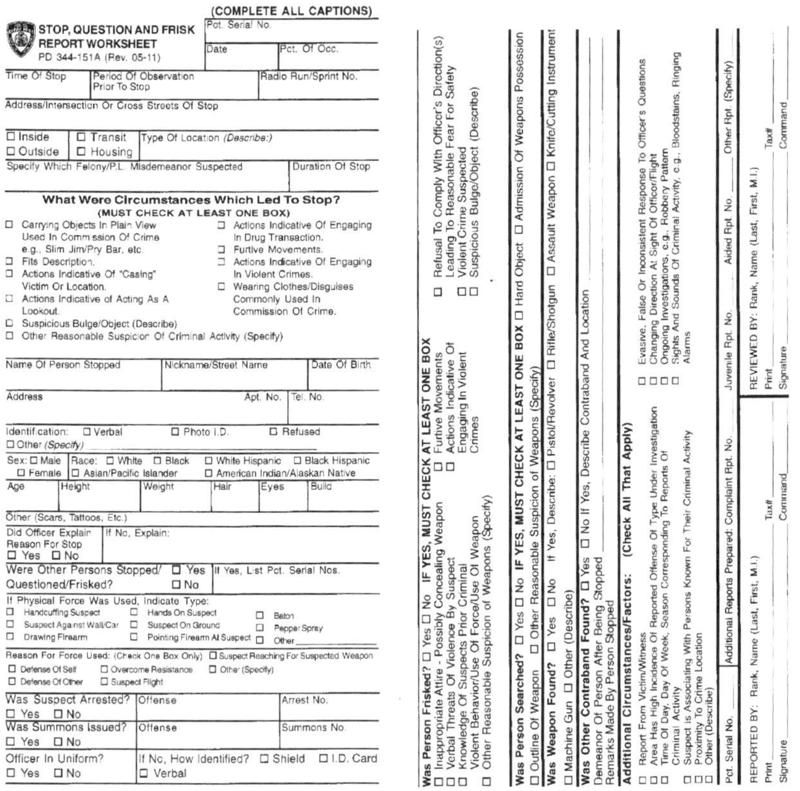

(COMPLETE ALL CAPTIONS)

STOP, QUESTION AND FRISK REPORT WORKSHEET
PD 344-151A (Rev. 05-11)

Pct. Serial No. | Date | Pct. Of Occ.
Time Of Stop | Period Of Observation Prior To Stop | Radio Run/Sprint No.
Address/Intersection Or Cross Streets Of Stop
☐ Inside ☐ Outside | ☐ Transit ☐ Housing | Type Of Location (Describe:)
Specify Which Felony/P.L. Misdemeanor Suspected | Duration Of Stop

What Were Circumstances Which Led To Stop?
(MUST CHECK AT LEAST ONE BOX)
☐ Carrying Objects In Plain View Used In Commission Of Crime e.g., Slim Jim/Pry Bar, etc.
☐ Fits Description.
☐ Actions Indicative Of "Casing" Victim Or Location.
☐ Actions Indicative of Acting As A Lookout.
☐ Suspicious Bulge/Object (Describe)
☐ Other Reasonable Suspicion Of Criminal Activity (Specify)
☐ Actions Indicative Of Engaging In Drug Transaction.
☐ Furtive Movements.
☐ Actions Indicative Of Engaging In Violent Crimes.
☐ Wearing Clothes/Disguises Commonly Used In Commission Of Crime.

Name Of Person Stopped | Nickname/Street Name | Date Of Birth
Address | Apt. No. | Tel. No.
Identification: ☐ Verbal ☐ Photo I.D. ☐ Refused ☐ Other (Specify)
Sex: ☐ Male ☐ Female | Race: ☐ White ☐ Black ☐ White Hispanic ☐ Black Hispanic ☐ Asian/Pacific Islander ☐ American Indian/Alaskan Native
Age | Height | Weight | Hair | Eyes | Build
Other (Scars, Tattoos, Etc.)
Did Officer Explain Reason For Stop ☐ Yes ☐ No | If No, Explain:
Were Other Persons Stopped/Questioned/Frisked? ☐ Yes ☐ No | If Yes, List Pct. Serial Nos.
If Physical Force Was Used, Indicate Type:
☐ Handcuffing Suspect ☐ Suspect Against Wall/Car ☐ Drawing Firearm ☐ Hands On Suspect ☐ Suspect On Ground ☐ Pointing Firearm At Suspect ☐ Baton ☐ Pepper Spray ☐ Other
Reason For Force Used: (Check One Box Only) ☐ Suspect Reaching For Suspected Weapon ☐ Defense Of Self ☐ Defense Of Other ☐ Overcome Resistance ☐ Suspect Flight ☐ Other (Specify)
Was Suspect Arrested? ☐ Yes ☐ No | Offense | Arrest No.
Was Summons Issued? ☐ Yes ☐ No | Offense | Summons No.
Officer In Uniform? ☐ Yes ☐ No | If No, How Identified? ☐ Shield ☐ I.D. Card ☐ Verbal

Was Person Frisked? ☐ Yes ☐ No IF YES, MUST CHECK AT LEAST ONE BOX
☐ Inappropriate Attire - Possibly Concealing Weapon ☐ Verbal Threats Of Violence By Suspect ☐ Knowledge Of Suspects Prior Criminal Violent Behavior/Use Of Force/Use Of Weapon ☐ Other Reasonable Suspicion of Weapons (Specify) ☐ Furtive Movements ☐ Actions Indicative Of Engaging In Violent Crimes ☐ Refusal To Comply With Officer's Direction(s) Leading To Reasonable Fear For Safety ☐ Violent Crime Suspected ☐ Suspicious Bulge/Object (Describe)
Was Person Searched? ☐ Yes ☐ No IF YES, MUST CHECK AT LEAST ONE BOX ☐ Hard Object ☐ Admission Of Weapons Possession ☐ Outline Of Weapon ☐ Other Reasonable Suspicion of Weapons (Specify)
Was Weapon Found? ☐ Yes ☐ No If Yes, Describe: ☐ Pistol/Revolver ☐ Rifle/Shotgun ☐ Assault Weapon ☐ Knife/Cutting Instrument ☐ Machine Gun ☐ Other (Describe)
Was Other Contraband Found? ☐ Yes ☐ No If Yes, Describe Contraband And Location
Demeanor Of Person After Being Stopped
Remarks Made By Person Stopped
Additional Circumstances/Factors: (Check All That Apply)
☐ Report From Victim/Witness ☐ Area Has High Incidence Of Reported Offense Of Type Under Investigation ☐ Time Of Day, Day Of Week, Season Corresponding To Reports Of Criminal Activity ☐ Suspect is Associating With Persons Known For Their Criminal Activity ☐ Proximity To Crime Location ☐ Other (Describe) ☐ Evasive, False Or Inconsistent Response To Officer's Questions ☐ Changing Direction At Sight Of Officer/Flight ☐ Ongoing Investigations, e.g., Robbery Pattern ☐ Sights And Sounds Of Criminal Activity, e.g., Bloodstains, Ringing Alarms
Pct. Serial No. | Additional Reports Prepared: Complaint Rpt. No. | Juvenile Rpt. No. | Aided Rpt. No. | Other Rpt. (Specify)
REPORTED BY: Rank, Name (Last, First, M.I.) Print Tax# Signature Command
REVIEWED BY: Rank, Name (Last, First, M.I.) Print Tax# Signature Command

Figure 7.3 NYPD Stop and Frisk Form.

is committing, or is about to commit a felony or a Penal Law misdemeanor …" [italics added]. The level of proof needed is reasonable suspicion. Officers are well trained as to what reasonable suspicion is and how they can achieve it. Arguably, the Stop-and-Frisk form itself gives guidance as to what is necessary by listing acceptable criteria for officers to simply check off such as furtive movements by a suspect or high-crime area. Thus, officers are keenly aware and trained that they can *only stop criminal suspects for whom they have developed some level of evidence to support their forcible stop, namely, reasonable suspicion* (see Figure 7.3).

The sheer number of stop-and-frisk reports along with illogical reasoning by the NYPD has raised very serious issues with respect to officers following legal parameters. The NYPD has forcibly stopped more individuals in 2010 than at any other time in its recent history—600,601 *(CCR, Floyd et al. v. City of New York et al.)*. From 2002 to 2010, the number of stop-and-frisks increased so markedly as to defy logic, rising from 97,296 in 2002 (Baker, 2007, November 21). Such an increase in stop-and-frisk reports at a time when the department also claims crime is down tremendously defies logic. Indeed, while we were both supportive of NYPD in this area, we are now far more skeptical. The NYPD has placed itself in a completely illogical position. Based on their official statistics, crime is down tremendously. That means, quite literally, that very few suspects are roaming the streets because there are so few criminals. Assuming their argument about crime is true, how can they possibly be finding suspects and lawfully stopping them on every corner? The argument is simply untenable. There is no sense to it. In the past, at a time when crime was much higher and suspects were roaming the streets in far greater numbers, hundreds of thousands of fewer stops were made. Furthermore, during this higher crime period, the NYPD was able to bring down crime tremendously *without the corresponding fantastic number of forcible stops*. Why the sudden need to stop hundreds of thousands of innocent people? Nearly 90 percent of forcible stops are of completely innocent people (see NYCLU, "Stop and Frisk Practices"). Such fatally flawed logic cannot stand. Even the most favorable reading of these numbers indicates something is fatally wrong at the NYPD.

The NYPD tries to justify the enormous increases in stop-and-frisk reports by claiming this tool is successful in the fight against crime. There are numerous problems with such an argument. First, police have successfully fought crime for many years, even under the Compstat system. It is only in very recent years under Commissioner Kelly that we have seen this indefensible increase in forcible stops skyrocketing to more than 600,000 a year from less than 100,000 a year. That is a huge 500-percent increase. Crime, of late, has not dropped nearly as much as it did when the police were using the tactic much less often. Indeed, as of this writing, we are seeing slight increases in violent crime. Second, the number of stops per violent crime in New York City is staggering. When crime was dropping at a far greater rate in 2002, there was approximately one stop for every violent crime (97,296 forcible stops compared to 95,030 violent crimes). In 2009, however, with crime drastically down there were approximately eight stops for every violent crime (576,394 forcible stops compared to 75,176 violent crimes). Approximately 85 percent of these forcible stops are of innocent people (NYCLU, "Stop and Frisk Practices").

However, the evidence of problems comes from other sources as well. The NYPD has also had liability issues with its stop-and-frisk practices. For example, it is currently being sued by the Center for Constitutional Rights (CCR) (and has been in the past as well). CCR decided to raise the issue again when it was so patently clear that there are issues. Jeffry Fagan of Columbia University issued a scathing report of NYPD's forcible stop practices (see Center for Constitutional Rights [CCR], Report: NYPD Stop and Frisk Program Based on Race Not on Crime). While his earlier report for the Attorney General in 1999 was effectively fended off by the NYPD, it is not clear how they can defend more than 600,000 forcible stops mostly in minority areas at a time when crime is supposedly at an all-time low. CCR, in the case *Floyd et al. v. City of New York et al.*, claims that, "These NYPD practices have led to a dramatic increase in the number of suspicion-less stop-and-frisks per year in the city, with the majority of stops in communities of color."

Minority areas including housing developments seem to be a particular concern for the NYPD. These areas are high-crime locations and should be focused on. However, the NYPD answer may be somewhat simplistic and perhaps even illegal. The simplistic answer seems to be to send a few officers in to do some forcible stops. Evidence of NYPD abuse of stop-and-frisk is also available in these areas. Recently, for example, the city agreed to pay out more than $150,000 to 9 of 16 plaintiffs who claim they were illegally stopped on housing development property (Shifrel, 2011, March 5). Mindless enforcement is much easier than working with tenant associations and community groups. Simplistic solutions are not the answer.

Beyond all this, the New York City Civilian Complaint Review Board has reported on the problem of abuse of authority related to stops for years. In a recent press release, it states, "... 'stop, question and frisk' complaints still account for roughly 30 percent of the CCRB's total intake, and they have since 2005" (CCRB, 2011, February 2).

Just as disturbing is the constant stonewalling of accurate and timely data from the NYPD. The NYPD failed to report these numbers for years until a successful lawsuit by the Center for Constitutional Rights. The NYPD was required by law to report stop-and-frisk figures to the City Council for years (see New York City Administrative Code 14-150—Vallone Bill).

The City Council certainly did not own up to its responsibilities to check police power either. They did nothing for years about NYPD complacency in this area. While one can give some time to the police department to computerize the reports, the failure to report went on for years. As soon as earlier years were computerized, they should have been released on a timely basis. The City Council did little or nothing when they were entitled to the figures. One has to wonder about this blatant lack of transparency by the police department as well as the mindset of a City Council unable or unwilling to do its job in overseeing police power.

Like any tool, stop-and-frisk can be abused. Theory tells us that there is a tradeoff between crime control and due process models. When crime control becomes the ultimate goal of law enforcement, a reasonable interpretation of theory is that we need to be watchful of due process rights. In this case, the sheer volume of forcible stops in New York City should raise caution flags. The NYPD's position of wildly increasing forcible stops at a time of supposed low crime is totally illogical. Lawsuits, CCRB complaints, and a lack of transparency are further complications. The house of cards created by

NYPD management will eventually fall. What is more logical—that suspects are peering out of every corner or that NYPD pressures from Compstat are leading to wild increases in stop-and-frisk citywide? Compstat is surely driving this, just as it is driving summons and arrest numbers. Perhaps we can justify some of this, but as a society, we must draw a line. Thus far in this chapter, we have quite possibly seen illegal quotas and illegal stops. These are not trivial concerns. As holocaust survivor Martin Neimoller cautions,

> First they came for the Socialists, and I did not speak out—Because I was not a Socialist. Then they came for the Trade Unionists, and I did not speak out— Because I was not a Trade Unionist. Then they came for the Jews, and I did not speak out—Because I was not a Jew. Then they came for me—and there was no one left to speak for me. (United States Holocaust Museum, Martin Neimoller, n.d.)

We cannot remain silent. Silence is not the answer to these nagging concerns. There is too much here to ignore. We must stand up, understand, learn, and voice our concerns. Our next question is, who is suffering from such police behaviors?

Minority Communities

There are unquestionably longstanding issues between the NYPD and the minority communities of New York City. Widely reported incidents in minority communities confirm the difficulties that the department has had especially *after* the first two years of the Compstat innovation. Haberman (1997, September 12, B1), for example, reports, "Citizens are locked up because of their race or their politics, as in Nazi Germany, one man asserted." He continues with similar statements, "'They say China is bad?' said Mrs. Baez, a huge button picturing her dead son pinned to her shirt. 'They have to take a good look at New York City.'" Anthony Baez died during a struggle with police after a football was thrown at a police car. Officers were fired and convicted of civil rights violations in the case. Because of these and other incidents, the NYPD developed policies aimed at protecting due process rights such as the *Courtesy, Professionalism and Respect Program*. These policies, however, do not appear to be enforced by the NYPD compared to their crime control methods nor are they emulated by other police agencies (Eterno, 2001).

Negative reports of NYPD practice are far more pronounced from minority communities. Other names that come to mind include Abner Louima, Amadou Dialllo, Patrick Dorismond, Sean Bell, and Police Officer Omar Edwards. Abner Louima was a Haitian immigrant who was arrested and subsequently sodomized with a broomstick by a police officer. As Chan

(2007, August 9), writes, "The case became a national symbol of police brutality and fed perceptions that New York City police officers were harass-
ing or abusing young black men as part of a citywide crackdown on crime."
Amadou Diallo was an unarmed black man shot by the aggressive citywide
Street Crime Unit. Patrick Dorismond was another unarmed black male shot
by the NYPD, "… in a confrontation with plainclothes police involved in a
controversial anti-drug crackdown that has netted more than 18,000 arrests
and cost the police department more than \$24 million in overtime over the
last two months" (Vann, 2000, March 22). Sean Bell was also killed by officers in yet another controversial police shooting. This shooting took place
in Jamaica Queens and Mr. Bell, who was also an unarmed black man, had
50 shots fired at him. In all three shooting incidents, officers were found not
guilty although the city paid significant monies in civil suits. Interestingly,
NYPD officer Omar Edwards, also black, was shot and killed by fellow officers thinking he was a perpetrator in May 2009 in East Harlem. All of these
incidents are tragic. What do all of them have in common? Minority members being shot in relatively high-crime areas. With so many incidents all
closely related, our interpretation of theory strongly suggests that there is too
much focus on crime control especially in minority areas and not enough
attention to due process rights.

Since Compstat began in 1994, the NYPD has made no secret that it
focuses on high-crime communities that happen to be minority. Since 2003,
for example, rookie officers are sent to "Impact Zones," which are 20 high-
crime areas throughout the city (Best Practice, 2010). As we have learned,
Compstat is a data-driven program that focuses resources on crime-ridden
areas. Officers target those areas for enforcement. NYPD then champions a
reduction in crime as a success and even suggests other locales emulate their
practices, taking care not to expose possible problems with a myopic focus
on crime. For example, the NYPD claims under Operation Impact that,

> The majority of New Yorkers had never experienced crime rates as low as
> they were when Operation Impact was launched in 2003. Driving crime rates
> even lower was a challenge. … Operation Impact addresses those challenges
> by assessing how best to allocate the resources of the largest police force in
> the country toward specific crime-zones and against specific trends. These
> strategies … would be transferable to a police department equipped with the
> resources. … (Best Practice, 2010)

Was it necessary to continue to focus on crime control without, at this
point, examining what theory tells us is a critically important aspect of being
a police officer—due process rights?

Note the NYPD yet again is trumpeting its crime control programs and
policies. Stopping crime is important, but what about other issues? Are there

side effects to continuing a complete focus on crime control through "super enforcement?" For example, crime was already substantially down before Operation Impact. Should crime control have been the focus of the program? Were community members concerned more about crime at this point, or about police behavior gone wild? Could officers have achieved the results without constant enforcement? Were there other strategies that could have been equally effective? What about abuse of authority? How about possible side effects on those targeted for enforcement of minor violations such as marijuana or forcible stops? Were Constitutional rights violated because of the operation? Did this operation meet the needs of the community or did it cause more problems? These questions are far more important to address than simply trumpeting the value of a program because it brings crime down. As we alluded to earlier in this chapter, bringing down crime is simple; it is bringing down crime while at the same time respecting and defending basic rights that makes policing in democracies such a high calling and difficult.

When Compstat first began, commanders were given full and complete discretion to determine what was necessary for their respective areas (Silverman, 2001). Today, however, the system has been reduced into iron control from Headquarters. Officers are required to conduct forcible stops, summonses, and arrests to be reflected in the Compstat figures. Field commanders no longer have much discretion to determine their own actions.

This legalistic, top-down style translates itself at the field level into requiring officers to formally sanction offenders so that the numbers can be used by hapless precinct commanders to defend themselves at Compstat. Local conditions become less important in a pressure-packed managerial environment mindlessly focused on numbers. This means that sworn officers at the NYPD who are working at the local level are being forced to act like automatons. What may be illegal quotas pushed down by Compstat to local levels have been a constant complaint by the union (see, for example, Murray, 2005). Police officers, sergeants, lieutenants, and other members of the police department downgrading or not taking reports is just one symptom of a department-wide problem. Detectives are burdened with closing out cases as well. With accurate intelligence information not being taken (crime report manipulation), detectives do not have appropriate information to develop patterns and properly do investigations. All ranks at the precinct level are under pressure, not to help communities but to ensure the numbers look good for higher-ups. Regardless of the overall consequences of an action, the NYPD has ripped discretion away making local conditions problematic.

Certainly, the large numbers of forcible stops of mostly minorities exacerbate the situation. The claims of racial profiling, driving while black, etc. are commonplace. As we reported, incidents regarding issues of police abuse of power seem to come almost exclusively from minority areas. Bittner (1974, 37), for example, writes this about American policing, "Police usually arrest the Black, the poor, the young, the Spanish speaking, and the rest of the urban 'proletariat.'" Does the way Compstat has been operationalized in New York City and emulated worldwide lead to unexpected side effects such as those espoused by Bittner?

Some commentators in the black community adamantly argue in the affirmative. Some go so far as to say the NYPD in minority areas is like an army of occupation. For example, Ford (2010) asserts,

> The New York City police force systematically withholds protective services from minority victims of crime, while simultaneously stopping and frisking hundreds of thousands of innocent black and brown citizens on the streets for no legitimate reason. Hundreds of hours of secret recordings by a disgruntled New York City cop prove beyond question that the most aggressive forms of institutional racism are the guiding management principles of the NYPD. Just as the Black Panther Party and others charged two generations ago, the New York City police are revealed as an occupying army that views residents of color as an enemy population. The predatory nature of New York City policing is captured, digitally, in a police lieutenant's exhortation to his officers at the beginning of their shift. "You're working in Bed-Stuy," says the shift supervisor, "where everyone's probably got a warrant." (Ford, 2010)

The idea of police being an army of occupation is sad exposition on what may be the state of affairs at the NYPD.

Lawsuits, Law, and Case Exemplar

At this point, most people of reason who have kept an open mind will agree there are issues that need to be explored carefully at the NYPD. We point out, however, that there is even more reason to be concerned. Regarding many of the issues we discuss, various parties currently engage the NYPD in civil litigation. Some of the issues include lack of transparency, racial profiling, and illegal stop-and-frisk. Some of the lawsuits against the NYPD are by the *New York Times* for failing to release information (see Barron, 2010, December 21). The New York Civil Liberties Union (NYCLU) is suing for access to shooting records (see *NYCLU et al. v. NYPD et al.*), and the Center for Constitutional Rights (CCR) is suing for racial profiling and unconstitutional stop-and-frisks (see *Floyd, et al. v. City of New York, et al.* as well as their expert report [Fagan, 2010] based on data that had to be extracted from the NYPD by the CCR through a lawsuit as well).

Other than the aforementioned lawsuits, some are trying to change New York State law. Due to the exceedingly high number of marijuana arrests for possession in New York City, State Senator Mark Grisanti, a Republican, has sponsored a bill in the State Legislature. He wants to make smoking marijuana in public view a violation of the law resemble a traffic ticket (see Precious, 2011, May 14 and testimony on the bill by Levine, 2011).

While we have shown many pertinent examples in this chapter and in this book, there is one example that stands out among others—the City of Baltimore, Maryland. The National Association for the Advancement of Colored People (NAACP) named former Deputy Commissioner in New York City Edward T. Norris, among others, in a lawsuit against the city. Norris reportedly got the job as Police Commissioner in Baltimore after Jack Maple and William Bratton lobbied then Mayor Martin O'Mally (Levitt, 2003, November 24). Norris brought NYPD-style Compstat to Baltimore. As one expert on Baltimore policing stated, "Norris implemented a New York-style Compstat approach mixing a combination of aggressive enforcement and strategic results driven policing" (Berlin, 2011). While there are many other issues with Baltimore, we focus here on a settlement that the city made in a lawsuit in the United States District Court for the District of Maryland, *Maryland State Conference of NAACP Branches, et al. v. Baltimore City Police Department et al.*

The case is very important because the Baltimore Police Department was being sued for actions that nearly mimic what we have seen in New York City. Fenton (2010, June 23) states,

> A lawsuit filed in 2006 on behalf of 14 people alleged that their arrests indicated a broad pattern of abuse in which thousands of people were routinely arrested without probable cause. The suit also alleged that the so- called "zero-tolerance" system was endorsed and enforced by city officials. ...

Court documents indicate that zero tolerance means, "the policy by which all Quality-of-Life Offenses are enforced by means of custodial arrest, regardless of any discretion to address the infractions through other available means, including, but not limited to, counseling, verbal warning, or written citation" (*Maryland State Conference of NAACP Branches, et al. v. Baltimore City Police Department et al.*, n.d.). This nearly mirrors NYPD's policy on marijuana—make arrests, no discretion. Officers must reach their numerical goals to be reflected in the Compstat performance management system. People, mostly minorities, are being treated as if there is one community standard. The social contract is disregarded.

The stipulation agreed to by the City of Baltimore has many parts to it including establishing policies to handle properly Quality of Life violations, training, tracking compliance, and having effective oversight. Some of the training that the stipulation agreement grants importantly includes,

> ... develop training curricula for pre-service and annual in-service regarding Quality of Life Offenses, assessing probable cause, rights protected by the First

Amendment to the U.S. Constitution, especially the lawful exercise of rights on City sidewalks and other public areas, and appropriate officer response … the range of appropriate responses to various factual scenarios involving Quality of Life offenses … (*Maryland State Conference of NAACP Branches, et al. v. Baltimore City Police Department et al.*, n.d.,24)

Incidents we describe earlier at Housing Developments (which the NYPD paid out a sum but little was mentioned about policy changes in the NYPD case) where officers abuse their stop powers, arrests for marijuana supposedly in public view, numerous forcible stops, summonses that call for warnings (at best) are NYPD behaviors that are similar to the issues in Baltimore. Baltimore emulated the NYPD Compstat process and, wisely, the NAACP sued.

We also note that while Baltimore is used as an example, similar actions have been taken in nearly every other city with which former high-ranking NYPD Compstat inquisitors are associated. Officers in Philadelphia are now under court monitoring and retraining because of a stipulation agreement (see Leach, 2011, June 21). In 2010, the New Orleans Police Department was found to have violated civil rights (Giamboso, 2011, May 7). Lastly, Newark, New Jersey has recently come under investigation by the Justice Department. The pattern is clear (Giamboso, 2011, May 7). The aggressive style of New York City was emulated in each of these locations as the main players of Compstat at NYPD commanded all of them. This strongly supports what we have exposed in this chapter.

Conclusion

By no means do we feel that we live in a police state—far from it. Further, based on our qualitative interviews, we argue that the NYPD is probably not purposely engaging in racist policing. Rather, the evidence from our study strongly suggests that the high pressures of Compstat as operationalized by the NYPD have unexpected side effects. An understanding of criminal justice theory helps us to unveil them. A reasonable interpretation of our data and events in New York City leads us to strongly suggest that caution flags must go up when police departments are not transparent, claim reducing crime is their main mandate, and, for all intents and purposes, judge commanders' almost exclusively on numbers. This has been the message emanating from Compstat—make the numbers look good at any cost. Women eating doughnuts in parks, the elderly issued a summons on a bitterly cold evening, summonses and arrests wildly increasing for minor violations even when crime is markedly down, uncontrollable and unimaginably high numbers of forcible stops also when crime is down, crime report manipulation, incidents that occur almost exclusively to minorities and in minority areas, many police departments emulating the NYPD model either under court order or investigation, and more, are only the symptoms of a far larger problem. Police work should not be all about numbers; they should be about people. Understanding theory helps us more fully to grasp the ramifications of the NYPD's Compstat pressures directed from Headquarters. Based on our research, the NYPD has lost its direction in this area. As social scientists, we illuminate these issues such that they are more visible. This, we hope, will lead to more discussion and change. We are a government of the people, by the people, for the people, and we want to keep it that way.

References

Baker, A. (2007, November 21). "City Police Stop Whites Equally but Frisk Them Less: A Study Finds," *New York Times,* http://www.nytimes.com/2007/11/21/nyregion/21rand.html?fta=y. Retrieved July 25, 2011.

Barron, J. (2010, December 21). "Times Sues City Police, Saying Information Has Been Illegally Withheld," *New York Times,* http://www.nytimes.com/2010/12/22/nyregion/22nypd.html?_r=1&partner=rss&emc=rss. Retrieved July 18, 2011.

Bayley, D. (1994). *Police for the Future.* Oxford: Oxford, UK: University Press.

Bayley, D. (2001). "Democratizing the Police Abroad: What to Do and How to Do It," *Issues in International Crime,* https://www.ncjrs.gov/pdffiles1/nij/188742.pdf. Retrieved July 25, 2011.

Berlin, M. (2011). "The Compstat Experience in Baltimore, Maryland." Unpublished manuscript.

Best Practice (2010). "Using Data to Target High-Crime Areas." New York City Global Partners' Innovation Exchange Web site, http://www.nyc.gov/html/unccp/gprb/downloads/pdf/NYC_Safety%20and%20Security_OperationImpact.pdf. Retrieved on July 21, 2011.

Bittner, E. (1970). "The Police Charge." Reprinted in Lundman, R.J. (1980). *Police Behavior: A Sociological Perspective.* New York: Oxford University Press. 28–42. From Egon Bittner, "The Functions of the Police in Modern Society." National Institute of Mental Health. 36–47.

Bittner, E. (1974). "Florence Nightingale in Pursuit of Willie Sutton: A Theory of Police." In: Jacob, H., Ed., *The Potential for Reform of Criminal Justice.* Beverly Hills, CA: Sage.

Bode, N. (2011, January 6). "NYPD Appoints Investigative Panel after Claims Police Downgraded Crime Stats," *DNAinfo,* http://www.dnainfo.com/20110106/manhattan/nypd-appoints-investigative-panel-after-claims-police-downgraded-crime-stats. Retrieved on July 14, 2011.

Bouza, A.V. (1990). *The Police Mystique: An Insider's Look at Cops, Crime, and the Criminal Justice System.* New York: Plenum Press.

Braithwaite, J. (1995). "Reintegrative Shaming, Republicanism, and Policy." In: Barlow, H. D. Barlow, Ed., *Crime and Public Policy: Putting Theory to Work* (191-205). Boulder, CO: Westview Press.

Bratton, W.J. (1996). "Great Expectations: How Higher Expectations for Police Departments Can Lead to a *Decrease in Crime*." Unpublished paper.

Bratton, W.J. (1998). *Turnaround: How America's Top Cop Reversed the Crime Epidemic.* New York: Random House.

Burleigh, M. and Wipperman, W. (1991). *The Racial State: Germany 1933-1945.* Melbourne, Australia: Cambridge University Press.

CBS News. (2011, January 24). "Queens Widow Blames NYPD for Husband's Death," *CBS News,* http://newyork.cbslocal.com/2011/01/24/queens-widow-nypd-responsible-for-my-husbands-death/. Retrieved on July12, 2011.

Center for Constitutional Rights. (2010, October 26). Report: NYPD Stop and Frisk Program Based on Race Not Crime, http://ccrjustice.org/newsroom/press-releases/report:-nypd-stop-and-frisk-program-based-race-not-crime. Retrieved on July 19, 2011.

Center for Constitutional Rights. (n.d.). *Floyd et al. v. City of New York et al.,* http://www.ccrjustice.org/floyd. Retrieved on July 19, 2011.

Chambliss, W. (1994). "Policing the Ghetto Underclass: The Politics of Law and Law Enforcement," *Social Problems,* 41(2): 177–194.

Chan, S. (2007, August 9). "The Abner Louima Case, 10 Years Later," *New York Times,* http://cityroom.blogs.nytimes.com/2007/08/09/the-abner-louima-case-10-years-later/. Retrieved July 21, 2011.

Churchill, W. (1947, November 11). "Speech to the House of Commons." In: James, R.R., Ed. (1974). *Winston S. Churchill: His Complete Speeches, 1897-1963.* Vol. 7, 7566.

City of Greenbelt Maryland. (2011). "Department Values, Oath of Office," http://www.greenbeltmd.gov/police/oath_of_office.htm. Retrieved July 11, 2011.

Civilian Complaint Review Board (CCRB), New York City. (2001). "Street Stop Encounter Report: An Analysis of CCRB Complaints Resulting from the New York Police Department's Stop and Frisk Practices," http://www.nyc.gov/html/ccrb/pdf/stop.pdf. Downloaded on July 18, 2011.

CCRB. (2003). "Status Report January–December 2003," http://www.nyc.gov/html/ccrb/html/reports.html. Downloaded on July 23, 2011.

CCRB. (2009). "Status Report January–December 2009," http://www.nyc.gov/html/ccrb/html/reports.html. Downloaded on July 23, 2011.

CCRB. (2010). "Status Report January–December 2010," http://www.nyc.gov/html/ccrb/html/reports.html. Downloaded on July 23, 2011.

CCRB. (2011, February 2). Press release, http://www.nyc.gov/html/ccrb/pdf/CCRB_Press_Release_20110202.pdf. Retrieved on July 25, 2011.

Cloward, R. and Ohlin, L. (1960). *Delinquency and Opportunity.* New York: Free Press.

The Commission on Accreditation for Law Enforcement Agencies, Inc., (CALEA). (2011). http://www.calea.org/content/commission. Retrieved July 25, 2011.

DelSignore, J. (2011, February 23). "NYPD Stop and Frisks Reach Record High in 2010," *Gothamist,* http://gothamist.com/2011/02/23/nypd_stop_and_frisks_reach_record_h.php. Retrieved on July25, 2011.

Dougherty, G. (2011, June 1) "Top Cops Plans May Include Controversial NYPD Measures," *Chicago Current,* http://www.chicagocurrent.com/articles/31651-Top-cop-s-plans-may-include-controversial-NYPD-measures.

Dussault, R. (1999, March 31) "Jack Maple: Betting on Intelligence," *Government Technology*, http://www.govtech.com/magazines/gt/Jack-Maple-Betting-on-Intelligence.html?page=1. Retrieved on June 17, 2011.

Dwyer, J. (2011, June 16). "Side Effects of Arrests for Marijuana," the *New York Times*, http://www.nytimes.com/2011/06/17/nyregion/push-for-marijuana-arrests-in-ny-has-side-effects.html?_r=1&ref=marijuana.

Eck, J.E. and Maguire, E.R. (2000). "Have Changes in Policing Reduced Violent Crime? An Assessment of the Evidence." In: Blumstein, A. and Wallman, J., Eds., *The Crime Drop in America*. New York: Cambridge University Press.

Eterno, J.A. (2001). "Zero Tolerance Policing in Democracies," *Police Practice and Research*, 2(3): 189–217.

Eterno, J.A. (2003). *Policing within the Law*. Westport, CT: Praeger.

Eterno, J.A. (2008). "Interview with Malme Odd Berner, Ministry of Foreign Affairs, Norway." In: Marenin, O. and Das, D.K., Eds., *Trends in Policing: Interviews with Police Leaders throughout the World*. Boca Raton, FL: CRC Press/Taylor & Francis.

Fagan, J. (2010). Expert report in the case of *David Floyd et al. v. NYPD et al.*, http://ccrjustice.org/files/Expert_Report_JeffreyFagan.pdf. Retrieved on July 22, 2011.

Fenton, J. (2010, June 23). "City Approves Settlement with NAACP, ACLU in 'Mass Arrest' Case." *Baltimore Sun*, http://articles.baltimoresun.com/2010-06-23/news/bal-naacp-settlement-0623_1_arrests-by-city-police-zero-tolerance-naacp-and-aclu. Retrieved on July 22, 2011.

Ford, G. (2010). "Secret NYPD Tapes Document Routine, Massive, Police Racism," http://www.blackagendareport.com/content/secret-nypd-tapes-document-routine-massive-police-racism. Retrieved on July 21, 2011.

Giamboso, D. (2011, May 7). "U.S. Justice Department to Launch Formal Investigation into Newark Police," *NJ.com*, http://www.nj.com/news/index.ssf/2011/05/us_justice_department_to_launc.html. Retrieved on July 26, 2011.

Golub, A., Johnson, B., and Dunlap, E. (2007). "The Race/Ethnicity Disparity in Misdemeanor Marijuana Arrests in New York City," *Criminology and Public Policy*, 6(1): 131–164.

Gray, K. (2011, June 13). "How Cops Turn 'Stop and Frisk' into 'Stop and Arrest,'" *The Root*, http://www.theroot.com/views/how-cops-turn-stop-and-frisk-stop-and-arrest?page=0,0. Retrieved July 26, 2011.

Haberman, C. (1997, September 12). "NYC; Civil Tones On a Topic Of Violence," *New York Times*, http://www.nytimes.com/1997/09/12/nyregion/nyc-civil-tones-on-a-topic-of-violence.html. Retrieved July 25, 2011.

Hammond, B. (2011, May 17). "The NYPD's Reefer Madness: Marijuana Busts Give Thousands a Record They Don't Deserve," *Daily News*, http://articles.nydailynews.com/2011-05-17/news/29570010_1_marijuana-busts-nypd-arrests-drug-conviction. Retrieved on July 26, 2011.

Henry, V.E. (2002). *The Compstat Paradigm*. New York: Looseleaf Law.

Johnston, G. (2011, June 8). "Doughnut Tickets: NYPD Doesn't Track Unaccompanied Adults In Playground Summonses." *Gothamist*, http://gothamist.com/2011/06/08/police_dont_track_unaccompanied_adu.php. Retrieved July 12, 2011.

Kelling, G.L. and Bratton, W.J. (1998). "Declining Crime Rates: Insiders' Views of the New York City Story," *The Journal of Criminal Law and Criminology*, 88(4): 1217–1232.

Kelling, G.L. and Coles, C.M. (1996). *Fixing Broken Windows.* New York: Simon & Schuster.

Leach, S. (2011, June 21). "New Guidelines for Controversial Stop and Frisk Policy," *Metro,* http://www.metro.us/philadelphia/local/article/896343--new-guidelines-for-controversial-stop-and-frisk-policy. Retrieved July 26, 2011.

Levine, H. (2011). "Testimony to New York State Regarding Marijuana Arrests," http://dragon.soc.qc.cuny.edu/Staff/levine/Testimony-Memo-NYS-Senate-Marijuana-Arrests-June-2011.pdf. Retrieved on July 22, 2011.

Levitt, L. (2003, November 24). "Maryland Troubles Have New York Link," http://nypdconfidential.com/columns/2003/031124.html. Retrieved on July 22, 2011.

Linn, E. (2009). *Arrest Decisions.* New York: Peter Lang.

Liska A.E. and Messner, S.F. (1999). *Perspectives on Crime and Deviance,* 3rd ed. Upper Saddle River, NJ: Prentice Hall.

Litigation and Settlement News. (2011, June 23). http://litigationandsettlementnews.com/?p=484. Retrieved on July 14.

Lundman, R.J. (1998). "City Police and Drunk Driving: Baseline Data," *Justice Quarterly,* 15(3)(September): 528–546.

Madison, J. (1961[1787–1788]) "Federalist # 48 & 51." In: *The Federalist Papers,* Rossiter, C., Ed. New York: New American Library.

Maryland State Conference of NAACP Branches, et al. v. Baltimore City Police Department et al. (n.d.) United States District Court for the District of Maryland. Civil Action No. 06-1863 (CCB), http://www.aclu-md.org/aPress/Press2010/Stipulation_of_Settlement.pdf. Retrieved on July 22, 2011.

Mac Donald, H. (2010, February 17). "Compstat and Its Enemies," *City Journal,* http://www.city-journal.org/2010/eon0217hm.html.

Manning, P.K. (1977). *Police Work: The Social Organization of Policing.* Cambridge, MA: MIT Press.

Maple, J. (1999). *The Crime Fighter.* New York: Doubleday.

Murray M. (2005). "Why Arrest Quotas Are Wrong," *PBA Magazine,* http://www.nycpba.org/publications/mag-05-spring/murray.html. Retrieved on July 14, 2011.

Nevins, A. and Commager, H.S. (1986). *A Pocket History of the United States.* New York: Washington Square Press.

New York Civil Liberties Union (NYCLU). (2011). "Stop and Frisk Practices," http://www.nyclu.org/issues/racial-justice/stop-and-frisk-practices. Retrieved on July 26, 2011.

New York City Police Department (NYPD). (1998). "The Compstat Process," NYPD document explaining Compstat.

Ortiz, E. (2011, July 17). "Many City Agencies Flout Law by Withholding Public Info from Press," *amNewYork.com,* http://www.amny.com/urbanite-1.812039/many-city-agencies-flout-law-by-withholding-public-info-from-press-1.3031728. Retrieved July 18, 2011.

Packer, H. (1966). "The Courts, the Police, and the Rest of Us," *Journal of Criminal Law and Criminology,* 57: 238–240.

Patrol Guide, New York City Police Department. Unpublished guide for New York City police officers.

Police state. *Merriam-Webster Dictionary,* http://www.merriam-webster.com/dictionary/police%20state. Retrieved on July 13, 2011.

Precious, T. (2011, May 14). "Grisanti Seeks to Reduce Public Marijuana Penalty," *BuffaloNewscom,* http://www.buffalonews.com/city/politics/article423121.ece. Retrieved on July 22, 2011.

Rashbaum, W. (2010, February 6). "Retired Officers Raise Questions on Crime Data," *New York Times,* http://www.nytimes.com/2010/02/07/nyregion/07crime.html. Retrieved on July 25, 2011.

Rayman, G. (2011, July 13). "Hey Ray Kelly, NYPD Commish, Norwood News Wants to Know Why You Won't Release Crime Stats," *Village Voice,* http://blogs.villagevoice.com/runninscared/2011/07/hey_ray_kelly_n.php, Retrieved on July 26, 2011.

Schaefer, R.T. (2001). *Sociology,* 7th ed. New York: McGraw-Hill.

Schifrel, S. (2011, March 5). "NYPD Stop and Frisk Policy in public housing leads to $150k in settlements." *New York Daily News.* Retrieved October 22, 2011 from http://articles.nydailynews.com/2011-03-05/local/28677337_1_public-housing-nycha-housing-residents

Silverman, E.B. (2001). *NYPD Battles Crime.* Boston: Northeastern University Press.

Skolnick, J. (1966). *Justice without Trial.* New York: John Wiley & Sons.

Skolnick, J. and Fyfe, J.J. (1993). *Above the Law.* New York: The Free Press.

Social contract. (2011). In: Encyclopædia Britannica, http://www.britannica.com/EBchecked/topic/550994/social-contract.

Spitzer, E. (1999). "A Report to the People of the State of New York from the Office of the Attorney General." New York.

United States Holocaust Museum. (n.d.) Martin Neimoller, http://www.ushmm.org/wlc/en/article.php?ModuleId=10007392. Retrieved on July 19, 2011.

Vann, B. (2000, March 22). "The Killing of Patrick Dorismond: New York Police Violence Escalates in the Wake of the Diallo Verdict," http://www.wsws.org/articles/2000/mar2000/nyc-m22.shtml. Retrieved July 21, 2011.

Warren, E. (1959). "Unanimous Opinion That Confessions Obtained Under Duress Must Be Excluded From Criminal Proceedings." Cited in Simpson, J.B. (1992). *Webster's II: New Riverside Desk Quotations.* Boston: Houghton Mifflin.

Weisburd, D., Mastrofski, S.D., McNally, A.M., Greenspan, R., and Willis, J.J. (2003). "Reforming to Preserve: Compstat and Strategic Problem Solving in American Policing," *Criminology and Public Policy,* 2(3): 421–456.

Westley, W. (1970). *Violence and the Police: A Sociological Study of Law, Custom, and Morality.* Cambridge, MA: MIT Press.

Wilson, J.Q. (1977). *Varieties of Police Behavior.* Cambridge, MA: Harvard University Press.

Worden, R.E. and Shepard, R.L. (1996). "Demeanor, Crime, and Police Behavior: A Reexamination of the Police Services Study Data," *Criminology,* 34(1): 83–105.

Zanoni, C. (2010, November 17). "Chess Players Ticketed by NYPD for Using Inwood Hill Park Chess Tables," *DNAInfo,* http://www.dnainfo.com/20101117/washington-heights-inwood/chess-players-ticketed-by-nypd-for-using-inwood-hill-park-chess-tables. Retrieved August 9, 2011.

Court Cases

Floyd et al. v. City of New York et al. Downloaded on July 19, 2011 from http://www. ccrjustice.org/floyd.

Maryland State Conference of NAACP Branches, et al. v. Baltimore City Police Department et al. United States District Court for the District of Maryland. Retrieved on July 26, 2011 from http://www.aclu-md.org/aPress/Press2010/ Stipulation_of_Settlement.pdf.

Mapp v. Ohio 367 U.S. 643 (1961).

Miranda v. Arizona 384 U.S. 436 (1966).

NYCLU v. NYPD (2009). Supreme Court of the State of New York, County of New York. Retrieved on July 18, 2011 from http://www.nyclu.org/files/releases/ NYCLUShootingPetition_11-12-09.pdf

Terry v. Ohio 392 U.S. 1 (1968).

Silence Is Not An Option

8

There has been a love affair with performance management in many sectors such as education, health care, policing, and much more. Compstat has been the epitome of police performance management. Its success is driven by enormous reductions in official crime reports. The sentiment of the last two decades is embodied by the statement, "Let's get tough and declare a war on crime." In New York City, reported index crime is down 80 percent. This leads acolytes to declare, "Who dares to challenge the 'wisdom of Compstat?'"

In 2007, two social scientists set out on a journey to empirically assess Compstat's police performance management system. Our research is the first scientific study to unveil what has been occurring behind NYPD closed doors for many years. Our study reveals the aura of Compstat for what it is—a human innovation with strengths and weaknesses. Compstat as an innovation is a success; however, like any human creation, it is not perfect.

Some very serious issues require attention by the NYPD and other agencies. Certainly, a billionaire mayor (see Powell, 2011, August 4, for a fascinating discussion on the mayor's personal money and governing), a wildly popular police commissioner, and those devoted to Compstat will attack us as they have in the past. Their failure to examine carefully or refusal to acknowledge the evidence or the implications of our findings does not diminish the validity of our research. As opposed to being viewed as enemies of a management system—for Compstat is simply a tool, and a good one at that—we see ourselves as good friends to those who champion performance management done the right way. Friends let friends know, sometimes boldly and loudly, when they do not realize that there is a problem. NYPD is like an alcoholic, fixated on its version of Compstat—the numbers game. It has become its drug. In this volume, we stand up to the bully alcoholic, NYPD managers, and tell others willing to listen that there are problems. Constantly in denial, they will likely spin the truth yet again. However, the problems are not insurmountable; we have solutions. Compstat is a good innovation, but it needs careful attention; it needs to be understood. More importantly, for Compstat to work properly in a police department, it requires much more transparency. The status quo is not an option for the health of the NYPD. In this chapter, we suggest those changes.

Lesson Learned

The NYPD and media backlash to our publicized study is instructive. The media blitz against us from the usual reporters known for their love affairs with the NYPD was documented in an earlier chapter. The attempt to silence us was even more pronounced at what was to be an open and professional conference on crime data. In late August 2010, we were invited to an international seminar at John Jay College of Criminal Justice—the same college where one of us worked for many years. We decided to accept the invitation. It was co-sponsored by the FBI and was on the topic of crime data. Our topic of NYPD crime manipulation was not only on point but also clearly a topic of great interest. We were informed that the media were welcome. After getting the okay from the organizers (we still have the e-mail indicating that reporters would be allowed access), we transmitted this permission to members of the press who contacted us.

After arriving at a get-together the night before, we noticed a professor who has strongly supported the NYPD position on their crime statistics. Apparently, this professor was a last-minute invitee as he was not on any previous lists. No matter, the evening was enjoyable as a professional dialog is always welcome. The next morning, the very first speaker was the same professor present the night before. That was interesting because he was not listed on the program. No matter, soon it would be our turn. We treated him professionally and with great respect as he delivered his NYPD advocacy presentation. We note, for the record, that we were consummate professionals, making no attempt to embarrass him or the college. Our interviews with the press were the same—we trumpeted our research findings already peer-reviewed and published in a respected scientific journal at the time.

Regardless, we let it go and awaited our turn at the podium. Of course, as long-invited guests the press was aware of our presentation time. As they sought entry into the college, we received phone calls from some of them telling us that the college would not let them in. At this point, after we approached the organizers to ask them about what was happening we were abruptly told that there was a change in plans and that no press would be allowed. Why? One can only ponder (for the view of one of those denied entrance, see Levitt, 2010, August 30).

During a short break, we were interviewed just outside the college perimeter and then returned to present our findings at this professional conference. Our presentation started well, but when we discussed some provocative parts about how the NYPD fudged statistics, an unprecedented action occurred that has never happened to either of us at a professional conference before or since. An organizer tried to silence us! Yes, that is correct. The organizer told us our already accepted presentation topic was unacceptable—that our research clearly had nothing to do with crime data. Caught off guard by the lack of professionalism, we noted that a previous speaker presented the NYPD's version on the same exact topic. Others in the audience agreed. After some disruption, our presentation was allowed to continue but precious time had been taken from us. As if this were not enough, at the end, of course we were ready to take questions. The professor supporting the NYPD then asked an obviously confrontational question. We proceeded to answer and were then shut down, being told that we could not respond and that there would be no more discussion on this. Several other questions were allowed and there was one interesting comment from a European scholar. This scholar noted that our hospital data certainly is very important and then he proceeded to say that if a police department is doing its job, crime reports should actually go up as this shows that people trust the police. It was a good point. Many times crime declines because victims do not report their incidents. This is because they feel the police will do nothing or the police are simply not open to them (e.g., sex crimes victim's experiences with the NYPD [see Chapter 2]). The conference was on crime statistics. Our position was well known. The organizer apologized later that day after one of us approached and questioned her interpretation of events. While we forgive the organizer for a lack of professionalism, we will never be silenced. We are adamant that our position must be heard and understood. Silence is not an option.

We have presented our research at numerous professional venues: two annual meetings of the Academy of Criminal Justice Sciences (2009 and 2010), the annual meeting of Criminal Justice Educators of New York State (2010, where we were invited speakers), at several colleges (all of them as invited speakers), and at the annual meeting of the International Police Executive Symposium (IPES; in 2011). All of our presentations were well received. We also currently have two peer-reviewed articles published on the topic.

It would be very easy for us to join the NYPD prevailing narrative. Why do we stand firm and dare to disagree with the NYPD spin? The evidence is so overwhelming that any moral person cannot turn away. Even in the face of this enormous adversary, we are as confident today as when our data first emerged. In this chapter, we begin by setting an example—we openly address some issues raised regarding our study. We offer this in the spirit of transparency, which is so dreadfully lacking in the NYPD. We hope that this helps readers make their own decisions on the value of our study. Further, the survey, letter, and other information are openly placed in the Appendices for all to inspect. We then discuss each chapter's ramifications and make very specific recommendations.

Issues

Our research, like all studies, has constraints. As social scientists, it is important to note freely those constraints. Nevertheless, the entire study is scientifically sound as evidenced by our publications in two peer-reviewed scientific journals. The citations for those publications are:

> John A. Eterno and Eli B. Silverman. (2010). "Understanding Police Management: A Typology of the Underside of Compstat," *Professional Issues in Criminal Justice,* 5(2&3): 11–28.
>
> John A. Eterno and Eli B. Silverman. (2010). "NYPD's Compstat: Compare Statistics or Compose Statistics?" *International Journal of Police Science and Management,* 12(3): 426–449.

These articles discuss very important features of our methodology. The absolute necessity of maintaining anonymity (which countless studies show helps promote truthful answers to sensitive questions) and keeping the questionnaire of reasonable length (which studies show makes it more likely that people will respond) were indispensable (see, for example, Babbie, 1989; Bradburn, 1983; Dillman, 1983; Neuman, 2000). However, this leads to tradeoffs. Importantly, space constraints mean we can only include a finite number of questions. We make up for this through our in-depth interviews. Furthermore, questions were omitted purposely to protect anonymity.

The NYPD model, to some extent, has been emulated throughout the world; perhaps not exactly, but certainly reasonably copied by many jurisdictions worldwide. This means our study has some generalizability to other locales.

It is important to point out to readers that our question about commanders being aware of manipulation was precise and answered according to the commander's experiences. We are quite confident of this. The reasons for this confidence are:

1. The survey was extensively tested and retested in development. Every focus group and individual reported that they completely understood that they were being asked about their personal experience.
2. The first question of our survey states, "With respect to the following criteria and *based on your personal experience.* …" For further questions such verbiage is repetitive, a waste of valuable space, and, most importantly, unnecessary because the instructions are already clear to respondents.
3. One respondent wrote this unsolicited remark, "In regards to Question #4, I think everyone in NYPD is 'aware' of instances in which crime reports were changed due to Compstat. However, I

marked 'No' for my answer because the instances that I heard of could have been only rumors and I have no factual information of such occurrences."

4. Further evidence that our interpretation is accurate is based on many respondents marking "no" for their answer to this question (strongly buttressing our view). Since changing reports happens every day in precinct commands—ethical changes occur all the time—it is very unlikely that anyone would answer "no" unless they did not have a precinct command assignment (Headquarters, Police Academy, etc.) That is, because this was a contingency question, we allow for awareness of any changes up front (see Appendix B for wording). Those who answer "no" were obviously not in an assignment to observe changes. This is the advantage of a contingency question. We can weed out those with no awareness.

5. Beyond this, as stated earlier, the wording is by design to protect respondents. If anything, it is most likely that our method of collecting crime report changes *undercounts* the level of manipulations known to commanders because we allow for multiple events. This means our results are *exceedingly conservative*.

6. Further, respondents retired over a 15-year period and worked in numerous commands. This makes it highly unlikely that events are conflated.

7. The letter to the respondents included with every questionnaire clearly states, "Due to your experience and expertise, we are inviting you to participate in this project by completing a short questionnaire that asks a variety of questions about *your management experience*" [italics added]. (See letter to respondents in Appendix A.)

Our study examined the managerial process. We were not looking to prosecute anyone. Therefore, the questions reflect our needs, not the needs of the NYPD or a prosecutor. For example, we do not need exact frequencies of manipulation, only knowledge about its basic extent. We now know it was widespread. We have that data.

We did not collect data regarding the outcomes of the numerous manipulations that were reported by our respondents. One reason for this is that such collection could threaten anonymity. A second reason is that this is not the objective of this research study—we only need to know that an extraordinarily high amount of manipulation was taking place in the NYPD.

We feel quite fervently that the evidence is so overwhelming that our conclusions are absolutely accurate. We now explain each chapter's ramifications followed by very specific recommendations.

Chapter Ramifications

Crime Report Manipulation

First and most importantly are the victims of crimes. Had our study not gone public, many of these victims may still not be heard. Sex crimes, in particular, are very difficult for victims to report due to the nature of the crime. Domestic violence also is underreported. Reprehensible as it may seem, even after our report went public in February 2010 and victims came forward, the NYPD was still in denial. Their followers still maintain there was no manipulation. Eventually, sex crimes victims groups met with Commissioner Kelly and numerous e-mails were sent. In response to the overwhelming cry of the public, Kelly formed a working group. In response, belated changes were made to reporting practices. Why? Because there was a problem.

While we are still concerned about reporting practices, this is a step in the right direction. We wonder, however, about the victims of sex crimes for the previous 15 years. We are glad to see change, but how about listening to constructive criticism in the first place? In addition, is the new practice working? Who is going to make that determination—an NYPD that for years was not taking reports accurately?

The NYPD has not and does not take criticism well. They consistently "circle the wagons," make denials, and distribute essentially useless reports by invited guests. They rarely admit error. One must read between the lines to see it. There are still many concerns. We ponder the reporting of sex crimes that occur to non-traditional groups; for example, prostitutes, gay, lesbian, or transgender groups, the poor, minorities, and others. Are their pains not heard because they may not be powerful enough to organize or send e-mails to the Commissioner? How about children? Victims of child sexual abuse need the police to seek them out aggressively. While we do not question the ethics of officers, we do question whether the system currently in place encourages officers actively to seek out and make complaint reports for such victims. Without these reports, no investigation takes place. Victims continue to suffer. How about prostitutes? Can a prostitute be raped? Of course. However, do police always take reports when they claim rape? Debbie Nathan was a white, middle-class victim and her complaint was not properly taken. Even after Kelly's changes, we have concerns.

Victims of all sorts of crimes are not the only ones hurt by all this. Certainly, the NYPD's reputation is hurt. Beyond this, detectives and others trying to investigate and develop patterns are unable to do so because crime reports either were not taken or were downgraded. Detective Harold Hernandez is an example of this (see Chapter 2). Therefore, the NYPD efforts at curbing crime are also hampered. Compstat itself is hampered because its main foundation is "accurate and timely intelligence." Other investigations and police work may be weakened as well. If the NYPD is not taking these reports, exposing terrorist activity is also negatively influenced.

Fighting Terrorism

Fighting terrorism is particularly important in this day and age. Some may claim that the high pressure of Compstat is necessary. We respectfully disagree. The 2010 terrorist attack in Times Square in New York City provides an excellent example.

Although the attempted terrorist attack in Times Square has heaped deserved praise on the NYPD, the cornerstones of its success were bystanders, vendors—Lance Orton and Duane Jackson, who both served during the Vietnam War. The police cannot possibly be everywhere; they need everybody's assistance. They need people from every community to help—to work with them in the fight on terrorism.

How police officers treat ordinary people determines how citizens respond to the call for assistance. Advertisements stating, "If you see something, say something" are an excellent way to inform the public on what to do. However, as with the "just say no" policy on drugs, its call is muted when it fails to address crucial social issues such as fear of police, the influence of peers, deviant subcultures, and the like. The manipulation of crime statistics occurs throughout New York City. For example, in the 81st Precinct, documented by the Schoolcraft tapes, precinct officers were being told to turn away victims, including robbery victims, who would not travel to the station house to make a report. What message does this send to people? Not to report, not to approach, not to advise police!

Precincts do not decide on their own simply to turn away victims of crimes. Rather, commanders and precinct personnel are likely engaged in such activities due to the extreme pressures of headquarters' Compstat meetings. Such activities (recorded on the tapes) have no place in policing. Even if victims do not want to prosecute, reports should be taken. Why? One important reason is intelligence gathering. It is information that can be used to fight crime and terrorism. Without these crime reports, the NYPD is getting a false and incomplete reading on what is occurring on the streets.

Importantly, such reports can lead investigators to possible terrorist activity. As terrorism expert Jonathan White (2012, p. 439, paraphrasing a study by Smith and Roberts, 2005) writes, "When a group prepares an attack, they commit about four crimes three or four months before the actual attack." Law enforcement will be in a far better position to prevent an attack if they are taking reports of crimes. Therefore, they will have the necessary information possibly to stop a terrorist attack before it occurs. For example, terrorists might give away their activities while committing these other crimes. Given the activities we document, not taking reports, or downgrading them, the vital information about those crimes is lost. By refusing to take the report, or downgrading reports, police are possibly enabling terrorists. The information is the key. Fear of increasing the number of crimes due to upper-management pressure is deterring officers from taking reports and citizens from approaching police.

The connection between the community and the police is vital and needs to be respected. A police officer needs to take every complaint seriously. When this does not occur, victims feel as if they are being victimized again—this time by the police when they experience three levels of call-backs, reports not being taken, and being told that they must go to the detective squad or nothing will be done.

Due to management pressures, officers seem far more concerned about crime numbers rather than people. We have seen evidence of this throughout this book. In 2010 with more than 600,000 documented forcible stops by police, one can only ponder whether such stops are targeted activities. We show the extreme pressures on officers to produce a certain "number" of stop-and-frisk reports (documented, for example, by various audiotapes by officers). Since many of the stops are based on furtive movements, it seems likely that the police are simply throwing a wide net and thus unnecessarily alienating law-abiding citizens. Indeed, approximately 85 percent of the stops are of completely innocent people (see New York Civil Liberties Union). In addition, a policy forcing officers to achieve targets such as getting a certain number of "C" summonses (summonses for minor violations of the law) or a quota on the number of stop-and-frisk reports fails to address the vital human element essential to citizen crime reporting.

For whatever reason, many cultural groups do not trust the police. A simple message of "see something, say something" fails miserably. The police need to reach out, to work closely with communities, to take reports from victims, to attract people to the democratic message of equality, liberty, and rights. The police are the front line of democracy. From what we see here, there is a need for change.

Recommendations

The auditing practices of the NYPD fail to address key issues. The most important is officers not taking reports or downgrading by changing a few words. In our interviews with officers, few fear the department's auditing system. This is confirmed by our quantitative analysis in which commanders in the pre-Compstat era are more concerned about integrity in crime statistics than in the Compstat era. Currently, the department has a Data Integrity Unit that examines the written report. That is nearly useless as the reports are being changed or not taken up front. While Quality Assurance is tasked with taking a sample of reports and contacting complainants, few commanders fear being caught. One reason commanders are unconcerned is that the number of reports that are sampled are few. Self-inspection, precinct checks, and Integrity Control Officers (ICO) calling back some complainants are other examples of integrity checks. However, these are all under the control of the commanding officer. Rarely will an ICO who works directly for the commander of the precinct be willing to charge an officer or supervisor with manipulating reports. Rather, the ICO will more likely informally handle the situation—doing the will of the commander who is directly supervising the ICO. Obviously, none of the commanders fears the lieutenant (a lower rank) ICO who works for him or her. We do not feel that more pressure on commanders is needed from the audit side. Rather, all our evidence suggests easing pressure from Compstat for the numbers to look good will help curtail the need to fudge. The inadequacies of the current system are a cause for concern.

One of the best methods to address this problem is the use of integrity testing. That is, undercover officers or others working with Quality Assurance or Internal Affairs need to test precincts. These tests, to the extent possible, should be accomplished for the major index crimes. A female officer should be disguised as a complainant and act as if she were raped. Various scenarios should be worked up and officers need to know that this will be done. Each precinct needs to be tested regularly and a hit list can be developed at Quality Assurance. We recommend this list not be shared with the commands. Those commands that fail or are at higher risk need to be targeted for more in-depth audits. In this way, money is not wasted on conducting superficial audits on every command (the current NYPD practice). Rather, a targeted approach is more likely to have success compared to the random audits conducted throughout the city with little or no reason.

Currently, the NYPD also seems to be taking a ticket-fixing scandal far more seriously than the manipulation of crime reports. First, the NYPD went directly to the Bronx District Attorney with its information. Has a district attorney been asked to investigate complaint report manipulation? Second, based on interviews with currently working police officers, we are aware that integrity testing of officers is now taking place at traffic court in an attempt to control officers' testimony. That is, undercover officers are asking officers who are about to testify if the testifying officer would change his or her testimony as a favor to a fellow officer. If the officer who is about to testify fails to testify properly or if the officer even fails to report the encounter, the testifying officer is disciplined. One must ask why such tactics are used for ticket fixing as opposed to crime report manipulation. Are victims of crimes less important to the NYPD? Is gathering accurate intelligence not necessary to fighting crime and terrorism? How long is this practice to continue?

Ensuring accurate report taking is not simply a matter of auditing and integrity testing. It involves changing a culture. Numbers have become the dominant theme. In Chapter 3 (Performance Management: Pitfalls and Prospects), we deal more with the needed cultural changes.

Pitfalls and Prospects

Chapter 3 highlights the overall problematic Compstat themes we have exposed: top-down management style, hierarchical pressure, and commander morale, abuse, and embarrassment. These themes are woven throughout our research and ultimately are translated into problems on the street. These problems include, but are not limited to reduced discretion by field officers, a deliberate emphasis on the short term to the detriment of long-term investigations, quotas, and domination of numbers. We suggest that the strongest sustaining force in maintaining these negative behaviors is the department's reigning narrative.

The crime success story is the dominant New York narrative. Again, this narrative holds that New York City was the nation's epicenter of crime and disorder until the advent of Compstat and then, miraculously, crime subsequently declined more than 75 percent. The Mayor and the Police Commissioner constantly recycle this narrative. This narrative must change. Eventually crime will inevitably go up assuming reports are accurately taken. Therefore, the narrative becomes a constraining force that contributes to manipulation of crime reports. Since the police department has fewer officers, eventually the narrative and the department will crack.

In a 2000 *New York Times* article discussing "A Vulnerable Police Force," one of us was quoted:

> In 10, maybe 5 years, the consequences of losing so many good people are going to be felt," said Eli B. Silverman, a professor at John Jay College of Criminal Justice and author of *NYPD Battles Crime* (Northeastern University Press, 1999). "The consequence is that you may become far less effective as crime fighters, and the bad guys may reassume their ascendancy."

In a February 7, 2010 television interview (CBS Television News, 2010) one of us is quoted:

> There are so few officers out there because of the crime statistics indicating that there's not so much crime, and they've cut the police department an enormous amount," Dr. Eterno said. Dr. Eterno says a shrinking department puts officers, and the public, at risk. Accurate numbers would only help New York's Finest keep the streets safe.

Fast forward to March 2010. After repeated forays attacking our research and arguing that they could do more with less, the NYPD subtly shifted gears following media reports of sharp increases in crime. What was the response of the NYPD's chief spokesman? "The NYPD is fighting its own success," said Paul Browne. Anyone hear an echo to what we have been repeatedly saying? What did the Police Commissioner say the following day when the *Daily*

News reported that the "NYPD to set up detailed questioning of prisoners to fight back against a 22-percent increase in murders"? "Police Commissioner Kelly warned that proposed budget cuts could reduce the program's effectiveness." This apparently is the new line as Mayor Bloomberg's words indicate: "We have fewer police than we did before. More cops always helps" (Lucadamo and Lemire, 2010, March 25). Another echo anybody?

Since our research has been made public, we have repeatedly urged that the department focus on transparent and accurate crime statistics. We always felt that such revelations would provide the department with leverage to ward off additional budgetary reductions. Suddenly with attention surrounding this issue of accurate reporting, the NYPD seems to have adopted this strategy. The Captains Endowment Association's recent newsletter to its membership reflects this newfound emphasis on accuracy:

> There is inordinate media interest surrounding the Compstat process. If you are discovered to have intentionally misclassified a crime report you will be made an example of. This type of misconduct will cause permanent damage, and potentially the end of your career. Suffering through a "bad Compstat" is a much more desirable fate. (Richter, 2010)

When the *Daily News* reported that:

> Crime is up 13 percent at the Brooklyn precinct where a whistleblower cop accused his supervisors of ignoring felonies to artificially lower the area's crime stats. Lawyers for whistleblower Officer Adrian Schoolcraft say the spike in felonies at the 81st Precinct in the first months of the year shows officials are now being more rigorous about how they classify crimes. "It raises the question: How were they taking reports before Adrian came forward, and are they being more careful now that everyone is watching what they do?" said lawyer Kevin Mosley. Are they doing things now the way they were always supposed to be done? (Parascandola, 2010, March 29)

Recommendations

There is evidence, then, to suggest that the legitimacy of crime statistics may have acquired a newfound attention. If the department had invested more effort to prepare the public for the consequences of depleted resources, it might not have to resort to last-minute acknowledgment of the importance of accuracy. The department's overall narrative must change. It must stop looking back to 1990 and look forward. Let the numbers go where they may. Indeed, having them go up should not be seen as a negative because it may show that people are willing to report to the police. The new narrative must focus on transparency, crime fighting while at the same time protecting people's rights, long-term investigations, and support rather than berate field commanders. We suggest that focusing on its mission statement as articulated on its Web site is far more valuable (we note that the mission statement in its Patrol Guide is worded differently showing the lack of focus on these issues in the immediate past):

> The Mission of the New York City Police Department is to enhance the quality of life in our City by working in partnership with the community and in accordance with constitutional rights to enforce the laws, preserve the peace, reduce fear, and provide for a safe environment. (NYPD, 2011; emphasis added)

Now that's a narrative! Unfortunately, it appears that the NYPD does not live by its mission. Stop the unrelenting focus on numbers and focus on communities—working with them—on protecting constitutional rights. Let commanders have discretion to determine what local conditions need. Headquarters must not mindlessly dictate. Support commanders in this mission. Explain at press conferences how rights are protected; do not demand more stop-and-frisk reports to be reflected at Compstat meetings. Do not berate and belittle their work. If commanders must be punished, fine, but this should rarely be done at Compstat in front of their peers.

An altered Compstat performance management landscape must shed its underbelly. The reformed management would embrace a wide array of police functions, inclusive membership involvement, and diverse participative management restoring closer police-community connections.

With proper reform, performance management can be multidimensional in featuring the long run as well as its current short-term quick fix solutions. For example, New York's Compstat does not have to resemble its current incarnation with its almost exclusive attention to immediate crime control statistics. Compstat's potential and beauty is in its diversity and multiplicity. This performance management system is capable of expanding beyond its current niche. For example, Compstat is a repository of a wealth of data, including citywide, borough, and precinct complaints of FADO (force, abuse, discourtesy, and obscene language). However, these data are rarely discussed at Compstat meetings. Similarly, preliminary domestic violence issues and data, sometimes provided at meetings but without critical review, remain only a blip on Compstat's radar screen. Compstat could also easily embrace other dimensions such as citizen satisfaction.

Over 50 years ago, Selznick observed efficiency's close linkage with means:

> There is a strong tendency not only in administrative life but in all societal action to divorce means and ends by overemphasizing one or the other. The cult of efficiency in administrative theory and practices is a modern way of overstressing means and neglecting ends ... it slights the more basic and

more difficult problem of defining and safeguarding the ends of an enterprise. (Selznick, 1957, pp. 134–135)

Difficult long-term solutions, not the quick fix, need to be the focus of police behavior.

The View from Abroad

In Chapter 4 (Police Performance Management: The View from Abroad), we find that many other countries that have adopted Compstat-like programs have had the same problems we note in New York City. Specifically, crime report manipulations were clear in Australia, France, and the United Kingdom. Downgrading and other manipulation of the figures, precisely the kind that we report in New York City, were rampant in other countries. It often took years to expose the problems as well as countless amounts of money spent on trying to make the performance management systems work.

In the United Kingdom, we find it interesting that they continually created additional units to conduct audits. The units kept growing. At the NYPD, the same can be said. The Data Integrity Unit was created after Compstat came on the scene. Yet, at the same time, commanders felt less pressure to ensure the crime statistics were accurate. In addition, the NYPD developed new bureaucratic rules on handling complaints, as did the United Kingdom. Indeed, the NYPD now boasts that it has numerous personnel assigned to audits:

> Mr. Browne estimated that about 1,000 officers and civilian NYPD employees are involved, in some capacity, in compiling its crime statistics or checking the accuracy of that data. Included in those 1,000 is a 100-employee unit that conducts about 50,000 audits of crime reports a year. (Gardiner, 2011, January 26)

The cost to taxpayers is enormous. We do not advocate ending Compstat but rather the pressures that lead to this lunacy. One thousand members of the service including 100 people in one unit dedicated to audits. This is an absolute waste. A targeted approach, combined with lessening the pressures, makes far more sense. Let the police do their job instead of counting beans.

Units within the department are weak substitutes for outside scrutiny. If the department finds a need to devote 1,000 of its personnel to auditing practices, we conclude there must be some issue with downgrading. Why go to the huge expense of setting up these elaborate mechanisms—much as the United Kingdom did—if nothing is occurring? Experience outside the United States indicates that independent audits are needed. The NYPD claims that a previously conducted and limited audit by a former state comptroller years ago is more than enough. In addition, the NYPD has invited guests whom they choose to examine selected information. These individuals are then held up as the pundits who ensure the purity of the statistics. An outside truly independent check should be welcomed by the NYPD.

In the United States, some manipulation has gone on for years and is well documented. However, Compstat provides a strong incentive to play with the numbers. It took many years for the U.K.'s Home Office to realize that targets simply exacerbated the problem of manipulation. We hope the NYPD will eventually come to this realization as well.

Leadership 101

In Chapter 5 (Big Bad Bully Bosses: Leadership 101), we document the bullying behaviors by the higher echelon at the NYPD. We carefully outline current research studies on bullying and how that affects an organization: over-protection of a public image, adversely influencing the promotion and award system, protection of bullies by the organization, and questionable behaviors that become routine. We discuss specific consequences of bullying at the NYPD such as abuse of authority, downgrading complaints, failure to develop criminal patterns so that criminals/terrorists go undetected, treating victims and innocent New Yorkers illegally and without respect, and employee dissatisfaction. The Compstat system has created an Us versus Them philosophy—commanders and field officers versus headquarters. We are very concerned about the influence of this on the department and its officers. The performance management approach has had problems in nearly every other country and in many other cities that have not carefully adopted it.

Our recommendations to stem these bullying behaviors are clear. Those who rise to the top must be leaders, not bully bosses. We outline many leadership principles such as punish in private and not in public, do not use fear as a motivator, establish an atmosphere of cooperation, set an example, do not micromanage, empower subordinates, and assist those with obstacles (do not berate them) just to name a few.

Importantly, leaders should also have humility. That is, give credit to others, do not brandish authority, and most importantly, the team comes first. Leadership should send out the message that we are all in this together, not Us versus Them. Compstat, as practiced by the NYPD, has become a showdown—commander of precinct versus upper echelon. This is not leadership. Rather, the NYPD should think collaboration—working together to fight crime while protecting rights. We work together to help others in order to get the job done. Baldoni (2009, September 15), for example, points out, among other things, that good leaders need to temper authority, look to promote others, and acknowledge what others do. At the NYPD, this critical element of leadership is sorely lacking. The NYPD's adversarial approach to Compstat has prevented collaboration. Those at the NYPD who lead should not be ego driven, thinking they are always right, but humble and open to other's ideas.

This will take years to develop, but we think it is an important if not critical trait for true leaders. It can all be summed up as "do unto others as you would have done unto yourself." NYPD would certainly be the finest if they would simply follow the golden rule.

We can also be instructed by the human relations school of management. That is, management needs to consider the roles, feelings, frustrations, and needs of those in the organization. Commanders and lower-ranking officers should be considered as part of a team rather than dispensable instruments to be yelled at when numbers are not looking right. Officers in this atmosphere will be more productive and innovative, will take responsibility for mistakes, and, most importantly, will be more likely to treat the public with respect.

The NYPD and the Media

Chapter 6 (NYPD and the Media: Curbing Criticism) unveils some stark truths. First, many in the media are more favorably disposed to the NYPD's perspective. This may be due to the symbiotic relationship that the media has with the NYPD. Certainly, the balance of power has shifted over the years to the NYPD. For example, most media stories on our research were quick to attempt to point out limitations of our research but failed to acknowledge the much more powerful weaknesses of research more favorable to the NYPD. Importantly, all other work in this area was conducted by academics who were invited into the NYPD fold. Further, these academics had no law enforcement experience—with the NYPD or other agencies. As invited guests, they spent little time studying the intricacies of the system or interviewing the foot soldiers. We, on the other hand, have worked and studied the NYPD in the field for many years. Our understanding is in-depth and not superficial. One of us is an accomplished field researcher who studied with the NYPD for many years and eventually published a key book on Compstat and the NYPD. The other worked with the NYPD rising through the ranks to Captain and worked closely with NYPD leadership for many years. We are aware, for example, that invited scholars who spend little time in attendance at the NYPD will not be privy to the types of behaviors of which we are aware and expose. It takes many years to develop those types of relationships and understandings. Further, these invited scholars have very different pressures on them. In addition, two key outside attempts at opening up the books were fatally flawed. First, the Comptroller's report, which even the NYPD's sponsored NYU study stated was weak, was hardly without stonewalling. As Gardiner (2011, January 26) writes,

> Among the first skeptics of the 20 percent crime drop was state Comptroller Carl McCall, who launched an investigation. Mayor Rudolph Giuliani ordered the heads of city agencies not to cooperate and had two state auditors

removed from city buildings. ... After a three-year legal battle during which Mr. Giuliani claimed the audits were politically motivated and Mr. McCall suggested Mr. Giuliani had "something to hide," the courts sided with Mr. McCall. ... Mr. McCall recently told the *Wall Street Journal* that the audit was limited by a lack of cooperation.

We note that the drop in reported index crime is now claimed to be approximately a whopping 80 percent. Additionally, the NYPD has been bleeding police officers for years. Their head count is now down approximately 6,000 officers, and thousands of other officers have been transferred from crime fighting assignments to terrorism, intelligence, and other newly created units. We do not question the wisdom of the transfers, only the likelihood that crime would drop so much while losing so many officers (see Chapter 2). We also note that a second attempt at an independent audit—this one was attempted by former federal prosecutor Mark Pomerantz—was also stymied. This time Mayor Bloomberg did not compel the NYPD to allow Pomerantz access. This one fatal stroke by the Mayor rendered the commission impotent.

Another stark and obvious truth is that requests for information from the media are often thwarted when it is a controversial issue. Numerous FOIL requests have been denied for seemingly frivolous reasons. Several journalists such as Paul Moses have tried to secure basic data from the NYPD. Recently, a local newspaper in the Bronx, the *Norwood News*, questioned one precinct's lack of transparency. They too filed a FOIL request and were thwarted. Lawsuits against the NYPD for such information continue to mount. the *New York Times* lawsuit for information is the preeminent example. Stonewalling on data release seems to be a common NYPD tactic. Even stop-and-frisk data were not released for years until a lawsuit by the Center for Constitutional Rights prevailed (see Chapter 7).

Press credentials have become bargaining chips. Non-mainstream media have been denied press credentials, although the department eventually relented on this. The story of Leonard Levitt is another stark example of how unfavorable reporters can be treated. The issue of editors changing and playing with stories has also been paramount as editors cozy up to the NYPD. The extent of this is unknown, but we are aware of several well-known reporters who changed their stories based on such pressures.

The press has been called the fourth estate. They are supposed to check and balance police power. Unfortunately, this has not been the case in New York. Even blog sites such as THEE RANT have been attacked by the NYPD. That Web site was attacked by city officials and told to remove NYPD from its title—the former title was NYPD RANT. How far does this go? What needs to be done?

Recommendations

Some of our recommendations are obvious and simple, others difficult, at best. For the NYPD, open the books. Slowly, lawsuit after lawsuit, the NYPD refuses or sometimes grudgingly releases selected information. We do not propose outright release of everything. We do propose far more transparency. Why does the public have to wait years for misdemeanor crimes, lost property figures, and stop-and-frisk numbers to be released? This is unconscionable. State legislation is necessary to compel police and other agencies to release certain easily attainable information. These data are collected with taxpayer money. Taxpayers have the absolute right to see what their dollars have paid for. There is no excuse here—none. This information must be released.

Let local commanders give interviews and some data where local conditions warrant. As is typical of the NYPD, no discretion is granted. Headquarters dictates everything—how many summonses, how many arrests, how many stop-and-frisks, what crime statistics can be given to the public. Nothing is allowed to vary. Headquarters should not stymie the Bronx command that was proudly supplying data all along. Perhaps they could ask permission, but generally, data should be released and not withheld. Data and information allow discussion in a free forum of ideas. Without that information, only guesses can guide outside discussion. It is not a question or even a request; it is a demand. The public has a right to know. They pay the salaries of the NYPD. The NYPD must be responsive. Again, they do not have to release everything, but far more information from the police should be regularly distributed.

Give local commanders discretion to react to local media and conditions in those precincts. This is an endemic problem in the NYPD. Local conditions lose out to centralizing forces on the department. Discretion at the local level is drastically diminished. Commanders and others should be encouraged to talk to the press. The Police Commissioner should not announce nearly everything. Rather, the spotlight should be shared with those who are in the field. The DCPI should not control information but, to the extent possible, assist in the release of information. The DCPI should help set up interviews with commanders and others (not just the favored few), and not prevent them. Citizens and media should have free access to those who serve them.

If a controversy occurs, the proper response is not closing all sources of information. Sure, investigations need to be done, but the DCPI could set up appropriate avenues for the press rather than withholding all information and then releasing selectively.

We have also documented that some members of the press are victims of their editors. Editors, too, feel pressures. We have seen stories edited to the point of changing their entire meaning. Reporters need to do their job— report. Editors, to the extent possible, should allow the truth to be exposed.

To that end, the Police Foundation money, which news reports suggest have paid for various lunches, dinners, and the like for upper management, might better be spent on studying what types of information can be released and how best to release it.

Specifically, the New York State Legislature should pen legislation requiring police departments throughout the state to release certain basic information to the public. For example, when it was revealed that only the NYPD and the Newburgh Police Department were not releasing misdemeanor crimes to the New York State Division of Criminal Justice Services, it should have set off alarm bells in Albany. All police departments in the state, to the extent possible, need to be transparent. DCJS and the Municipal Police Training Council (an arm of New York State) could help write this legislation such that it is not burdensome on departments yet allows maximum exposure. Given what we see in New York City, it cannot be left up to police departments to decide what taxpayers should know. Rather, some data and information should be required by law to be released. This legislation might also include a person to whom any reporter or other can appeal a decision of a police department not to release information. The person would have the power to force departments to release information after reviewing it. The person should be impartial and set in his or her position by the Attorney General or the Governor and approved by the State Senate. In this way, departments will not be able to continue hiding statistics and other information that the public deserves to know and the media can use to report.

Underpinnings and Implications

In Chapter 7 (Compstat: Underpinnings and Implications), we developed a deeper understanding of Compstat based on theory. We point out that like any other human-created system there are both strengths and weaknesses. Compstat strengths are well publicized. However, an understanding of the lesser-known weaknesses has rarely been the focus of research. Compstat has become popular among police agencies due to its success at crime fighting. Yet, from the beginning, few police leaders or scholars delve into the side effects of such a focus.

Based on criminal justice theory, we suggest that a focus (or over-focus) on crime can influence due process concerns. Even staunch proponents of Compstat who understand theory have recognized this issue (see Kelling and Coles, 1996). Under Compstat, the NYPD has policed the city as if there is one community standard. Local conditions and discretion of officers has been minimized. Instead, iron control from Headquarters has resulted. Compstat has been and continues to be a strong centralizing force. Police have targeted minority communities in particular. Numbers-crunching bureaucrats dictate policy from Headquarters without understanding or even trying to understand local communities. The result is a huge number of forcible stops of mostly innocent people, arrests for minor quality-of-life violations going through the roof, useless summonses and arrests, little transparency in the organization, and quite likely, alienating much of minority youth—if not outright destroying what chance they have of success by labeling them with criminal records for minor violations that occur in every community throughout the city. What can be done?

Recommendations

As we have continually stated, one of the most important recommendations that we make is that the NYPD must become more transparent. For example, withholding basic information such as misdemeanor crimes for many years is simply unacceptable. The department still needs to allow commanders and others to talk to the media openly without oversight or repercussions. Mr. Kelly must allow others to share the spotlight. Allowing others to experience the glory is part of the humility we discussed earlier that leaders need to exhibit (see Chapter 5).

FOIL requests should be answered quickly, succinctly, and truthfully. Oversight of the NYPD may be necessary on this particular issue due to its dismal record. For example, failing to release data on lost property for many years after numerous FOIL requests by the press including Paul Moses is bad enough. However, the NYPD decided when it was convenient for them to release the lost property figures, giving the *Wall Street Journal* a scoop on the numbers. If the numbers were so readily available, why were they not released many years earlier? Misdemeanor crime is another example. Why the sudden release of selected data after numerous requests? It is likely that the upper echelon felt it could not hurt after carefully vetting them. That is, they examined all the figures that were to be released beforehand and then decided it was in their best interest—not the public's best interest—to allow the public to see them. This is the antithesis of transparency. Data and information need to be released whether good or bad news results. The NYPD's record is dismal. Oversight of the NYPD from someone or some group outside the organization, at this point, is mandatory. The organization has become obsessed with its image and lost sight of its mission to serve the public.

The public is not served well by the gargantuan campaign "if you see something, say something." This may actually mean something to people if police work with communities rather than alienating them with ridiculous summonses, forcible stops, and nearly meaningless arrests. How often do people go to police officers with information? Many police officers are not viewed as professionals with the ability to decide when to write summonses and make arrests. Rather, the Compstat process encourages mindless automatons that do the bidding of Headquarters, which may be forcing them to submit to illegal quotas. Allowing local commanders and officers to address conditions without the foolhardy pressures of Compstat will be one of the best innovations the department can and should do.

This does not mean ending Compstat but developing a collaborative approach. Numbers can still be important but not looking for them mindlessly to head in the "right direction." Rather, Headquarters should be supporting officers in the field who have the ultimate authority to make decisions. Summons a woman eating a doughnut—no. Summons an elderly woman getting prescription drugs on a freezing cold night—no. How about injecting some common sense into the equation! The NYPD has created a story line from which it is now difficult to extract itself. Our recommendation—pull out and follow your new mission statement on your Web site.

Importantly, in attempting to follow their new mission statement, police officers from the top down need to appreciate their job's inherent balancing act. They must properly balance due process policies with crime fighting policies. This is a difficult task, at best, but it is what makes the job of police officer such a high calling in a democracy. The job is difficult and meant to be that way. Fight crime but balance protecting Constitutional rights. Where should the balance be drawn? That is the question. In times of fear, the power of police must expand such as 9/11. However, when there is no immediate danger, the balance must shift to protecting rights. This means it is fluid. It always has been in our democracy. For example, habeas corpus was suspended three times in our history—the Civil War, World War II, and 9/11. The gravity of 9/11 can be seen from this. Note, however, that the suspension is not indefinite. When the emergency subsides, powers should return to a healthy norm. In addition, even during the emergency, protections still exist. We do not suspend the Constitution. If we did that, terrorists can claim victory. In sum, the balance between crime/terrorist fighting and due process is a fluid one that will depend much on the times. Police need to be ever vigilant of this balance. By maintaining close ties to communities, they will be better able to maintain their mandate. As it stands now, we believe that the NYPD is dangerously close to losing (or has already lost) its mandate through the social contract especially in minority communities. We again point out that this is not easy, nor is it meant to be. Local commanders need the authority and discretion to work with people. Mindless number games from Headquarters do not help.

We also call on the NYPD immediately to begin the process of accreditation through the Commission on Accreditation for Law Enforcement Agencies (CALEA). This will show a willingness to be open and transparent. CALEA is not some sort of hoax organization. It was started by the International Association of Chiefs of Police (IACP), the National Organization of Black Law Enforcement Executives (NOBLE), the National Sheriffs' Association (NSA), and the Police Executive Research Forum (PERF). All of these organizations are highly respected in the democratic world of policing. The time has come for organizational awakening. We know what the NYPD is capable of, but they need to adopt a new culture, a new philosophy of democratic policing. It is not easy, nor is it meant to be.

Conclusions

In sum, we recommend the following:

1. Develop and regularly conduct integrity tests to address the problem of crime manipulation. This may include undercover officers, the use of fake radio runs, and developing lists of precincts that are problems. There is nothing unusual about integrity testing. The NYPD currently uses these tests with corruption and more recently with ticket fixing. In this way, much more thorough audits should be conducted on those precincts that fail or are doing poorly on the tests. The NYPD can then use very large samples on targeted precincts rather than the almost useless sampling method currently used. This targeted approach is far more cost effective and efficient. We point out, however, that this needs to be done in conjunction with our other recommendations. Otherwise, the NYPD is just adding yet another pressure on precinct commanders.
2. Ironically, by following recommendation Number 1—targeted auditing—the enormous gain in efficiency will allow the NYPD to transfer some of the 1,000 staff members they claim are devoted to auditing crime reports. It is suggested they go to precincts where communities will directly benefit and not to Headquarters units.
3. Adopt the mission statement on its Web site as the new narrative. Again, this mission statement reads:

The Mission of the New York City Police Department is to enhance the quality of life in our City by working in partnership with the community and in accordance with constitutional rights to enforce the laws, preserve the peace, reduce fear, and provide for a safe environment. (NYPD, 2011)

4. Immediately stop the unrelenting focus on numbers at Compstat. Develop a more comprehensive approach that takes into account the multifaceted aspects of policing.
5. Allow commanders to work more closely with communities. Focus on local conditions and do not follow mindless directives from Headquarters units that may have little understanding of local

conditions. Closer community cooperation will provide the NYPD with enhanced intelligence thereby strengthening their anti-crime and anti-terrorism efforts.

6. Focus far more attention on protecting rights. Hundreds of thousands of forcible stops of innocent people need to be something Headquarters questions, not promotes. How is it possible that police brought down crime for years without such aggressive behavior?

7. End the micromanagement. Iron control from Headquarters stifles efficiency and effectiveness. Transfers from one command to another within a borough, for example, must be permitted if a borough commander approves. These types of transfers should not be micromanaged from Headquarters.

8. Stop the bullying immediately. Think collaboration. Headquarters must support the field, not demand mindless numbers from them. This will mean, for example, immediately transferring many of the bloated units at Headquarters devoted to Compstat. There will be no need for detectives and other staff to be part of a Chief's personal squad. The "gotcha" game must end. Headquarters must learn to delegate power to the commanders it places in the field. This means leadership, not iron control. We also recommend peer evaluations and a system by which good performance is rewarded. This can be done in conjunction with supervisory evaluations; however, peer evaluations often promote good behavior without top-down dictates.

9. Legislation at the state level to force police departments to be more transparent must be penned. The press as well as taxpayers are entitled to basic information without having to initiate lawsuits. Oversight of this may be required.

10. Even without legislation, the NYPD must become more transparent. This means, at a minimum, respond promptly and fully to FOIL requests, provide access to redesigned Compstat meetings, provide press access to all personnel without first securing DCPI's permission, easily obtainable data should not be selectively released, allow local commanders authority to release data based on local conditions, and many others as seen throughout this work. Allow commanders to talk freely to the press and allow the press access to nearly every command with very few exceptions. DCPI's job should be to help create access, not to spin control over events.

11. The NYPD's upper echelon must be leaders. For example, they would benefit from greater humility. Allow commanders to share the spotlight at press conferences. They deserve to shine as much if not more than those currently in front of the microphone do.

12. The NYPD should immediately begin the process of accreditation through CALEA. This is a good first step toward a new and improved department.

13. If the New York City Police Department fails to adopt the previous recommendations, it is imperative that an independent commission with subpoena power and ability to grant immunity be established immediately. The Knapp and Mollen Commissions serve as precedence for this.

Silence is not an option. Policing a free society is not a simple exercise of "making the dots go away." Balancing rights with crime fighting, working with communities, serving the public, these are not shallow words. It is the duty of an informed citizenry to stand up for what they know is right. This is our history. We stand firmly behind our research and the constructive spirit in which this book is offered.

Officers are sworn to uphold what Americans cherish most—liberty— not mindless numbers, not unchecked police power, not crime control, not bullying. Will our critique be heard or will our words echo in the sounds of silence? When fear of crime and terrorism overcomes reason and freedoms, our society, our way of life, is forever lost.

References

Babbie, E. (1989). *The Practice of Social Research,* 5th ed. Belmont, CA: Wordsworth.

Baldoni, J. (2009, September 15). "Humility as a Leadership Trait," *HBB Blog Network,* http://blogs.hbr.org/baldoni/2009/09/humility_as_a_leadership_trait.html. Retrieved July 28, 2011.

Bradburn, N.M. (1983). "Response Effects." In: Rossi, P., Wright, J., and Anderson, A., Eds., *Handbook of Survey Research.* New York: Academic Press, pp. 289–328.

CBS Television News. (2010). "Controversial Study: NYPD Officials Cooked Books Research Claims Higher-Ups in Department Fudged Numbers to Improve Crime Rate Statistics." Hazel Sanchez, Reporter. Aired February 7, 2010.

Dillman, D.A. (1983). "Mail and Other Self-Administered Questionnaires." In: Rossi, P., Wright, J., and Anderson, A., Eds., *Handbook of Survey Research.* New York: Academic Press, 359–377.

Gardiner, S. (2011, January 26). "NYPD's Long War Over Crime Stats," http://online.wsj.com/article/SB10001424052748704698004576104203869313630.html. Retrieved on July 26, 2011.

Kelling, G.L. and Coles, C.M. (1996). *Fixing Broken Windows.* New York: Simon & Schuster.

Levitt, L. (2010, August 30). "Hiding the Truth at John Jay?" *Huffington Post,* http://www.huffingtonpost.com/len-levitt/hiding-the-truth-at-john-_b_698899.html. Retrieved on August 25, 2011.

Lucadamo, K. and Lemire, J. (2010, March 25). "Mayor Bloomberg Blames Spike in Murders in 2010 on Budget Cuts that Puts Fewer Cops on NYC Streets," *Daily News*, http://articles.nydailynews.com/2010-03-26/news/27060134_1_lowest-murder-murder-rate-budget-cuts. Retrieved on August 25, 2011.

Neuman, W.L. (2000). *Social Research Methods: Qualitative and Quantitative Approaches*, 4th ed. Boston: Allyn and Bacon.

NYPD. (2011). "About Us. Mission Statement," http://www.nyc.gov/html/nypd/html/home/mission.shtml. Retrieved July 28, 2011.

Parascandola, R. (2010, March 29). "Crime Is Up 13 percent in B'klyn's 81st Pct. Where Whistleblower Accused Chiefs of Lowering Felony Stats," *Daily News*, http://articles.nydailynews.com/2010-03-29/news/27060261_1_crime-victims-crime-stats-crime-rate. Retrieved on August 8, 2011.

Powell, M. (2011, August 4). "Governing New York by Writing a Check," *New York Times*, http://www.nytimes.com/2011/08/05/nyregion/for-bloomberg-governing-new-york-by-writing-a-check.html?emc=eta1. Retrieved August 9, 2011.

Richter, R.T. (2010). *CEA Newsletter,* III(2): 3.

Selznick, P. (1957). *Leadership in Administration: A Sociological Perspective.* Berkley, CA: Harper & Row.

Smith, B.L. and Roberts, P. (2005) "Pre-Incident Indicators of Terrorist Activities: The Identification of Behavioral, Geographic, and Temporal Patterns of Preparatory Conduct," *National Institute of Justice.* Cited in White, J.R. (2012). *Terrorism and Homeland Security,* 7th ed. Belmont CA: Wadsworth, 439.

Appendix A: Letter to Respondents Accompanying Survey

ROY T. RICHTER
PRESIDENT

233 BROADWAY – SUITE 1801
NEW YORK, NY 10279
(212) 791-8292

CHRIS MONAHAN
VICE PRESIDENT

July 14, 2008

Dear CEA member,

John A. Eterno, Ph.D. and Eli B. Silverman, Ph.D. are the Principle Investigators in a scientific research project aimed at studying the management styles of the New York City Police Department (NYPD). Due to your experience and expertise, we are inviting you to participate in this project by completing a short questionnaire that asks a variety of questions about your management experiences. We are asking you to look over the questionnaire and, if you choose to do so, complete it and send it back to the Captains Endowment Association (CEA) in the enclosed envelope. It should take you a few minutes to complete.

Your participation will help us to provide policy feedback to the NYPD and the CEA as well as advance the scientific study of police management. The results of this project will be published in various scientific journals and will be shared with the CEA.

We hope you will take the time to complete this questionnaire and return it. Your participation is voluntary (you are not required in any way to do this) and your answers are completely anonymous (we do not know who filled out questionnaires or even who returned them). The research is being funded completely by a grant from Molloy College. The CEA is incurring no expenses whatsoever and will benefit from the results.

If you have any questions or concerns about completing the questionnaire or about being in this study, you may contact Dr. John A. Eterno at (516) 678-5000 ext. 6138 or by e-mail at: jeterno@molloy.edu or Dr. Eli B. Silverman by e-mail at: estcompany@optonline.net.

We are looking forward to receiving your completed questionnaire so that we can better understand the management of the NYPD and also see how the CEA can better serve you. Please send the completed survey back to us in the envelope provided.

Very truly yours,

Roy T. Richter
President
Captains Endowment
Association

John A. Eterno
Associate Dean &
Director of Graduate
Studies, Molloy College

Eli B. Silverman
Professor Emeritus
John Jay College,
City University of New York

Appendix B: Survey Instrument

NEW YORK CITY POLICE DEPARTMENT RETIREE SURVEY

Principal Investigators John A. Eterno, Ph.D. and Eli B. Silverman, Ph.D. are conducting a survey to examine how the New York City Police Department (NYPD) operates with respect to the mid-level manager. We hope to assist those currently working by providing information from you. Your participation in the survey is strictly voluntary and you can stop at any time. **Please do not put your name or other identifying information on this survey**. The survey is being conducted anonymously (the investigators do not know who filled out a particular questionnaire). You indicate your **voluntary consent** to being questioned by filling out the questionnaire. This is a short survey and it should only take a few **minutes** to complete. If you have any questions, feel free to contact John Eterno at (516) 678-5000 ext. 6138.
SIMPLY CIRCLE YOUR ANSWER TO EACH QUESTION.

1) **With respect to the following criteria and based on your personal experience, on a scale of 1 to 10 (with 1 being the least and 10 the most), how much pressure was there from management/supervisors to**:

	Least Pressure									**Most Pressure**
Increase summonses	1	2	3	4	5	6	7	8	9	10
Increase arrests	1	2	3	4	5	6	7	8	9	10
Decrease index crime	1	2	3	4	5	6	7	8	9	10
(Basically index crime is murder, forcible rape, burglary, robbery, serious assault, GLA, Grand Larceny)										
Decrease other crime	1	2	3	4	5	6	7	8	9	10
Downgrade index crime to non-index crime	1	2	3	4	5	6	7	8	9	10
Improve Quality of life	1	2	3	4	5	6	7	8	9	10
Decrease CCRB complaints	1	2	3	4	5	6	7	8	9	10
Increase Stop and Frisk Reports	1	2	3	4	5	6	7	8	9	10
Detect victims of domestic violence	1	2	3	4	5	6	7	8	9	10
Detect victims of rape	1	2	3	4	5	6	7	8	9	10
Detect victims of child abuse	1	2	3	4	5	6	7	8	9	10

Skip to Question #5 if you retired in 1993 or earlier.

PLEASE TURN OVER

263

2) **On a scale of 1 to 10 (1 being very poor and 10 being excellent), what is your overall opinion of Compstat with respect to:**

	Very Poor									**Excellent**
reducing crime	1	2	3	4	5	6	7	8	9	10
reducing fear in the community	1	2	3	4	5	6	7	8	9	10
serving community needs	1	2	3	4	5	6	7	8	9	10
addressing quality of life issues	1	2	3	4	5	6	7	8	9	10
detecting *victims* of crime	1	2	3	4	5	6	7	8	9	10
improving management effectiveness	1	2	3	4	5	6	7	8	9	10
improving teamwork within management	1	2	3	4	5	6	7	8	9	10
improving teamwork among rank-and-file	1	2	3	4	5	6	7	8	9	10

3) **On a scale of 1 to 10 (with 1 being greatly reduces and 10 being greatly increases), to what extent does Compstat reduce or increase the following items:**

	Greatly reduces								Greatly increases	
tension among management	1	2	3	4	5	6	7	8	9	10
tension among rank-and-file	1	2	3	4	5	6	7	8	9	10
morale among rank and file	1	2	3	4	5	6	7	8	9	10

GO TO THE NEXT PAGE

4) Are you aware of any instances in which crime reports were changed due to Compstat?

YES ☐

NO ☐ (If no, continue to question 5)   If yes: on a scale of 1 to 10 answer
                                                         the following:

	Least									Most
Extent to which the change(s) was (were) due to pressure of Compstat	1	2	3	4	5	6	7	8	9	10
Extent to which change(s) was (were) legally inappropriate	1	2	3	4	5	6	7	8	9	10
Extent to which change(s) was (were) ethically inappropriate	1	2	3	4	5	6	7	8	9	10

5) On a scale of 1 to 10, rate the importance you place on the following criteria to explaining why officers under your command followed orders given by you:

	Least important									Most important
general management style of the NYPD	1	2	3	4	5	6	7	8	9	10
your personal management style	1	2	3	4	5	6	7	8	9	10

6) On a scale of 1 to 10, rate the importance of the following criteria to police work:

	Least important									Most important
Loyalty to officers	1	2	3	4	5	6	7	8	9	10
Loyalty to management	1	2	3	4	5	6	7	8	9	10
Controlling crime	1	2	3	4	5	6	7	8	9	10
Protect basic rights	1	2	3	4	5	6	7	8	9	10
Maintaining integrity	1	2	3	4	5	6	7	8	9	10
Service to the public	1	2	3	4	5	6	7	8	9	10

7) On a scale of 1 to 10, to what extent is promotion based on crime statistics within a manager's command?

Not based									Highly based
1	2	3	4	5	6	7	8	9	10

PLEASE TURN OVER

8) On a scale of 1 to 10, how would you rate the fairness of the promotion process above the

rank of Captain? Least Fair   **Most Fair**
                    1   2   3   4   5   6   7   8   9   10

9) **To what extent did management demand integrity in crime statistics?**
      Slight Demand   **High Demand**
                    1   2   3   4   5   6   7   8   9   10

10) **Should the Retiree's representative in the Captain's Endowment Association be divided into three areas: (1) recently retired and in the workforce, (2) general issues, and (3) Medicare eligible retiree?**   Yes   No

11) **As a retiree, how responsive is the Captain's Endowment Association to your needs?**
      Not responsive   **Very Responsive**
                    1   2   3   4   5   6   7   8   9   10

12) **Have you ever had contact with the Captain's Endowment Association's retiree representative?**   Yes
                    No

13) **Would you be interested in a Captain's Endowment Association alumni directory?**
            Yes   No

14) **Your gender:**   Male   Female

15) **Your age:** under 20   20-40   41-60   61+

16) **Your highest degree:**   High School   Some College   College Graduate   Graduate or Law School

17) **Your Marital Status:**   Single   Married   Divorced   Widowed   Other

18) **Your race:**   Asian   Black   Hispanic   White   Other

19) **Your rank when retired:** Captain   Deputy Inspector   Inspector   Deputy Chief   Other Chief

20) **How many years did you serve as a (answer only those that apply to you):**
Captain____; Deputy Inspector____; Inspector ____; Deputy Chief____.

21) **How many years of service did you do for the NYPD?** _____

22) **Do you have prior military experience?**   Yes   No

23) **Did you serve on NYPD after 1994?**   Yes   No

24) **Please make any comments that you feel are important to understanding the NYPD based on your experiences as a manager (attach other pages if necessary).**

Appendix C: NYPD Letter to Victims of Identity Theft

 POLICE DEPARTMENT

To Whom It May Concern:

The New York City Police Department requires specific documentation be submitted before a police report for Identity Theft or fraud-related crimes can be taken. The documentation is needed to aid in the proper investigation of the crime.

The documents that are need are as follows:

1. A letter on the company, bank or institutions letterhead, that states the person is disputing opening the account and/or the charges being billed; it should include:

   a. Account Holder's Name and Account Number
   b. Amount(s) or Services being disputed
   c. Name and address of person who opened the account (if available)
   d. Where merchandise was sent (if available)

2. A company affidavit, that is notorized, that states the complainant had no prior knowledge or involvement in the transaction of fraud or identity theft; this should include amount(s), account names, account numbers, services and/or any other item(s) being disputed.

3. A copy of your credit report from: Experian, TransUnion and Equifax, the credit reporting bureaus, to see if any other fraudulent transactions have occurred.

4. Any supporting documentation that can aid in your claim of fraud or identity theft.

Once the above documentation has been submitted and verified by our investigators, a police report can be taken. Please allow 24 to 48 hours after you file your report, for a complaint number to be generated and be made available.

Sincerely,

Police Administrative Aide
Complaint Room

COURTESY • PROFESSIONALISM • RESPECT
Website: http: nyc.gov nypd

Index

A

Aborn, Richard, 178
Abuse of authority, 117–118, 126, 202, 223, *See also* Police misconduct
Academic peer reviewed research, 9, 76, 144, 238, 239, 240
Academy of Criminal Justice Sciences, 239
Accreditation, 203–204, 256, 259
Ahmad, J., 129
Alejandro, Joseph, 28
Anderson, D., 130
Anonymity of respondents, 28, 34, 144, 240
Anti-social behavior (ASB), 70–71, 92
Anti-terrorism activities, 154, 243–244
Arantz, Philip, 2–3, 5–8
Argyris, Chris, 17
Arrest decisions, extralegal considerations, 205
Arrest quotas, 11, 28, 64–66, 169, 170
Arrests, questionable
    Baltimore lawsuit case, 228–229
    marijuana enforcement, 217–220
    Mauriello specials, 113–114
Arson, 30
Assaults
    felony versus misdemeanor trends, 43–44, 117
    firearms-related data, 41–42
    hospital data, 40–42, 165
    numbers following publication of Eterno & Silverman's study, 52
    U.K. police undercounting, 95
Assaults against police, 99
Audiotape evidence of crime report manipulation, 4, 49–52, 117, 121, 169, 170, 175
Australian police performance management, 97–102, 249, *See also* New South Wales (NSW) Police Force
    early computer system, 6–7
Australian workplace bullying, 116
Authoritarian leadership style, 131
Autocratic leadership style, 131
Auto theft reporting, 33, 46

B

Bacon, P., 66–67
Baez, Anthony, 224
Baker, A., 114
Baltimore CitiStat program, 15–16
Baltimore Police Department, 15, 228–229
Bayley, David, 194, 208
Bell, Sean, 225
Bernstein, J., 132–134
Best Value principles, 88
Bill of Rights, 199, 201
Blair, Tony, 88, 179
Bloch, P. B., 129
Bloomberg, Michael R.
    Commissioner Kelly's relationship with, 152–153
    Compstat and, 77
    confidence in power of statistics, 147–148
    criticism of state-mandated privacy protections, 177
    political ramifications of crime statistics, 151–153
    reelection campaign, 152
    responses to statistic manipulation allegations, 164
    response to Eterno-Silverman research report, 141
    safe city declarations, 73, 152
    Times editor Shipley and, 145
Bolanos, Joseph, 37
BorderStat, 16
Bouza, A. V., 201
Braithwaite, John, 212
Braton, Betty, 169
Bratton, William J., 192–194, 197, 198, 204, 217–220
    Baltimore PD and, 228
    leadership style, 131
    Newsday reporter Levitt and, 160
    NYPD re-engineering initiative, 13
    response to Eterno-Silverman retiree survey, 141, 145
Broken Windows theory, 192–198
Brotheridge, C. M., 115–116

Browne, Paul, 153, 155–157, 159, 161, 163, 164, 175, 246
Bullying behavior by senior management, 59–60, 109–112, 115–130, 250
  bully alliances, 119, 122–123
  bullying research, 115–116, 123
  Compstat meetings and commander embarrassment, 59–60, 110–112, 125
  fear as motivator, 132–134
  female officers and, 129–130
  leadership issues, 132
  Pinocchio incident, 197
  promotion and dissatisfaction, 119–121, 123–124
  protecting the bullies, 121–122
  public image preoccupation and, 116–118
  reform recommendations, 248, 250–251, 258
  reprisals against whistleblowers, 121–122, 127–128
  sociological perspectives, 125–129
Bureaucracy, Weberian sociological perspectives, 126–128
Bureaucratic leadership style, 131
Bureaucratic management, See Top-down management style
Buress, Plaxico, 42
Burglary trends, 43, 117
Burke, Kenneth, 77
Burleigh, M., 206
Business performance management model, 12–14, 72, 87, 97, 103

C

Campbell, Donald T., 10
Captains Endowment Association (CEA), 28–29, 247
Center for Constitutional Rights (CCR), 222–223, 227, 252
The Challenge of Crime in a Free Society (Arantz), 7
Chambliss, W., 205–206, 219
Chess players, NYPD persecution of, 216
The Chief/Civil Service Leader, 171
Child abuse victims, 71, 242
Churchill, Winston, 200
CitiStat, 15–16
Citizens Crime Commission, 105, 178

City Journal, 141, 142–144, 154
Citywide Accountability Program, 15
Civilian Complaint Review Board (CCRB), 117, 123, 178, 223
Civil liberties, 201
  crime control versus due process, 201–206, 254–255
  government and police powers, 198–200
  inappropriate summons examples, 214–216
  media coverage and, 161–162
  minority communities and, 224–227, See also Minorities
  mission of the police to protect, 201, 203, 256
  NYPD criticism of state-mandated privacy protections, 177
  police state versus, 205
  protection and fighting crime, 13
  rapid deployment units versus minorities, 205–206
  reform recommendations, 258
  reprisals against whistleblowers, 1–3
  security as safety for all, 79
  stop-and-frisk practices and, 220–224, See also Stop-and-frisks
Civil litigation, See Lawsuits
Cloward, R., 213
Coles, Katherine, 197–198
Commander accountability under Compstat, 24–26
Commander embarrassment and demoralization, 59–60, 110–112, 116, 125, 132, 197, See also Bullying behavior by senior management
Commissioner's panel appointed to examine NYPD crime statistics, 53–54, 67, 105, 172, 175, 177, 210
Commission on Accreditation for Law Enforcement Agencies (CALEA), 203, 256, 259
Commission to Combat Police Corruption, 143, 159, 166, 177–178
Community policing, 195–198, 202
Community Policing Consortium, 197
Community relations and policing, 68–71, 209, 213, See also Civil liberties; Minorities
  Broken Windows theory and, 192–198
  legalistic policing style, 70, 127, 209, 226

NYPD mission statement and, 248, 256, 257

Compstat, 14, 24–26, 202, 204, 237, 246, *See also* Performance management and accountability systems

adoption outside New York, 14, 16, 191, 249

Australian system, 5–7, 97, *See also* Australian police performance management

French system, 102–104

U.K. system, 94, 249, *See also* United Kingdom (U.K.), performance policing

archive infiltration to manipulate data, 169–170

authors' support for, 194

Broken Windows theory and, 192–198

commander accountability, 24–26

competing for resources, 135

computerized pin map, 208–209

conversions, 14–16

crime-fighting versus due process focus, 202, 204, 254–255, *See also* Crime control versus due process

crime-fighting versus quality-of-life focus, 195–196

crime statistic manipulation, *See* Crime report manipulation

FADO data, 248

index crimes, 30

leadership styles, 131–132

legalistic style of policing, 127, 129, 209, 212

mayoral support for, 77, 147–148

military model, 129

non-law enforcement implementations, 15–16

numbers focus, 24–25

origins of, 193–194

reform issues, *See* Reform issues and prospects

sacred cow mentality, 191–192

social science theory and, *See* Social science theory

Success Story and symbolism, 76–78

"The Trouble with Compstat" article, 165

threatening implications of critique, 148

as vindictive punishment tool, 59–60

Compstat bureaucratic management style, consequences of, *See* Bullying behavior by senior management; Hierarchical pressure; Top-down management style

Compstat meetings, 14, 24, 28

bullying and commander embarrassment, 59–60, 110–112, 116, 125, 132, *See also* Bullying behavior by senior management

closed to outsiders, 176, 206

fear resonation throughout police work, 24

"inquisitor" power and resources, 25–26

Pinocchio incident, 197

Comptroller's report, 251–252

Computerized crime reporting system, 6–7

Condon, Richard J., 65

Conflict theory, 213–214

Constitutional rights, *See* Civil liberties

Courtesy, Professionalism and Respect program, 202, 224

Cowper, T. J., 128–129

The Crime Fighter (Maple), 197, 204

Crime control versus due process, 201–206, 223–224, 254–255, *See also* Civil liberties

inappropriate summons examples, 214–216

law and lawsuits, 227–229, *See also* Lawsuits

marijuana enforcement, 217–220

minority communities, 224–227, *See also* Minorities

stop-and-frisk practices and, 220–224, *See also* Stop-and-frisks

Crime misclassification or downgrading, *See also* Crime report manipulation

criminal trespass, 39, 43, 159

District of Columbia, 12

evidence of crime report manipulation, *See* Crime report manipulation, evidence of

lost property, 4, 35, 52, 158–159, 166

media reports, 169, *See also* Media

Philadelphia and, 210

property value manipulations, 35

retiree survey item, 31–32

sex crimes, 37–40, 43, 118

Crime reduction trends, New York City, *See* New York City crime reduction
Crime report manipulation, 5, 23, *See also* Crime misclassification or downgrading
   Commissioner's panel appointed to examine NYPD crime statistics, 53–54
   Compstat archive infiltration, 168–169
   early reports, 12
   how to fake a crime decrease, 27, 165
   integrity testing, 210, 245, 257
   internal discipline for, 134, 168, 170, 211
   media reports
      2004, 162–164
      2005, 165–168
      2010, 168–171
   politician responses to allegations of, 171–174
   quiescent political establishment, 171–174
   ramifications for victims, 242–243
   rebuff of Mayor's Commission to Combat Police Corruption, 143
   recommendations, 244–245
   reprisals against whistleblowers, 1–3, 4–9
   terrorism fighting ramifications, 243–244
Crime report manipulation, evidence of, 26–28, 165
   abuse complaints and, 117, 118
   admitted problems, 48–49
   audio tapes, 4, 49–52, 121–122, 169
   crime victims coming forward, 36–39
   drug use data, 46–48
   enforcing letter of the law, 46
   French policing and, 103–104
   general versus personal awareness, 32–33
   Harold Hernandez, 39–40
   "historical" misdemeanor data reluctantly released, 43–45
   hospital data, 40–42, 46, 165
   NYPD's media friends and, 158–159
   NYPD's supported studies versus, 45–47
   police union statements, 27–28
   questionable scope of NYC crime reduction, 26–27, 146
   state non-index crime data, 42–43
   survey of retirees, 28–34, 169, *See also* Eterno-Silverman police retiree survey
   crime numbers following publication, 52–53
   interviews, 34–36
   U.K. and, 48, 67, 89, 93–96
Crime victims, *See* Victims of crime
Criminal Justice Educators of New York State, 239
Criminal justice theory
   Broken Windows theory and Compstat, 192–198
   crime control versus due process, 201–206, 254–255
   labeling theory, 211–212
   rational choice/deterrence theory, 208–211
   social contract, 200
   social science theory and Compstat, 208–214
   strain theory, 212–213
Criminal rationality assumptions, 210
Criminal trespass, 39, 43, 159
Customer-led management orientation, 88

D

Daily News
   crime report manipulation allegations, 4, 164, 168–169
   criticism of state-mandated privacy protections, 177
   murder increase report, 247
   NYPD relationship, 156
   response to Eterno-Silverman survey, 141, 144, 146
Data Integrity Unit, 31, 40, 48, 67, 211
Delegation of authority, 134–135, 258, *See also* Discretionary authority, Compstat-style management effects
Deming, W. Edwards, 18
Demoralization and embarrassment, 59–60
Deputy Commissioner for Public Information (DCPI), 153, 155, 160–161, 163, 175, 179, 253
Diallo, Amadou, 225
Discretionary authority, Compstat-style management effects, 61–62, 64, 126–127, 226
District attorneys, 50–51, 168, 177, 245

District of Columbia crime reporting, 11–12
Domestic violence reporting, 51, 135, 242, 248
Dorismond, Patrick, 225
Drug enforcement, 217–220, 227–228
Drug use data trends, 46–48
Due process versus crime control, *See* Crime control versus due process
Dunlap, E., 219
Dussautt, Raymond, 210
Dwyer, Jim, 154

E

Eck, J. E., 194
Economist, 13
Edelman, Murray, 74–75
Educational performance measurement, 10–11, 64–65, 79–80
Edwards, Omar, 225
Efficiency, means, and ends, 248–249
Emergency room visits data, 40–42, 53
Eterno-Silverman police retiree survey, 28–34, 80, 237
    attempts to silence in academia, 238–239
    cover letter, 261
    crime rates following publication of, 52–53
    focus groups, 29
    funding of, 29, 143–144
    generalizability outside New York, 240
    hierarchical pressure item, 59
    in-depth interviews, 29–30, 34–36
    matrix questions, 30
    media and NYPD responses, 141–146, 159, 164, 169, 175–176, 238
    morale-related item, 128
    peer-reviewed, 9, 76, 144, 238, 239
    peer-reviewed, citations, 240
    professional venues, 239
    reform calls following publication, 105
    respondent anonymity, 28, 34, 144, 240
    respondents' awareness of manipulation, 32–33, 240–241
    survey instrument, 262–266
    understanding NYPD-media spin, 146–148
    value neutrality, 9
Ethnic/racial minorities, *See* Minorities
Executive branch of government, 198–199

F

Fagan, Jeffry, 222
False statement allegations, 178
Favoritism in rewards and promotions, 119, 121, 135, 208
FBI crime statistics, 73–74, 164
Fear
    Compstat-related bullying, 110–112, 127
    crime reporting and public fear of crime, 75, 148–149
    making numbers look "right," 24
    as motivator, 132–134
Federal law enforcement agents, 11
Felony crimes downgraded to misdemeanors, *See* Crime misclassification or downgrading; *specific crime categories*
Field operations-level restriction effects, 60–68
Finn, Chester, 10
Finnegan, William, 154
Firearms assault hospitalization data, 41–42
Floyd et al. v. City of New York et al., 223, 227, 235
Focus groups, 29, 30, 144, 240
Forcible stops, *See* Stop-and-frisks
Forcible touching, 38, 43
France, police performance management system, 102–104, 249
Freedom of Information Law (FOIL) requests, 166–168, 252
Freedom of Information requests, 255, 258
Frost, J., xxv, 71, 81, 96, 106
The Fudge Factory," 36
Fyfe, James, 205

G

Gardiner, S., 251
Gatekeepers for police public information, 153, *See also* Deputy Commissioner for Public Information
Gestapo, 206
Giuliani, Rudy, 74, 77, 151–152, 168
    NYPD transparency concerns and, 207, 251–252
Glassner, B., 75–76
Glendinning, P. M., 124–125
GO-15 interview, 156
Goldstein, Herman, 12

Golub, A., 219
"Gotcha reporting," 179
Gotham Gazette, 15
Government and police power, 198–200
Government Performance and Results Act
        of 1993, 13
Grand larceny, 45, 158
Gray, K., 220
Greenspan, R., 128

H

Habeas corpus suspensions, 256
Hallam, S., xxv, 89, 94, 100, 106
Hammond, B., 220
Henry, V. E., 195–196
Her Majesty's Inspectorate of Constabulary
        (HMIC), 88, 89, 91, 93
Hernandez, Harold, 39–40, 43, 50, 118, 159
Hierarchical pressure, 58–59, *See also*
        NYPD top-down management
        style
    bullying and commander
        embarrassment, 59–60, 110–112,
        115–130, *See also* Bullying
        behavior by senior management
    Compstat "inquisitors" and, 25–26
    evidence of crime report manipulation,
        See Crime report manipulation,
        evidence of
    field operations restrictions, 61–62
    retiree survey item, 30–32, 59
    street-level officer morale and alienation
        effects, 62–64, 112–115
    Us versus Them environment, 58, 131,
        250
Hoffer, Jim, 51–52, 114, 121
Home Office Circular of 1983, 86–87
Homicide rates, 45–46, 247
Hospital data, evidence of Compstat-
        associated crime report
        manipulation, 40–42, 46, 165
Hudson, Robert and Doris, 216
Human relations school of management,
        251
Hutchinson, M., 116, 119, 121, 122–123

I

Iannone, M. D., 132–134, 136
Iannone, N. F., 132–134, 136

Identity theft report procedures, 36–37, 70,
        267
"Impact Zones," 225
Incentive plans, 16–17
Independent assessment of police crime
        data, 45–46, 54, 105, 168, 249–
        250, *See also* Eterno-Silverman
        police retiree survey
    Australian police and, 100–102
    Mayor's Commission to Combat Police
        Corruption, 143, 159, 166, 168,
        177–178
    NYPD supported studies, 45–47, 76, 80,
        142, 251
    U.K. audit bodies, 96, 249
Index crimes, 30, 42
    non-index crime rates and, 42–45
    pressure for downgrading, 31–32, *See
        also* Crime misclassification or
        downgrading
Innovations in American Government
        award, 16
"Inquisitors," 25–26
Integrity testing, 210, 245, 257
Intelligence gathering, 243
International Association of Chiefs of Police
        (IACP), 203, 256
International Police Executive Symposium
        (IPES), 239
Interview evidence of crime report
        manipulation, 29–30, 34–36, *See
        also* Eterno-Silverman police
        retiree survey

J

Jackson, D., 116, 243
John Jay college of Criminal Justice,
        238–239
Johnson, B., 219
Johnson's Presidential Commission on
        Law Enforcement and the
        Administration of Justice study, 7

K

Karmen, Andrew, 43
Kelley, David N., 54
Kelling, George, 192, 197–198
Kelly, Raymond
    criticism of cast as defamation of NYPD,
        153

criticism of state-mandated privacy
    protections, 177
declarations of NYC safety, 73–74
Mayor Bloomberg's relationship with,
    152–153
Newsday reporter Levitt and, 160, 206
panel appointed to examine NYPD
    crime statistics, 53–54, 67, 105,
    172, 175, 177, 210
Republican Convention of 2004 and,
    155
response to Eterno-Silverman retiree
    survey, 142
response to sex crime downgrading
    allegations, 39
Kennedy, M., xxiii, xxviii, 97–99, 106, 138
Knife crime statistics, 95

L

Labeling theory, 211–212
Laissez-faire leadership style, 131
Lawsuits, 227–229
    abuse of authority, 202
    Baltimore zero-tolerance policing case,
        228–229
    information access, 43, 117, 157–158,
        207, 227, 252, 253
    press credentials issuance policy, 160,
        252
    Schoolcraft and, 5, 170–171
    stop-and-frisk practices and, 222–223
Leadership issues, 109, 130–136, 250–251,
        See also Hierarchical pressure
    bullying, *See* Bullying behavior by
        senior management
    competing for resources, 135
    fear as motivator, 132–134
    reform recommendations, 250–251, 258
    styles of leadership, 131–132
Lee, R. T., 115–116
Legalistic style of policing, 70, 127, 129, 209,
        212, 226
Lessel, Harriet, 38
Levine, H., 218, 219
Levitt, Leonard, 40, 160, 206, 252
Litigation, *See* Lawsuits
Locke, John, 200
Lost property reports, 4, 35, 52, 158–159,
        166, 255
Louima, Abner, 224–225
Loveday, B., 71, 81, 93, 88–89, 94, 105–108

Loyalty versus bureaucratic management,
    128
Lundman, R. J., 205
Lutz, Bob, 18
Lynch, Patrick, 28, 163

M

MacDonald, Heather, 142–144
Madison, James, 199
Maguire, E. R., 194
Malme, Odd Berner, 207
Manning, Peter, 113
Maple, Jack, 15, 193, 196–197, 204, 210,
    228
Mapp v. Ohio, 199, 235
Marijuana enforcement, 217–220, 227–228
Marino, Michael, 122
Marlow, A., xxv, 67, 69, 81, 96, 107
*Maryland State Conference of NAACP
    Branches, et al. v. Baltimore City
    Police Department et al.*, 228–229,
    235
Maryland StateStat system, 16
Mastrofski, S., 128
Matrix questions, 30
Mauriello specials, 113–114
May, Theresa, 85
Mayor's Commission to Combat Police
    Corruption, 143, 159, 166, 168,
    177–178
McCall, Carl, 251–252
McCarthy, Gary, 195
McCarthy, Sharon L., 54
McNally, A., 128
Means, ends, and efficiency, 248–249
Media, *See also* NYPD and the media
    crime reporting and public fear of crime,
        75, 148–149
    crime statistic manipulation reports
        2004, 162–164
        2005, 165–168
        2010, 168–171
        U.K. popular press and, 95
    future prospects, 175–176, 179
    "gotcha reporting," 179
    nature of police-media interactions,
        148–151
    NYPD approach, 174–175
    police misconduct discussions, 161–162,
        175

political ramifications of crime statistics, 151–153
politician responses to crime report manipulation allegations, 171–174
press credentials issues, 160, 252
promoting NYPD-favorable stories, 153–155
recent crime increase reports, 247–248
responses to Eterno & Silverman's retiree study, 141–146, 159, 164, 169, 175–176, 238
suppression of critical coverage of NYPD, 155–162
understanding NYPD-media spin, 146–148
Medical Examiner (ME) data, 45–46
Merton, Robert, 212–213
Micromanagement, 63, 126, 258
Military command and control model, 128–129
Miller, Judith, 154–155
Minor crime, *See* Misdemeanor or minor crimes
Minorities, 224–227, 254–255
conflict theory, 213–214
marijuana enforcement and, 218
rapid deployment units versus, 205–206
stop-and-frisk practices and, 213, 214, 223
strain theory and policing priorities, 212–213
Miranda v. Arizona, 199, 235
Misdemeanor or minor crimes
assault trends, 43–44, 117
downgrading of more serious crimes, 4, 38–40, 43, *See also* Crime misclassification or downgrading
drug use data, 46–48
NY state non-index crime data, 42–43
transparency issues, 43, 117, 127, 157–158, 254, 255, *See also* NYPD transparency issues
trends, 118
vetted "historical" data, 43–45
Mission statement of the NYPD, 248, 256, 257
Mollen Commission, 168
Molloy College, 29, 143
Morale effects
Australian police, 99

commander embarrassment, 59–60, *See also* Bullying behavior by senior management
dissatisfaction with promotional system, 119–121
street cop alienation, 62–64, 112–115, 128
Morvillo, Robert G., 54
Moses, Paul, 52, 165–168, 252, 255
Murder rates, 45–46, 52, 247
Murphy, Jarrett, 166
Murrow, Edward R., 1

N

Nathan, Debbie, 37–39, 43, 242
National Association for the Advancement of Colored People (NAACP), 228
National Association of Black Law Enforcement Executives (NOBLE), 203, 256
National Centre of Policing Excellence (NCPE), 91
National Police Improvement Agency (NIPA), 93
National Sheriff's Association (NSA), 203, 256
Neimoller, Martin, 224
The New Yorker, 154
Newark, New Jersey, 229
New Orleans, 210, 229
Newsday, 160, 162
News media, *See* Media
New South Wales (NSW) Police Force, 97–100
computerized crime recording system, 6–7
NYPD's Compstat model and, 97
Philip Arantz case, 2–3, 5–8
responses to rising crime rates, 97
New York City, 2004 Republican Convention in, 154
New York City Corrections Department, 15
New York City crime reduction, 14, 23, 45, 73–76, 146–148, 235, 252
Broken Windows theory and, 192–198
Compstat Success Story, 76–78
contesting the dominant narrative, 77–78, 246
crime numbers following publication of Eterno & Silverman's police retiree study, 52–53

distortions of Eterno-Silverman
    findings, 76
dominant narrative, 73–76, 147, 246
downward trend without normal
    statistical fluctuations, 26, 158
FBI Uniform Crime Report, 73–74
force reductions and, 26–27, 72,
    246–247, 252
how to fake a crime decrease, 27, 165
media's investment in, 175
non-index crime rates and, 42–43, 118
number of forcible stops and, 44,
    221–222
NYC as safest big city in America,
    73–75, 152, 176
NYPD-supporting studies, 45–47
political ramifications of crime statistics,
    151–153
public and media expectations and, 147,
    161
questioning *scope* of decrease, not
    decrease itself, 23, 26–27, 45, 146,
    198
recent crime increase reports, 247–248
threatening findings, 146–148
New York City Department of Health and
    Mental Hygiene, 40–42, 47
New York City Department of Parks and
    Recreation, 15
New York City Police Department, *See*
    NYPD
New York City Police Department
    Retirement Survey, *See* Eterno-
    Silverman police retiree survey
New York Civil Liberties Union (NYCLU),
    207, 227, 235
New York Daily News, See Daily News
New Yorker, 13
New York Magazine, 170
New York Post, 141, 144, 146, 161, 164, 169,
    170
New York State Division of Criminal Justice
    Services data, 42–43
New York Times, 11–12, 52, 105, 157–158,
    207, 246
    crime statistic manipulation reports
        2004, 163–164
    Eterno-Silverman survey report and
        responses, 141–142, 144–145
    lawsuits against NYPD, 43, 157–158, 207,
        227, 252
    Republican Convention 2004 coverage,
        154
New York University crime statistics study
    (2006), 142
Ngo, E., 120
Nixon administration crime crackdown,
    11–12
No Child Left Behind law, 10, 64, 79–80
Non-index crimes, *See* Misdemeanor or
    minor crimes
Norris, Edward T., 228
Norwood News, 207, 252
Numerical performance measurement and
    standards, 9, *See also* Compstat;
    Performance management and
    accountability systems; Quotas
    accountability under Compstat, 24–26,
        See also Compstat
    consequences of unreliable statistics, 57
    management versus street cops, 114–115
    Mayor Bloomberg's reliance on, 147–148
    performance distortions, 64–67
    police officer concerns, 23–24
    private sector influence, 12–14
    public sector, 9–12
NYC Against Rape, 38
NYCLU v. NPD, 207, 227, 235
NYPD (New York City Police Department)
    admitted crime statistic manipulation,
        48–49
    antiterrorism actions, 154, 243–244
    auto theft reporting requirements, 36
    Data Integrity Unit and Quality
        Assurance Division, 31, 40, 48, 67,
        211, 244–245
    extraordinary media coverage, 174
    female officers, 129–130
    force reductions, 26–27, 72, 133, 246–247
    identity theft report procedures, 36–37,
        70, 267
    internal discipline for crime report
        manipulation, 134, 168, 170, 211
    lack of accreditation, 203–204
    lawsuits against, *See* Lawsuits
    leadership styles and issues, 130–136
    mission statement, 248, 256, 257
    public image preoccupation, 116–118,
        See also NYPD and the media;
        Public image issues for NYPD
    response to Eterno-Silverman retiree
        survey, 141–146
    turnover, 119–120, 123

NYPD and the media, 163, 174–175,
        251–252, *See also* Media; NYPD
        transparency issues
    future prospects, 175–176, 179
    manipulation reports
        2004, 162–164
        2005, 165–168
        2010, 168–171
    nature of police-media interactions,
        148–151
    Occupy Wall Street protests, 175
    police HQ access control, 160–161
    political ramifications, 151–153
    press credentials issuance, 160, 252
    promoting favorable stories, 153–155
    recent crime increase reports, 247–248
    reform recommendations, 253
    suppressing negative coverage, 155–162
    transparency concerns, 206–207, *See
        also* NYPD transparency issues
    understanding NYPD-media spin,
        146–148
    Wall Street Journal's privileged
        relationship, 157–159, 255
NYPD Battles Crime (Silverman), 144
NYPD bureaucratic management style, *See*
        Top-down management style
NYPD crime report manipulations, *See*
        Crime report manipulation
NYPD Deputy Commissioner for Public
        Information (DCPI), 153, 155–157,
        163, 175, 179, 253
NYPD leadership issues, 130–136
NYPD Patrol Guide, 46, 50, 131, 220
NYPD performance management system,
        See Compstat; Performance
        management and accountability
        systems
NYPD police retirement survey, *See* Eterno-
        Silverman police retiree survey
NYPD supported research, 45–47, 76, 80,
        142, 251
NYPD top-down management style, *See*
        Top-down management style
NYPD transparency issues, 43, 117,
        124–125, 157–158, 166–168,
        206–208, 239, 251–252, *See also*
        Independent assessment of police
        crime data
    bureaucratic management style and, 127
    closed Compstat meetings, 176, 206

    Commission to Combat Police
        Corruption, 143, 159, 166, 177–178
    FOIL requests, 166–168, 252, 255, 258
    Giuliani versus Comptroller, 251–252
    lawsuits, 43, 157–158, 252, 253
    misdemeanor or non-index crime data,
        43, 117, 127, 157–158, 255
    public image preoccupation and,
        116–117
    Rayman's questions, 5
    rebuff of Mayor's Commission to
        Combat Police Corruption, 143
    reform recommendations, 253–259
    THEE Rant website, 36, 252
NYPD whistleblowers, *See* Polanco, Adil;
        Schoolcraft, Adrian

O

Oath of office for police officers, 203–204
Occupy Wall Street protests, 175
"Offenses against public administration," 44
Ohio Department of Jobs and Family
        Services, 16
Ohlin, L., 213
O'Neill, T., xxix
Operation Impact, 225–226
Operations and Crimes Review (OCT), 97,
        98–99
Orde, H., xv, xxiii, xxviii
Organizational-managerial consequences,
        57–60
Ortiz, E., 207
Orton, Lance, 243
Overland, Simon, 101

P

Packer, Herbert, 201
Paddy's Book system, 6–7
Paris, France, police force, 102–104
Parks, excessive law enforcement in,
        215–216, 229, 256
Parkstat, 15
Participative leadership style, 131
Patrol Guide, 46, 50, 131, 220–221
Patrolmen's Benevolent Association (PBA),
        27–28, 62, 113, 163, 164–165
Pay-for-performance incentives, 16–17
Peer-reviewed research, 9, 76, 144, 238, 239,
        240
Performance contracts, 98

Performance culture, 64, 66, 71, 88, 89, 94
Performance management and
        accountability systems, 8–9,
        See also Compstat; Numerical
        performance measurement
        and standards; Top-down
        management style
    Australian policing, 6–8, 97–102, *See
        also* New South Wales (NSW)
        Police Force
    effects on field operations, 60–68
    French policing, 102–104
    incentive plans, 16–17
    law enforcement distortions, 11
    means, ends, and efficiency, 248–249
    organizational-managerial
        consequences, 57–60
    political pressures on crime recording,
        11–12
    private sector influence, 12–14, 72, 87,
        97–98, 103
    private sector shortcomings, 16–18, 72
    public sector, 9–12
    reform obstacles and prospects, 71–73,
        78–80
    reform recommendations, 247–249
    special considerations for law
        enforcement, 13–14
    U.K. policing, 85–97, *See also* United
        Kingdom (U.K.), performance
        policing
Personnel transfer powers, 126, 134
Peters, T. J., 87
Petty larcenies, 4, 45
Philadelphia, 210, 229
Pinocchio incident, 197
Polanco, Adil, 2, 49, 113–114, 117, 121,
        127–128
Police abuse of authority allegations,
        117–118, 126, 202, 223, *See also*
        Police misconduct
Police Commissioner's panel to examine
        NYPD crime statistics, 53–54
Police Executive Research Forum (PERF),
        203, 256
Police force reductions, 26–27, 72, 133,
        246–247
Police-media relations, 146–151, *See also*
        Media; NYPD and the media
Police misconduct, *See also* Crime report
        manipulation
    abuse complaints, 117–118, 126, 202, 223

    Compstat and FADO data, 248
    false statement allegations, 178
    media discussions, 161–162, 175
    minority communities and, 224–227
    Occupy Wall Street protestors and, 175
    stop-and-frisk practices and, 223, *See
        also* Stop-and-frisks
Police officer oath, 203–204
Police performance management, *See*
        Compstat; Performance
        management and accountability
        systems
Police personnel turnover, 119–120, 123
Police power, 199–200
    democratic society and, 200–201
    social contract, 200
Police priorities versus public needs, 68–71
Police Standards Unit, 91
Police state, 205
Police unions, *See* Patrolmen's Benevolent
        Association; Sergeant's
        Benevolent Association
Political establishment and crime statistics,
        11–12, 151–153, 176–178
Pomerantz, Mark F., 28, 143, 166, 252
Privacy protections for stop-and-frisk
        suspects, 177
Private sector performance management,
        12–14, 72
    Australian policing, 97–98
    French policing, 103
    shortcomings, 16–18
    U.K. policing, 87
Promotion issues, 32, 98, 208
    bullying and dissatisfaction, 119–121,
        123–124
    favoritism, 119, 121, 135, 208
    lieutenants taking the captain's test,
        123–124
Property crime rates, 52
Property value manipulations, 35
Prostitutes, 242
Protective custody, 206
Proust, Jean Paul, 102–103
Public health assessments, 11
Public image issues for NYPD, 116–118, *See
        also* NYPD and the media
    nature of police-media interactions,
        148–151
    promoting NYPD-favorable stories,
        153–155

suppressing critical media coverage, 155–162
understanding NYPD-media spin, 146–148
Public needs versus policing responses, 68–71
Public sector performance measurement, 9–12
Punch, M. 22, 24
Punishment as motivator, 132–134
Purtell, R., 45, 47, 142

Q

Quality Assurance Division, 31, 40, 48, 244–245
Quality-of-life policing issues, 193, 195–196
  Baltimore lawsuit case, 228–229
  Broken Windows theory and, 192–198
  NYPD mission statement, 248
Quotas, 11, 28, 64–66, 113, 226
  lawsuits related to, 170
  management "expectations" and, 126
  media exposure, 169
  police denials of, 117
  summonses, 28, 64–66, 215, 244

R

Racial conflict theory, 214
Racial/ethnic minorities, See Minorities
Rape or attempted sexual assault, 37–40, 43–44, 52, 118, 159
Rapid deployment units (RDUs), 205–206
Rashbaum, W., 48, 134, 142, 164, 166, 169, 172, 211
Rational choice/deterrence theory, 208–211
Ravitch, Diane, 10, 64–65, 79–80
Rayman, Graham, 4–5, 39, 169–170, 206–207
Reasonable suspicion standard, 66, 201, 220–221
Re-engineering, 13, 87
Reform issues and prospects, 71–73, 78–80
  integrity testing, 210, 245, 257
  leadership issues, 130–136
  media issues, 175–176, 251–253
  need for independent assessments, 54, 105, See also Independent assessment of police crime data
  NYPD accreditation, 203–204, 256, 259
  NYPD mission statement, 248, 256, 257

political establishment, 176–178
recommendations, 244–245, 247–249, 253–259
summary of recommendations, 258–259
Reintegrative shaming, 212
Republican Convention of 2004, 154–155
Research, NYPD supported, 45–47, 76, 80, 142, 251
Research evidence for NYPD Compstat-associated crime report manipulation, 28–34, See also Eterno-Silverman police retiree survey
Retirement trends, 119–120
Reuss-Ianni, E., 112–113
Rivera, R., 114
Robb, P., xxv, xxix, 96, 107
Robberies, downgrading or non-reporting, 4, 49–51
Rokeach, Milton, 78
Rousseau, Jean-Jacques, 200
Ryan, Peter, 98–99

S

Sarkozy, Nicolas, 103
Scarborough, K. E., 129
Schoolcraft, Adrian, 1–2, 4–5, 49–52, 113–114, 117, 121, 127–128, 169–171, 206
Scientific value neutrality, 9, 191
Scipione, A., xix, xxiii, xxviii
Selznick, P., 248
Sergeant's Benevolent Association (SBA), 28, 165
Serpico, Frank, 5
Service style of policing, 127, 209
Sex crimes, 37–40, 43, 118, 159, 242
  crime numbers following publication of Eterno & Silverman's police retiree study, 52
  felony versus misdemeanor trends, 43–44
  recently released "historical" NYPD data, 43
Sex Crimes Working Group, 39
Shaming, reintegrative, 212
Shipley, David, 145
Short-term versus long-term focus, 63, 65
  private sector performance management, 17–18
  public sector performance management, 11

Silverman, Eli B., 144, 246, *See also* Eterno-Silverman police retiree survey
Sims, B., 129
Skolnick, Jerome, 205
Smith, D. C., 45, 47, 142
Social contract, 200
Social science theory, 208–214, *See also* Criminal justice theory
   conflict theory, 213–214
   labeling theory, 211–212
   rational choice/deterrence theory, 208–211
   strain theory, 212–213
Societal effects, 68–71
Societal reaction theory, 211
Sociological perspectives, 125–129
Staff transfer powers, 63
Staten Island Advance, 171
StateStat, 16
Stolen property possession, 44
Stop-and-frisks (forcible stops), 28, 44, 66, 68, 212, 220–224
   abuse complaints and, 117, 118
   civil liberties versus, 203
   criticism of state-mandated privacy protections, 177
   huge numbers, 118, 123, 126, 221–222, 244
   lawsuits related to, 222–223
   media reports, 169
   minorities and, 213, 214
   NYPD data release, 117, 252
   reasonable suspicion standard, 66, 201, 220–221
Strain theory, 212–213
Street-level officer alienation, 62–64, 112–115, 128
Sullivan, W., 54
Summonses
   dismissals, 68, 159
   filings, 118
   inappropriate enforcement examples, 214–216, 255
   quotas, 28, 64–66, 170, 244
Sydney Morning Herald reports, 8
Symbolic language, NYC crime success story, 73–76

T

Teachers' incentive pay plans, 16–17
TEAMS program, 15
Terrorism, fighting, 154, 243–244

Terry v. Ohio, 201, 220, 235
THEE Rant website, 36, 252
Ticket-fixing, 245
Times Square terror attack (2010), 243
Timoney, John, 110, 210
Tink, A., 83, 99, 107
Top-down management style, 57–60, *See also* Compstat; Hierarchical pressure
   bullying behaviors, 109–112, 115–130, *See also* Bullying behavior by senior management
   centralization and reduced field flexibility, 61–62
   management versus street cops, 62–64, 112–115, 128
   micromanagement, 63, 126, 258
   military model, 128–129
   no delegation of authority, 134–135
   NYPD public image preoccupation, 116–118
   officer discretionary authority versus, 61–62, 64, 126–127, 226
   organizational-managerial consequences, 57–60
   societal/community effects, 68–71
   sociological perspectives, 125–129
   U.K. policing reforms, 85–86
Total Efficiency Accountability Management System (TEAMS), 15
Trafficstat, 135
Traffic ticket quotas, 11
Turnover of police personnel, 119–120, 123

U

Uniform Crime Report, 73
Uniform Crime Reporting (UCR) index, 12
United Kingdom (U.K.), performance policing, 85–97, 249
   anti-social behavior and, 70–71, 92
   auditing bodies, 91, 249
   budget reductions, 72
   Coalition Government's reforms, 85–86
   community consequences of Compstat-like policies, 68–71
   evidence of crime report manipulation, 48, 67, 94–96
   government revelations and problem intensification, 89–93

Her Majesty's Inspectorate of
    Constabulary (HMIC), 88, 89, 91,
    93
HMIC's "Valuing the Police" study, 93
Home Office Circular of 1983, 86–87
Labour Government and Best Value
    principles, 87–88
National Policing Plan, 2003-2006,
    90–93
performance indicators and monitoring
    system, 90–91
private sector model, 87
responses to rising crime rates, 86–87
scholarly analysis, 93–94
similarities with NYPD Compstat
    model, 94
top-down bureaucracy, 66–68
U.S. Border Patrol, 16
U.S. Constitution, police mission to protect,
    201, 203
U.S. General Accounting Office (GAO), 11
Us versus Them environment, 58, 131, 250

V

Vallon, Peter, Jr., 171–174, 176, 177
Vallon, Peter, Sr., 172

Value neutrality, 9, 191
Vann, Albert, 170
Vickers, M. H., 116
Victims of crime
    auto theft reporting requirements, 46
    evidence of crime report manipulation,
        36–39
    identity theft report procedures, 36–37,
        70, 267
    police discouragement from making
        complaints, 4
    ramifications of crime report
        manipulation, 242–243
    seeking out, 71, 242
Victoria Police Force, 100–102
Village Voice, 4, 165–166, 169–170, 175

W

Wall Street Journal, 144
    privileged NYPD relationship, 157–159,
        255
Warren, Earl, 206
Washington GMAP system, 16
Watchman style of policing, 127, 209
Waterman, R. H., Jr., 87
Weapons-related crime rates, 44
Weber, Max, 126–128, 191
Weisburd, D., 128
Whistleblowers, *See* Arantz, Philip;
        Polanco, Adil; Schoolcraft, Adrian
White, Jonathan, 243
Wilkes, L., 116
Willis, J. F., 128
Wilson, J. Q., 127, 192, 209
Wilson, O. W., 12
Wipperman, W., 206
Woman officers, 129–130
Workplace bullying, *See* Bullying behavior
        by senior management

Z

Zero tolerance policing, 64, 77, 97, 228
Zimring, Frank, 45–47
Zink, Robert, 27, 165

A Call for Authors
Advances in Police Theory and Practice

AIMS AND SCOPE:

This cutting-edge series is designed to promote publication of books on contemporary advances in police theory and practice. We are especially interested in volumes that focus on the nexus between research and practice, with the end goal of disseminating innovations in policing. We will consider collections of expert contributions as well as individually authored works. Books in this series will be marketed internationally to both academic and professional audiences. This series also seeks to —

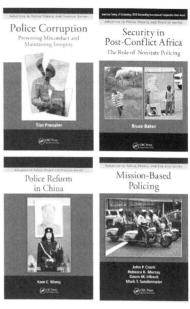

- Bridge the gap in knowledge about advances in theory and practice regarding who the police are, what they do, and how they maintain order, administer laws, and serve their communities
- Improve cooperation between those who are active in the field and those who are involved in academic research so as to facilitate the application of innovative advances in theory and practice

The series especially encourages the contribution of works coauthored by police practitioners and researchers. We are also interested in works comparing policing approaches and methods globally, examining such areas as the policing of transitional states, democratic policing, policing and minorities, preventive policing, investigation, patrolling and response, terrorism, organized crime and drug enforcement. In fact, every aspect of policing, public safety, and security, as well as public order is relevant for the series. Manuscripts should be between 300 and 600 printed pages. If you have a proposal for an original work or for a contributed volume, please be in touch.

Series Editor
Dilip Das, Ph.D., Ph: 802-598-3680
E-mail: dilipkd@aol.com

Dr. Das is a professor of criminal justice and Human Rights Consultant to the United Nations. He is a former chief of police and, founding president of the International Police Executive Symposium, IPES, www.ipes.info. He is also founding editor-in-chief of *Police Practice and Research: An International Journal* (PPR), (Routledge/Taylor & Francis), www.tandf.co.uk/journals. In addition to editing the *World Police Encyclopedia* (Taylor & Francis, 2006), Dr. Das has published numerous books and articles during his many years of involve-ment in police practice, research, writing, and education.

Proposals for the series may be submitted to the series editor or directly to —
Carolyn Spence
Acquisitions Editor • CRC Press / Taylor & Francis Group
561-998-2515 • 561-997-7249 (fax)
carolyn.spence@taylorandfrancis.com • www.crcpress.com
6000 Broken Sound Parkway NW, Suite 300, Boca Raton, FL 33487